ELIZABETH I, QUEEN OF ENGLAND

Neville Williams

"He is particularly good on the social life and habits of the Court."—*The Observer*

"A careful and balanced interpretation of her reign and personality."—*The Economist*

"The book is lively with quotations and full of stray pleasures."—*The Times*

Neville Williams is Deputy Keeper of Public Records, a member of the council of the Royal Historical Society and a Fellow of the Society of Antiquities. He is the author of seven historical books, including *Elizabeth I, Queen of England* which is regarded as the finest study of the Virgin Queen since Sir John Neale's work.

ELIZABETH I, QUEEN OF ENGLAND

For Alison

Elizabeth I, Queen of England

NEVILLE WILLIAMS

SPHERE BOOKS LIMITED
30/32 Gray's Inn Road, London WC1X 8JL

First published in Great Britain in 1967 by Weidenfeld &
Nicolson Ltd.
© Neville Williams, 1967
First Sphere Books edition 1971

Set in Monotype Bembo

Printed in Great Britain by
Hazell Watson & Viney Ltd.
Aylesbury, Bucks

CONTENTS

LIST OF ILLUSTRATIONS

(The numbers in the left hand column refer to the page numbers of the illustrations.)

PREFACE

A FRIEND warned me some twenty years ago that since so much of the past had still to be explored properly, one needed real justification for rewriting the life of any individual who had already merited an entry in *The Dictionary of National Biography*. The reader may well ask himself at the outset why the most famous of all England's queens should deserve another biography.

The justification is more than an apologia for tackling a subject of immense personal interest. There has been no full-scale life of Elizabeth for a generation, during which time Tudor studies have flourished as never before. The leading statesmen of the reign, and many lesser figures, have had important volumes devoted to them and detailed research on broad topics of political, administrative, social and economic history, as well as a host of minutiae, have added enormously to our knowledge of the period and all throw light, in varying intensity, on the Queen herself. (A select list from this considerable literature of what, in this writer's opinion, are the hundred best books on the reign, is given on page 371 and it is remarkable how many of these have appeared within the last thirty years.) Were this process to be continued indefinitely, we should be in the extraordinary position of having *Hamlet* without the Prince.

Parallel to this development in historical studies, and in part its cause, great strides have been made in making available the original sources, be they official records or private papers, resulting in some cases in series of stout printed calendars, in others to typescript handlists or even briefer reports, pointing to a great body of new material to be taken into account.

This book, then, is a new synthesis; a reinterpretation of Elizabeth Tudor in the light of recent scholarship and of new evidence. To help to advance knowledge still further it has been fully documented. How much it differs from what we have come to regard as the traditional portrait is a matter for readers themselves to judge. What follows is specifically a life of the Queen, not a chronicle of her times, certainly not a social history of her age. As a result certain events that feature in general histories would be out of place here and parts of this book are not strictly chronological. For the sake of clarity in all quotations from contemporary material both spelling and punctuation have been modernized and the use of capital letters rationalized.

Her Majesty the Queen has graciously permitted the reproduction of plates 1 and 6. Other illustrations are reproduced by permission of His Grace the Archbishop of Canterbury, the Marquess of Salisbury, the Marquess of Bath, the Earl of Winchilsea and Nottingham, Mr. G. M. Dent-Brocklehurst, Captain F. Tyrwhitt-Drake, the Controller of Her Majesty's Stationery Office (including the illustration on the jacket from the Victoria and Albert Museum), the Trustees of the British Museum, the Trustees of the National Portrait Gallery, the Trustees of the London Museum, the Trustees of the Wallace Collection, the Stopford-Sackville Collection and the Director of the Bibliothèque Nationale, Paris. Unpublished material in the Public Record Office in which Crown copyright is reserved is reproduced by permission of the Controller of Her Majesty's Stationery Office.

My interest in Tudor history was first aroused as a schoolboy by two great teachers, N. P. Birley and A. B. Jeffries, and was further stimulated at Oxford, and since, by A. G. Dickens, G. D. Ramsay, A. L. Rowse, R. B. Wernham and the late Claude Jenkins. Work at the Public Record Office has brought the dual benefits over the years of colleagues who have willingly shared their specialist knowledge of the records and of helpful discussions with visiting scholars, of whom I must mention in particular the late Conyers Read. I am once again indebted to Mrs. D. Steer for typing my manuscript. As always my wife has given me the constant encouragement necessary to bring a work to completion.

N.W.

Hampstead Garden Suburb,
August 2nd, 1967

MERE ENGLISH

Like Eve it had all begun with an apple. The courtiers who had gathered in the whispering gallery of politics, outside Anne Boleyn's chamber in Whitehall Palace, one February morning in 1533 first heard the news. As she came out of her apartment the Lady Anne caught sight of an old flame, the poet Wyatt, and cried out to him with excitement that for three days now she had had 'such a violent desire to eat apples, as she had never felt before, and that the King had told her it was a sign that she was with child; and she had said it was not so at all.' Then she turned on her heel with a burst of hysterical laughter, leaving her audience 'abashed and uneasy'.[1] Understandably, Anne could no longer keep the secret of her triumph from those about her, and they, solving her conundrum, knew that conceiving an heir to the throne would win her a crown.

Anne's secret marriage to King Henry was already a month old,[2] solemnized when the infant she was carrying was still but a month. By Easter their union was recognized at court, and Queen Anne was prayed for at the Chapel Royal, though not until the end of May did Archbishop Cranmer pronounce Henry's marriage to Katherine of Aragon incestuous and proclaim Anne to be his lawful wife in the eyes of church and state. Her coronation followed on Whitsun Day, with the folds of the heavy crimson brocade concealing her altered figure and all eyes on the string of pearls 'bigger than chick peas' round her neck.[3] There remained but one thing to set the seal on her extraordinary success and Greenwich Palace was accordingly made ready for the birth of that prince, for whose sake Henry VIII had defied the Pope. On Sunday, 7 September 1533, between 3 and 4 p.m., Anne was delivered of her baby, who confounded her parents and astounded the astrologers by being a girl.4

'God has forgotten him entirely, hardening him in his obstinacy to punish and ruin him', commented the imperial ambassador with satisfaction.5 Indeed, it seemed as if the words of St Paul in the epistle for the day which Henry had heard at mass, mocked him: 'To Abraham and his seed were the promises made.'6 A female heir; a woman ruler? It was unheard of. Yet it was to be this child of the English Reformation, this seed of England's Abraham, that would live to become one of the most remarkable sovereigns the world had ever seen.

When three days old she was christened Elizabeth by Stokesly, Bishop of London, at the church of the Franciscans at Greenwich. The Lord Mayor and city fathers had come down by river to add to the pomp and ceremony of a royal occasion. The dowager Duchess of Norfolk, as senior godmother, carried the child in a christening robe of purple velvet to an area which had been screened off from the choir; here there was 'a pan of fire' to keep the infant warm while she was made ready. The silver font stood raised in the middle of the church with a fine canopy of crimson satin, fringed with gold, and after baptism Garter King of Arms made proclamation that 'God of his infinite goodness send prosperous life and long to the high and mighty Princess of England, Elizabeth.' Then Archbishop Cranmer, her godfather, proceeded at once to administer the sacrament of confirmation. 'Then the trumpets blew and the gifts were given; after which wafers, comfits and hypocras were brought' into the church for the main party, before the procession formed for returning to the palace.7 Henry had not himself attended the service. A critic of his regime testily noted that there were no bonfires in the streets that night and hinted that the whole proceedings had been 'very cold and disagreeable to the court and to the city.'8

Elizabeth was named after her grandmother, the consort of Henry VII, who had been born in the purple as the child of Edward IV and Elizabeth Woodville. In the Italian states they called her 'Ysabel', but in Spain and the Empire she was spoken of bluntly as 'the wench's baby' or even 'the concubine's little bastard'. Tales would soon be told that Henry was not her father – that she was a suppositious child stolen from poor parents, even that she was the incestuous progeny of Anne Boleyn and Lord Rochfort.[9] Two friars were in trouble for saying the Princess had been christened 'in hot water, but it was not hot enough'.[10] Thus she began her life to the sniping shots of detractors and the bellicose taunts of false accusers, who saw her as the symbol of England's breach with Catholic Europe and the threat to Mary's cherished birthright. These rumblings would continue for a quarter of a century, yet they provoked in turn incredible loyalty so that in years to come she would realize that her 'mere Englishry' was the fount of her popularity.

Within a few weeks of the christening a separate household was established for the Princess, so that she could be sent away from plague-ridden London to the safer air of the home counties, and on 10 December she left Greenwich for Hatfield in the care of Lady Bryan, who had looked after Mary from her earliest days.[11] At first no expense was spared, but in time her cofferer realized he had a far larger staff in the Princess's livery than he had bargained for, since several of the household servants kept more of their own personal servants than was allowed.[12]

By January Mary had been forced to remove herself to Hatfield. She had been deprived of her title of Princess of Wales and to add insult to injury her father required her to become a maid of honour to her baby half-sister.[13] But Mary, now nearly eighteen, was obstinate. When ordered to pay her respects to the Princess, she answered that she knew no other princess than herself; she would call Elizabeth her 'sister', just as she called her half-brother, the illegitimate Henry Fitzroy, duke of Richmond, 'brother', but to bow the knee to her as heir to the throne was anathema to Mary.[14] Thus began the cold war between the two sisters that lasted until Mary's death. Henry used bullying words to get her to renounce her title, Anne Boleyn demanded that her ears be boxed 'for the cursed bastard she is' and they even went to the lengths of confiscating her jewels.[15] It would be fascinating to read 'the ballad made of the Princess by my Lady Mary', which Thomas Cromwell, Lord Privy Seal, knew all about, but not a line survives.[16] More tactfully, as the months went by she reported to her father that Elizabeth was 'such a child toward as I doubt not but Your Highness should have cause to rejoice in time coming.'[17]

Mary's presence tended to put the household staff on edge in those early days at Hatfield, at neighbouring Hunsdon House or on the visits to Eltham Palace in Kent. Mary Hilton, Elizabeth's laundress, had plenty to gossip about with Mary Norris and Blanche Parry, two other servants of her household. The atmosphere was highly charged when Henry came down to see his heir and completely ignored his elder daughter or when Mary stood squarely on a trivial point of etiquette.

Anne Boleyn had chosen the crimson satin and fringe for Elizabeth's cradle and paid for the white and purple caps, embellished with gold, and the needle ribbands 'to roll her hair', once it was long enough.[18] At six months 'her grace is much in the King's favour, as a goodly child should be' and at twenty-five months both parents decided Elizabeth must be weaned 'with all diligence'.[19] Mother and daughter were still in high favour as the turbulent year 1536 opened. On Sunday, 9 January, Henry began a fantastic round of festivities, almost a second Twelve Days of Christmas, to celebrate Katherine of Aragon's death. Dressed from top to toe in yellow he conducted his little daughter to chapel 'with trumpets and other great triumphs' and, dinner over, he carried her in his arms, showing her off to his courtiers.[20] Before January was out, however, Anne Boleyn had signed her own death warrant by giving premature birth to a stillborn infant; it was an unpardonable offence against the dignity of the crown, for she had miscarried of a son. The witch-hunt began at once, while Jane Seymour waited in the wings and Elizabeth lay forgotten.

A day or so before Anne was sent to the Tower she was seen at an upper window of Greenwich Palace for the last time. A Protestant refugee from Germany vividly recalled the scene years afterwards, as he watched from the courtyard while the hapless Queen attempted to plead with the King while she fondled her baby.[21] On 20 May, the day after her execution, Henry married Jane Seymour and when Parliament met in July Elizabeth was degraded to the same status of illegitimacy as Mary, in order to pave the way for a male heir, as yet unconceived.

In all these changes one factor remained constant, and for Elizabeth it was of fundamental importance: she remained in the care of Lady Bryan, who was devoted to her. Unswervingly she looked after the child's interests, interceding with Cromwell and, if need be, the King himself to have things as they should be. Her son, Sir Francis Bryan, by contrast, lived by intrigue, working as ruthlessly for the downfall of Anne Boleyn as he had plotted for the divorce from Katherine, so that he had earned himself the merciless nickname of 'the vicar of hell'.

These were troubled times for Lady Bryan. She was a cousin of the disgraced Anne Boleyn and her second husband had just died. On top of all this there were the difficulties caused by her charge's altered status which disrupted Hunsdon House. She understood that Elizabeth was no longer Princess of Wales, but 'what degree she is now, I know not, but by hearsay.' And then there was Sir John Shelton, the pompous steward, lording it over her, claiming to rule the household over her head, yet she had never seen anything in writing to give him this authority. 'Master Shelton', she complained to Thomas Cromwell:

would have my Lady Elizabeth to dine and sup every day at the board of estate. Alas! my Lord, it is not meet for a child of her age to keep such rule yet. I promise you, my Lord, I dare not take it upon me to keep her in health, and she keep that rule. For there she shall see divers meats and fruits, and wine, which would be hard for me to restrain Her Grace from it. Ye know, my Lord, there is no place of correction here. And she is too young to correct greatly. I know well, and she be there, I shall neither bring her up to the King's Grace's honour, nor her's – nor to her health, nor my poor honesty.

What the child needed was some wholesome nursery fare on her own in the nursery under proper supervision, not spoiling by her elders at table in the hall.

Whatever her rank might be Elizabeth was disastrously short of clothes; perhaps she had been growing so fast:

She hath neither gown nor kirtle, nor petticoat, nor no manner of linen, nor foresmocks, nor kerchiefs, nor sleeves, nor rails, nor bodystichets, nor handkerchiefs. . . : I have driven off as long as I can, that be my troth, I cannot drive it no longer; beseeching you, my Lord, that you will see that Her Grace may have that is needful for her.

Finally the little girl was having:

great pain with her great teeth, and they come very slowly forth, and causeth me to suffer Her Grace to have her will more than I would. I trust to God, and her teeth were well graft, to have Her Grace after another fashion that she is yet; so as I trust the King's Grace shall have great comfort in Her Grace, for she is as toward a child, and as gentle of condition, as ever I knew any in my life.[22]

Lady Bryan got her own way at least about meal times and Sir John Shelton was told the King wished Elizabeth to eat in her chamber.[23]

She was, however, allowed to partake of the wine and spiced dainties following her brother Edward's christening at Hampton Court in October 1537, late in the evening, even though she was only just four. She had borne the chrisom, or baptismal robe, in procession, being herself carried by Viscount Beauchamp and as her train was heavy Lord Morley lent a hand.[24] Edward's had supplanted her name in the bidding prayers and it was the baby who was now the centre of Lady Bryan's attentions; she worried now not about Elizabeth's scanty wardrobe, but about the Prince's need for 'a good jewel to set in his cap'. Yet knowing child that she was, Elizabeth accepted unquestioningly that she must give way to the brother who would one day be King and grew very fond of him. Jane Seymour's death in childbed had left him motherless, like his sister, and this was a further bond between them, as she watched uncomprehending and from afar her elders performing the fantastic steps in the courtly dance of life. She fondly sewed Edward a little cambric shirt with as neat stitches as she could.[25]

Despite the label of bastardy the two sisters were still royal children and were accounted vital pieces in the great game of dynastic politics. The question of Elizabeth's marriage had first been raised in 1535, when the Duc d'Angoulême, youngest son of Francis I, had been suggested, though no one had taken the nego-tiations very seriously. The fact that Mary and Elizabeth were no longer styled 'Princess' devalued them on the European marriage market and accordingly the Privy Council advised their father that they ought 'to be made of some estimation, without which no man will have any great respect for them.'[26] Not until 1544 were they reinstated in the succession by act of Parliament.

Together so often at Hunsdon or the manor of the More, near Rickmansworth, the sisters had little in common, the one half Spanish, the other 'mere English', and there were seventeen years between them. Mary taught Elizabeth various card games, some involving stakes, and so now and again she gave her money 'to play her withall'. Then there were the antics of Jane the Fool and Lucretia the Tumbler to make her laugh. On New Year's Day they exchanged presents, Elizabeth, for instance, receiving a gold pomander with a watch inside, and giving Mary a pair of gold and silk stockings. They each had their minstrels and musical accomplishments ranked second only to sound study in their household.[27] Soon after Edward's birth Katherine Champernowne was appointed Elizabeth's governess; she very quickly gained the child's confidence and 'Kat', as she was affectionately called, was to remain in her service for many years. She later married John Ashley, who held a confidential position in the princess's household and was a close friend of Roger Ascham, the Cambridge scholar. Katherine laid the foundations for that remarkable grasp of languages and classical scholarship which the Princess was to acquire from Cheke and Ascham. When she was no more than six years old Sir Henry Wriothesley, who was no flatterer, said she would still be an honour to her sex if her formal education were to cease then and there. She talked to him with as much assurance as a woman of forty. 'If she be no more educated than she now appeareth to me, she will prove of no less honour and womanhood, then shall be seen her father's daughter.'[28] She was always her father's daughter.

In these years her visits to court were rare. Sometimes she stayed at Chelsea and would be taken in a litter to Richmond or Hampton Court to visit her father, but never for long. It was as well that she escaped the corrupting influence of life at court during the fiasco of the King's marriage to Anne of Cleves, in

January 1540, which was annulled next July, while Katherine Howard waited in the wings. Queen Katherine, executed for adultery after a sordid trial in February 1542, repeated so nearly the tragic pattern of her cousin Anne Boleyn – but there was this exception, that Katherine left no infant behind her.

We can never pierce the mystery of how these events were related to Elizabeth, the phrases used, the tone of voice, the nuances, or know her immediate reaction to the tidings. At any event Henry was always her hero, a figure who could do no wrong, and even though she saw so little of him she was to him much more than just a dutiful daughter. His might, majesty, dominion and power hypnotized her with their grandeur. How magnificent to have as father the King of Great Britain, France and Ireland, Defender of the Faith and Supreme Head of the Church, the living embodiment of the new monarchy of the reformation, even though he had become corpulent and sickly. This more than cancelled out the slur of a bar sinister before she came to the throne and for the rest of her life she revered Henry's memory for what he had achieved in church and state.

In the summer of 1543 Henry married his sixth and last wife, Katherine Parr, a widow of thirty who was recognized as one of the most cultivated women of the Renaissance. She proved an ideal stepmother, for she insisted on bringing the royal children to court and so, for the first time in her life, Elizabeth had a settled home for long periods, with apartments, when she was at Whitehall, next door to the Queen's. Katherine and her stepdaughter were to remain close together for five years.

Thanks to the Queen the princess's formal education was extended and her tutors discovered that she had a natural bent towards learning. She shared with her brother Edward classical lessons from John Cheke and French from Jean Balmain, but studied Italian alone with Battisti Castiglioni. Elizabeth's earliest surviving letter was written to Katherine Parr from St James's on the last day of July 1544 and shows how apt a pupil she was. Composed in Italian and penned in a beautiful Italic script it is a remarkable performance for a girl of her years. She sent her bounden duty and hoped that the Queen would intercede with her father, away in France, to end some piece of misunderstanding.[29] By Christmas she had completed an English translation of Queen Margaret of Navarre's *Le Miroir de l'Âme Pecheresse*. This 'godly meditation of the christian soul concerning a love towards God and His Christ' she gave to Queen Katherine as a New Year's gift. The manuscript is carefully written and the binding splendidly embroidered, with the initials K.P. in the centre of a diamond bearing flowers of heartsease at the corners.

But her masters had instilled in her the question of standards. In a covering letter she regretted the imperfections of her translation; she undertook it to keep her wit from getting rusty, putting it 'out of French rhyme into English prose, joining the sentences together, as well as the capacity of my simple wit and small learning could extend themselves.' She knew it needed polishing, and left that to her stepmother's keen mind, but hoped there was nothing in her work worthy of reprimand. After that she came down to earth with wishes for 'a lucky and prosperous year'.[30]

A year hence her present was more personal – a translation in Latin, French and Italian of Queen Katherine's own prayers and meditations, which she finished at Hertford on 20 December 1545. This time there was no apologia, nor could it possibly need one. This manuscript is a superb example of the renaissance in miniature.[31] (See plate 3.)

In the classroom hexameters and pentameters, paradigms and particles, optatives and subjunctives were mastered without tears. Before long Elizabeth was launched on commentaries on the Greek new testament, studies of the early fathers, Plato's *Republic*, Cicero's orations and such classics of the age as More's *Utopia* and Erasmus's *Paraphrase*. This was a tough diet for a thirteen-year-old, but Edward, four years her junior, was digesting the same fare. When her father was her age Erasmus had told him he hoped that by infecting others with his love of scholarship he would one day turn the court into a university, and now it seemed to have come to pass. Nothing was done by halves. Romances were forbidden but story books based on classical mythology, the bible and history were allowed to be read provided they pointed a moral. Elizabeth and Edward would write stilted little letters to each other when they were separated, sometimes in French but usually in Latin, much as brothers and sisters of today send cheery postcards. For relaxation there was music and dancing, needlework, riding and archery, in all of which – except needlework – the Princess excelled.

There was practical relevance in much of the godly learning so thoroughly, if not always effortlessly, acquired, since in the age of the reformation theological controversy was high politics. As Supreme Governor of the Church Elizabeth was little less read in the holy scriptures, the early fathers and the by-ways of divinity than her bench of bishops, and her religious knowledge was of fundamental importance in her efforts to achieve a settlement. Yet for these prodigies working under John Cheke and his friend William Grindal the lump was leavened by the fact that they loved learning for its own sake. As Queen of England Elizabeth would still make time in her early sixties to translate Boethius' *Consolations of Philosophy* and works of Horace and Plutarch.[32] The scholar's habit of reading, translating, annotating never left her. It is important to dwell on the range and the depth of her studies which went steadily forward from the age of six, with little interruption, until her accession. Her fluency in languages enabled her when the need arose to deal with ambassadors without need of interpreters, to read despatches, draft instructions and even love-letters without leaning on secretaries. And yet despite this very formidable linguistic technique acquired as princess and her wide knowledge of continental scholarship of her own day, she remained insular – 'mere English'. An English sovereign, with no trace of foreign blood in her veins, she was never to set foot outside her native country, not even to visit the Wales of her grandfather, Henry Tudor. In this insularity no less than in her sex lay much of her strength and part of her weakness.

The earliest-known portrait, now at Windsor, belongs to these blue-stocking years. A pale-faced girl, with innocent eyes and fair auburn hair, wearing a simple patterned gown of crimson cloth of gold and a few jewels, is holding a small book, and at her side on a reading-desk there is a large opened volume.[33] For all her self-assurance and regal bearing, she is still a child. The closing years of King Henry's reign were the most peaceful of her whole childhood. Busy at her books, the months went by all too quickly. Despite all the turmoils since her earliest days, her father had been the one constant factor in her life and once he had gone there would be endless troubles facing this fourteen-year-old princess.

As Henry lay dying, Edward Seymour, Earl of Hertford and uncle to Prince Edward, made his dispositions for seizing power. The Howards, his chief enemies, had already played into his hands, for the follies of the Earl of Surrey at dabbling with treason had enabled Seymour to secure his attainder and send his father, Lord Treasurer Norfolk, to the Tower and, but for King Henry's death in the night, to his execution. The Succession Act of 1533, settling the crown in turn on Edward, Mary and Elizabeth, had reserved to Henry the right of altering the succession by his testament. In his will he confirmed the order of succession of his own children, but went on to provide for the possibility – so remote it must have seemed in 1547 – of all three of them dying childless; in such a case he laid down that the crown should descend to the heirs of his younger sister Mary, who had first been betrothed to the Emperor Charles V and then wedded to Louis XII of France. Widowed after three months, she had a runaway match with Charles Brandon, Duke of Suffolk, by whom she had a son, who died young, and two daughters, Frances and Eleanor. Frances, the elder girl, married Henry Grey, subsequently created Duke of Suffolk, and gave birth to three daughters, the eldest of them being Lady Jane Grey. The other Brandon sister, Eleanor, married Henry Clifford, Earl of Cumberland, and produced a daughter, Margaret. Such was 'the Suffolk line' preferred at the last by Henry VIII to the children of his elder sister Margaret ('the Stuart line'). In his will he also nominated the councillors who were to govern the realm during Edward's minority, but immediately on Henry's death Seymour assumed power as governor of the boy king and Lord Protector of the kingdom, with the title of Duke of Somerset. He soon embarked on an ambitious programme of religious and social reform, forcing the pace of a Protestant Reformation, and he was too much of an idealist to realize that the councillors whom he had excluded from power would stop at nothing to overthrow him.

Elizabeth remained for the time being with her stepmother in Chelsea, but the peace of their household was soon shattered by the arrival of a suitor. Thomas Seymour, the Protector's younger brother, was in some ways the most eligible bachelor in England. He was an old flame of Katherine Parr's and they had been on the point of marrying four years back when Henry VIII had trumped his jack and he had discreetly withdrawn from court. Now, nearing forty, he was still a dashing figure, his mouth full of pretty phrases but his head crammed with madcap schemes. 'Wise and liberal,' wrote a friend, 'he through malice went to pot.'34 Before Edward's coronation he had been created a Knight of the Garter, elevated to the peerage as Lord Seymour of Sudeley and appointed Lord High Admiral. Yet over-loaded with honours, he bitterly resented the fact that his brother Somerset had succeeded in drawing the reins of power into his own hands instead of following the letter of King Henry's will and he was determined to attempt to oust him.

Seymour moved fast. In the first weeks of the new reign he chanced his arm to win one of the princesses; either Mary or Elizabeth would serve his purpose,35 but as the Protector would have none of it he turned to the Queen Dowager. Katherine was overwhelmed with joy that she should once again be the centre of Seymour's universe but, like him, realized the need for extreme caution. He tried to handle his brother Somerset, 'to creep into his favour to bring our matters meet to pass',36 yet, as he soon found it useless to expect he would consent to the match, he went ahead and married Katherine secretly, probably in mid-April.

Elizabeth knew about the marriage long before her sister, for Seymour was always in and out of Chelsea Palace. She was thrilled both by the excitement of the secret romance and by the idea of having the Admiral as a stepfather. Mary, away at Wanstead, was quite out of things. To break the news to her, Seymour wrote at the end of May, imploring her to help influence Katherine to accept him, but Mary declined to meddle; 'I being a maid am nothing cunning' in wooing matters, besides it was an exceptionally delicate matter, 'considering whose wife her Grace was of late'.[37] When the news eventually leaked to court Somerset was 'much offended',[38] but with other matters on his hands he could not but accept the *fait accompli*, though the affair drove the brothers even further apart, for Katherine Parr and the Duchess of Somerset could not abide each other. Katherine would refer to the Duchess as 'that hell' and she hated the Protector as much as she despised his wife; 'Your brother', Katherine once wrote to Seymour, 'hath this afternoon a little made me warm. It was fortunate we were so much distant else I should have bitten him.'[39] She meant what she wrote.

Once installed at Chelsea Seymour began to flirt with Elizabeth and tease her mercilessly; he snatched kisses from the fourteen-year-old girl, smacked her indecorously and pocketed the key of her bedroom. There was indecent horseplay in the garden at Hanworth when he cut the black dress she was wearing into a hundred pieces while Queen Katherine held her.[40] No one outside the house knew that the Queen Dowager and the Lord Admiral would come into the Princess's bedroom and tickle her in bed; and then he started coming in alone. Quite often, reflected Katherine Ashley, pained by the recollections drawn out of her, Seymour would barge into her room of a morning:

before she was ready, and sometimes before she did rise, and if she were up he would bid her good morrow and ask how she did, and strike her upon the back or on the buttocks familiarly ... and sometimes go through to the maidens and play with them, and so go forth. And if she were in her bed he would put open the curtains and bid her good morrow and make as though he could come at her, and she would go further in the bed so that he could not come at her.

One morning he tried to kiss her in bed, but Mistress Ashley was on duty and bade him go away for shame; another time at Chelsea, Elizabeth, hearing his key in the lock, ran out of bed to hide behind the bed-curtains, until he gave up waiting. Katherine Ashley spoke out to him in the gallery that he was ruining the girl's reputation, but the Admiral swore, 'God's precious soul!

He would tell my Lord Protector how it slandered him.' He lost
his temper again with the governess when she reproved him for
coming into the Princess's room at Seymour Place bare-legged
and in his nightgown to wish her good day, though by now
Elizabeth had taken care to be fully dressed before he arrived and
generally had her nose in a book.[41]

Elizabeth was undoubtedly attracted to Seymour and the
startling effect of a single kiss would have quickened her sexual
instinct; but he affronted her girlish modesty with his mock
attempts at seduction and the routine of his flirtation soon palled,
shaming her innocence. A rather naughty escapade had degener-
ated into a bedroom farce, with the same old pathetic jokes and
gestures, so Seymour for all his charm became repulsive, and
Elizabeth dreaded the thought of being caught quite alone by the
Admiral, though Mistress Ashley would see to it that the chances
of this happening were remote.

Katherine Parr, too, felt the joke was wearing thin; she became
jealous of the Princess who saw so much of her husband and this
jealousy increased with Katherine's pregnancy. It was the last
straw when at Whitsun 1548 she came across the two of them 'all
alone, he having her in his arms'.[42] Next day Elizabeth left the
household for good and moved to Cheshunt under the wing of
Sir Anthony Denny. After a day or so she wrote to Katherine to
set things in perspective: she was too sorrowful on leaving her to
be able to thank her properly for all her many kindnesses 'and
albeit I answered little, I weighed it more deeper when you said
you would warn me of all evils that you should hear of me. For if
your Grace had not a good opinion of me you would not have
offered friendship to me that way, that all men judge the contrary. But what may I more say than thank God for providing
such friends to me.'[43] She and Seymour had been playing with
fire and it was a blessing she was no more than scorched; for all
his advances she was a virgin still.

There was more continuity in Elizabeth's everyday life than the
change of residence would suggest, for besides the Ashleys she
was accompanied by her new tutor, Roger Ascham. The previous
January William Grindal, who had supervised her studies for

three years, had died of the plague. The Queen Dowager was in favour of appointing a Mr Goldsmith to succeed him, but Ascham wanted the post for himself and, thanks to his close friendship with the Ashleys, the influence of Cheke and the determination of the Princess to be taught by Ascham and no other, he was successful. He congratulated Mistress Ashley on the academic attainments of 'her noble imp'; not yet fifteen, her knowledge of Latin was exceptional, her Greek good and her fluency in French and Italian very remarkable – *benissimo*, thought a Venetian of the latter. 'Her study of true religion and learning is most energetic', but it was he who set the pace. They began the day with a passage or two from the Greek new testament, and spent the rest of the morning reading from the tragedies of Sophocles or speeches of Demosthenes. In the afternoon they would turn to Latin authors, principally Cicero and Livy, and selected works of the early fathers, like the *De disciplina virginum* of St Cyprian. The key to Ascham's method was 'double translation', turning a speech from Cicero, for instance, into English and back again into Latin; but there was more to humane letters than vocabulary and grammar. The pupil studied a work selected for its content and style, for together these would help form character.[44] As a result of this method, said Ascham, she came to prefer:

style that grows out of the subject; chaste because it is suitable, and beautiful because it is clear. . . . Her ears are so well practised in discriminating all these things and her judgement is so good, that in all Greek, Latin and English compositions there is nothing so loose on the one hand and so concise on the other which she does not immediately attend to, and either reject with disgust or receive with pleasure as the case may be.[45]

Of all the pupils of the author of *The Scholemaster*, Elizabeth was his 'brightest star', and in listing her accomplishments the difficulty lay in setting bounds to his praise. When he had left her service after a quarrel, probably with her cofferer, Parry, Ascham enlarged to a friend on the prudence and industry, dignity and gentleness and many other virtues of this princess of sixteen. No womanly weakness here, since 'her perseverance is equal to that of a man.' Her memory was prodigious and she is 'as much delighted with music as she is skilful in the art. In adornment she is elegant rather than showy', spurning fashionable head-dresses and gold ornaments. Later on he admitted to Bishop Aylmer with pardonable exaggeration that he learnt more of Elizabeth every day than she of him. 'I teach her words and she me things. I teach her the tongues to speak, and her modest and maidenly looks teach me works to do. For I think she is the best disposed of any in all Europe.' This, surely, answers the accusations that she was a shameless hussy in her romps with Seymour. Her penmanship in the Italic script Ascham had taught her could be singularly beautiful, when she took pains with it, using the silver pen he had given her. Alas, when she became Queen the paperwork of the palace proved too demanding for her to devote the time to write a sweet Roman hand for everyday affairs and though Ascham, now her Latin Secretary, practised it himself in his letters to foreign courts, he must have sighed when he read some of his old pupil's scribbling.[46]

At Cheshunt Elizabeth continued to work hard at her books, undistracted by Seymour. She had plenty of physical exercise, too, when her health permitted it, for Ascham was the author of *Toxophilus*, the standard book on archery, and John Ashley was destined to write a similar manual on the art of riding. A young Cambridge mathematician, William Buckley, wrote for her a Latin treatise on the use of horary rings and sent her one of the 'ring dials' he had devised as a primitive form of watch.[47] Busy at her books and her virginals, at the butts and in the saddle she all but forgot the Lord Admiral.

Seymour, too, was preoccupied and his naval duties and political intrigues kept him too much from Hanworth and Sudeley, where Katherine awaited the birth of their child. The Queen Dowager wrote fond letters telling him of her progress. 'I gave your little knave your blessing. . . . Mary Odell being a'bed with me had laid her hand on my belly to feel it stir.'[48] But in August 1548 Queen Katherine died in childbed at Sudeley, feverishly accusing those around her of neglect, and thus Seymour was free to court Elizabeth for a wife.

Now he is free again 'you may have him if you will', suggested Mistress Ashley, eager to cast herself in the role of match-maker. 'Nay', blushed the Princess. 'You will not deny it if my Lord Protector and the Council were pleased therein', chided the elder. What news from London? Elizabeth asked her on another occasion and was told the rumour was that she and Seymour were to be married, but the girl smiled and said 'It was but a London news.'⁴⁹ When they played the parlour game of 'drawing hands, she chose my Lord and chased him away', provoking much teasing.⁵⁰ The men knew from the women's whisperings that something was in the wind and Master Ashley advised his wife to be circumspect, 'for he did fear that the lady Elizabeth did bear some affection to my lord Admiral',⁵¹ for she blushed now whenever his name was mentioned; yet the governess could not help herself from gossiping to Thomas Parry, the cofferer, about it all and then forcing him to promise to say nothing to a soul on the topic. Tactfully Elizabeth put Seymour off a proposed visit to her at Hatfield.⁵²

At this time, Durham Place in the Strand, which had been temporarily assigned to Elizabeth, was commandeered by the Protector for a mint and she badly needed accommodation in the capital for herself and her growing household. A fortnight before Christmas Seymour sent a message through her cofferer, offering her the use of his mansion, Seymour Place; and when Parry saw her delight at this suggestion he went on to ask her whether, if the Council agreed, she would marry the Admiral. The response was one of her 'answerless answers', but Seymour, to whom it was reported, interpreted it favourably. He had whispered discussions on tactics with Mistress Ashley in St James's Park and sent Parry to find out when the grant of lands, due to Elizabeth under the terms of Henry VIII's will, was to be sealed and whether those estates lay near his own domains. He argued with the Lord Privy Seal on whether the man who married the Princess could be assigned her entire income and he even asked Fowler, a crony at the palace, to discover the views of the boy King, whom he kept supplied with pocket money. Accordingly, when Edward was asked whom Seymour should marry he first answered 'Anne of

Cleves' for a joke and then, more seriously, 'Mary, to turn her opinions.'53 But much more than matrimony was at stake, for Seymour was stopping at nothing to overturn his brother Somerset. He had secured the wardship of Lady Jane Grey whom he intended should marry King Edward and even planned to secure the King's person. He was always in and out of St James's Palace, drinking with Fowler and others in the privy buttery, and one morning he observed 'A man might steal away the King now'. It was not a disinterested comment.

The Lord Admiral had overreached himself. His designs were almost an open secret by now; he had dismissed the warnings of friends and in the end he was accused at the council table. When he ignored a summons to an interview with his brother he was sent to the Tower on 17 January. Much was suspected of the household at Hatfield and next day Mistress Ashley and Cofferer Parry were arrested in the hope that they would supply incriminating evidence to substantiate current hearsay.

Sir Robert Tyrwhit, sent to Hatfield to interrogate the Princess, sensed a general conspiracy against him. She was 'marvellous abashed and wept very tenderly a long time' when she heard that two stalwarts of her household were in the Tower. 'She will not confess any practice by Mistress Ashley or the Cofferer concerning my Lord Admiral,' he wrote to Somerset, 'and yet I do see it in her face that she is guilty, and do perceive as yet, she will abide more storms or she accuse' her governess. By next day Tyrwhit had come to realize he was dealing with an extremely able opponent: 'she hath a very good wit and nothing is gotten of her but by great policy.'54 He hoped Lady Browne might extract something from her, but Elizabeth remained circumspect and Tyrwhit feared there was a secret pact among the principals 'never to confess to death.' After seven days of preying on her nerves, Elizabeth at last agreed to write to the Protector. She began coolly, denying that Mistress Ashley had ever advised her to marry Seymour, 'but said always when any talked of my marriage that she would never have me marry ... without the consent of the Council.' And then she turned to the attack. The sordid rumours that she was herself in the Tower and even with child by

Seymour degraded her honour and honesty. 'My Lord, these are shameful slanders'; to end them she demanded to come to court and show herself there.[55]

Another week of despair went by and then to try and break her spirit Tyrwhit was ordered to show her the confessions of Kate Ashley and Parry, written, as she could see, in their own hands. The Princess read the pages through 'much abashed and half-breathless'. Her Kate began with the escapade in the garden at Hanworth where her gown had been slashed and went on to relate other episodes, conversations with Parry and asides to her husband about Seymour's relations with her. All this made embarrassing reading but worst of all was the final paragraph in which she pleaded with the Protector for another prison, 'for by my troth it is so evil that I cannot sleep in it and so dark'; there was no glass in the windows and to keep out the cold she had stopped them with straw. The cold and the eeriness of the Tower which Kate Ashley was enduring for her sake seemed very dreadful to the young girl. At least she had not been browbeaten into writing that Elizabeth had been prepared to accept Seymour's proposal without waiting for the Council's consent. When Tyrwhit told her that her retainers had made a promise not to confess until death, she answered very calmly that it was 'a great matter for Master Parry to make such a promise and then to break it.'[56]

In the hope of alleviating Mistress Ashley's wretchedness Elizabeth set down on paper a few more harmless points about the Lord Admiral; she had not 'wittingly concealed them', but they seemed so trivial (they were) that she had overlooked them. Somerset concluded that Mistress Ashley had proved herself a most unreliable servant. His wife had thought so all along and had chided her for allowing Elizabeth to go in a barge on the Thames by night 'and for other light parts', unworthy of the governess of a King's sister, and so Lady Tyrwhit was appointed to succeed her. When she reported her appointment the Princess cried out that 'Mistress Ashley was her mistress and that she had not so demeaned herself that the Council should now need to put any more mistresses into her.' All that night she wept and 'lowred all the next day.' After a while she plucked up courage and wrote to

Somerset again. She was ashamed to press the point, but it was the Council's business to issue an official proclamation discountenancing the evil rumours against her and awarding punishment for those who maintained them. She then asked him to be kind to Katherine Ashley, because of her long service in her household; and St Gregory, she remarked, says we are bound to those that bring us up as much as to our natural parents. Moreover, if she failed to support her governess people would think that she were herself guilty. In fact Somerset failed to keep his promise about issuing a proclamation, but after a few weeks Mistress Ashley was released and in the summer was allowed to return to her old post at Hatfield, though Sir Robert Tyrwhit remained as controller.[57] A French cleric who had translated St Basil's epistle sent her his manuscript with a touching dedication – 'being now quite alone' – . It was a task after the Princess's own heart.[58]

The lengthy catalogue of Seymour's high treasons, which was easily compiled, ranging over all his activities since Edward's accession, included his attempt by crafty means to marry Elizabeth. Before he went to the block on 20 March he succeeded in writing letters with makeshift materials to both the princesses, urging them to rise against the Protector before it was too late, but the letters were discovered and laid before the Council. Innocent of intrigue with Seymour, his fall none the less left Elizabeth in semi-official disgrace and for nearly two years Edward did not receive her at court. Years afterwards she provided Seymour's epitaph – 'a man of much wit and very little judgement'. The strain of events from the death of Katherine Parr the previous summer, reaching a climax in Tyrwhit's interrogations had exhausted her, and she was ill. At fifteen she had endured the experience of losing the man who had aroused her love to the executioner and she had begun to tread the strange steps of the dance of love and death, romance and tragedy, in which her mother had stumbled and fallen. Thanks to rest and relaxation at Cheshunt under the care of Dr Bill, whom the Protector sent to attend her, she recovered, but she would not lightly forget Seymour or the political dangers which his rashness had placed her in.[59]

Although under the terms of her father's will Elizabeth was to receive an adequate income until such times as the councillors nominated by him should provide her with a suitable marriage, she was merely assigned *ad hoc* sums until 1550. That summer, however, she was at last granted her own estate as Princess – the patent which Seymour had fretted over eighteen months before. This comprised an extensive group of lands, principally in the home counties, worth £3,106 a year, including Berkhamsted manor, Ashridge College, Missenden Abbey and the lordship of Ewelme and, as her town house, Durham Place in the Strand, which hitherto she had rented. A few months later she exchanged some property in Lincolnshire for Hatfield House where she had spent much of her childhood.[60] To administer this property she very shrewdly sought the help of William Cecil, appointing him her surveyor. He, equally shrewd, asked to be allowed to put in a deputy to do the donkey work, for he was on the eve of becoming Secretary of State; but an alliance had been formed which was to survive the difficult years of Mary's reign and would be put on a different footing on Elizabeth's first day as Queen.[61]

Elizabeth had Cecil's help in putting the affairs of Ewelme hospital in Oxfordshire on an even keel. Because Ewelme manor was part of the crown estate the hospital or almshouse there had escaped dissolution under King Henry and since Elizabeth had been granted the lordship, she regarded herself as protectress of the almshouse which was in sore need of reformation. The villain of the piece was Thomas Key, a warden who cheated the old men out of their dues, and when the Princess heard of it she determined 'to remove the violence and oppression and to have the poor on every hand thoroughly contented.'[62]

Elizabeth at Hatfield contrived to keep clear of politics. John Dudley, Earl of Warwick, had succeeded in bringing down Somerset's Protectorate in the autumn of 1549 and though subsequently pardoned and back in the Council from the Tower, Somerset knew he was no match for the unscrupulous Dudley. 'At the Council board no man dare utter a word unless he had Warwick's countenance', and in due course there was evidence enough to send Somerset to his execution for high treason.

Dudley, created Duke of Northumberland in 1551, accumulated all the key offices of state, though he did not assume the title of Lord Protector. Elizabeth was too obvious a figurehead for intrigues, and the lesson of Seymour was not lost on her; hence her excessive cautiousness in word and deed. When the Venetian ambassador came to Hatfield to pay his compliments and hunt in the park she hastened next day to send the Protector a report of the visit via Parry, now reinstated, 'not for that the talk did import weight, but that her Grace will neither know nor do anything in matters that either may sound or seem to be of importance without doing of my Lord's Grace to understand thereof.'[63] She was again dogged by long spells of ill health; as Parry told Cecil in September 1550 'Her Grace hath been long troubled with Rheums.'[64] Only a false rumour that her brother was near to death brought her out of retirement and she rode in state to London, overjoyed to find him improved.

Northumberland, bent on retaining supreme power after the sickly Edward's death, toyed with the possibility of making Elizabeth a pawn in his dynastic game. At one time he considered forcing his brother Warwick to divorce his wife so he would be free to marry the Princess, at another he wondered about marrying her to his son Guildford Dudley, yet the Protector could not ignore the hard political fact that if Mary's right to the throne was to be set aside, so must Elizabeth's. Besides, he realized the younger princess was too clever to agree to any plans of his, too wary of traps, abundantly circumspect in her letters and conversation, cautious far beyond her years. Youth was on her side; she could afford to wait and watch him make a fatal move, and in this contest for the succession she knew the intrinsic value of a lord protector was as nothing beside a true daughter of royal genealogy. Northumberland hurriedly married off Guildford to Lady Jane Grey, the eldest claimant of the Suffolk line of succession. (See the Genealogical Table, opposite p. 354.) Edward was tricked into signing a document attested by twenty-six peers, altering the succession to Lady Jane, and the conspirators restlessly awaited his demise.[65]

Ignorant of Northumberland's scheming, the last months of Edward's reign were comparatively uneventful for Elizabeth. Her household at Hatfield or Ashridge was under the nominal direction of Sir Walter Buckler,[66] who had succeeded Sir Robert Tyrwhit, but in fact was largely run by Thomas Parry. An artist, George Tarling, came down to paint her portrait for £10 and she dutifully sent it to Edward with a letter that pleased him: 'For the face, I grant I may well blush to offer, but the mind I shall never be ashamed to present', and she wished it were she herself and not her picture that shared his company. She would write in Latin, laced with allusions to Pindar and Homer, glad that he was feeling stronger or reproaching herself for not writing more often.[67] The news of his final illness was first kept from her by Northumberland, but when he at last ordered her to the boy's bedside she smelt a rat and sent word that she was herself too ill to travel, backing this up with bulletins from her doctor.[68] Undoubtedly, had she gone to court she would have found herself in the Tower. Within the week there was good Bishop Ridley telling his astonished hearers at Paul's Cross that Mary and she were both bastards in justification of a Protestant succession. Edward died at St James's on 6 July 1533 and when four days later Lady Jane Grey was proclaimed Queen in London, Elizabeth was able to wait upon events from Hatfield. The testing-time was to begin in earnest.

MUCH SUSPECTED

NORTHUMBERLAND, apparently secure in the capital, had not counted on the country at large coming to Mary's support and the army he had mustered to oppose the loyal following in East Anglia dwindled away, so that he was taken prisoner at Cambridge, desperately trying to save his life by a sudden recantation. With the collapse of his conspiracy within a fortnight and Lady Jane Grey in the Tower, the succession devised by Henry VIII took its course, even though the sovereign was a woman. Throughout her sister's reign Elizabeth was to find herself the figurehead of the opposition, and for those who plotted to depose Mary, whether on grounds of religion or because of her Spanish marriage, the Princess was the only practical alternative. The experiences of Edward's reign had taught her the art of being on her guard and in the next five years she was to need all her calculated dissimulation, masterly procrastination and native cunning to preserve herself both from the wrath of Mary and from the wiles of the hot heads weaving plots about her. Secretly she rejoiced at her popularity, which grew with the return of the Roman rite and the announcement of Mary's plans to marry Philip of Spain, but she took pains to disown it. Compared with the Queen, age and personality were all on her side and she must beware lest they become a liability. 'Her figure and face are very handsome, and such an air of dignified majesty pervades all her actions that no one can fail to suppose she is a Queen', wrote a visiting ambassador, who could only say of Mary 'were not her age on the decline she might be called handsome.'[1] Hence Elizabeth's danger to Mary. The position of heir to the throne was an invidious one, for everyone who found the government wanting turned as of course to the rising sun; and Elizabeth as Queen never would acknowledge her successor for this very reason.

Once the pretender had been routed Elizabeth wrote to her sister congratulating her on her succession and tactfully begged her to let her know whether or not she should be wearing mourning for Edward when she came to court to salute her. She entered London 'with a goodly company of mounted men, and well-accoutred' and Mary, in token of her happiness that her throne was secure, gave her a brooch of diamonds and rubies, depicting the tale of Pyramus and Thisbe – that tale of Ovid's made popular by several English authors half a century before Shakespeare made a burlesque of it. London prepared for all the pageantry of the coronation and the master of the great wardrobe was required to issue the Princess with crimson velvet, lace, silk and gold buttons and tassels and powdered ermines for making into her robes for the service in the Abbey, at which she would carry Mary's train. At this time, in rummaging among the crates and packages left in Westminster Palace were found two little dolls in a wooden box, one dressed in crimson satin, the other in white velvet; one would like to think that years before Elizabeth had played with 'Lancaster' and 'York'.[2]

Though alterations in religion awaited the meeting of Parliament in October, from the beginning of the reign mass was celebrated in the palace and a full requiem had been sung for King Edward in the chapel of the White Tower. Already on 9 August, Antoine de Noailles, the French ambassador, was reporting home about Mary's attempts to reduce her sister '*à semblable dévotion. Mais elle est si obstinée . . .*' By the end of the month the Princess and Anne of Cleves were conspicuous for their absence from mass. The warm, sisterly affection of the Queen for her stepsister was cooling rapidly and the latter began to sense danger. When Mary again asked her to forsake the error of her ways, early in September, she sought a private audience. On her knees, in tears, she begged to be forgiven for holding such views but she had been brought up very differently from Her Majesty and 'had never been taught the doctrine of ancient religion.' During this interview, which apparently lasted some hours, Elizabeth asked to be sent books of doctrine that she might learn from them 'if her conscience would allow her to be persuaded' or for a learned man to come and instruct her. At last she promised to attend her first mass on 8 September, the Nativity of the Blessed Virgin Mary, as earnest of her change of heart.³

When the day came she began by feigning sickness, and then 'complained loudly all the way to church that her stomach ached, wearing a suffering air.' As another onlooker put it, 'The event did not take place without a certain amount of stir.' Mary had set her heart on converting her, as a preliminary to the reconversion of England, and now that the Princess had started to give way her sister was exceedingly relieved and, treating her as a child, gave her more jewels, though Elizabeth did not wear any of them for some weeks. Her attendance at chapel was erratic by design and soon Mary felt bound to question her closely about her conversion. Was it without dissimulation? She answered there had been no pretence, she had merely followed her conscience, yet to a devout woman like Mary the Princess's behaviour seemed equivocal: 'She only went to Mass out of hypocrisy', she blurted out, and were not her household staff all heretics?⁴

The Queen heeded the advice given so insistently by Simon Renard, the imperial ambassador, that Elizabeth's 'presence at court would cause endless trouble', and not only on the score of religion. Parliament was considering the succession and, while it left the Princess a bastard, had not excluded her from the throne, for the Commons 'would not stand for it'. There was a heated conference between Mary, Renard and Paget, the Secretary, in which the Queen came to the conclusion that she ought to debar Elizabeth from the succession on account of her 'heretical opinions, and illegitimacy, characteristics in which she resembled her mother, and as her mother had caused great trouble in the kingdom' she feared the daughter might do the same. As autumn drew into winter the girl experienced all kinds of disfavours. She lost her precedence at table to claimants like the Countess of Lennox, people began to shun her company, there was overmuch whispering. Though full of mistrust Mary was unable to take any decisive action against her sister. It was all very well Renard hinting darkly

that the Tower was too good for her, but there was as yet nothing
to justify extreme measures. In the end Elizabeth herself took the
initiative and asked for leave of absence from court and Mary,
with a sigh of relief, allowed her to go to her house at Ashridge on
6 December. She took leave of the Queen 'very courteously', was
given a rich coif of sable and then off she went with a splendid
escort. Some ten miles out of London she stopped and wrote a
letter to Mary asking for 'copes, chasubles, chalices and other
ornaments for her chapel'. It was a gambit worth trying, but the
Queen was not deceived; bitterness welled up in her and sometimes she let slip that the girl was no half-sister at all, for she noticed
in Elizabeth's features a likeness to Mark Smeaton, the musician
at her father's court 'who had been a very handsome man'.[5]

That winter conspiracies were afoot, with the object of marrying Elizabeth to Edward Courtenay and placing them on the
throne. Born in 1526 Courtenay had been in the Tower from the
age of twelve until Mary released him a few days after her accession and created him Earl of Devon. As a grandson of King
Edward IV, 'well-proportioned' and a good linguist, he seemed
to many people an ideal husband for Mary herself; indeed, when
the Commons in mid-November petitioned her to marry 'within
the realm' the unspoken name was Courtenay's. Instead of hark-
ing to this advice she had pressed forward with her plans to accept
Philip II's proposal. Within her Council, however, were men such
as Bishop Gardiner, the Lord Chancellor, who now angled for a
match between Earl and Princess with the Queen's blessing, but
as her opposition was adamant Gardiner carried on intriguing
behind the scenes. More desperate plots were hatched by men who
feared the Spanish marriage and all it would involve for the
kingdom, and the ringleaders, Sir James Croftes, Sir Thomas
Wyatt, Sir William Pickering, Sir Nicholas Throgmorton and
William Thomas, were determined to act speedily. Both Croftes
and Throgmorton visited Elizabeth, though no one will ever
know what passed, and they also wrote to her, yet she was too
cautious to commit anything to writing. At any rate the leaders
made free use of her name because of its sheer popular appeal. Their
scheme was to stage risings in the shires which would converge

on the capital; Croftes would take charge of Herefordshire and the Marches, Wyatt would see to Kent, while Leicestershire was to be led by the Duke of Suffolk and Devon would rise as a man under Carew and Courtenay. The rising was staged for Palm Sunday and there were promises of French support. 'The heretics are constantly trying to rouse up the people against the Queen and foreigners, in order to prevent the marriage' (with Philip), lamented Renard at the turn of the year. 'They are trying to induce Courtenay or Elizabeth to act as their leader.' And no one knew with Elizabeth, for 'she was too clever and sly'. In the event the government became alarmed and the plotters panicked into premature action: Courtenay defected, having been so long in prison, he had 'neither that spirit nor experience which his position would require',[6] so that all that was left of this grand strategy was Wyatt's rising in Kent, which broke out on 25 January.

Mary had written to her sister with a reproof for not sending news from Ashridge and by reply learnt that she had been poorly. 'I have been troubled since arriving at my house with such a cold and headache that I have never felt their like, and especially during the last three weeks I have had no respite because of the pain in my head and in my arms.' She went on to comment on Mary's marriage-treaty with Philip, which was 'a deep and weighty matter', made a none too felicitous contrast between houses built on sound foundations with those built on sand, but ended on a happier note. 'Though comparisons be odious', no one could be found 'more ready to pray God for you or more desirous of your greatness' than her sister. This letter arrived just before Wyatt raised his standard. A peremptory order came from St James's on 26 January to 'our right dear and entirely beloved sister', requiring her to come to court:

We tendering the surety of your person which might chance to be in some peril if any sudden tumult should arise, either where you now be, or about Donnington, whither (as we understand) you are about shortly to remove, do therefore we think expedient you should put yourself in readiness with all convenient speed to make your repair hither to us, which we pray you, fail not to do, assuring you, that as you may more surely remain here, so shall you be most heartily welcome to us.

There could be no doubt about the tone of the letter, but Elizabeth ignored the summons, sending a verbal message that she was too ill to move. There was awkward circumstantial evidence against her. In London there were rumours that Ashridge was being prepared for a siege, and the tale that Croftes had urged her to move to Donnington – hence the pointed aside in Mary's letter. Worse, the French ambassador's diplomatic bag was rifled by the government and with his despatch home was found a copy of Elizabeth's own letter to Mary of the previous week. Its presence there remains a mystery, but in those hectic days, when Wyatt was so near to victory, it seemed only natural to suppose that the Princess was in active communication with de Noailles. 'Much suspected', indeed; and when a second time she was ordered to London she again pleaded illness.[7]

With the rebels defeated and Wyatt in custody, the Lord Admiral (Lord William Howard), Sir Edward Hastings and Sir Thomas Cornwallis, all privy councillors, were sent down to Ashridge on 9 February, demanding an audience with the Princess. Two of the Queen's doctors went ahead of them to report on her condition. They found her ill, for her body was badly swollen – a recurrence of the trouble she had had four years before – but in the opinions of Dr Owen and Dr Wendy she could be moved without danger. Lord William Howard and the others then went in to her to deliver the Queen's command and she appeared 'very willing and conformable' to Mary's wishes but asked for the journey to be postponed, to which Howard agreed. He worked out an itinerary which would bring her to Westminster by easy stages, no more than eight miles a day, which he forwarded to the Council, together with Elizabeth's request to Mary that she might have a lodging in Whitehall 'rather further from the water than last time'. (Was it that she feared the cold air from the river would aggravate her condition or that being near the Thames meant being nearer to the Tower?) In a day or so she prepared to leave Ashridge, for all she knew to her doom.[8]

After the fourth night, when she had stayed at Mr Cholmondeley's house at Highgate, her litter was escorted down Highgate

Hill, from which the Tower and old St Paul's were visible, and on past the Charterhouse in Smithfield, along Fleet Street to White-hall. Cold though it was, she had the curtains on both sides of the litter drawn back so that people could see her and Londoners disturbed by the clatter of the horses came out of their houses for a glimpse of this fairy-tale princess, dressed all in white, ashen pale, and they feared for her safety, though even with her illness and anxiety she managed to appear 'proud, haughty and defiant'. At the palace Mary refused to see her and the request to be away from the river had been ignored. Here she was a prisoner for just over a month, while Wyatt and his fellows were examined.[9]

At first nothing could be gleaned from them that would in any way implicate Elizabeth. Sir James Croftes, for one, was 'marvellously tossed' but revealed no secrets, so the government grasped at straws. It sifted a report sent in by the Sheriff of Gloucestershire of one of the local gentry who after denouncing the Spanish marriage 'had gone on to talk of the Lady Elizabeth', but as the sheriff was hard of hearing he could not be more specific. In the Tower Chancellor Gardiner and Sir John Bourne 'laboured to make Sir Thomas Wyatt confess concerning the Lady Elizabeth', but extracted nothing. Renard was amazed at the slackness in bringing her to trial and thought 'delays were being created in the hope that something may come up to save them', and he was adamant that so long as Elizabeth was kept alive Philip II could hardly come to England in safety. At his trial on 15 March Wyatt alleged he had written to Elizabeth but that her reply was verbal and non-committal. Under torture, after his con-viction, he is said to have signed a full statement implicating both the Princess and Courtenay, in hope of a pardon, yet on the scaf-fold on 11 April he denied this. But the day following his trial, Elizabeth was herself ordered to the Tower. The privy councillors argued fiercely about the precise reasons for her imprisonment and about which of their number was to accept the responsibility for her custody. At all costs they decided she must be sent by water, not through the streets, as she had too many well-wishers in the city. Earlier that week Londoners in their hordes had gone to hear the miraculous spirit in the wall, which made no response to the loyal cry 'God save Queen Mary!' but replied to 'God save the Lady Elizabeth!' with an assured 'So be it!' The Marquess of Winchester and the Earl of Sussex came to bid her make ready and she was dumbfounded. She could not believe this was her sister's command and begged to be allowed to see her, but the peers refused. Then could she write her a letter? Winchester said it was out of the question, but Sussex could see no harm in it, so in the end pen, ink and paper were provided. They must have agreed that it was not an easy letter for anyone to have to write and it was going to take time for Elizabeth to collect her thoughts, and time was what she desperately needed; time to appeal to her stepsister who had still ignored her person since she had been brought to Whitehall. Delay might mean salvation – if she could spin her writing out until the tide turned it would mean that the barge to take her to the Tower would be unable to shoot London Bridge.[10]

If any ever did try this old saying, that a King's word was more than another man's oath, I most humbly beseech your Majesty to verify it in me, and to remember your last promise and my last demand, that I be not condemned without answer and due proof, which it seems that now I am; for that without cause proved I am by your Council from you commanded to go into the Tower, a place more wonted for a false traitor than a true subject; which though I deserve it not, yet in the face of all this realm appears that it is proved, which I pray God that I may die the shamefullest death that any died afore I may any such thing.

And to this present hour I protest afore God, who shall judge my truth, whatsoever malice shall devise, that I never practised, counselled nor consented to anything that might be prejudicial to your person anyway, or dangerous to the state by any means. And I therefore humbly beseech your Majesty to let me answer afore yourself, and not suffer me to trust to your councillors; yea, and afore that I go to the Tower, if it is possible; if not, afore I be further condemned. Howbeit, I trust assuredly your Highness will give me leave to do it afore I go, for that thus shamefully I may not be cried out on, as now I shall be, yea, and without cause. Let conscience move your Highness to take some better way with me, than to make me be condemned in all men's sight afore my desert known.

Also I most humbly beseech your Highness to pardon this my bold-
ness, which innocency procures me to do, together with hope of your
natural kindness, which I trust will not see me cast away without
desert: which what it is I would desire no more of God than that you
truly knew, which thing, I think and believe, you shall never by report
know, unless by yourself you hear. I have heard in my time of many
cast away for want of coming to the presence of their Prince; and in
late days I heard my Lord of Somerset say that if his brother had been
suffered to speak with him, he had never suffered; but the persuasions
were made too him to great, that he was brought in belief that he could
not live safely if the admiral live, and that made him give his consent to
his death. Though these persons are not to be compared to your
Majesty, yet I pray God as evil persuasions persuade not one sister
against the other and all for that they have heard false reports, and not
hearken to the truth known.

She read through the first page – and as we read it through we
can sense the effort it cost her, even the recollection of Seymour's
folly – while Winchester and Sussex waited beside her. Those last
half dozen words had been squeezed in to leave no space, but
apart from this the first page is faultless, in a beautiful hand. But
once she had turned over her agitation began to show; she left
out various words and made spelling mistakes which she would
never have done at the age of six:

Therefore, once again kneeling with all humbleness of my heart,
because I am not suffered to bow the knees of my body, I humbly crave
to speak with your Highness, which I would not be so bold to desire if
I knew not myself most clear as I know myself most true. And as for the
traitor Wyatt, he might peradventure write me a letter, but on my faith
I never received any from him. And for the copy of my letter sent to
the French king, I pray God confound me eternally if ever I sent him
word, message, token or letter by any means. And to this my truth I
will stand to my death.

She had said all she could, yet the writing went no more than a
third of the way down the second page. To leave a blank space
courted danger, for a cunning forger might undo all her work by
adding a sudden recantation, a blatant admission of guilt. So she

made eleven diagonal lines across the sheet, leaving just enough room for a final appeal:

I humbly crave but only one word of answer from yourself.

Your Highness's most faithful subject that hath been from the beginning and will be to my end, Elizabeth.[11]

By then the tide had risen too high for the barge to go in safety that day and so she had won her day's grace.

Mary was unmoved by her appeal and furious with Sussex and Winchester. 'They would never have dared to do such a thing in her father's lifetime, and she only wished he might come to life again for a month.' The same two peers came next morning, a wet Palm Sunday, and as she walked beneath the Queen's apartments she looked up, hoping for a chance of seeing her sister, but Her Majesty was taking part in a procession of palms. This was the very day that the conspirators had originally chosen for the rising, but no one was about to cheer on the waterside as the Princess was rowed downstream. At the water gate of the Tower, since those days called 'Traitor's Gate', the river was running very high and she was anxious not to wet her ankles in getting ashore. This, she knew, was the way her mother had come, and she felt very near to death; it was an effort to speak up bravely to the warders and soldiers, 'Oh Lord! I never thought to have come here as a prisoner; and I pray you all, good friends and fellows, bear me witness that I come in no traitor, but as true a woman to the Queen's Majesty as any is now living, and thereon will I take my death!' A few steps on and she asked Sir John Gage 'What, are all these harnessed men for me?'

'No Madam', the lieutenant shook his head.

'Yes,' she insisted, 'I know it is so. It needeth not for me, being alas but a weak woman.'

She was desperately afraid that she would be quietly put out of the way – like little Edward V and his brother. Once in her chamber in the Bell tower, the Earl of Sussex gave her some words of encouragement – many of the Privy Council pitied her, 'and as for me (casting his hands abroad . . .), sorry I am that ever have lived to see this day.' He gave out that her door was not to be' locked, 'for she is a King's daughter and the Queen's Majesty's sister.' The morrow of Wyatt's execution two London apprentices were in trouble for spreading the rumour that in his last speech he had cleared the Princess of treason.[12]

'Much suspected', and Mary had in truth to agree that 'Nothing proved can be.' She had begun the investigations of the Kentish conspirators full of distrust; 'she is what I have always thought her', she told Renard, but after Wyatt's execution she had to admit to the ambassador that there simply was not sufficient evidence to convict her sister, for the judges had gone through all the documents and declared as much. Gardiner was even cheated of the chance of producing the copy of Elizabeth's letter to Mary found in the French ambassador's diplomatic bag, because the despatches which it accompanied made reference to the Chancellor's own interview with Courtenay, so he gave out that the documents had been 'lost' when the rebels ransacked his library. After a while Elizabeth was given greater liberty, first to walk in the gallery, then to take the air in the lieutenant's garden. A gaoler's son brought posies, a little girl came up to her with tiny keys 'so she might unlock the gates'. Perhaps she was able to see Sir John Harington who was imprisoned nearby, for carrying a letter to her – 'one deed of special goodwill' that Elizabeth later remembered when she agreed to stand godmother to his son. Early in May Sir Henry Bedingfield came to take over her custody and she was alarmed that he brought a hundred soldiers with him, not realizing that arrangements were being made for her removal to the country.[13]

Mary's dilemma was that since she had no evidence to send Elizabeth for trial she had no justification for confining her any longer, yet the political situation required her to be kept under close surveillance away from court. Her position as *de facto* heir to the throne, whatever her religious affiliation, made her the focal point of opposition to the Spanish marriage and within a week of Wyatt's execution broadsheets were being circulated in London warning all true Englishmen to stand firm to 'keep the Prince of Spain from entering the kingdom.' Certainly the Princess must be out of the way before Philip landed and Renard suggested she might be sent to the Court of Brussels presided over by his remarkable Aunt Mary, the dowager Queen of Hungary. Mary of Hungary was asked for her views and replied, 'As for the Lady Elizabeth, it is quite possible that our characters may be different', but like a good aunt she agreed to give it a trial if it really would serve Philip's interests to have the Princess under her wing. The proposal foundered, however, on the belief that Elizabeth's removal to Brussels would provoke a further rising in England. At this time the Queen once more began referring to her as 'sister' and her portrait in Whitehall was restored to its usual place. After many discussions it was decided to send her, not to Ashridge, which was too near London for Mary's peace of mind, but to Woodstock in Oxfordshire, a rather tumble-down overgrown hunting-lodge, near the site of what would one day be Marlborough's Blenheim Palace. She was taken by water to Richmond on the day before Trinity Sunday and the Hanseatic merchants, bolder than their English brethren, gave her a royal salute as her barge passed the Steelyard, quite sure that she was being set free. Yet that very night at Richmond (if we are to believe Foxe), she was equally certain that she was about to meet her end.[14]

Bedingfield, her custodian for the next nine months, was a Norfolk squire who was a privy councillor. Mary had chosen him with care, for he had been keeper of Katherine of Aragon during the last years of her life at Kimbolton, the days of Anne Boleyn's triumph and Elizabeth's birth. Bedingfield did not set out to make the Princess's life a misery but he was a stickler for rules and did nothing without reference to the Council, maddening Elizabeth by his lack of initiative and imagination.

From Richmond Elizabeth was taken in a litter to Windsor, where she spent the night in the dean's house, 'a place more meet indeed for a priest than a princess.' The scholars of Eton came out to gaze on her next day when she crossed the Thames into Buckinghamshire and in every village and hamlet through which she passed she was right royally welcomed with loyal shouts of 'God Save Your Grace!' Her presence scotched old rumour that she had been put out of the way and what Mary had envisaged as retreat into disfavour turned into a royal progress. At High

Wycombe the housewives passed cakes and wafers into her litter until, rather embarrassed by the quantities, she had to ask them to stop. After a night at Sir William Dormer's house at West Wycombe she moved on to Rycote, Lord Williams' mansion near Thame, and as she passed through Aston four men ran to the church to ring a peal in her honour, but were later in trouble for their greeting. Next morning she explored the gardens and orchard at Rycote in search of shade and solitude. As she approached Islip men were drawing home a load of wood, the annual gift of the lord of the manor to the church; it was always a red-letter day in Islip, for the children cheered on their fathers, but this year, when a minstrel played while the Princess passed by, none would ever forget. All too soon she was at Woodstock, palatial only by name, as no more than four rooms could be found for her use.[15] Sir Henry Bedingfield fussed when he found that only three doors were capable of being locked and took elaborate precautions to prevent anyone from the outside world passing messages to the Princess. A troop kept nightly watch on a hill in case of attempted escape and rumour was rife. Here Elizabeth was to remain until the end of April 1555 in solitary state.[16] Her own establishment was weeded and pruned, and even her faithful cofferer, Thomas Parry, who was responsible for the running of the house, was not allowed to sleep there, but made the *Bull* in the town his headquarters, which soon became frequented by the Princess's well-wishers, like Francis Verney.

Pin-pricking restrictions goaded Elizabeth into stubbornness. Some Latin books she asked Parry to send her had first to be taken to London to be scrutinized for messages written inside them. She demanded to have the right to roam beyond the gardens over the entire park, claiming that Winchester and Sir John Gage had permitted this. She complained of the changes Mary had insisted upon among her women servants and by sheer persistency got her way in some cases, though she was unable to get back Mistress Ashley, her favourite, as Mother of the Maids. She demanded permission to write to her sister and this was eventually granted just before Mary's wedding; though the letter she wrote has not survived we can deduce from the Queen's reply that it restated her innocence. Mary thereupon decreed that she was not to write any more of these 'colourable letters', but instead to pray for God's grace. Bedingfield read it through to his captive twice and when she asked him to write on her behalf to the Council he said he had no authority for this. She cried out in a fury that it was worse at Woodstock than in the Tower, for there 'the prisoners be suffered to open their mind to the lieutenant and he to declare the same to the Council – and you refuse to do the like!' Next day she returned to the charge – if he refused to write 'I shall be in worse case than the worst prisoner in Newgate.' All this he reported in his turgid missives to court and within a week Elizabeth had won her point, yet having won it she characteristically delayed for three weeks before asking Bedingfield to act as her scrivener. At last on 30 July she made him set down a petition to the Council to mediate with the Queen to end her captivity; she asked either to face a trial or be given liberty to come to court 'which she would not desire were it not that she knoweth herself to be clear even before God for her allegiance.' If these courses were not acceptable then she hoped some councillors might be allowed to come down to Woodstock and talk with her, 'whereby she may take a release not to think herself utterly desolate of all refuge in this world'; these final words are so obviously the Princess's, not those of the bumbling Bedingfield. After a fortnight of waiting for a reply she demanded to send a servant to court with a further message, but this was naturally forbidden ('and her grace saith she is sure your lordships will smile in your sleeves when you know this my scrupulousness', reported Sir Henry). And so the duel of wits, wearing each other down, went on. Tradition has made the captive Princess envy the carefree, happy life of the milkmaid.[17]

In June she felt quite ill with swellings and asked if the Queen's own physicians could come to her, but she was told that this was not at present possible and it was suggested that a well qualified Oxford doctor might do just as well. This infuriated her: 'I am not minded to make any stranger privy to the state of my body, but commit it to God.' Soon Mary relented and sent Dr Owen to attend her. He examined her swollen face, arms and hands and reported 'Her Grace's body is replenished with many cold and waterish humours', which required purging, but midsummer was the worst season for this treatment. A careful diet alleviated her condition and she stuck it out bravely until October when she was given purgatives and bled.[18]

That summer, while Elizabeth kept up her spirits by keeping up her feud with Bedingfield, Mary awaited Philip's arrival. From Babylon, by devious routes known only to the merchants of the spice trade, came news of the birth of Antichrist, a male child which spoke at eight days, and nearer home were phenomena just as strange which men interpreted as ill auguries for the Spanish match. John Dee and other astrologers were arrested for daring to cast the Princess's horoscope with those of the Queen and her fiancé. In prayer and fasting Mary bade her time, fretting lest she would be too old a bride to bear a child, until at last on a rainy July day she was married to Philip in Winchester Cathedral and took him off to Hampton Court for the honeymoon. The large number of Spaniards who accompanied him, bent on profitable places at court, did nothing to increase his popularity. Like their master, these Spaniards were far from enamoured of the English or the country. The Englishwomen of the court seemed to them ill-bred and badly dressed, with short skirts that showed their legs to the knee, 'so that they really look quite indelicate when they are seated or riding' and 'their dancing consists only of ambling and trotting.' Perhaps, indeed, there were 'too few Orianas and many Mavilias'. One of these critical southerners within a week or two of their cool welcome predicted that the marriage 'will indeed have been a failure if the Queen has no children.'[19]

At any rate Mary soon believed she was pregnant in answer to her prayers before holy shrines and that however numbered her days she would produce an heir to keep England Catholic in faith in place of her heretical stepsister. In the autumn Cardinal Pole returned after twenty years' absence to absolve England from the papal interdict and undo the work of King Henry's reformation. Meanwhile Parliament authorized the Church to undertake a heresy hunt against the recalcitrant clergy, and under the direction of Edmund Bonner, Bishop of London, the fires of Smithfield began to burn from February 1555. Many of the Edwardian clergy fled to the continent, the rest faced conformity or the Bishop's bonfire, lighting with the Oxford martyrs that candle which Latimer trusted by God's grace would never be put out in England.

Elizabeth conformed; she would find her niche in John Foxe's *Acts and Monuments* not as a martyr but as the personification of God's providence. On the last Sunday in August she went to confession for the first time and received the sacrament of the altar. Renard shrewdly surmised the character of her 'conversion' to Catholicism, when later on he was told that she had obtained indulgences, attended mass every day and spent many hours in private devotions; she was doing her utmost, he said, 'to give the impression that she had changed her religion ... However, she is too clever to get herself caught.' She required her chaplain at Woodstock to read the litany and many of the prayers of the mass in English, until Mary heard of this and told her she must be content with the Latin service used at court and throughout the land. The Princess thereupon expressed horror at the error of her ways and promised 'with all my heart to obey'.[20]

The last few months of Elizabeth's sojourn at Woodstock were uneventful, for she and Bedingfield had become used to each other's ways, while Mary had other matters on her mind. There is a delightful tale of Foxe's that on her accession Elizabeth forbade Bedingfield to come to court, telling him to go home to Norfolk; 'and if we have any prisoner whom we would have sharply and straitly kept, then we will send for you.' To Sir Henry such a prohibition must have come as a relief, for there was no spite in it since the Queen with a twinkle in her eye nicknamed him her 'jailer', and twenty years on seems to have invited herself to his home in Oxborough during her prolonged progress of the eastern counties. Just after Easter 1555 Mary ordered Bedingfield to bring his charge to Hampton Court, for, ill and mentally troubled, she felt her time was approaching and old fears nagged her. What if she died in childbed? What if she faced her Maker unreconciled with her stepsister? Philip, anxious to leave England, wanted the question of the succession settled and even Renard was beginning to eat his words and think that the Princess should now be restored to favour. At least she had been restored to health by her year in the country, away from the smoke and germs of London. It was shortly before leaving Woodstock, according to the traditional story of Holinshed which dies hard, that Elizabeth scratched on a windowpane with a diamond from her ring the three lines:

> Much suspected, by me,
> Nothing proved can be.
> Quoth Elizabeth, prisoner.[21]

She came to court 'very privately, accompanied by three or four of her women' and was received at Hampton Court by Lord William Howard, who placed her in the custody of the Duchess of Alva, a notable slight. She had not seen Mary for eighteen months, when she had left to spend the first Christmas of the reign at Ashridge, and Philip she had never set eyes upon. Mary was in no hurry to give her an audience and Bedingfield's troops still guarded her door. After three days, if we are to believe the French ambassador, Philip could restrain his curiosity no longer, and Mary went so far as to lend her a rich gown to wear for this meeting. Soon Bishop Stephen Gardiner, the Chancellor, came to her rooms to try and persuade her to acknowledge her complicity in Wyatt's rebellion, but she refused to ask for forgiveness as she had committed no offence, and when Gardiner reported these words to Mary she 'marvelled that she would so stoutly stand on her innocence.' If the Princess were blameless, then her imprisonment would have been unjust, and justice must seem to have been done, so she told the Chancellor that the Princess 'must tell another tale'. Elizabeth refused to be tricked and stuck to her story. The battle of wills continued and after a fortnight at Hampton Mary was weakening.[22]

One night about 10 o'clock, Susan Clarence, Mary's mistress of the robes, came up to Elizabeth's room to fetch her by torchlight across the garden and up to the Queen's bedchamber. Going down on both knees as soon as she entered, Elizabeth repeated that she was innocent.

'You will not confess your offence but stand stoutly in your truth', said her sister. 'I pray God it may so fall out.'

'If it doth not,' answered the Princess, 'I request neither favour nor pardon at Your Majesty's hands.'

'Well, you stiffly still persevere in your truth', said Mary. 'Belike you will not confess but that you have been wrongfully punished.'

'I must not say so, if it please Your Majesty, to you.'

'Why then,' retorted the Queen, 'belike you will to others.'

'No, if it please Your Majesty. I have borne the burden, and must bear it. I humbly beseech Your Majesty to think me ever to be your true subject, not only from the beginning hitherto, but for ever, as long as life lasteth.'

Thus, face to face at last, a reconciliation was achieved. Mary accepted her sister's profession of loyalty and spoke 'a few comfortable words'. Perhaps Philip heard it all from behind the arras. Shortly afterwards Elizabeth was allowed to be at court without restriction, though she did not as yet appear in public, and later that summer she was allowed to leave for the country with her household attendants. To make matters easier Edward Courtenay, Earl of Devon, had been sent abroad.[23]

That wet summer of 1555, when the corn failed to ripen – 'the like is not remembered for the last fifty years' – various ex-associates of Wyatt began meeting in London to plan a further rising that once more aimed at setting Elizabeth and Courtenay on the throne in place of Philip and Mary. The plot was anti-Spanish, as much as anti-papal, for the key objective was to stop the scheme for crowning Philip as King. The development of Dudley's conspiracy, as it is called, which came to a head the following spring, is confused, and much of the evidence for it comes from the French ambassador's despatches, for he was up to his neck in the intrigues, largely to counter the Hapsburg designs in England. Henry Dudley was a distant relative of the late Duke of Northumberland and had been captain of the guard at Guisnes under King Edward. He and his henchman, John Throgmorton, contemplated robbing the Exchequer, seizing the Tower and killing the Queen. The English exiles in France under Courtenay were to land in the Isle of Wight and there were to be risings in the provinces, notably in the west country. It was all rather gentlemanly and amateurish; the secrets were not well kept, supporters were in the main too lukewarm to act and the rising never really got off the ground. The one feature which saved the affair from utter bathos was the steadfastness of Throgmorton, who endured the rack without confessing the names of his fellows.[24]

Elizabeth knew enough about what was afoot to want to steer clear of this dubious enterprise and her captivity resulting from Wyatt's revolt was too recent for her to want to risk her neck. Certainly some of her household were involved, such as the hot-headed Francis Verney, her Italian tutor and possibly Mistress Ashley. We do know that when the Princess was at Whitehall for a week early in December, François de Noailles, the new French ambassador, wanted to speak urgently with her 'to ascertain the state of her patience and whether she is moving any designs for next summer', but he considered a visit to her apartments to be too dangerous. Instead, he used the Countess of Sussex as a go-between and the lady wearing disguise called on him to say that Elizabeth's servants were urging her to flee to France. Some of her household, indeed, feared she was about to be sent to Spain as an eventual bride for the hapless Don Carlos, then but eleven years old. To flee, said Noailles, would be utterly disastrous and in later years he claimed that had Elizabeth not hearkened to his advice she would never have succeeded to the throne. Even so, Lady Sussex crossed the Channel to spy out the land with Dudley and others and found herself in jail on her return to England. As in Wyatt's rising, Elizabeth's name cropped up in the host of rumours and a handful of depositions: 'to set up the Lady Elizabeth and Lord Courtenay, whereby that God's word prosper and be set up again, and to banish Spaniards and Popery.' 'Elizabeth', said one, 'is a truly liberal dame and nothing so uncharitable as her sister is, and she taketh this liberality of her mother, who was one of the bountifullest of women', and another, on a more personal note, maintained, 'If my neighbour of Hatfield might once reign, then should I have my lands again.'[25]

Yet this time there was no danger of Elizabeth going to the Tower, for she was in far too strong a position. Philip knew full well that Parliament would never consent to his coronation if Elizabeth were imprisoned at home or banished abroad, while Mary sensed that if anything should happen to her sister there was a very real danger of a popular rising much more broad-based than the schemes of Dudley and Throgmorton. A message reached the Princess that Mary had refused to believe the stories of her complicity in the plot – so very different from the Queen's attitude in 1554 when she assumed her to be guilty unless she could prove her innocence. Mary certainly believed she was in as great personal danger now as when Wyatt marched on London; she doubled her guard, rarely appeared in public and, it was said, even wore armour. But the danger lay not from her sister and she realized this. Two years after the Dudley conspiracy Simon Renard wrote a memorial on the state of affairs during his tour of duty as Charles V's ambassador in London. 'All the plots and disorders that have troubled England during the past four years have aimed at placing its government in Elizabeth's hands sooner than the course of nature would permit.' The Princess survived them but not, as Renard suggested, through the support of 'an organized and influential party', for such did not exist. What did exist was a loyal personal following in her household and, understandably, the household at Hatfield was remodelled in June 1556.[26]

Mistress Ashley was arrested and her collection of Protestant tracts at Somerset House aroused great suspicion. She denied all knowledge of the conspiracy, asserting that her loyalty was too well known for her to have trusted two 'such naughty fellows' as Dudley and Throgmorton. Sir Edward Hastings, the master of the horse, was sent down with a token ring to Hatfield to explain on Mary's behalf that Elizabeth was well rid of servants who were put in danger of evil suspicion. A fortnight later Sir Thomas Pope rather reluctantly came to take charge of the house. The Princess found him a much more sympathetic custodian than Bedingfield, for he was a cultured man, still anxious about his new foundation of Trinity College, Oxford, a man with a very different outlook from the Norfolk squire, and her few months under his tutelage were in consequence uneventful. Her faithful cofferer, Thomas

Parry, was still at his post and there were welcome visits again from Roger Ascham. No dull dog, Sir Thomas; he knew the young – even so diligent a scholar as the Princess – liked merriment, and Shrove Tuesday was a good excuse for a pageant in Hatfield Hall with music and dancing.[27]

Sir Thomas had been asked to relate to his charge the tale of a man who suddenly appeared in Essex proclaiming Elizabeth Queen 'and her beloved bedfellow, Lord Courtenay, King', and this prompted Elizabeth into writing a splendid paean of loyalty to her sister on 2 August:

When I resolve in mind, most noble Queen, the old love of Paynims for their Prince, and the reverent fear of the Romans for their Senate, I can but muse for my part, and blush for theirs, to see the rebellious hearts and devilish intents of Christians in name but Jews in deed, toward their anointed King, which methinks if they had feared God (though they could not have loved the State), they should for the dread of their own plague, have refrained that wickedness, which their bounden duty to Your Majesty had not . . .

She agreed with St Paul that seditious folk were the sons of the devil, and she congratulated her sister on divine deliverance from rebellion, like a lamb from this bull of Basan.

Oh that there were good surgeons for making anatomies of hearts, for then, I doubt not, but know well, that whatever others should subject by malice, yet Your Majesty should be sure by knowledge that the more such mists render obfuscate the clear light of my soul, the more my tried thoughts should glisten to the dimming of their hid malice.

One wonders what Mary made of it all. But at least the closing words were as clear as day: as Elizabeth had been faithful and true since the very beginning of Mary's reign, 'so shall no wicked person cause me to change to the end of my life.'[28] Later in the year news reached England of the death in Padua of Edward Courtenay, whom the man in the street had chosen as her consort, and this event helped to ease her position even further.

By now it had become clear to everyone except Mary that Philip had married her for no other reason than to obtain dominion in England, and with the Queen's deteriorating health the question of Elizabeth's own marriage became more important. Various Hapsburg princes had been suggested at different times as most suitable candidates for her hand. There was the Archduke Ferdinand, ruling at Prague, who was reported to be 'high-spirited and lusty ... his magnificence and generosity being no less noteworthy than his Catholicism.' Don Carlos's name was bandied about a good deal, even after Elizabeth had plainly said 'she would not marry, even were they to give her the King's son.' Next it was Emmanuel Philibert of Savoy, a kinsman of Philip's and a pensioner of Spain. Philip pressed his suit very hard on Mary and when he revisited England in March 1557, after an absence of nineteen months, he brought with him the Duchess of Lorraine whom he planned should take the Princess back with her to Flanders for the wedding with Emmanuel Philibert. When this intelligence reached the King of France he exclaimed 'I really don't know how these people will stand it.' Warning of this was sent to Elizabeth by the French ambassador through the Marchioness of Northampton and the Princess firmly replied that she would sooner die than bend England to Philip's will. For her part Mary called her to court to discuss the project, but was herself almost as opposed to it as the Princess, and she told Philip it would be quite impossible to arrange such a match without Parliament's approval. Philip still hoped he might make all of them see reason before long but could make no progress before he left England. Out of the blue at Easter there arrived an envoy from the King of Sweden to propose his son Eric as a suitor for Elizabeth, and Mary, fearing Philip's displeasure if the scheme were even discussed, became dreadfully agitated. 'After Madam Elizabeth had replied that she had no wish to marry,' reported the new Imperial ambassador, Feria, 'she calmed down, but she is still in a terrible talking about it.'[29]

Philip's departure made Mary more dependent on her sister's company and for a few weeks in the summer of 1557 they were perhaps closer together than at any time since their father's death. Some say that at this time the Queen once more imagined she was pregnant and that Elizabeth out of compassion began making baby clothes for her. Londoners saw the Princess return to favour as she travelled down the river to Richmond to keep midsummer with Mary in a barge decked out with fresh flowers, and in Richmond Palace gardens Mary gave a splendid banquet in a pavilion where the centrepiece was a veritable confectioner's triumph – an edible pomegranate tree bearing the arms of Spain. Later that year the Queen paid her a state visit at Hatfield where she showed herself a most considerate host. Together the sisters watched bear-baiting in the courtyard, from a safe distance, and for the evening's entertainment she had arranged for the choristers of St Paul's to come down on an excited excursion and act plays in front of them; one of the boys had so enchanting a voice that Elizabeth asked if she could accompany him on the virginals.[30]

Philip of Spain had not, as Mary still secretly hoped, left an heir behind him, but that final visit of his to England provided a legacy no less portentous, for he had persuaded Mary to join him in his war against France, which the kingdom was in every way ill-equipped to undertake. Six months later Calais was lost. According to one Englishman it fell by 'negligence of the Council at home, conspiracy of traitors elsewhere, force ... of enemies, helped by the rage of the most terrible tempests of contrary winds and weather.' It was a national disaster of the first magnitude and Mary, who bore the brunt of the blame, knew that instead of raising the stature of England by her marriage with Philip she had in fact brought the kingdom's prestige to the lowest point in living memory. Calais, the bastion on which her father had spent a fortune, gone, and England had shrunk to a size it had not known since the days of King Harold. One devout Catholic attributed the calamity to Calais being 'a great town for heresy', and he hoped the beads, hallowed by the Abbess of Sion, which he sent his mother would help her to pray for the reversal to be overcome. But most of his contemporaries spoke of it in the same terms of astonished depression that later generations of Englishmen would reserve for Van Tromp's sailing unchallenged to Nore buoy, General Burgoyne's surrender at Saratoga, the death of Gordon and the fall of Singapore. It was this burning indignity at the loss of the French fortress, and all it implied, that provoked the popular outburst of nationalist fervour which greeted Elizabeth's accession later that year; it was all the stronger in that its tone was militantly Protestant, but it would be wrong to underestimate the nationalist element, and for years to come Elizabeth would scheme and negotiate for the return of Calais.[31]

For Mary military defeat was the final straw. She felt Philip had utterly deserted her and her illness, dropsy, fever or whatever it was, became progressively worse. That autumn as she lay wasting away at St James's, Elizabeth at Hatfield awaited her summons. She was leaving nothing to chance; too much was at stake for her to be an entirely passive spectator of events. It mattered little now if she were 'much suspected', for the initiative in her duel with her sister had passed to her. In the late summer, when a rumour of Mary's death was abroad, Sir Nicholas Throckmorton had sent Elizabeth a lengthy secret memorandum on the tactics she should follow 'to succeed happily through a discreet beginning', with suggestions for appointments to offices (not all of them disinterested proposals) and useful hints about the ways in which she could make sure of capturing the machinery of government in the first awkward hours of her reign. She should, for instance, immediately require the Chancery clerks to attend on her with the great seal, still 'the key of the kingdom'. Caution and deliberate vagueness about policy had been the way recommended by Throckmorton: 'It shall not be meet that either the old [Mary's] or the new [Elizabeth's Council] should wholly understand what you mean, but to use them as instruments to serve yourself with.' Elizabeth was to follow the spirit, though not the letter, of that memorial and for years to come her apparently purposeless vagaries would succeed in overturning the calculated negotiations of seasoned statesmen.[32]

Before the end of October the Princess was confirming supporters in their loyalty to her and assuring them that their past service and professions of faithfulness would not be forgotten. She made plans to counter any moves by those who would deny her her inheritance, whether in the Spanish interest or the French, whether from claimants from the Suffolk line or the Stuart. Her cofferer Parry was closely in touch with Sir John Thynne, who could guarantee her a stout following in Wiltshire if trouble should arise; a biblical quotation sufficed to make Elizabeth's point – 'Blessed is the servant to whom the master when he cometh may say I have found thee a good and faithful servant.' She had even arranged with various captains of the Berwick garrison to march their troops all the way to Hertfordshire 'for the maintenance of her royal state, title and dignity'. Mary's troubles in July 1553 were too recent for the Princess to assume that hers would be a peaceful accession, though she prayed she would not have to fight for her throne.[33]

Philip's special envoy, Count de Feria, who had visited Elizabeth in June, came post haste from Brussels as Mary neared the end of her unhappy life. On 9 November he called the Privy Council together and in Philip's name approved the choice of Elizabeth as heir to the throne, and Mary recovered sufficiently to give her concurrence, asking that her sister be made to promise to maintain the old faith and to pay her debts. The Master of the Rolls and the Controller rode off to Hatfield to impart the news to her and next day de Feria arrived there, aiming from the start to dominate proceedings. She must realize, he told her, that she would owe her throne to her brother-in-law's intercession, but she answered him back that it was the English people who had placed her where she was, not a foreign prince. 'She is much attached to the people,' de Feria noted with amazement, 'and is very confident that they take her part.' 'She is a very vain woman, but a very acute one. She evidently has great admiration for her father and his way of doing things', he added. Perceptive about people, he misjudged events. Once the accession had gone smoothly forward, he simply could not understand what had happened. It pained him beyond measure when he had to report to his master:

but what can be expected from a country governed by a Queen, and she a young lass, who though sharp, is without prudence, and is every day standing up against religion quite openly.... She seems to me incomparably more feared than her sister, and gives her orders and has her way as absolutely as her father did.[34]

Mary died before dawn on Thursday, 17 November and in the afternoon the bells rang out for the new reign, as they would ring out on every anniversary of her accession, long after Elizabeth's death, even. At last, at the age of twenty-five, she had come into her own. For this she had never known a mother's love, had borne the stigma of bastardy, had endured the terrors of suspicions under two lords protector and faced the peril of the Tower under Mary. She had triumphed in the face of endless difficulties. caused by well-wishers as well as foes. All her training and experience, her self-discipline and abnegation, her loneliness and sorrows endured, had been for this 'crown imperial', which was hers of right. She was determined never to give it up and for the rest of her life self-preservation became her first care.

3

GOD'S CREATURE

PARLIAMENT was sitting on 17 November and it fell to Nicholas Heath, Archbishop of York and Lord Chancellor, to announce the demise of the Crown to the assembled Lords and Commons, who then went in procession to the door of Westminster Hall for the accession proclamation. 'Elizabeth by the grace of God, Queen of England, France and Ireland, Defender of the Faith et cetera', Garter King of Arms cried out, had succeeded 'as the only right heir by blood and lawful succession' following 'our dearest sister's death'. All subjects were charged on their allegiance to the new Queen, who for her part promised 'no less love and care' towards her people than any of her predecessors. All were warned to keep the peace and not to attempt upon any pretext the alteration of any order or usage established. The heralds then rode on to the city to repeat the proclamation before the Lord Mayor and Aldermen at Cheapside Cross. The effect was electric. Joyous bonfires were lit, at great risk to the timbered and thatched houses, church bells pealed out and Londoners with undisguised relief at the passing of the old order brought out tables into the narrow street to 'eat and drink and make merry for the new Queen'. As the news spread to the provincial cities and country villages it was greeted in similar vein. Even in the north, so strongly Catholic in sympathy and so remote from royal processions and all the trappings of majesty, her accession was greeted with enthusiasm. She is 'a princess, as ye wot', the people of York heard, 'of no mingled blood of Spaniard, or stranger, but born mere English here among us, and therefore most natural unto us.' Never had a sovereign come to the throne on a greater wave of popularity.[1]

The Queen herself could not witness the loyal demonstrations. Earlier that day a select band of councillors and courtiers had ridden to Hatfield to kiss her hand. There is a pretty tale, told by Naunton years afterwards, that were it true would rank with that other scene in Kensington Palace in 1837 when another Princess heard of her destiny; when they came to salute her in the park she sank on her knees and exclaimed the psalmist's verse 'This is the Lord's doing; it is marvellous in our eyes.' She once said she cried and cried on hearing of her sister's passing. Orders were issued for closing the ports and for keeping a careful watch on the coasts of Kent and Sussex, for England was still at war with France, and Dr Bill, the Queen's chaplain, was chosen to preach the Sunday sermon at Paul's Cross, as he was known to be a man who would not stir up trouble. By a stroke of fortune Elizabeth had not been Queen for many hours before Cardinal Pole, the arch-priest of the counter-reformation in England, died, thus ridding her of an implacable enemy. Convention demanded a hiatus of mourning before formal government began and it was not until Sunday 20 November, when in churches all over the country a solemn *Te Deum* of thanksgiving was sung, that she called her first meeting of the Privy Council. William Cecil was sworn as Secretary of State, being required by his sovereign 'without respect of my private will' to give 'that counsel that you think best.' Though a Protestant by conviction, Cecil had conformed during the late reign and at thirty-eight he was by Tudor standards already a man of great experience in public affairs. Queen and Secretary thus entered on a partnership that was to be unique in English history, for he was destined to serve her diligently for another thirty-eight years.[2]

Later that Sunday Elizabeth addressed the chief members of Mary's Council:

My lords, the law of nature moveth me to sorrow for my sister, the burthen that is fallen upon me maketh me amazed; and yet, considering I am God's creature, ordained to obey his appointment, I will thereto yield, desiring from the bottom of my heart that I may have assistance of His grace to be the minister of His heavenly will in this office now committed to me.

She aimed at a small body of councillors, and wanted to make as few immediate changes as possible, but for the present hesitated to show her hand. Those whose appointments were not confirmed she required to be steadfast in their loyalty. It surprised no one that Thomas Parry should become comptroller of her household and that other faithful ally, Kate Ashley, first lady of the bedchamber, but the elevation of Lord Robert Dudley to the high office of Master of the Horse caused some speculation.[3]

On the Wednesday, after three more Council meetings, she set out for the capital with an entourage of 'a thousand and more lords, knights, gentlemen, ladies and gentlewomen', headed by the young Earl Marshal, her cousin of Norfolk and England's only duke. As she approached Lord Northe's fine mansion at the Charterhouse, where she broke her journey, 'the whole of London turned out and received her with great acclamation.' 'They tell me her attitude was more gracious to the common people than to others', commented the haughty Spaniard de Feria, who was intriguing for all he was worth to be given a set of rooms actually in Whitehall Palace. After five days at the Charterhouse Elizabeth went with great pomp and ceremony through the streets to the Tower, to take formal possession of the citadel that had once been her prison, and en route captured the citizens' hearts with friendly words and gestures. Thence by water to Somerset House until Whitehall was ready to receive her for Christmas.[4]

There was soon to be the more prolonged pageantry of the coronation, for Elizabeth wanted to be crowned with little delay, to remove all doubts about the legality of her succession. While the act of 1544 had placed her in the succession after Mary, it had left unrepealed an earlier statute barring her from the throne. At Lord Robert Dudley's suggestion Dr John Dee made an astronomical calculation for the most auspicious date for the coronation and hit upon Sunday, 15 January, a date giving little time for the many preparations to be made. 'Soon work began in the city on the building of scaffolding for the pageants, while the customs officers down at the wharfs were secretly ordered to impound any crimson silk that was landed, so the Queen could have the pick of them.'[5]

The most important question was, who was to perform the ceremony? With Pole's death the see of Canterbury was vacant and Heath, Archbishop of York, who was thoroughly alarmed at rumours of coming doctrinal changes, refused to act. Eight sees were already vacant and if the Protestant exiles returning from Geneva and Zurich regarded Elizabeth as their Deborah, a saviour to rescue the realm from abysmal darkness, the remnant of the old episcopate looked on Mary's death as the end of an epoch; they were fearful for the state of the Church, their own preferment and even their heads. Tunstal of Durham could not easily be reconciled to the new order and in a tactful letter Elizabeth dispensed with his services in the Abbey. White of Winchester had been placed under arrest for his outspoken sermon at Mary's funeral; though spoken in Latin, his contempt for the new Queen was obvious: 'the dead deserved more praise than the living, for Mary had chosen the better part.' Eventually Owen Oglethorpe, Bishop of Carlisle, was appointed to perform the ceremony as a suffragan of Heath, Archbishop of York. The remaining thirteen English and Welsh bishops, with the exception of Bonner of London, attended the coronation but took no part in the service. Elizabeth had an especial enmity towards Bonner and ordered him to lend Oglethorpe his richest vestments.

Fine materials of all kinds were being bought up from city merchants to clothe the court; £3,958 was spent on cloth of gold, cloth of silver, velvets and satins provided by the mercer William Chelsham, and in mid-December an official was sent over to Antwerp to buy such things as London could not provide, all of which were turned into gorgeous and stately robes and furnishings by an army of craftsmen. Cutlers, saddlers, bitmakers and chariot-makers busied themselves for the processions, under Lord Robert Dudley's eagle eye. All was prepared from the £5,794 worth of scarlet cloth for the lesser household staff to the shillingsworth of cottonwool 'to dry up the oil after the Queen's anointing'; from the 672 ounces of spangles of fine silver and gold for garnishing the guardsmen's coats to the eighteen yards of cloth of silver incarnate used to cover St Edward's chair in the Abbey. Everyone at court received a new set of clothes for the occasion – the jesters, Will Somers and Jane, were rigged out in orange-coloured velvet, splattered with purple and gold tinsel; the eighteen henchmen in cloth of gold with helmets boasting red, white and yellow plumes of ostrich feathers; and the three kings of arms, five heralds and four pursuivants who were to play so conspicuous a part in the ceremonies had their distinctive arms painted in oils on their robes by the serjeant painter. Velvet crimson gowns were made for the great officers of state, like the Lord Great Chamberlain; while privy councillors paraded in crimson satin. Each of the thirty-nine ladies attendant on Her Majesty on the eve of the coronation was granted sixteen yards of velvet for a gown and two yards of cloth of gold, plain, 'for turning up the sleeves'.

For the Queen herself the most splendid robes imaginable were devised. On the eve of the coronation, when she drove in state through the City of London, Elizabeth appeared in a 'mantle of estate' made from twenty-three yards of gold and silver tissue with fur trimmings and a lace of silk and gold. During the coronation she changed her robes twice. Her parliament robe was of crimson velvet with a fur of powdered ermines. Her Robes of State were of purple velvet, consisting of a kirtle and a surcoat 'made round to the shoe with tabard sleeves'[6] and a mantle with a long train: with them she wore ermines and a silk and gold mantle with tassels. On her head in the procession to the Abbey she wore a hat of crimson velvet, embroidered with Venice gold and a few pearls, with taffeta tassels and a hatband of silken gold. Also in her wardrobe for that day were a velvet cloak, with twisted lace of gold, a pair of silk and gold stockings and a pair of gloves knitted with the finest white thread. We can but feel that the officials of the great wardrobe, who received £27 for measuring cloth, gave their services very cheaply!

All the trappings for the procession were newly produced too. A magnificent litter was made of yellow cloth of gold, with a quilt of white damask and a satin lining, and eight cushions to match. Ladies riding on horseback were to sit on red velvet saddles. £154 was spent on 700 yards of blue cloth as a carpet between the upper end of Westminster Hall and the choir door of the Abbey; while inside a lesser length of 'mean silk, crimson and green' covered the steps to the throne. The Surveyor of Works had timber brought up from Windsor and from the New Forest for constructing seats for the great congregation. Seventeen trumpeters had new tabards, and the many standards ordered included six St George's crosses, three of damask and three of taffeta, with white and green staves.

It is not surprising that all this pageantry cost £16,741. 19s. 8¾d. – quite apart from the unknown cost of the great banquet.[6] Elizabeth I has a bad reputation among historians for parsimony, but it is quite clear that nothing was stinted at her coronation. Comparatively few would be able to witness the actual crowning, but countless Londoners and other subjects would see the various processions and spectacles. A sovereign was expected to be lavish in the provision of such pageantry, which brought warmth and colour to the drab lives of ordinary men and women. One who witnessed the great scenes put into words a maxim practised by princes of the renaissance throughout Europe; 'in pompous ceremonies a secret of government doth much consist.' And at her coronation Elizabeth stirred the hearts of her people as none of her predecessors.

There was considerable interest in the appointment of the Lord High Steward of England for coronation day. This was an office of very great authority, the right of governing the realm immediately under the sovereign, which for the last two centuries had only been revived for coronations. For this post Elizabeth selected Henry, Earl of Arundel, who rather fancied himself as a possible suitor for her hand, though whether she played to the gallery by honouring him in this way, or whether the rumours about his ambitions only started in earnest after his appointment, we have no means of knowing. Of meagre intelligence, he had already buried two wives and at forty-seven was past his prime; certainly rank was the only thing that commended him, especially his close family connexion with young Norfolk, the Earl Marshal, with whom inevitably the Lord Steward had to work very closely. Arundel was also made Lord Great Chamberlain for the eve of the coronation, with power to create thirty Knights of the Bath at the Tower.

Elizabeth came to the Tower by water on 12 January, landing, not at the water gate as in 1554, but at the private stairs on Tower wharf. Next day, Friday, she drove out to Cree Church Place, Aldgate to bring the heralds up to strength by a new creation, and returned for the investiture of the Knights of the Bath. On the morrow, before leaving the Tower, she gave a heartfelt prayer of thanks to God for having been spared 'to behold this joyful day', comparing herself with the prophet Daniel – 'even so was I overthrown and only by Thee delivered.' She began her triumphal progress through the streets of the city at 2 p.m., a prolonged state drive with many halts for formal speeches and informal acclaim, during which she won Londoners' hearts. She knew by instinct when to speak and when to listen attentively, when to smile and when to be solemn. It was to be the same throughout her reign on her annual summer progresses, just as it had been on that journey in a minor key to Woodstock. She inspired fervent loyalty in the loving hearts of humble folk and made them feel their love for her was amply reciprocated. Such was the secret of kingship. Before her went her household staff, lesser officers of state, the bench of bishops and temporal peers and foreign ambassadors. Then came the kings of arms, followed by Arundel, as Lord High Steward, bearing the sword of state, Norfolk as Earl Marshal and Oxford as High Constable. Over her chariot was a fair canopy, carried by four knights, and on either side marched an escort of pensioners with axes. Immediately behind came Dudley, as Master of the Horse, leading a spare horse. He was followed by the thirty-nine ladies of honour, twenty-four of them on palfreys, the rest in three chariots. Chief amongst them were the Countess of Lennox – soon to be a thorn in the Queen's side – and the Duchesses of Norfolk, Suffolk and Somerset, with other wives and daughters of the chief peers of the land. The henchmen on 'stirring horses' rode behind and the royal guards brought up the rear. It was a splendid sight.

As she entered the city the Queen was 'of the people received marvellous entirely, as appeared by the assembly, prayers, wishes, welcomings, cries, tender words, and all other signs which argue a wonderful earnest love of most obedient subjects toward their

sovereign.' The streets were richly decorated, and colourful hangings, banners and streamers fluttered out of the windows of every
house on the route. At various stages of the progress *tableaux* were
arranged for Her Majesty's delight. At Fenchurch a boy spoke his
poem of welcome from a gaily furnished scaffolding; while at
the upper end of Gracechurch Street the citizens had erected a
magnificent ark, with the actors representing the Queen's genealogical tree: the whole pageant proclaimed the marriage of the
houses of Lancaster and York, and the stage was fittingly strewed
with red roses and white. Here, as at the other *tableaux*, a child
interpreted the scene; and for the benefit of Her Majesty, and
others equally learned, the theme was also proclaimed in Latin
hexameters from hoardings. At the end of Cornhill a pageant
portrayed the 'seat of worthy governance' – with Pure Religion
treading upon Superstition, Wisdom upon Folly, and Love of
Subjects trampling down Rebellion: Her Majesty graciously
promised her good endeavour to maintain these virtues. All along
the route there was cheering from the crowds and music.

In another pageant eight children represented the Beatitudes of
St Matthew's Gospel, as applied to Elizabeth. At the upper end of
Cheapside the Recorder of the City offered the Queen a purse of
one thousand marks as a demonstration of the city's goodwill. In a
characteristic reply Elizabeth said:

I thank my Lord Mayor, his brethren, and you all. And whereas your
request is that I should continue your good Lady and Queen, be ye
assured that I will be as good unto you as ever Queen was to her people.
No will in me can lack, neither, do I trust, shall there lack any power.
And persuade yourselves that for the safety and quietness of you all, I
will not spare, if need be, to spend my blood. God thank you all.

The pageant by the Little Conduit contrasted the differences
between a decayed commonwealth and a flourishing commonwealth: here the child-interpreter presented the Queen with an
English bible, which she kissed and laid upon her breast. By St
Paul's churchyard a scholar of St Paul's made a Latin speech which
would have warmed the heart of Dean Colet, the school's
founder. Farther on, at Ludgate, there was yet another *tableau* –

'Deborah, the judge and restorer of the house of Israel,' who governed the land in peace for forty years – this indeed needed little interpretation. By St Dunstan's Church stood all the charity children of the hospital: one of them reminded Elizabeth that after these great spectacles had been forgotten in the city there would yet remain the everlasting spectacle of mercy shown to the poor by her father. The Queen kept a copy of his speech and promised to send relief to the poor and needy. At Temple Bar, where the city of London gives way to the city of Westminster, the giant figures of Gogmagog the Albion and Corineus the Briton held welcoming verses high in their hands; and on the south side a children's choir sang a farewell. 'Be ye well assured I will stand your good Queen', came the answer.

The citizens of London had provided a splendid show, but the hearts of all had been won by Elizabeth's brilliant performance: her words of thanks to the Lord Mayor, her kissing the English bible, her smiles and numerous little incidents had brought tears of joy to many eyes. It was observed that a simple branch of rosemary given to her by a poor woman near Fleet Bridge was still in her chariot when it reached Westminster. Within ten days a full account of this happy and glorious progress through the capital was on sale in Fleet Street, written by George Ferrers, who had taken part in the procession. The city's triumphal day would not merely be a matter for personal reminiscence: it would be read and re-read by those who witnessed it and by many yet unborn who would serve as loyal subjects of the Queen.

On the morrow, Sunday, 15 January, Londoners who rose early in order to catch a glimpse of the stately procession from Westminster Hall to the Abbey Church found the streets freshly gravelled, for it was a cold, frosty day.[7] The lords spiritual and temporal robed in the House of Lords and were conducted over to the Abbey. The Dean and Chapter of Westminster in rich copes, together with all the officials of the Abbey and the choir of the Chapel Royal, moved across to the Palace, led by the serjeant of the vestry; the Dean of the Chapel Royal, George Carew, carried the crown of St Edward the Confessor, the founder of the Abbey, and other dignitaries carried the rest of the regalia – two further crowns, the sceptre, orb, ring, bracelets and St Edward's spurs and staff, all of which had been delivered to them by the master of the jewel house.

In Westminster Hall the officers at arms marshalled the illustrious gathering into an orderly procession. It began very humbly with gentlemen, squires and knights without liveries, and proceeded by degrees to include the most eminent in the land. After the knights came the sewers of the chamber, the aldermen of London, the squires for the body and the clerks of the privy seal, signet and privy council. Then followed chaplains having dignitaries, knights of the bath, serjeants-at-law, barons of the exchequer, the Solicitor-General and Attorney-General, the judges, knights commissioners, and privy councillors and knights of the garter not being peers. Next came the Chief Baron of the Exchequer, the Lords Chief Justices of the Courts of Queen's Bench and Common Pleas, the master of the rolls and ambassadors of foreign states. Then walked together the serjeant of the vestry and the serjeant porter of the palace; and preceded by three crosses came the canons and prebendaries of Westminster 'in their best robes', followed by the choir of the Chapel Royal chanting *Salve Festa Dies*. Behind the choir walked the bishops in scarlet copes, wearing their mitres, barons of the realm, the two secretaries of state and the comptroller and treasurer of the royal household. After them came viscounts, earls and marquesses, 'in their robes and caps of estate, with coronets in their hands'; their ladies were already seated in the Abbey. Norroy and Clarenceux, Kings of Arms, in their brilliant dress, embodying the coronation itself, preceded the regalia; the Earl of Huntingdon carried the spurs, the Earl of Bedford St Edward's staff, and the three unsheathed swords of state were borne by the Earls of Derby, Rutland and Worcester. Garter King of Arms followed on their heels, walking in step with the Lord Mayor of London and a gentleman usher. The Earl of Oxford, the Lord Great Chamberlain, walked alone. Behind him came Henry, Earl of Arundel, with the sceptre in his left hand, and the aged Marquess of Winchester, the Lord Treasurer, with the orb in his right. The Duke of Norfolk followed with St Edward's crown. And then Queen Elizabeth herself, supported by the Earls of Pembroke and Shrewsbury, her train borne by the Countess of Lennox, assisted by the Lord Chamberlain; the thirty-two barons of the Cinque Ports supported the canopy over Her Majesty. With great solemnity the splendid host walked along the blue carpeting into the Abbey to see their Queen crowned after the rites of her forefathers. One bizarre touch. This splendid carpet, provided at a cost of £145 to cover the route from the upper end of the Hall to the choir door of the Abbey, attracted the souvenir hunters. 'As Her Majesty passed the cloth was cut by those who could get at it', and the Duchess of Norfolk, who walked behind the Queen, was very nearly tripped up.[8]

About a number of important points in the lengthy coronation service we are surprisingly ignorant; for the religious ceremony is documented far less satisfactorily than the secular pageantry. Much significance attaches to the order of service followed:[9] it was the last coronation conducted in the Latin service of medieval times, and it was performed before Parliament met to settle the religion of the land and approve a new prayer book.

Elizabeth, having first seated herself on a chair of state in front of the high altar, to the sound of trumpets, was at four different places proclaimed Queen of England, and was four times acclaimed by the people. She was then led before the altar to make her final oblation, offering a piece of gold to the value of 20s. and a beautifully-worked crimson and gold pall, which was placed over the paten. A sermon followed – doubtless a lengthy exposition – then a bidding prayer in English (the bidding of the beads). Afterwards the Bishop of Carlisle administered the coronation oath, which Cecil held up for him to read. By this she undertook to keep the law and customs of the realm, to keep peace to the Church and people and execute justice in mercy and truth. The litany was then sung, and several long prayers, culminating in the anointing. A tabard of white sarsenet was put over Her Majesty's gown, and the pall she had offered was held over her while the Bishop anointed her with the holy oil: a coif of fine cambric protected the oil on her head, and a pair of gloves that on her hands. After Elizabeth had changed her apparel and returned to .the coronation chair that enclosed the Stone of Scone, the Bishop began the investiture. A sword was first hung by her side and two 'armills' or bracelets were placed on her arms. With fanfares sounding, the Bishop placed St Edward's crown on her head, the ring on the fourth finger of her right hand and the sceptre and orb in her hands. Her Majesty next delivered the sword to the Bishop, who laid it upon the altar.

The peers of the realm now made their homage to their Queen. First the Bishop of Carlisle 'put his hand to the Queen's hand', then the lords temporal knelt before her, and with a kiss on her left cheek promised to become her liege men 'of life and limb and of earthly worship'. Significantly, on this occasion the remaining bishops had to wait until after the temporal peers – an indication of Elizabeth's attitude towards the individuals who had refused to crown her themselves. The service concluded with the saying of mass by Bishop Oglethorpe. Both the epistle and gospel were read in English as well as in Latin. Preceded by three naked swords and a sword in its scabbard, Elizabeth left her throne to make her offertory on her knees before the high altar, and to kiss the paten. Various prayers were said over her there. Instead of returning to her throne, as the rubrics stated, she withdrew to a traverse (or pew secluded by a curtain) in St Edward's Chapel, where she remained until the consecration of the elements and the elevation of the host were completed. It was probably during the *Agnus Dei* that she returned to the throne, and there received the pax. She did not communicate. She absented herself from the choir during the consecration as a protest against Oglethorpe's elevation of the host according to the Roman rite. At the recent Christmas Day mass at the Abbey he had been ordered to omit the elevation, and when he refused the Queen left the service. The Bishop had agreed to crown the Queen, but he was adamant about the elevation. As a result Elizabeth could not but withdraw from the service while ritualistic practices so repugnant to her were performed. The mass over, the Queen removed to another traverse behind the high altar and again changed her robes. Meanwhile the procession formed again and slowly filed out of the great west door of the Abbey.

After the long service in the Abbey was ended, the equally long secular ceremony began. The dignified procession escorting the Queen, now indeed 'God's creature', wearing her crown of state, re-entered Westminster Hall for the traditional banquet. All was performed under the direction of the Earl Marshal and High Steward. In the seating arrangements the ladder of precedence was followed as strictly as in the processions. The royal table stood at the upper end of the Hall on a raised floor, and at 3 p.m. the Queen sat down to feast, clad in violet velvet. On the west side sat the great officers of state, peers above the rank of earl, and two unnamed gentlemen of the court, wearing the ancient dress of ducal peers of France, as 'representing' the Dukes of Normandy and Guienne, to maintain Elizabeth's claim to the fealty of her French 'subjects'. Her Majesty was duly served by the great household officers and those whose claims to special tasks had been admitted by the Court of Claims: for instance, the Lord of the Manor of Addington in Surrey brought to the royal table with the first course the special mess of pottage he was bound by the tenure of his lands to supply.

During the banquet the Queen's champion, Sir Edward Dymoke, rode into the Hall on a magnificent beast, in full armour, ready to battle against anyone who might dispute the Queen's legal right to her crown. He was the most striking relic of the age of chivalry. A herald proclaimed the challenge; the champion threw down his gauntlet; and, so it was said, 'took end with great joy and contention to all beholders.' Fresh dishes were produced, more barrels of wine were broached. All the while trumpeters and other musicians performed in the gallery. At the end of the meal there was probably a masque or a play, as the Master of the Revels, the court entertainment officer, subsequently received £408 for the expenses of his department 'at the coronation and the triumphs following it'. The celebrations lasted till 1 o'clock in the morning. An Italian who was there thought all the ceremonial splendid, in contrast to the music, which 'not being remarkable, and having heard better, I will say nothing about it.' During the day the Council Office issued the Coronation Proclamation of Pardon of all treasons, certain

felonies, and other offences committed before 1 November 1558.
A number of individuals, knowing full well that a general pardon
was always issued at coronations, had been leading a life of petty
crime since the Queen's accession; and on 12 November it had
been necessary to issue a special warning of dire consequences
which might follow. The pardon now published on 15 January
did not extend to offences committed after the previous 1 November, and those guilty of housebreaking and highway robbery
were excluded from its provisions.

There was to have been a joust in the tiltyard at Whitehall next
day, but Elizabeth, mortal creature, was still weary from the
strain of the last two days and so it was postponed until the
Tuesday. Other festivities followed. After the gloomy months of
the end of Mary's reign, life at court seemed one long party – so
much so that a Mantuan visitor lifted a reproving finger at 'the
levities and moral licentiousness practised at the court in dances
and banquets.' One night, he reported, a double mummery was
played, when 'one set of mummers rifled the Queen's ladies and
the other set, with wooden swords and bucklers, recovered the
spoil.' Thence to the business of government, for Parliament
opened on 25 January, determined to effect a new reformation.

4

WINDOWS IN MEN'S
SOULS

From the beginning of her reign Elizabeth was determined that her religious policy should effect a permanent settlement in church and state, ending once and for all the uncertainties and up-heavals of the last two decades, in which the orthodoxy of one reign became the heresy of the next. She tackled the problem essentially as a statesman, knowing that to attempt a settlement purely on religious considerations would court disaster. As she told Parliament with an especial glare at her bench of bishops in 1566, 'It is said I am no divine. Indeed, I studied nothing but divinity until I came to the crown; and then I gave myself to the study of that which was meet for government.' Politics was the art of the possible, and though she was hampered at many turns from bringing to pass exactly what she envisaged, her settlement of 1559, grounded on the Acts of Supremacy and Uniformity and the prayer book, was a remarkable achievement. To attain national unity it was necessary to enforce religious conformity; they were not separate issues, but different aspects of the same phenomenon. Her mission, as she saw it, was to maintain the Church's continuity, to give stability to its character and to re-quire it to minister in such a way as would gain the assent, if not the full support, of all reasonable believers. She was cautious in shaping her policy, but at each stage hers was no passive role, and despite having to sacrifice various features of that policy to meet the demands of extremists in Parliament, the settlement remained in essence her own. Conceived as a compromise, the Anglican Church thus generated has endured; and perhaps in our own ecumenical age, where the desire for Christian unity is so marked, we can appreciate more readily than previous generations the young Queen's ideal and achievement.

Her past had conditioned her thinking, made her what she was. Reconciliation with Rome was out of the question, for she could have no tenderness for a church that had abased her as Anne Boleyn's daughter. She had been nurtured in the rich soil of the new learning and her teachers had brought her to view the reform of the Church in the light of a full understanding both of holy scripture and of the early fathers. Long ago Bishop Hooper had told Bullinger that Elizabeth was 'enflamed with . . . zeal for the religion of Christ.' But the humanist, no less than the politician, tempered the zealot in her and, remaining insular, she had escaped the powerful influences of the militant continental reformers, who so changed the outlook of the English Protestant exiles under Mary. She could not identify herself with a party, with a particular brand of theology, but with nothing less than the nation of which she was leader. She looked on herself as the instrument of 'God's providence', but it was no part of her mission to introduce Calvinistic theology or a Presbyterian system of church government. John Knox with his trumpet blasts from across the Cheviots was as much anathema to her as papal supremacy. In the evening of her life a Frenchman told her that in his country people said she read nothing but the works of Calvin. 'She swore to me that she had never seen one, but that she had seen the ancient fathers, and took great pleasure in them; all the more because later writers are full of disputes and strivings, and the others have only the good interest of rendering service and profit to God.'[1] She was bent in 1559 on ending disputes and strivings by a reformation which took as much account of the early fathers and the Western tradition of Christendom as of the English bible.

Fundamentally she sought to heal the divisions rending the nation by making her church so comprehensive in its theology that there was room in it for all sorts and conditions of men. In place of the Protestant extremism of Edward's reign or the Catholic exclusiveness of Mary's, she would steer a middle course.

Those closest to her appreciated that it required 'great cunning and circumspection both to reform religion and to make unity between subjects'; she knew that the children of this world were wiser in their generation than the children of light, and intended to take for herself the role of a '*politique*'. Such a policy was easier for her to follow than for some of her contemporary rulers, for though she was sincere in her belief, and intensely interested in doctrinal problems, she was not deeply religious – the very opposite, in fact, of her sister. She believed *au fond* that religion was a personal affair and that within the framework of a broad national church men could satisfy their very varying spiritual needs. As Supreme Governor she had no wish, as she said, to 'open windows in men's souls.' Unfortunately, moderation did not appeal to the Protestant exiles returning from Zurich and Geneva, Frankfurt and Strasbourg, now that the fires of Smithfield were out. Elizabeth must beware of false prophets. 'The wolves be coming out of Geneva', snarled Bishop White in his funeral oration for Queen Mary, well aware that an epoch had passed, 'and have sent their books before, full of pestilent doctrines.' Their 'Deborah's' mission was unmistakable. As the ballad writer John Awdley put it, God looked out of heaven at England in ruins as Mary died, and called Elizabeth to her duty:

> With that the skies their hue did change
> And light out shone in darkness stead,
> Up (said this God, with voice not strange),
> Elizabeth this realm now guide.
> My will in thee do not thou hide
> And vermin dark let not abide
>   In this thy land.[2]

These ministers of the word, who had taken London by storm, could not wait for Parliament to put their new reformation on a legal footing, but began 'to sow abroad the doctrine of the gospel more freely, first in private houses, and then in churches, and the people greedy of novelties began to flock unto them in great number and to wrangle amongst themselves and with the papists, about questions contraverted in religion.' Such vigorous partisanship was a stab in the back for a Queen seeking unity and comprehensiveness; and to prevent matters getting more seriously out of hand she issued a proclamation forbidding clergy and people from taking the law into their own hands. They could have the Lord's Prayer, the Ten Commandments, the Apostles' Creed, the Epistle and the Gospel in English, but for the rest they must continue to use the Latin service, and there was to be 'no exhortation', or preaching, which merely provoked further wrangling.[3] This in turn was a bitter cup for those who thought the 1552 prayer book insufficiently radical – it was not godly enough. John Jewel, the future bishop, just returned from Zurich, lamented to his friend Peter Martyr the Queen's slowness to act. She 'openly favours our cause, yet she is afraid of allowing any innovations'; and his letter hinted at a compromise, a golden mean, in highly disapproving terms: 'Others are seeking after a golden, or as it rather seems to me, a leaden mediocrity, and are crying out that the half is better than the whole.'[4]

Besides the *revenants* from Geneva and Zurich, continental reformers of all kinds of persuasions flocked to England from the moment of Elizabeth's accession, some to escape persecution, others in hope of preferment, but one and all to offer their zealous assistance in fulfilling the word of God. They could not possibly allow England's salvation to be regarded as a domestic affair. They fulminated against anything remotely resembling the Roman rite, often, one suspects, voicing their opinions in very imperfect English. Most made for London, and were attached to the Dutch church in the Austin-friars, where they argued minutiae of doctrine, but all too soon the minister of that church was to be excommunicated by the mild Bishop Grindal for favouring Anabaptists. Typical of these reformers was Justus Velsino, a man who never failed to stir up trouble in every church he entered, calling down God's vengeance on all who refused to receive his pet ideas.[5] A rather different case was Jacopo Acontio who regarded all dogma as 'a stratagem of Satan'. Essential truth, he held, was embodied in the apostles' creed, which no Christian could reject, and the warring confessions of faith were nothing less than sheer devilry. Elizabeth was at first rather taken with

Acontio, who alone among reformers maintained that capital punishment for heresy was a sin against the holy ghost. She gave him a small pension but, on reading a book he had dedicated to her, found his doctrine wanting. Such continental reformers, and the Scots, were slow to grasp the essential point that the Queen was determined to achieve a truly national church, whose right to decide upon its doctrine, ritual and organization, without external interference, was self-evident. *Cujus regio, ejus religio*, as the tag had it; and Elizabeth would keep them guessing. 'God keep us from such a visitation as Knox has attempted in Scotland', prayed Matthew Parker fervently.

To reduce the temperature of controversy Elizabeth's injunctions of 1559 chided the 'rash talkers of scripture' and once the revised Thirty-Nine Articles of Religion had been formulated, she decreed that 'all curious further research' into matters theological should cease. In her view too many sermons and disputations, with laymen demanding a right to be heard, and public worship could degenerate into 'prophesyings' – the equivalent of a present day teach-in. That way led to presbyters, elders and congregations believing themselves to have the divine right to rule the body politic; it would spell the end of a comprehensive church and sound the knell of episcopacy and, ultimately, of monarchy.

On the first day given to public business a markedly Protestant House of Commons began to debate the state of the Church and in the days which followed made very significant amendments to the government's Royal Supremacy bill, such as that permitting priests' marriages. Meanwhile Convocation under Bonner's lead passed articles affirming belief in transubstantiation and papal supremacy and roundly declared that the authority for defining matters of faith belonged to the Church alone. It was a bad beginning for those seeking unity, peace and concord. Her father had been able to carry the bench of bishops with him in his severance from Rome, but Elizabeth knew she could not hope for such support. She needed the co-operation of the Commons, but not at the price which the radicals there demanded, for she 'was resolved to restore religion as her father had left it', intending a

reissue with the most minor modifications of the first Edwardian
prayer book. But the Commons in defiance passed a bill to allow
the religion 'as used in King Edward's last year', that is the
second prayer book. There might have been no Act of Uniformity
and no Elizabethan Book of Common Prayer until much later in
the year had not news reached London on 19 March that peace
had been signed with France, placing England out of immediate
danger, so the Queen could risk allowing the extremist elements
in the Commons to have, not indeed its own way, but more of a
say in the settlement than she had dared to envisage. Instead of
following her original plan of going down to Westminster to
give her assent to the revised Supremacy bill, she now adjourned
Parliament until after Easter, and in the interval of the recess a
series of disputations on dogma were held.[6]

When the Sessions reopened, the Royal Supremacy bill, embodying further revisions, was at last passed and, following it, an
Act of Uniformity for enforcing a new prayer book. In this latter
act the radicals had secured the reissue of the 1552 book, but with
one very important addition for which Elizabeth herself was
responsible. It reads in the act as a small enough concession – 'two
sentences only added in the delivery of the sacrament to the com-
municants', but it made the world of a difference. The 1552
sentences at the administration of the sacrament, 'Take and eat
this in remembrance that Christ died for thee and be thankful'
and 'Drink this in remembrance that Christ's blood was shed for
thee and be thankful', plainly showed that the communion was a
commemorative act. But now these words were to be preceded
by the sentences from the more conservative prayer book of 1549:
'The body of Our Lord Jesus Christ which was given for thee,
preserve thy body and soul unto everlasting life' and 'The blood
of Our Lord Jesus Christ which was shed for thee, preserve thy
body and soul unto everlasting life.' Herein lay the essential compromise. For Elizabeth to have agreed to have only the words of
the 1552 book would not only have been personally distasteful to
her, she knew it would have alienated at a stroke a great number
of her subjects, not least the more moderate of the Marian bishops
whom she hoped could be persuaded to accept her position. For

her, on the other hand, to have insisted on the 1549 sentences by themselves, as had been her original intention, would have been far too strong for the radicals to have stomached. The interpretation of the traditional words *Hoc est corpus meum*, so conveniently shrouded in a dead language, had become the central point of the reformation, but now Elizabeth had shelved the issue in a masterly way. Her liturgy contained as wide a selection from the doctrinal welter of the sixteenth century as possible and for Anglican doctrine to be so comprehensive it must necessarily remain incomprehensible. She herself did not 'desire a thorough change' of religion as Jewel, for one, fondly imagined. She believed, as she told the Spanish ambassador, 'in the sacrament of the eucharist, and only dissented from three or four things in the Mass.' Her Church of England, though reformed had not ceased to be Catholic, and the Thirty-Nine Articles, when they were eventually revised, contained no denial of the real presence,[7] any more than they contained an explicit belief in that doctrine.

The Act of Supremacy, which repealed Mary's Heresy Act and revived various statutes of the Reformation Parliament, emphasized the continuity of Anglicanism with the medieval Church in England, for it was an act 'for restoring and uniting to the imperial crown of this realm the ancient jurisdictions, authorities and pre-eminences.' Archbishop Heath had made some ripe remarks in the Lords about a woman being 'supreme head' of the Church, but as government policy unfolded, the 'et cetera' in the royal style of the Accession proclamation was expanded into the title 'Supreme Governor'. Title apart, it endowed her with the same authority as her father had wielded. She looked on herself as 'the nurse of God's religion, the "over-ruler"' of his Church; and the articles of 1563 expounded this theme:

Where we attribute to the Queen Majesty the chief government (by which we understand the minds of some slanderous folk to be offended), we give not to our princes the ministry either of God's word, or of the sacraments . . . but that only prerogative which we see have been given always to all godly princes in holy scripture by God himself; that is, that they should rule all estates and degrees committed to their charge by God, whether they be ecclesiastical or temporal, and restrain with the civil sword the stubborn and evil-doers.

As Queen, Elizabeth could hardly have brought herself to accept any position that was not supreme, yet the concept of 'supreme governorship' was basic to a national church, and without it no settlement could have achieved any effective degree of unity. From this flowed a divine right of kingship. 'She is our God in earth', wrote Lord North to Bishop Cox of Ely, in 1575; 'if there be perfection in flesh and blood, undoubtedly it is in Her Majesty!' For her the sacramental anointing and crowning in Westminster Abbey made her different in kind as well as in degree from any subject, even an archbishop.[8]

Whatever the hotheads had hoped for, episcopacy was retained as the only valid form of church government, though the filling of sees was to be a major problem. The system of church courts, from archdeacon to archbishop, remained and these were bolstered by a new secular tribunal, the Court of High Commission, charged with the duty of securing conformity in religion. Elizabeth postponed for as long as she could the issue of a definitive set of articles of religion, for to spell out matters of doctrine would at this stage emphasize divisions and what she wanted was an amalgam of divergencies. She had been compelled by circumstances to accept the position of the 1552 prayer book, with the important modifications on which she had insisted, though clearly she would have preferred the Act of Uniformity to have read 'the first prayer book of King Edward with two sentences added.' She never would forget the strength of this Parliamentary opposition to her conservatism, which had almost humiliated her at Easter 1559, and when in the future clergy and laity sought to move further left from her *via media*, whether in opposition to vestments or in favour of prophesying, she would give them short shrift. The reformers for their part were ill-satisfied with their half-a-loaf, and called the Anglican Church 'a cloaked papistry or a mingle-mangle'. Their goal was to secure a root and branch reform of the Church in the next Parliament, but Elizabeth would see to it they had not the slightest chance of doing anything except talk.

Before then, in 1562, appeared Bishop Jewel's *Apology*, the first of a series of works justifying the Anglican settlement, giving the *via media* a philosophy of its own. 'Of a truth, unity and concord' doth best become religion; yet is not unity the same and certain mark whereby we know the Church of God?' Jewel's was a question expecting the most emphatic 'yes'. A generation later Richard Hooker, whose judicious mien gave him the appearance of being above the heat and dust of controversy, looked back in a golden haze to the foundations of the settlement: 'By the goodness of Almighty God and his servant Elizabeth, we are.' The sweet reasonableness of Hooker would have shaken the reformers of the Parliament of 1559, yet in spite of the Queen's difficulties with them and with the Marian bishops, the whole transition from the romanism of Mary's reign had gone as peaceably as her accession. As Camden noted, 'All Christendom admired that it was wrought so easily and without commotion', lasting from 27 December 1558, when she issued her proclamation about the modified use of a vernacular liturgy, until July following, when the Oath of Supremacy was first administered to the bishops. There was one drawback, as yet imperfectly understood. As Supreme Governor Elizabeth would resist to the end the idea that she might open windows in men's souls; but as Queen it would be necessary to pry into men's political beliefs, and as a result of the overlapping of the secular and the ecclesiastical spheres, heresy would become scarcely distinguishable from high treason.[9]

'We do not mean, nor ever meant, to make change of the order of our religion, as per case the adversaries have bruited to impair the good will of our best subjects and friends', wrote Elizabeth to her ambassador in Paris in May 1561. Her church, she told him, was a national church, so she could not allow a papal nuncio bringing letters from the Council of Trent to set foot in England. Rome's very internationalism threatened the incipient nationalism of the English people; yet 'if a general and free council might be had by consent of all Christian princes, without admitting the supreme authority which the pope claims ... she would gladly be a party to it.' She could not regard the council of Trent, which was redefining Catholic doctrine, as a 'general council, when none shall have voice but the clergy that are sworn to the pope, and where the ambassadors of princes like herself shall be but beholders of them who will decree acts against Christ's religion, and consequently against her who profess the same.' She was 'Defender of the Faith' as well as 'Supreme Governor', and on a par with the 'Most Christian' King of France, 'His Catholic Majesty' of Spain and the 'Holy' Roman Emperors of the house of Hapsburg. But her dilemma was that on the continent the dogmas of each of the rival camps was hardening: post-Tridentine Catholicism was as rigid and exclusive in its approach as latter-day Calvinism, and this at the very time when the Elizabethan Church was attempting to be broad and comprehensive. If England were not to enjoy its religious experiment in splendid isolation, there would be endless difficulties in the sphere of foreign relations. There are not a few asides illustrating her approach to the practical problems of easing the strain between the warring faiths, though often on a modest level. It was characteristic that she should encourage her subjects to give alms to help a Macedonian Christian whose property had been despoiled by the great tartar.[10]

At the beginning of 1559 there were seventeen Marian bishops still in office, some of whom Elizabeth hoped she could win over to her settlement, but of these in fact the only one to take the Oath of Supremacy was Anthony Kitchen, once a Benedictine monk, who despite the sundry and manifold changes in religion had clung to the bishopric of Llandaff ever since 1545. The first bishop to be deprived was Bonner of London, who mocked at the law by keeping the old Roman rite going in St Paul's, and by mid-August, apart from Kitchen, only Tunstal of Durham and three others remained at their posts. The main task was to consecrate an archbishop, and from the outset the Queen had had her eye on Matthew Parker. At first he wrote his '*nolo episcopari*' from Cambridge on the grounds of ill health, for he had fallen rather badly from his horse, and then, when pressed again, he had pleaded that Canterbury was 'above the reach of mine ability'. Elizabeth's injunctions, issued as guidance for visitations of the entire Church, alarmed him, since they advised against clerical marriage, and he had himself taken a wife. But eventually Parker gave way: 'If he had not been so much bound to the Mother' (Anne Boleyn), he said years afterwards, 'he would not so soon have granted to serve the daughter.' Not until July was the royal assent given for his election and his consecration was delayed until a week before Christmas 1559.[11]

As the first panel of bishops, led by Tunstal, who had been required to consecrate Parker, refused to act, a second set had to be brought together. Elizabeth, sensing Parker's consecration might well be questioned by Romanists, made a point of including in her order to the bishops administering the rite the comprehensive phrase, 'the Queen by her supreme authority supplying any legal defect in their actions or themselves.' Accordingly, in Lambeth Palace chapel on 17 December Miles Coverdale, the Edwardian Bishop of Exeter, William Barlow, the former Bishop of Bath and Wells, John Scory, the former Bishop of Chichester, and John Hodgkin, the suffragan of Bedford, laid their hands on the Archbishop elect in due canonical form, as links in a chain of episcopal succession stretching from St Augustine. Miles Coverdale, who objected to vestments, wore just a long woollen gown that reached to his ankles, while Scory, Bishop of Chichester, appeared in full canonicals and Hodgkin of Bedford, bent on doing the right thing, dressed himself like Scory for the first part of the service and like Coverdale for the latter – this would have pleased the Queen. The scurrilous tale of an invalid consecration performed in the *Nag's Head* tavern did not originate until after Elizabeth's death and the once interminable wranglings about the authenticity of Matthew Parker's orders have long been silenced. Before Christmas the election of six other bishops had been confirmed and by the end of the following year all the sees in the southern province, except Oxford, were filled. Barlow went to Chichester, Scory to Hereford, Grindal to London and Jewel to Salisbury, but Coverdale, whom Elizabeth wanted to appoint to Exeter, refused, as he objected so strongly to vestments. Archbishop Parker's main trouble with his clergy was to be on that score.[12]

Supreme Governor was no empty title. Immediately, she issued her own injunctions for visitations, had her say in the choice of lessons for the revised lectionary and took an active part in making ecclesiastical appointments. For 'the edification of the simple people' she insisted on substituting 'more profitable portions of scripture' to be read at morning and evening prayer in place of some of the old select passages, particularly from the old testament, which were confusing and often irrelevant to Christian doctrine. As yet she would have no cleric on her Privy Council – not even Parker. She resisted the extremists' demands for dealing with the Marian clergy who would not conform when, in 1563, the pains and penalties in the Act of Supremacy were increased and the Oath of Supremacy was extended to all in holy orders, graduates, schoolmasters, MPs and lawyers. The government bill was transformed in the Commons by the left-wing Protestants, who added scorpions by prescribing death for those who refused the oath when tendered to them a second time. Elizabeth gave the bill her assent but at the same time required Parker to instruct all his bishops to see that no individual was faced with taking the oath a second time without his written instructions; in this she undoubtedly saved the lives of many Romanist clergy and her tactics showed that she was indeed supreme. In later years she was to suspend Archbishop Grindal for failing to prosecute the 'prophesyers' and when she was thoroughly dissatisfied with the state of her church she recalled the bishops to their duties in no uncertain terms: 'If you, my lords of the clergy, do not amend' these faults, 'I mean to depose you. Look ye therefore to your charges.' She meant it.[13]

If the religious settlement was essentially the work of the Supreme Governor, the dominant voice in Anglican worship was still that of Cranmer. The shape of the English liturgy, with its strong scriptural content and the characteristic cadences of its collects, which Elizabeth's godfather had been inspired to pen, survived his martyrdom. Indeed, nothing that the prayer book revisers of 1662, 1928 or even 1966 achieved in due season would effectively drown his voice. Elizabeth revered his memory – as her mother's chaplain, her father's archbishop and as a very English hero against papal intolerance under her sister. If he had deserted his flock in 1554 for asylum on the continent and thus been able to return to Canterbury, there would have been many difficulties for each of them, yet she was too like her father for them not to have reached an accommodation. As it was, she could only keep his name green. In 1563 she heard that Cranmer's commonplace book had escaped the burning of so many of his papers and she eagerly sought to borrow it. 'Such a rare and precious treasure', she said, 'should not be hid in secret oblivion as a candle under a bushel, but rather ought to be set abroad to the public use of the Church of Christ.'[14]

On certain specifically ecclesiastical matters she held very decided views, though she was wise enough to refrain from insisting on their universal adoption, for such would have narrowed the Church. She would have liked to have required all her clergy to be celibate, for in her estimation their vocation demanded the single life. As we noticed, Matthew Parker's reluctance to accept the archbishopric was in part due to his disagreement with the Queen on the topic of clerical marriage. Without warning, in the summer of 1561 Elizabeth issued an injunction ordering all wives of canons and of fellows to leave their cathedral closes and college precincts. But for Cecil's influence the prohibition would have been much wider. 'Her Majesty', he told the astonished Archbishop, 'continueth very ill-affected to the state of matrimony in the Clergy. And if I were not therein very stiff . . . would utterly and openly condemn and forbid it.' Parker was 'in an horror to hear such words come from her mild nature and Christianly learned conscience, as she spoke concerning God's holy ordinance and institution of matrimony.' Richard Cox, Bishop of Ely, whose daughter Joanna was to marry Parker's son, warned that the injunction would encourage non-residence in cathedral churches, and hoped that Elizabeth might be tactfully reminded of St Paul's respect for marriage. Parker had already written a tract on the subject in Mary's reign, in answer to a broadside of Stephen Gardiner's, and to forestall any extension of the royal injunction he now brought his essay up to date and published his *Defence of Priests Marriages, Established by the Imperial*

Laws of the Realm of England. Elizabeth pressed the point no further; clerical marriages were permitted, yet discouraged. As the system settled down a minister intending to marry had to have the lady vetted by the bishop and two justices of the peace, besides obtaining the consent of her parents. Significantly, Whitgift, the archbishop with whom the Queen had fewest disagreements, was single. Her snide remarks to Mrs Parker on taking her leave from Lambeth Palace are clearly a literary invention of her godson Harington. '*Madam* I may not call you, and *Mistress* I am ashamed to call you, so I know not what way to call you, but yet I do thank you'; yet the fact that Harington could have perpetuated such a tale is a pointer to Elizabeth's attitude. She may have feared too much of the Church's income would be squandered by family men, or that clerical nepotism would run riot; but in fact the first generation of sons and daughters of the Anglican parsonage grew to be the staunchest supporters of the Elizabethan settlement. The five young clerics who married the five daughters of the Bishop of Chichester all became bishops.[15]

The Supreme Governor regarded preaching as a doubtful blessing. Some pulpits could be 'tuned', so that government propaganda could effectively reach ordinary men and women – many of them illiterate – and at times the sermons at Paul's Cross were merely expositions of government policy. The anniversary of the Queen's accession each year was often the occasion for a trumpet call to loyalty, particularly in the first half of the reign. But certain divines were a hopeless liability once they touched on politics and in 1579 her Council required the Archbishop of Canterbury to admonish ministers 'that in their sermons and preachings do not intermeddle with any such matters of the state, being in very deed not incidental or appertaining to their profession'. Being so thoroughly grounded in theology herself she delighted in 'a good sermon', provided it were on a theme to her liking and not too long; besides it gave her the chance of discovering whether particular prelates merited higher preferment. An able preacher could indeed capture her with his eloquence, as did Thomas Dove of whom she remarked 'the holy ghost had again descended in a dove.' But it was a stern test being called on to preach before Her Majesty. She would answer back if the preacher said something with which she disagreed, call out 'To your text, Mr Preacher' or in extreme cases close the window of her closet to shut out offending words, as Anthony Rudd found to his cost when he rather tactlessly expounded on the theme of death. When Dean Nowell, preaching at court in Lent 1565, made sweeping remarks about the crucifix in her chapel, she interrupted him with 'Do not talk about that!' But the Dean apparently did not hear her so she broke in again more loudly. 'Leave that; it has nothing to do with your subject and the matter is now threadbare.'

Shortly after his appointment as Dean of Durham, Toby Matthew drew attention in a royal sermon to the very unequal distribution of clerical preferment, remarking that 'rewards were not given in the Church to those who deserved them, and that no man should so live as that his labour should be lost.' Before he left the pulpit, the Queen addressed him: 'Well! whosoever have missed their rewards, thou hast not lost thy labour.' We can sympathize with Bishop Jewel, a most effective preacher and one who clearly enjoyed the pulpit, when he begged to be excused from being chosen as Lent preacher at Whitehall in 1565. The risks of displeasure were too great.[16]

A sermon at the Chapel Royal before the Supreme Governor was one thing, but regular sermons for the laity at large in parish churches were an entirely different proposition. They had not her theological grounding and could too easily be indoctrinated, which involved the considerable risk of them being seduced by false doctrine. At the opening of the reign, indeed, she had closed the pulpits entirely for a season. Parker's advertisements of 1566 had admonished all those admitted to preach 'to use sobriety and discretion in teaching the people, namely, in matters of controversy; and to consider the gravity of their office, and to foresee with diligence the matters which they will speak, to utter them to the edification of the audience.' The reading of the homilies he prescribed as the best means of 'quiet instruction', not the glossing of the scriptures every man in his own way. This was asking too much of too many. When Archbishop Grindal told her in 1576 that preaching was 'the only mean and instrument of the salvation of mankind', she strongly disagreed. All the teaching a flock needed was in the prayer book, the lessons from the bible and the book of homilies, and three or four 'preaching ministers' to a county was, she thought, quite sufficient. The homily on obedience, after all, stated quite emphatically that clergy ought 'especially and before others' to be obedient to their princes. Sermons from hotheads too easily led to schisms, and it was the 'preachers of the word of God' who before long were undermining the establishment with their 'prophesyings'.[17]

The question of the Queen's personal belief has often been shrugged off. Was there no window into her own soul? Was she nothing more than a *politique*, for ever subordinating religious considerations to political ones; a Supreme Governor regarding her control of the Church as no more than a compartment of statecraft; an Erastian leader with no positive mission, bent on appearing all things to all men? The words 'God's providence' which recur so frequently in her speeches were not meaningless. In her own day, and since, Elizabeth has been dubbed 'the deliverer', 'heretic', 'papist', 'Lutheran', 'Calvinist', 'Zwinglian', 'Arian', 'Socinian', 'deist' and 'quietist', and was even described (by John Wesley[18]) as being as just and merciful as Nero and as good a Christian as Mahomet. In fact, though for very obvious reasons of state she was often deliberately vague in controversial matters, enough of her own likes and dislikes are known.

On the central issue of the sacrament, the precise nature of Christ's presence at the consecration of the bread and wine in the holy communion, the words of the 1559 prayer book were, as we have seen, intentionally all-embracing. But the Queen's own interpretation of the sacrament is less of an enigma. Her name has always been linked with a poignant verse, which, it is said, she quoted by way of answer to a question addressed to her in Mary's reign on her opinion of Christ's presence. The exact placing of the occasion is irrelevant; so is the question whether or not she was the author of the stanza, which is possible, though unlikely. The verse gained wide currency and as early as 1565 was being written down by ordinary folk in letters:

Hoc est corpus meum
As Christ willed it and spake it
   And thankfully blessed it and brake it
And as the sacred word doth make it
   So I believe in it and take it
My life to give therefore
In earth to live no more.[19]

The meaning of the '*hoc est corpus meum*' of the Vulgate was the high point of theological controversy in the age of the reformation, but the exposition of doctrine in this verse is remarkably Lutheran in tone, though the Queen would no doubt have denied this on principle.

. A collection of Latin prayers purporting to be the Queen's own compilation was published by Christopher Barker in 1582, but it is impossible to sample from them any strong doctrinal flavour.[20] Biblical phrases and allusions are there in plenty, and it was this appeal to scriptural authority which was most characteristic in her approach to dogma, though she always insisted that the early fathers were the handmaid to the old and new testaments. When she gave Ann Poyntz, a lady-in-waiting, a new testament, Elizabeth wrote inside it these lines;

Among good things I prove and find
The quiet life doth much abound
And sure to the contented mind
There is no riches may be found.[21]

Ceremonial played a great part in everyday life at court, where many of the humblest tasks, even laying the table, were elevated by a peculiar ritual into a quasi-religious office. Much of this was time-honoured and a good deal was common to all the monarchies of the West, and Elizabeth had no desire to clip the wings of majesty by curtailment, simplicity or innovation. It was natural that she should carry the regard for ceremonial in secular affairs into the religious sphere – which her critics called 'the scenic apparatus of divine worship'. When Bishop Aylmer and Dean Nowell received the Queen at the thanksgiving service for the defeat of the Armada in old St Paul's in November 1588, they were preceded by fifty clergy, all in rich copes. She always liked processions and expected the celebrant to be wearing a cope when she attended divine service. Jewel had thought vestments 'relics of the Amorites', and felt it too Roman a practice to have the crucifix on the altar: 'There is a little too much foolery. That little silver cross of ill-omened origin still maintains its place in the Queen's chapel.' Certain other bishops grudgingly agreed to use the sign of the cross in baptism and kneeling for communion only 'until the Lord shall give us better times.' Though essentially a 'broad churchwoman' as regards the realm at large, she very much had her own way in the royal peculiars. Here the altars remained, with candles burning on either side of the crucifix. She had, under pressure, issued an order for the removal of stone altars from parish churches, but was very angry with the ecclesiastical visitors for carrying it out. She had very different views, compared with the average parliamentarian, on the interpretation of the phrase 'superstitious uses' in the statute; for her images and shrines, incense, sanctuary bells, tapers and anniversaries for the dead, were, like the elevation of the host, Roman practices. On the other hand much that had been expunged under Edward VI she regarded as a helpful, though not a necessary, part of church worship – for instance vestments and altar frontals. Bishop Cox of Ely condemned such insignia as 'marks of the beast', and at first refused to celebrate the communion service clad in what he termed 'the golden vestments of popery' and 'dared not minister in her grand chapel, the lights and cross remaining', and yet in the end he gave way. Knollys, vice-chamberlain of the royal household, kept nudging Parker to do something about 'the enormities in the Queen's closet retained'. The crucifix disappeared for a season but then returned. In the chapels royal surpliced choirs sung Latin motets and even plainsong psalms. At Westminster Abbey 'the canons wear the amice and surplice, as also the others, and have copes; and it seems [noted a foreigner] that there is little difference between their ceremonies and those of the Church of Rome.' That 'little' meant a lot to the Queen. There was room enough within the ample folds of the Church of England for all sorts and conditions of men, not least for the Queen herself who, though no *dévote*, within her own chapels liked to indulge in what a later age would classify as moderately high-church tastes, and in this she restored the balance, tilted so strongly in the capital to austere Protestantism.[22]

Elizabeth's policy of not making windows in men's souls is most clearly visible with regard to the Catholic recusants. In general, during the first decade of the reign, provided they lived peaceably, put in a statutory appearance at the parish church or paid their fines for absence, they could seek the administrations of a Catholic priest without fear of prosecution. Outward conformity was sufficient. It was well known that the chapels of the French, Spanish and Imperial ambassadors in London were full of Englishmen and women; even some of the ladies of the royal household contrived to attend mass with some regularity while the court was in London. In the provinces, especially the west and the north country, there was not wanting a succession of priests who kept cells of the old faith alive in great houses. The government knew a good deal about these activities, but though well-wishers of ardent Protestantism on the Privy Council, such as Cecil, Knollys and Leicester, and some of the more militant bishops wanted to pursue a repressive policy, the Queen at this stage preferred to let sleeping dogs lie, for repression and amity were uneasy bedfellows. Not until Mary Queen of Scots took refuge in England in 1568 was there any real menace from the Catholics and at once the government issued orders to local justices and others to keep known papists under close observation and to press the court of high commission and the ecclesiastical courts into vigorous action. The fact that the majority of the Catholics sympathized with Mary's cause, and many in 1569–70 were to die for it in the Northern Rebellion, made recusancy a serious political offence and it could no longer be tolerated as merely a religious deviation. The untimely papal bull of 1570 excommunicating Elizabeth, and the position of Mary Queen of Scots as her prisoner opened the wound still further, so that the devoted bands of missionary priests from Douai and elsewhere, who landed with the object of reconverting England to Rome, met their death as traitors.

But the challenge to religious unity in these early years came not from the right but from the left, and the cause of it was opposition to the injunctions enforcing the vestments which priests of the established Church should wear. To Protestants, many of them still under the spell of Zurich or Geneva, the surplice was anathema, a vestige of papistry, 'the livery of Antichrist' – an outward and visible sign that the New Jerusalem was a long way off. They slightingly called surplices 'porters' coats' and nick-named those that obeyed the injunctions 'whitecoats' and the wearers of the regulation caps 'tippet gentlemen'. Thus arose the vestarian controversy, the first of a series that has troubled the Church of England. Not a few of the bishops, like Pilkington of Durham, were sympathetic. There were other grievances: they were against using the sign of the cross, they wanted freedom to preach at will instead of having to read from Parker's new book of homilies and they preferred singing metrical psalms, like the Scottish Calvinists, to hearing the organ; yet the dispute centred on vestments.

Archbishop Parker would have been happier to have kept to his study at Lambeth or Croydon, continuing the preparation of the Bishops' bible, the new translation that Elizabeth hoped would oust the Geneva bible from its popularity, but she sensed the danger and prodded him into action. A strongly-worded petition on the subject of vestments had been put up to Convocation in January 1563 and the Queen counter-attacked by requiring the Archbishop 'to take effectual measures that an exact order and uniformity be maintained in all external rites.' She had had to compromise with the extreme Protestants in Parliament in 1559 and only just staved off their threat to capture the Church and reform it root and branch, and she saw the vestarian menace for what it was – a threat to undermine the established supremacy and uniformity. In this Elizabeth could hardly expect support from the Privy Council, where several prominent members had close connexions with the Protestant camp. The previous year the terms of the court of high commission had been extended to deal with 'those obstinate persons who still refuse to acknowledge the Queen's supremacy and the established religion',[23] but it was against the Catholic right, not the Protestant left that the Council intended the law should be directed. In time Matthew Parker issued his *Book of Advertisements* 'for the preservation of order and decency', but propaganda was not enough. There were notable secessions from the Church, particularly in London, and deprivations of those clergy who would not conform. The laity, too, were 'divided into various parties and are loud in their abuse of godly ministers.' And so cracks appeared in the walls of the Anglican Church. These congregations, separating themselves out of choice from the establishment, were the founding fathers of English nonconformity and the Queen soon found she was having to face the ardent criticism of the nonconformist conscience. Fines and imprisonment were of no avail in ending the schism. 'These precise folk', Parker told Elizabeth with feeling, 'would offer their goods and bodies to prison rather than they should relent.'

Meeting in private houses, 'in the fields and occasionally even in ships', these separatists of the mid-1560s, with their own ordained ministers, their own government of elders and deacons, worshipped God in their own ways, without bowing the knee to the Supreme Governor. They had made a breach in the unity of the Church and by denying the Queen the right to regulate their lives as Christian worshippers would one day be led to deny the right of monarchy itself. The fearless Peter Wentworth dared to say in her presence in 1576 that he 'chose to offend your earthly Majesty, rather than to offend the heavenly Majesty of God ... Remember, Madam, that you are a mortal creature and although you are a mighty prince, yet that He who dwelleth in heaven is mightier.' 'No Supreme Governor' would mean 'No Queen.' Very much later Elizabeth wrote to James VI of Scotland:

Let me warn you that there is risen, both in your realm and mine, a sect of perilous consequence, such as would have no kings but a presbytery, and take our place while they enjoy our privilege, with a shade of God's word, which none is judged to follow right without by their censure they be so deemed. Yea, look we well unto them. When they have made in our people's hearts a doubt of our religion, and that we err if they say so, what perilous issue this may make I rather think than mind to write ...

John Knox's third trumpet blast of a generation back had indeed pointed the way. Presbyterianism was a pistol pointed at the heart of the Anglican settlement.[24]

A curious aspect of English religious life was the tendency to 'prophesy' – in fulsome old testament manner – with utterances rich in verbal imagery. As a Spaniard noted 'They are so full of prophecies in this country that nothing happens that they immediately come out with some prophecy that foretold it so many years ago, and it is a fact that serious people, and good Catholics even, take notice of these things and attach more importance to them than they usually warrant.' (In fairness he might have remembered that at Philip II's court was a soothsayer whose views. were held in great esteem.) Elizabeth's peaceful accession, her church policy, her successes and her mistakes were indeed all 'foretold' by someone or other. In certain of her speeches she adopted this very technique herself and the predictions of Dr John Dee and other soothsayers, to which she paid rather more than lip service, showed that she was not so different from the preachers who thumbed their English bibles for parallels to current politics and claimed to have heard the voice of the spirit over the waters: The burning of Old St Paul's in 1561 seemed to many an act of divine wrath against the Church, episcopacy and the Supreme Governor.[25]

But 'prophesyings' took on a rather different aspect in the 1570s, with Edmund Cartwright, the learned Lady Margaret Professor of Divinity at Cambridge, leading a movement for Church reform, which was based exclusively on scriptural authority. 'Prophesyings' took the form of public questions and answers between clergy and laity – a mixture of a 'brains trust' and a 'teach-in', which certainly nurtured study, but gave ready opportunities for disseminating doctrines and opinions that were obnoxious to the established Church. Elizabeth rightly saw it as a challenge to 'kingly rule' and the prophesying movement was the more dangerous because so many of the bishops themselves were ardent supporters. This strong puritan movement overshadowed Matthew Parker's last years at Canterbury and proved the stumbling-block for his successor, Edmund Grindal.

Grindal had long ago helped to tutor Elizabeth in godliness and renaissance studies, but where she had developed by broadening her outlook, he had rather stagnated, and did not recognize the change in her. He had been dejected at being asked to put up a French cardinal on a diplomatic mission at Fulham Palace, and successfully pleaded that his house was too small; it would, surely, have been a bizarre affair for Grindal to have been hobnobbing with a cardinal! His weakness in tackling the early separatists in the capital had led to his promotion from the seething see of London to the relative quietude of the archbishopric of York, where nonconformity was exclusively Catholic. For perhaps the first time, the Queen regretted following Burghley's advice in having Grindal posted from York to Canterbury. Far from eradicating the prophesying movement, the Archbishop defended its leaders, in direct opposition to the Queen. She reproved him and required him to take immediate action to suppress the prophesyings, but Grindal shuffled his feet, saying that such exercises were advocated in holy scripture and were important for improving the general tone of the ministry and for educating laymen. 'If it be Your Majesty's pleasure for this or any other cause to remove me out of this place, I will with all humility yield thereunto', he added. If he meant to bluff her by this threat he was grievously mistaken; neither Burghley's nor Leicester's support was of the slightest use, for in May 1577 Elizabeth wrote direct to the various bishops ordering them to put an end to all prophesyings and soon afterwards sequestered Grindal from office for six months. He had been found guilty of disobedience to his Queen in 'her supreme authority ecclesiastical'. To all intents and purposes the Church was without its primate, yet its Supreme Governor remained.

At the end of the six months efforts were made to bring an accommodation, and there was talk of Grindal, if reasonably penitent, making a personal confession of his faults before the Lords of the Council and asking members to intercede with the Queen. But she refused to pardon him as she considered his letter to the Lords too much in the vein of self-justification and there was nothing in it about amending his conduct. To depose him seemed impolitic, so she left him sequestered hoping he might

resign of his own free will, but he was slow to come to any
decision and his sight was deteriorating. 'My case dependeth
long', he had written in February 1579; 'and yet if a man may
believe in court promises, I was at no time so near an end of my
troubles as at this present.' Convocation petitioned for his restoration, but this made the Queen urge him to consider his resignation more seriously. In April 1583 he wrote at long last express-
ing his determination to resign, but it had come too late. Grindal's
death in July 1583 relieved the Queen from this impossible
situation; he left her in his will a Greek new testament, 'having
nothing worthier to present her'. His eventual successor at Canterbury, John Whitgift, had been vice-chancellor of Cambridge
University at the time Cartwright had issued his 'Admonition to
Parliament'. Whitgift had attacked this tract as being 'fantastical
... leading to the overthrow of learning, religion, yea the whole
of the commonwealth.' Those were views which the Queen fully
endorsed. Her dealings with Whitgift, whom she nicknamed 'her
black husband', were less strained than with any other cleric in
her entire reign. He shared with her, as we shall see, a violent
distaste for puritanism, which he was bent on suppressing with
unremitting zeal. But Queen and Archbishop did not always see
things eye to eye, and when she read his Lambeth Articles of
1584 for issuing to the clergy in his province she detected Calvinistic views of predestination and election and insisted on their
removal.[26]

The first to die for their faith were two Dutch Anabaptists, in
1575. The term 'Anabaptist' covered a multitude of sinners in
sixteenth century parlance, from the fanatics of Münster a generation earlier, whose year of profligacy shocked all Europe, to the
sect led by John of Leyden, who preached the necessities of a
socialist republic. All governments regarded them as the extreme
left wing of Protestantism, whose tenets were politically dangerous. On Easter Day 1575 a house outside Aldgate was raided and
twenty-seven of the Dutch congregation were sent to prison. A
few of these later recanted their heresies at Paul's Cross; the
others, mostly women, were tried in the Bishop of London's

consistory court and 'after great pains taken with them, only one woman was converted.' Most of the remainder were whipped from Newgate to the river side, where a boat was provided to ship them back to Holland, but on 22 July John Peters and Henry Turwent, described as 'men of Flanders' went to the stake in West Smithfield near to where Bonner's fires had raged nineteen years before, 'in great horror, with roaring and crying.' Elizabeth had herself signed their death warrant, naming the very place of execution. Had Archbishop Parker not died before their trial there was a chance that they might have been spared.[27]

Disregarding those of the rebels in the north, who rose and fell with the Earls of Northumberland and Westmorland and met their fate as traitors, the first of the Catholics to suffer death was Cuthbert Mayne in November 1577. By then penal legislation, provoked by the papal bull of 1570 excommunicating Elizabeth, had widened the scope of high treason, and no priest owing allegiance to Rome could hope for mercy once he were caught. Mayne was the nephew of a conforming priest who hoped to place him in a family living once he had graduated. He was sent to St Alban Hall, Oxford, but very soon became chaplain of St John's College, where he came under the spell of the most brilliant of the fellows, Edmund Campion and his friend Gregory Martin. Rome beckoned him and he went to the newly founded English seminary at Douai to continue his study and became ordained a Roman Catholic priest there in 1575. The prime objective of Douai was to train priests who would return to England and begin the dangerous task of ministering to the faithful and winning others to the Church of Rome. Cuthbert Mayne was one of the first band of these seminary priests and worked for several months in Cornwall, in that delightful stretch of country between St Austell and Truro. He found shelter in Golden Manor, a fine early-Tudor farm house, that had belonged to the 'golden prebend' of Probus collegiate church until its dissolution. (The house is little altered today and in what are now the barns across the way one can see where the chancel step was and where the east window.) After some months of eluding capture Mayne's hiding place was discovered, and he was sent to Launceston for

therfor ons agam with humblenes of my hart, bicause I am not
suffera to bow the knees of my body I humbly crave to speke
with your higthnis wiche I wolde not be so bold to desier
if I knewe not my selfe most clere as I knowe my selfe most
tru. and as for the traitor Wiat he might parauentur writ
me a lettar but on my faithe I neuer receiued any from him and
as for the copie of my lettar sent to the freche kinge I pray
God cōfonn me eternally if euer I sent him Word, message
toke or lettar by any menes, and to this my truth
I will stande to my dethe.

I humbly craue but only one worde
of answer fro your selfe.

Your highnes most faithful subiect that
hathe bine from the begininge and wylbe
to my ende.   Elizabeth

trial as a traitor. He was not a militant campaigner, but one of the meek; yet his offences easily came within the terms of the rigorous act of 1571, for he had 'upheld the authority of the Bishop of Rome, published a papal absolution and introduced the use of a superstitious emblem called an *Agnus Dei*, of stone and silver, consecrated by the Bishop of Rome, whereby indulgences and immunities were alleged to be bestowed.' From Launceston Castle he went to his death on 29 November 1577. Some half-dozen of his flock who had been found guilty of aiding and abetting him to prevent capture were subsequently pardoned, one of them as late as 1586, but the owner of Golden Manor, Francis Tregon, suffered life imprisonment. Before long Mayne's mentor, Edmund Campion, would tread the same path to martyrdom in 1581.[28]

In their very different ways the burning of the Dutch Anabaptists and the execution of Cuthbert Mayne exemplify the breakdown in practice of the Elizabethan theory of the equivalence of church and state. Under the strain of political life, the political settlement of religion of 1559 was found to be wanting. But Elizabeth, Supreme Governor, held to her ideal, for there was indeed nothing that could take its place. The state was too weak to survive the existence of a permitted, radical nonconformity, whether from the left or the right. Not opening windows into men's souls to spy on the private religious exercises of outward conformists could not extend to benign acceptance of rival loyalties and organizations. 'The state within the state', as, for instance, the Huguenots erected in France, led to and helped perpetuate a series of disintegrating French civil wars that stretched the whole length of Elizabeth's reign. By contrast, England during the same period endured but one rebellion. Individuals like Campion and Mayne suffered for their idealism, there was imprisonment, crippling fines, banishment for extremists, but as a result of this policy the country escaped civil war.

Semper eadem, the Queen's personal motto, which Camden interpreted as 'to hold an even course in her whole life and actions',[29] was in effect synonymous with the golden mean of her churchmanship. The Protestant ethic could go too far and, appreciating more readily than anyone its inherent dangers to monarchy, she would always be on the side of the angels. She wanted a learned church, spiritually strong, cleansed from worldliness and capable of inspiring men and women. Though her government was conducted by laymen, the Church was the essential partner of the crown.

The Church thus buttressed by the state paid dearly in money and in kind. Elizabeth perforce had to turn to the still considerable revenues of bishoprics and deaneries because the crown was by contrast so needy. The richest spoils of the dissolution of the monasteries had passed by sale or lease to courtiers before her accession and as the years went by she found herself hampered by lack of money. The medieval idea that the sovereign could live off his own, the crown estate, and finance the government of the realm out of its own ancient revenues, was already a forlorn hope by the year 1500. But successive devaluations of the currency and the growth in the state's spheres of activity, the revolution in national defence and in the conduct of foreign affairs, as England emerged as a nation state, made the pressure on the royal purse unbearable. Elizabeth herself reiterated how Parliament had tied her down to traditional taxation – tonnage and poundage for life, and grants on out-dated scales of subsidies from laity and clergy in exceptional circumstances. To balance her budget the Queen plundered the Church; and her demands became increasingly oppressive.[30]

By an Act of 1559 archbishops and bishops were forbidden to lease lands in their possession for longer than three lives, or twenty-one years (instead of the more usual ninety-nine years), unless the leases were made over to the Queen. In other words long leases of church lands became the province of the crown and the course of this rich stream of patronage was turned so that it flowed right through the court. The same Act also made abundantly clear the Queen's right to the temporal possessions of bishops' sees during a vacancy, and authorized exchanges of lands between the crown and any vacant see. This statute, dubbed by

Strype 'The Act for the Plunder of the Church', enabled Elizabeth to remain solvent at the expense of church property. It was
now very much in her interest to keep bishoprics vacant for as
long as possible. There was no Bishop of Oxford between 1568
and 1589 and again from 1592 until after her death. Ely, the
richest of plums, was vacant for nineteen years, Bristol for
fourteen.[31]

Episcopal leases to reward courtiers, civil servants and even an
exiled King of Portugal cost Her Majesty not a penny. Favourites
such as Leicester and Hatton, Oxford and Heneage acquired most
of their rewards from this source. Sir Christopher Hatton in a
cause célèbre made off with the best portion of the Bishop of Ely's
London residence. For long he and others had coveted Ely
House, Holborn, with its spacious gardens, but old Bishop Cox
bravely kept the 'harpies and wolves' at bay until Hatton
established himself as royal favourite. In 1577 he was forced into
granting him a lease for twenty-one years and almost at once, at
the favourite's prompting, he was required to demise 'the place
to the Queen', for letting off to Hatton, and foot a bill of £2,000
for improvements.

Ecclesiastical promotion usually involved making over lands to
the Queen or granting annuities to her nominees, or both.
Thomas Godwin would not have become Bishop of Bath and
Wells in 1584 unless he had made a ninety-nine years' lease to the
Queen of property which she could then pass on to Sir Walter
Raleigh. Richard Fletcher, when he exchanged Worcester for
London in 1595, was required to make 'gratifications' out of his
Worcester revenues 'to divers of the court, by the Queen's
appointment' – up to £2000, and Fletcher did as he was bidden
rather than 'lose the least mite of her grace'. Thomas Bilson,
author of *Perpetual Government of Christ's Church*, a tract on the
divine right of episcopacy which he dedicated to Her Majesty,
received due acknowledgement in elevation to a bishopric, but he
had to part with £400 a year from one of his richest Winchester
manors as a pension for Sir Francis Carew. 'We request therefore',
wrote the Queen, 'a speedy lease in reversion to him, such as shall
reward his long service and be least hurtful to the bishopric' – an

euphemistic phrase – 'leaving the choice to you.' Poor Bilson grovelled 'at the lowest step of her princely throne', as he put it, but the Carew lease, together with other annuities, reduced the Bishop's income from £2,513 to £500. Again, Gervase Babington, bent on being translated from Exeter to Worcester in 1597, found the price required of him was a lease of his most valuable estate, the manor of Crediton, while Bishop Scambler of Norwich had to sign away the bulk of his lands to Sir Thomas Heneage for eighty years in the year of the Armada. When Martin Heaton was promoted to the much attenuated see of Ely the wits made puns of his signature 'Mar Ely' or worse 'Mart Ely', and others said the bishopric of Llandaff should be renamed 'Aff' as the land had gone – indeed its income had sunk to £154. But the value of the richer bishoprics had fallen even more alarmingly. Durham, one of the wealthiest, had lost £1,000 of its wealth, Lincoln's value had halved and Winchester seemingly withered away.[32]

Deans and chapters found they were subject to the same pressures as the bishops. Thus the coffers of the Church became a reserve for the exchequer that was always being tapped, a pension fund for government servants and the jackpot from which the highest stakes in the gamble of court life would emanate. Church finance, as big business, became the province of developers, contractors and agents. In the same way impropriated tithes were sold off at an alarming rate and Elizabeth herself disposed of such tithes in no fewer than 2,216 parishes. As a result the average parson's income slumped. One of the few ways – certainly the simplest – for clerks in holy orders to make ends meet was by holding more than one benefice, and in the three years 1559–62 the Queen granted as many as 414 licences to individual ministers, from deans down to perpetual curates, to hold benefices *in commendam*.[33]

Bishoprics and deaneries were auctioned to the highest bidder. The Bishop of Durham, late in the reign, dared indirectly to accuse the Queen of simony, when he was asked to put in a bid for the vacant archbishopric of York. Matthew Hutton, the prince bishop, was reproved by young Cecil for his squeamishness as much as for his outspokenness: it was 'absurd to make the person of a prince' obey the same rules as her subjects. 'These niceties will hardly be admitted where such a prince vouchsafes to entreat', he added.[34] So Hutton reviewed his conscience and his position and became Archbishop of York. The Supreme Governor had not been able to predict how the system under the Act of 1559 would develop, and her own rapaciousness – rather her ready ear for the rapaciousness of others – did not become insistent until the last fifteen years of her reign. There had been too few effective protests. In her plunder of the Church Elizabeth was no doubt a child of her own age, carrying to its logical conclusion the nationalization and secularization of monastic and guild property under her father, yet she bears full responsibility for weakening so disastrously the finances of the Church and thus paring away the props of monarchy itself. Not for a century after her death did another Queen regnant begin to restore the balance by founding Queen Anne's Bounty.

ANSWERS ANSWERLESS

WITH the religious issue settled in 1559 to the satisfaction of the vast body of Englishmen, the most pressing problem was the succession. Since Elizabeth was young and it was assumed that, unlike her sister, she was capable of bearing children, the succession to the throne was at first looked on essentially in terms of her marriage. Whom she would marry and who might succeed her in the event of sudden death before she produced an heir, she regarded as matters of her prerogative – a matter, indeed, of life and death. When pressed on either topic by Parliament or Council, she would give an 'answer answerless'. Her adamant refusal from the beginning to name her successor set in train all kinds of intrigues. Bent on overturning her *via media*, Catholics supported the Stuart claim, stemming from Henry VIII's elder sister, Margaret, and in retaliation the more extreme Protestants argued the merits of the Suffolk claim, yet the Queen impartially gave them both short shrift. Any claimant to the succession she branded as a potential traitor. For her own experience had taught her that never so reluctant a claimant to *eventual* succession, he or she might, as the puppet of faction, challenge Elizabeth's rule here and now, and then she would again be in the Tower 'within a month'. Before discussing the many suitors for her hand it is as well to identify the various offending limbs in the Tudor genealogical tree (opposite p. 354) and see how the Queen dealt with them.

Unlike her father, Elizabeth regarded the Stuart claim as the more satisfactory, and hence the more dangerous to herself. Four days after her accession, when news of Mary's death reached France, Henry II had proclaimed his daughter-in-law as Queen of

England. At once Mary Queen of Scotland and of the Isles and Dauphine of France, then aged seventeen, began to quarter the royal arms of England on her own, first privately, then in public. When Throgmorton, the ambassador in Paris, complained to the Constable of France, the great man shrugged his shoulders. He knew nothing about it, he said, for at the time of Mary's marriage to the Dauphin he had been in prison, and in any case Throgmorton should not forget that his Queen still styled herself 'Queen of France' and quartered the fleur-de-lis on her arms. Mary's claims were not claims to the succession on the failure of Elizabeth to produce an heir, but claims to be rightful Queen of England in her place.

> The arms of Mary Queen Dauphine of France
> The noblest Lady in earth, for till advance
> Of Scotland Queen and England, also
> Of Ireland, as God hath provided so.

The subsequent history of those lines[1] dominates the relations between the two Queens and was a key factor in international politics.

The death of Henry II of France on 10 July 1559 made Elizabeth's position extremely critical, for his successor, Francis II, husband of Mary Queen of Scots, was a puppet of the Guise, who were bent on re-establishing Mary's power in Scotland over a factious nobility and on supporting as effectively as they could her claims to the crown of England. Never had the 'auld alliance' presented so alarming a situation as when Francis of Guise and his brother, the Cardinal of Lorraine, ruled France while their sister Mary of Guise was Regent in Scotland. The Lords of the Congregation in Scotland, inspired by John Knox, deposed the Regent but as they were powerless to expel her French troops they appealed to Elizabeth for aid. After a six-month campaign against the French north of the border in what was called the War of the Insignia – the arms of England which Mary had unlawfully used – in July 1560 the Treaty of Edinburgh was signed, by which the Scots recognized Elizabeth's right to her throne and undertook that their own Queen should relinquish her claim to the crown of

England. But the sudden death of Francis II on 5 December increased Elizabeth's difficulties, for Mary decided to return to Scotland. Perhaps in refusing to allow her to travel through England on her way to Edinburgh Elizabeth inflicted a wound that never healed, as Mary consistently refused to ratify the Treaty of Edinburgh unless Elizabeth would name her as her successor, and the widowed Queen's search for another husband further aggravated the situation. ·...

There was another claimant of the Stuart line nearer home in the person of Lady Margaret Douglas, Countess of Lennox, first cousin of the Queen. After the death of James IV of Scotland, Margaret Tudor had married Archibald Douglas, Earl of Angus. Margaret, their only child, had been placed by Henry VIII in the household of Princess Mary to whom she became devoted. Her staunch Catholicism and her marriage to Matthew, Earl of Lennox had forced Henry to exclude her from the English succession. Theirs was, truly, a formidable alliance, for Lennox himself had a claim as heir presumptive to the Scottish throne. The Countess had chosen to live on her Yorkshire estates at Temple Newsam and here her son Henry, Lord Darnley had been born in 1545; in her eyes his English birth gave his claim to the English crown precedence over Mary's and so long as Mary was still Queen of France the English Catholics favoured Darnley. One great obstacle to this claim, which Elizabeth successfully exploited, was the papal annulment of the marriage between Margaret Tudor and Angus, for it made Lady Lennox a bastard. She, however, had her own grand design which would more than paper over the cracks – no less than for her Darnley to espouse the widowed Mary – and no sooner did she learn of Francis II's death than she began intriguing at the French court. A lanky, handsome youth, good at sports and courtly accomplishments, but with a brain no bigger than a pea, Darnley was destined to captivate Mary, and Elizabeth found herself having to accept as a *fait accompli* his luckless marriage with the Queen of Scots which produced her successor to the throne of England.

After Lady Jane Grey had been so fatally beguiled into Northumberland's conspiracy in 1553 the Suffolk claim to the succession passed to her sisters Katherine and Mary Grey. Lady Katherine, born in 1538, had been married to Henry Herbert, later Earl of Pembroke, but the marriage was never consummated, and with the execution of her father and elder sister, Herbert divorced her. On her accession Elizabeth kept Lady Katherine Grey at court under close supervision; for there were tales of a madcap scheme in August 1559 for her to be enticed abroad and sent to Spain as a bride for Philip II – or even Don Carlos – 'since she is supposed to be the next heir to the realm.' And then in the last weeks of 1560 she was secretly married to Edward Seymour, Earl of Hertford, at Hertford House in Canon Row, Westminster; the ceremony performed rather remarkably by a Catholic priest, was unknown to all but a few until the following August when Katherine was great with child. Elizabeth promptly despatched her to the Tower and Hertford, on returning from France, was also sent there, though to different quarters from his wife, who gave birth to a son, Edward, on 24 September. Cecil thought the Queen unnecessarily harsh in her treatment of Lady Katherine; she saw 'some greater drift' in this match than mere love, and he was unaware of any conspiracy. The following spring a commission headed by the Archbishop of Canterbury investigated the marriage and as neither priest nor witness could be produced, the union was declared invalid. As a result Hertford was fined £15,000 in the Star Chamber for the crime of 'seducing a Virgin of the blood royal'.[2]

But though they were not man and wife in the eyes of the law, the couple continued to meet, thanks to bribes to jailers, and in February 1563 Lady Katherine was delivered of a second son within the Tower, thus dashing any hope she might have had of the Queen's mercy. Worse was to come, for John Hales, a chancery clerk and MP with marked Protestant leanings, published a tract on the succession favouring Lady Katherine's claim, which cost the author his liberty and Sir Nicholas Bacon his seat on the Privy Council. Elizabeth was greatly alarmed that there was a conspiracy afoot to legitimize Katherine's marriage. She had been permitted to leave the Tower while the plague was raging in London and continued her captivity in the country, but now she was deemed too dangerous a figure, with her two healthy infant sons, to be allowed this comparative freedom, and only left the Tower for periodic visits to the lieutenant's house at Cockfield Hall. Fuller's 'Lady of Lamentations', Lady Katherine was seldom seen with dry eyes for years together, until in 1568 she died. Elizabeth, much relieved at her passing, paid £76 to give her a stately funeral in Salisbury Cathedral. At one time her boys appear to have been brought up in Cecil's household. Much later their father remarried Frances Howard but in 1595, when he sought to have this marriage set aside to clear his sons' claims to the throne, he was arrested. For such matters, so closely touching her regality, Elizabeth had a long memory – and so did her successor, for Katherine Grey's grandson, William Seymour, was sent to the Tower by James I for presuming to marry Arabella Stuart.[3]

Lady Katherine's younger sister, Lady Mary Grey, fared no better. She had stayed on at court as a maid of honour, despite her sister's disgrace, so Elizabeth could keep an eye on her. Alas, after six years of life at court, fearing at twenty-five that she was becoming an old maid, Mary clapped her eyes on Thomas Keys, the Queen's serjeant porter. It was an incongruous match, for Lady Mary was petite and Keys an enormous fellow with a huge girth. One evening in August 1565, after a quiet supper in her rooms in Whitehall Palace with Lady Stafford's daughters, she walked over to the privy chamber and thence to the council room where she found a messenger to take a prearranged token to the serjeant porter. At 9 p.m. they were married by candlelight in Keys' chamber near the water-gate, by an unidentified priest, 'apparelled in a short gown, being old, fat and of low stature'. But Elizabeth soon heard and she was furious. That a maid of honour – let alone a candidate for the succession – should marry without her permission was *lèse majesté*, but that she should marry so far beneath her, and right under the Queen's nose, was unpardonable. Keys was packed off to the Fleet Prison, where he spent three miserable years, hoping in vain to be given a second chance; he even volunteered to serve in Ireland. His health suffered, particularly after eating a rib of beef which had been immersed in a liquid wash prepared from mangy dogs. At length he was freed, on condition that he lived quietly at Lewisham and did not attempt to see his wife. Even a letter of Keys sent with Archbishop Parker's blessing, begging for the Queen's mercy to live with his wife 'according to the laws of God' was flatly refused.[4]

Lady Mary meantime had been placed in the custody of William Hawtrey at Chequers in Buckinghamshire. Then she was allowed to live at Greenwich with the Dowager Duchess of Suffolk, a kindly soul, who bemoaned that she had no decent furniture 'for the dressing up of' the girl's room. Out of loyalty to the serjeant porter Mary continued to sign herself 'Mary Keys' and on his death unsuccessfully petitioned Elizabeth to be allowed to wear mourning. The hapless Mary died in 1578.[5]

A weaker claim in the Suffolk line, but still sufficiently strong to perturb the Queen, was that of Lady Margaret Strange, first cousin to the unfortunate Grey sisters, being the only child of their Aunt Eleanor, who had married the Earl of Cumberland. In Queen Mary's time some regarded her claim as far more weighty than her Grey cousins, for her side of the family had stood aloof from Lady Jane's conspiracy; and the Venetian ambassador of the day, dismissing Princess Elizabeth's title under bastardy, wrote of Margaret as 'the nearest of all to the blood royal – and to her the succession belongs.' She had already married Henry Stanley, Lord Strange, later to become Earl of Derby, though theirs was a far from happy union. They were ever squabbling about money. A postscript of a letter to her Derby in-laws was so blotted with tears that it could not be read. For the first dozen years of the reign Lady Margaret attended at court, but when given leave of absence on her father's death in 1570, she was reluctant to return to Whitehall. Yet Elizabeth peremptorily required her attendance 'as one very near in blood to us'. This was written in the aftermath of the northern rebellion, but though her late father had been warm in support of Mary Queen of Scots, Lady Margaret was about the last candidate the rebels would have favoured and the Queen's summons shows her touchiness about the succession. She wanted possible claimants, who were not already in the Tower, under her eye at court just as compulsively as Queen

Victoria needed all her relatives about her. Unhappy to the end, Margaret tried to find consolation in the company of magicians and wizards.[6]

There was one other claimant – a man, and he caused no trouble at all. Henry Hastings, Earl of Huntingdon was descended on his father's side from Edward III, and through his mother, who was a Pole, to George, Duke of Clarence, brother of Edward IV, who had ended his days in a butt of malmsey. Though the Plantagenet line through the Poles had alarmed Henry VIII, Elizabeth never regarded Huntingdon as a serious contender. Others were less doubtful and when the Queen was feared to be dying in 1562, the Earl's candidature seemed the most promising; his sex, his Protestantism and his connexions with the greater nobility were all decisive factors. When his wife came to court (as he told Leicester) the Queen would 'give her a privy nip, especially concerning myself.' A fanatic Puritan, 'always finding money for hot-headed preachers', he tried to persuade Elizabeth to let him sell his lands and join the Huguenot army in France in 1569, but she had work for him at home and never once had occasion to doubt his loyalty. The fact that he had married Leicester's sister counted for much. A vigorous Lord President of the Council in the North, he contented himself with writing his family history instead of fretting about the succession.[7]

Right to the end there were shadows. Just before her death Elizabeth heard word of a proposed match between another generation of Stuart and Suffolk claimants. Intriguers were putting forward Arabella Stuart (the daughter of Darnley's younger brother) as a bride for William Seymour, Katherine Grey's grandson. There is a tale that in the year of the Armada, when she was fourteen, Arabella had been brought to court as a lady in waiting, but no one could stomach her haughtiness, and she had been sent away.[8] But in 1603 as her last defensive action, Elizabeth kept the girl in confinement.

'Here is a great resort of woers and controversy among lovers', wrote Cecil in October 1559, already heartily sick of a masquerade that, had he known it, was in its infancy. As Elizabeth was

reckoned the greatest match in Christendom, the suit for her hand
became a key question of international politics. The stakes were so
high that the most unlikely candidates entered the lists, and a
month after Cecil's observation there were 'ten or twelve ambassadors competing for her favour'. 'So many loose and flighty
fancies are abroad', wrote one of the principal match-makers, that
serious negotiations were degenerating into sheer pantomime;
were it not so important it might be absolutely laughable. Amidst
all the confused tales of diplomatic despatches and court gossip one
point is abundantly clear; everyone at home and abroad expected
Elizabeth to marry, and most thought the matter would be cut
and dried in a matter of weeks rather than months. The Queen
herself revelled in it all; the more suitors the merrier, and she
played off one against the other with a deft hand.[9]

Count de Feria, Philip II's pompous ambassador, who had
married Jane Dormer, one of the late Queen's maids of honour,
was quite sure there would be no serious opposition to his master's
own proposal. In the first days of the reign he reported, 'If she
decides to marry out of the country, she will at once fix her eyes
on Your Majesty.' Before the coronation Philip had sent him
various notes to guide him in his tactics with Elizabeth; he was
even to tell her there would be 'no difficulty in obtaining a dispensation from the Pope for their marriage' if she should by then
still be regarded as a 'heretic'. When this approach failed miserably, Count de Feria was told to show Philip 'as a good and true
brother, who really wishes her well', and if she adopted 'perni-
cious novelties' in religion 'all idea of my marriage with her must
be broken off.' Elizabeth shelved the issue with fair words, for she
could not risk alienating him by an outright refusal while peace
negotiations with France were in progress and she was counting
on his active help to secure the return of Calais. Philip himself
simply could not understand why she was hesitating about
accepting him, the great master of two continents, and de Feria,
too, was astounded that she should behave so curiously. He began
to realize he was the wrong person for discussing so personal a
matter with this 'young lass' and asked for Bishop Quadra to be
sent over to help him. While the peace preliminaries were being

signed at Cateau-Cambrésis, the Count in Whitehall was having his fourth private audience on the vexed topic. This time Elizabeth told him plainly that she had no desire to marry, claiming she had intimated as much from the start. She readily appreciated that for her to become Philip's wife would be 'advantageous to her honour' and the security of both their kingdoms against France, but good friendship as brother and sister could achieve this just as well. Then she brought up the impediment of Philip having married her sister, with unspoken hints of King Henry's doubts about marrying Katherine of Aragon, Prince Arthur's widow; true there was the possibility of a papal dispensation, but now she roundly denied the Pope's authority. Again, her beloved people were against her marrying a foreigner and amidst laughter she told the Count that many of them were saying Philip would just come for the nuptials and go off to Spain directly. Finally, as if all these reasons were not enough, she said it was impossible for her to take him as a husband for she was 'a heretic' – she used the word with pride. When Philip heard of this considered, multiple refusal he put forward the names of the Holy Roman Emperor's sons, the Archdukes Ferdinand and Charles, either of whom would do very well for her, and he himself lost no time in courting Elizabeth de Valois, the beautiful daughter of Katherine de Medici.[10]

Meanwhile the House of Commons, always more worried than their sovereign about the succession, had been discussing the question of royal matrimony. Early in February a number of members asked for a humble address to be made to the Queen to marry an Englishman, though with commendable tact Mr Speaker had watered this down to a request to marry, without limitations. Within a few days he read to the House her gracious, and lengthy, reply. Whenever it should please God to incline her heart to another way of life than spinsterhood, they might rest assured she would 'never conclude anything that shall be prejudicial to the realm, for the weal, good and safety whereof I will never shun to spend my life. And whomsoever may chance shall be to light upon, I trust he shall be as careful for the realm and you.' Her faithful Commons could put clean out of their heads

any fear of another marriage like Mary's, in which national and
religious interests had been sacrificed:

> And albeit it might please Almighty God to continue me still in this
> mind to live out of the state of marriage, yet it is not to be feared but
> He will so work in my heart and in your wisdoms as good provision by
> His help may be made in convenient time, whereby the realm shall not
> remain destitute of an heir that may be a fit governor, and peradventure
> more beneficial to the realm than such offspring as may come of me.
> For, although I be never so careful of your well doings and mind ever
> so to be, yet may my issue grow out of kind and become perhaps un-
> gracious. And in the end, this shall be for me sufficient, that a marble
> stone shall declare that a Queen, having reigned such a time, lived and
> died a virgin.[11]

One name that was in some MPs' minds when they asked for
her to choose an English consort was Henry, Earl of Arundel,
Lord High Steward of the coronation, whom she certainly never
contemplated. The other was Sir William Pickering, who had
been getting over a fever in Flanders and did not appear at court
until May. The son of Henry VIII's Knight Marshal, Pickering
had for a time been a boon companion of the poet Surrey and
then became a diplomat. He had played a part in that plot long
ago to marry Elizabeth to Edward Courtenay, Earl of Devon, and
now, in between embassies, appeared to be wooing her himself.
Although nearly forty-three he was tall, well-proportioned and
had a reputation as a ladies' man. On his first visit to court Elizabeth saw him secretly, next day he spent nearly five hours quite
openly at the palace and Londoners, jumping to conclusions,
reckoned he would court her in one; 'they are giving 25 to 100
that he will be King.' Soon the Queen assigned him lodgings at
Greenwich Palace. He spent a fortune on clothes, entertained
lavishly and 'always dines apart with music playing.' None the
less, strait-laced Bishop Jewel thought him prudent and upright
– perhaps because he had once been a pupil of Cheke at Cambridge – and even detected 'a royal countenance'.[12]

But Pickering was a nine days' wonder. His swaggering and
disregard for court protocol upset several of the nobility. He had a
brush with Dudley early on and when Bedford spoke out against

him at a banquet in September Pickering apparently challenged him to a duel. One day next month Arundel stopped him on the threshold of the Queen's apartments, telling him that his place was the presence chamber, not the inner sanctum, which it was the privilege of peers alone to enter. The knight admitted he knew the rule as well as he knew that Arundel was 'an impudent, discourteous knave', and went on in. Rumour had it that the Earl was ready to leave the realm for good if Pickering became consort. Elizabeth liked his company but never dreamt of marrying him. Even that summer he had whispered to the Spanish ambassador that 'he knew she meant to die a maid.' A few more diplomatic tasks and Sir William faded out of history. He died in London in 1575, a bachelor, leaving his splendid library to his natural daughter, Hester.[13]

Foreign suitors were in fact more pressing. With the reign only a few weeks old there was much speculation about Adolphus, Duke of Holstein, whose Protestantism was reckoned his strongest suit, though de Quadra had grudgingly to admit that he was reckoned 'not a worse looking man' than his own Catholic candidate, the Archduke Charles. For weeks on end there were rumours of his imminent arrival in England to court Elizabeth, though in fact he did not come until April 1560, when he took up a ten weeks' residence in Somerset House. She saw as little of him as she could, pleading a fever. His ardour cooled very little for he proposed again from Germany, hoping she might change her mind, but she told him courteously 'she must sing the same song.' The Duke of Saxony also made a half-hearted attempt to press his attentions on her, and a French prince was supposed to be interested, for an agent bustling between France and England had a secret audience with her during which he produced a portrait 'which she gazed on intently.'[14]

Eric XIV of Sweden was much more persistent. While both he and she were heirs to thrones he had pressed his claims by proxy, and immediately after her accession he sent an envoy to prepare the way, but the man completely misinterpreted the Queen's politeness, by reporting to Eric that 'her countenance, her voice, her words and gestures had evinced her good will and love to-

wards him.' In May 1559 he asked for a special embassy to be received to discuss arrangements and Elizabeth desperately hoped it
could be put off; if not, she trusted 'the refusal which they will
receive' for his proposal would not damage the friendship of the
two countries. But the Swede could not take a hint and in July
wrote her a passionate love letter in Latin: 'He is bound by an
eternal love towards her, having loved her hitherto faithfully and
constantly', without knowing her sentiments towards him. Ad-
versity will not shake him, since she has given him 'these great
tokens' of her favour and affection – 'Your Serenity's most
loving Eric'. This was followed up by formal letters announcing
the departure of a special embassy, led by his younger brother,
Duke John of Finland, which would expect 'a favourable answer'.
So the comedy had to be played out.

Duke John landed in September and was lodged in the Bishop
of Winchester's house. He hobnobbed with the Lord Mayor,
scattered money very freely wherever he went and forced his
company on the Queen whenever he could. The Imperial ambassador, hard put to it to interest Elizabeth in the Archduke Charles,
tried to make the Duke a laughing stock, telling everyone that his
father was 'only a clown who had stolen his kingdom' from the
Danes, whereupon John threatened to kill him. 'The matter has
reached such a point that the Queen is careful they should not
meet in the palace, to avoid their slashing each other in her
presence.' Bishop Jewel noted with amazement that the Swedish
and Imperial proxies were 'courting at a most marvellous rate.
But the Swede is most in earnest, for he promises mountains of
silver in case of success. The lady, however, is probably thinking
of an alliance nearer home.' Elizabeth certainly enjoyed leading
them all a dance. At one time de Quadra panicked, in case she
should suddenly decide to accept Eric, because she was 'only a
passionate, ill-advised woman'. Eric would not believe that she
was really turning him down and accused his brother John of
wooing her on his own account; he was recalled and promptly
married the King of Poland's daughter. His successor arrived with
gifts of bullion and piebald horses sent with a lover's message that
Eric would quickly follow in person to lay his heart at her feet.

Envoys, presents and messages were still coming over from Sweden two years later, and at Michaelmas 1561 the King was expected to make his long postponed visit. She would receive him at Richmond after dinner and hear his protestations of love by the bay window in her presence chamber. Alas, he never came; he lost heart in Elizabeth and after rapidly turning his attentions first to Mary Queen of Scots then to a French princess, the great lover fell for the charms of one of his own subjects, Karin the nut girl, a common soldier's daughter. Elizabeth was perhaps well rid of her Swede.[15]

There was another less passionate suitor nearer home in the second half of 1560. The Treaty of Edinburgh, which ended England's war against the French in Scotland, breaking 'the auld alliance' once and for all, brought England and Scotland closer together than ever before, and the Lords of the Congregation sought to extend this friendship by a marriage. They had no King, alas, to offer, but they presented Arran as being a most suitable candidate; he was a thorough gentleman, well brought up and trained since childhood in war. But Elizabeth was impressed neither with the qualities of Arran nor with the scheme, and the damages of alienating Spain as well as France by embarking on such a marriage would undo all the solid achievement of the Treaty of Edinburgh. She delayed her formal reply until early in December. 'Finding herself not presently disposed to marry' she did not want to prevent Arran from accepting any other proposal which might be made to him. Before the letter reached Scotland she had heard of the sudden death of Francis II of France which meant that his widow, Mary, would return to her Scottish kingdom.[16]

All this time the Spanish and Imperial ambassadors were singing in unison the praises of the Emperor's sons. First it was the eldest, Ferdinand, and at times she gave them the impression that she would 'only accept a great prince' – a category into which the Archduke certainly fitted. But from what was known in London, Ferdinand was reputed a thorough bigot and Elizabeth commented that all he was fit for was praying for his father and brothers, so the ambassadors quickly dropped him for the Archduke Charles.

When they began to rush preliminaries, she said quite firmly she would never agree to marry a man she had not seen and (no doubt recalling the sorry story of her father and Anne of Cleves) said she 'will not trust portrait painters.' Some who knew said Charles had a monstrous head far bigger than the Earl of Bedford's, which was rather dampening. He must be a good rider and thoroughly masculine, she insisted, not the kind of fellow 'who sits at home all day amongst the cinders.' She asked whether he could pay her a visit, preferably incognito, and the next day Will Summers, her fool, joked that the Archduke Charles was already in London, disguised as the chamberlain at the Imperial embassy, waiting for the chance to look the Queen over. Baron Rabenstyn came over from Germany at the end of May to sound opinions. Elizabeth told him she had not yet determined upon marriage, but asked him to talk with her councillors. Next day the English Ambassador in Augsburg was required to make searching enquiries about Charles – his age, height, weight, strength, complexion, nature, personal affections, education, judgement in matters of religion and 'whether he hath been noted to have loved any woman, and in what sort.' But before the ink was dry the Queen had herself written to the Emperor Ferdinand: conscious of the honour of the proposed match she:

has no intention of abandoning a single life. Her age and position may possibly make this appear strange, but it is no new or suddenly formed resolution on her part. There were times when marriage ... would have rescued her from great griefs and dangers, but she could not be moved thereto either by the apprehension of peril nor the desire of liberty. So much for the past. God will direct the future; she will act for the good of the realm.

Tu felix Austria nubes, as the saying went, but not as yet in England. The fact that negotiations were afoot had, however, increased her status in Europe very considerably. She admitted, quite honestly that Charles was the best match for her in Christendom, but had no intention of things going beyond the talking stage. The door was deliberately left open for political reasons, and many more advances and discussions about Charles were to be made before she took the matter up in earnest four years later in very different conditions.[17]

It was in April 1559 that Lord Robert Dudley, seemingly over-night, became established in Elizabeth's affections, and their special relationship was to endure, despite the quarrels, the mis-understandings and the upheavals of life at court, down to his death in the year of the Armada. The fifth son of John Dudley, Duke of Northumberland, he had married Amy Robsart in 1550 at the age of seventeen. With his father's ascendency he became master of the buckhounds to Edward VI, but was implicated with the rest of his family in the scheme for his younger brother Guild-ford to marry Lady Jane Grey in his fatal bid for the succession. In January 1554 Robert and his brothers were tried and sentenced to death as traitors, but Queen Mary stayed sentence against all except Guildford and after a further ten months in the Tower they were pardoned. Robert sought to win his way back to favour at court by military service, and Philip's war with France gave him the opportunity of showing his worth. After the battle of St Quentin he was rewarded with the post of Master of the Ordi-nance and the slur for his father's attainder was removed when Mary restored him in blood, with the rank of a duke's son. At last with Elizabeth's accession his meteoric career began in earnest. Other favourites came and went, but he remained constant, to the dismay of grave statesmen and the amazement of seasoned diplomats.

Portraits amply bear out the contemporary comments on his striking appearance – the 'comely feature of body and limb'. His sudden rise to fame made him the target for a thousand malicious stories: this *nouveau riche* who had captured the Queen's heart and was to be showered with honours and wealth was always under suspicion, for ever liable to arouse intense hatred. He was unpre-dictable, a dangerous man, even, and because he was a *parvenu* many credited him with no principles whatsoever. His ambitions seemed boundless and there was every likelihood that he would fulfil them. He was an outsize character whom men saw in terms of black and white. Because it was his masculinity that appealed to Elizabeth, enemies made out that his lust was a byword; 'seeking pasture among the waiting gentlewomen of Her Majesty's chamber, he hath offered £300 for a night.' His concupiscence, said others, was only equalled by his violence and he relieved the monotonies of a life of adultery by poisoning people. The sustained bitter attacks on this level that form the ground swell of that unsavoury work, *Leicester's Commonwealth*, were all summed up by the Earl of Sussex on his deathbed, when he counselled his friends to avoid Dudley: 'Beware of the gipsy, for he will be too hard for you all. You know not the beast as well as I do.'[18]

By mid-April the master of the horse 'has come so much into favour that he does whatever he likes with affairs and it is even said that Her Majesty visits him in his chamber day and night', wrote de Feria. 'People talk of this so freely that they go so far as to say that his wife has a malady in one of her breasts and the Queen is only waiting for her to die to marry Lord Robert.' Amy Robsart had never come to court, though that may have been from personal choice, as she was already ailing and in the country she was her own mistress.[19]

Scandalous tales spread quickly. Soon Sir Thomas Chaloner was writing from Brussels to Cecil: 'These folks are broad-mouthed where I spoke of one too much in favour, as they esteem. I think ye guess whom they named. ... As I count the slander most false, as a young princess cannot be too wary what countenance or familiar demonstrations she maketh, more to one another.' Kate Ashley, whose scholarly husband had been made keeper of the jewel house, went down on her knees to implore her mistress to put an end to the evil rumours by marrying her beau – how Lady Dudley was to be dealt with, she did not say. But Elizabeth defended herself with spirit: her relations with him were quite open, she was well-chaperoned by her ladies all the time, so there could be nothing indiscreet, nothing wrong in her conduct towards a man of so honourable a nature. 'If', however, 'she ever had the will or had found pleasure in such a dishonourable life – from which God preserve her – she did not know of anyone who could forbid her.'[20]

Camden, writing years afterwards, could but try and explain their mutual attraction in terms of astrology – 'the hidden courses of the stars at the hour of his birth, and thereby a most straight conjugation of their minds – a man cannot easily say.'[21] Both of them certainly dabbled in astrology, but love works in a mysterious way. By some strange fortune Dudley struck the right note in his flattery, pandered to her whims when she needed distraction from cares of state, amused her, above all treated her as a young woman who desperately needed the warmth of personal affection, not as the Queen ruling the loyal hearts of a people. Lonely and unloved for so long, Lord Robert gave her the inner assurance for which she had yearned. Not surprising, then, that she was gay and vivacious in his company, moody and ill at ease when he was not at her side. At this stage it was a purely platonic friendship. The strength of it and the attraction of the affair for her lay in the fact that while Dudley had a wife living, she was insured against the danger of surrendering herself to him. So as yet the question, 'Was she sufficiently in love with him to want to marry him?' did not arise. Innocent flirtation was one thing, unbounded passion was in another category, and people who could not distinguish between the two were fools.

Feelings about Lord Robert were running very high at court that autumn of 1559, when there were ill-founded rumours of plots to murder him, which centred round the Duke of Norfolk. 'The Queen and Robert are very uneasy about the Duke of Norfolk, as he talks openly about her lightness and bad government. People are ashamed of what is going on, and particularly the Duke', wrote Bishop Quadra. He had apparently written to Dudley, telling him that if he did not abandon his pretensions and presumptions he would not die in his bed. 'The duke and the rest of them cannot put up with his being king' – this last statement was certainly as true as the threats of murder were false. As Christmas approached, Norfolk had it out with Dudley, speaking out 'so plainly' in advocating Elizabeth's marriage with the Archduke Charles that they separated abruptly and Lord Robert told him 'he was neither a good Englishman nor a loyal subject who advised the Queen to marry a foreigner.' Within a few days of that strained meeting the Duke was forced by Elizabeth to take the post of lieutenant-general in the north, for the coming war against the French in Scotland and it is hard to resist the conclusion that Dudley engineered this appointment to get him as far away from court as possible. In his absence in the first six months of 1560, Dudley went from strength to strength. An absurd story gained currency that he was 'laying in a good stock of arms and every day is assuming a more masterful part in affairs. They say that he thinks of divorcing his wife.' It was reported that Queen and favourite spent days shut up together 'without coming abroad' and that under his spell she was unable to concentrate on matters of state. 'Not a man in England but cries out at the top of his voice this fellow is ruining the country with his vanity.' Such were not, of course, impartial reports, but they show what those at court feared.[22]

In mid-June there was old Mother Dowe of Brentwood embroidering odd tales she had picked up as she wandered about south-east Essex. Dudley, said she, had given the Queen a rich petticoat. 'Thinkest thou it was a petticoat?' chimed in a crony; 'No, no, he gave her a child, I warrant thee', and Mother Dowe repeated this yarn in the next village she came to. Lord Robert and Elizabeth had played legerdemain together and he was the father of her child. 'Why, she hath no child yet?' 'No,' said old Annie, 'if she hath not they have put one to making.' When arrested, the local magistrates wanted her tried in secret session to prevent the scandalous stories from reaching the public. Ten years later there were still folk rash enough to spread slanders that Elizabeth had had a child by Dudley, and some lost their ears for it. Even in the 1580s he was still so troubled by mischievous gossip that the Privy Council leapt to his defence with an order.[23]

Cecil was at his wits' end when he returned to court after negotiating with the Scots and poured out his troubles to the Spanish ambassador. The Queen, he told him, was ruining the realm through her association with Dudley and the country was not going to put up with it very much longer. He himself was seriously considering retiring before the storm broke out in earnest, for Elizabeth simply would not listen to him, yet perhaps the ambassador could try and remonstrate with her. Twice in the conversation Cecil moaned 'Lord Robert would be better in paradise than here.' Then suddenly on 8 September the entire situation was transformed when Amy Robsart was found at the bottom of the staircase at Cumnor House with a broken neck, by her servants returning from a day's holiday.[24]

Foul play was at once suspected. Had not the scandalmongers and soothsayers been hinting at Dudley wanting her dead? The news reached Lord Robert at Windsor and Elizabeth sent him away from court until the coroner had held his inquest. He went off under this dark shadow, utterly dazed, to his house at Kew: 'Methinks I am here all this while as it were in a dream and too far, too far, from the place where I am bound to', he lamented. There was no disputing the evidence that Lady Dudley had died from a broken neck in the empty house, no question of somebody having pushed her down the stairs, and so the jury brought in a verdict of death by misadventure. Modern medical research has, however, been able to provide a satisfactory explanation of the old mystery and it is now reasonably certain that Amy was suffering from cancer of the breast in an advanced stage, which caused a spontaneous fracture of the spine. Robert Dudley, though cleared by the law, still lived under a cloud and many were shocked that he failed to attend his wife's funeral, though in his troubled state such may have been far too great a strain for him.[25]

The cynical whispers about Elizabeth and Dudley in the capitals of Europe now took on a sinister note. Poor Throckmorton could not hold up his head in Paris; he wrote 'with weeping eyes' about the scandalous statements being made and wished himself dead, 'for every hair of my head stareth out and my ears glow to hear ... Some let not to say "what religion is this, that a subject shall kill his wife and the Prince not only bear withal but marry with him?"' and the whole stock of the Dudleys, back to the grandfather, were reviled. Amongst the babel and ululations there was one sane voice, coming unexpectedly from the Earl of Sussex in Ireland. He had not the slightest regard for Dudley, but he was passionately devoted to the Queen. He told Cecil that her relationship with Lord Robert was entirely her own affair: 'If the Queen will love anybody, let her love where and whom she list', he demanded. Her marriage was most necessary and if her choice fell on Dudley, then let her go through with it, for the maxim *omnes ejus sensus titillarentur* should ensure that their union gave England 'a blessed prince'. By the time Cecil read Sussex's words he knew the immediate danger was over, for he mentioned to de Quadra that Elizabeth had decided not to marry Lord Robert and hoped the match with the Archduke Charles could go forward.[26]

Throckmorton was still thundering from Paris. 'The bruits be so brim and so maliciously reported' that if Elizabeth went ahead and married the wretched man, 'God and religion, which be the fundamentals, shall be out of estimation; the Queen, our sovereign, discredited, condemned and neglected; our country reviled, undone and made prey.' He needed circumspect advice on how to dismiss these stories and, unable to leave his post, sent over Robert Jones. At Greenwich courtiers quizzed Jones about the rude remarks made by the Queen of France that Elizabeth was to marry 'her horse-keeper', but when he saw her in the presence chamber, looking quite poorly, she told him in a matter of fact way that the affair had been tried by the coroner's inquest 'and it fell out as it should touch neither Lord [Dudley's] honesty nor her honour.' 'The matter of my Lord Robert doth much perplex her and it is never like to take place; and the talk thereof is somewhat slack', noted Jones. Some of the Council decided the time was ripe to press forward with the negotiations with the Archduke, but 'she uses all means not to marry.' Clearly she was not going to marry 'on the rebound', like Robert Jones, home from Paris, who that month was turned down by one young lady, but was accepted by another three weeks later – 'and the wedding gear is already provided for the first Sunday before Lent.'[27]

The strain of those weeks between the tragedy at Cumnor and Christmas was beginning to tell on Elizabeth. Foreign and domestic politics seemed to be solely concerned with her marriage. She decided to reinstate the favourite by making him an earl in November, but when the warrant for his creation was brought for her signature she had second thoughts and cut the parchment in pieces with a penknife. Then after a while she began to relent. Those about her thought she would elevate him at twelfth night and gossips already predicted the title 'Earl of Leicester', yet once more she changed her mind. Reason overcame emotion after all, for it was still not yet politic to bring him back into full favour.[28]

Elizabeth still loved him and perhaps would marry him yet, but Amy Robsart's death made the world of difference. Had she ended her days peaceably in her bed in circumstances entirely free from suspicion, the way ahead would have been clear for her. She was, as she put it, 'no angel' and the measure of her conduct was that she had been deeply attached to a man who was already married and he was at her side when his lawful wife was dying. 'Nothing improper ever passed between them', she maintained; had it, we may be sure the postbags of foreign envoys in London would have been full of the details, for they had plenty of people in the palace in their pay. 'Although it was a love affair,' commented Henry Sidney, Lord Robert's brother-in-law, 'the object of it was marriage and there was nothing illicit about it.' She scorned those barbed questions from foreign princes about her honour, as if she had demeaned herself to become Dudley's mistress, and told one 'she will count it a favour if he will believe none of the rumours which he hears, if they are inconsistent with her true honour and dignity.'[29] She put on a brave face now and told de Quadra in February 1561 that she liked Dudley for his good qualities, but had never decided to marry him 'or anyone else', although with each day that passed she saw more clearly the necessity for her to marry someone. After all, what would King Philip have thought of her if she had run off with one of her servitors, like the old Duchess of Suffolk marrying her groom, Adrian Stokes.[30] The ambassador just could not make her out and fell back, when writing to Philip, on the suggestion 'which certain physicians confirm' that she was incapable of bearing children – a point to which we will return.

At midsummer Lord Robert organized a splendid fête on the Thames to amuse her, and while watching the pageantry they both teased Bishop de Quadra, who had joined them. Dudley jokingly said they should get him to perform the marriage service

himself and Elizabeth capped this by saying she doubted whether
he had sufficient English to do it! The favourite had most certainly not given up hope. Henry Sidney, with his brother-in-
law's blessing, angled for Philip II's support for his suit, which the
latter would give if he made a solemn promise to restore Catholicism. In one of their last talks on this delicate topic Elizabeth told
de Quadra she was as free from any engagement to marry as the
day on which she had been born, whatever the world might
think. She most certainly would never wed anyone she had not
seen or come to know well and in consequence might be obliged
to take an Englishman as husband; in that case, she added, she
could find no more fitting person than Lord Robert. Perhaps all
the princes of Europe could petition her to marry him, so that if
she did do so she could claim she acted on their advice. Bishop
de Quadra played on manfully; the fact that the Queen was still
single, he wrote in June 1562, was not from lack of good offices
on his part, though at that very time the old fox was spreading a
tale that the nuptials had been celebrated in great secrecy at Lord
Pembroke's London house. By then Dudley was high in favour,
the death of Amy Robsart, never forgotten, was being seen in
perspective, and as the number of suitors from abroad narrowed
he still reckoned he could win a consort's crown. 'The Queen
would like everyone to be in love with her,' commented the new
ambassador from Spain (after poor de Quadra had to be removed
for intrigue), 'but I doubt whether she will ever be in love with
anyone enough to marry him.' By then she had almost certainly
come to the bitter conclusion that she could never marry her
'sweet Robin'; he was too controversial a figure in personality
and politics for her to take him without irredeemably dividing
her Council and her people, though she remained emotionally tied
to him to the end.[31]

The question of the succession became critical in October 1562,
when Elizabeth was dangerously ill. Feeling out of sorts while at
Hampton Court, she took a bath, hoping to shake off her indisposition, but instead she caught what was diagnosed as a chill,
which soon developed into a high fever. In fact she had caught

smallpox, that dread disease from which the Countess of Bedford had recently died, but for some days there was no sign of a rash. Her cousin, Hunsdon, sent for Dr Burcot, a German immigrant who had earned his praise for attending him when he had been ill. He told her, 'My liege, thou shall have the pox', but she swore at him to get out of her sight. The Queen grew worse and death seemed near at hand. In desperation those about her risked recalling Burcot – almost too late. The doctor called for some scarlet cloth, 'laps all her body in it, save one hand', in which he put a bottle of 'a comfortable potion'. Whatever the effects of his ministration, the spots began to appear before long, her feverish temperature subsided and she began to turn the corner. Lady Sydney, who nursed her so faithfully, herself succumbed and was left so disfigured that she chose to live out her days in seclusion.[32]

In nearby rooms at Hampton Court there were hectic, informal meetings with 'nearly as many different opinions' about the succession to the crown 'as there were councillors present', though no one apparently espoused Mary's candidature. Dudley, we know, favoured the Earl of Huntingdon's title and was supported by Bedford and Pembroke; a few, most probably including Cecil, preferred Lady Katherine Grey, even though she was in the Tower. Old Winchester, the Treasurer, wanted to have the rival claims submitted to the lawyers, but others were against this as the jurists were suspected of being Catholics, and in consequence would probably turn down both Lady Katherine and Huntingdon in favour of Lady Margaret Douglas and her son. Nothing had been decided by the Council by the time Elizabeth recovered and in her very first words she hoped that in case of an emergency they would make Lord Robert Dudley protector of the realm, with an income of £20,000 a year and a suitable title. A few days later Dudley was sworn a member of the Council and, to balance him, Cecil secured the appointment of the Duke of Norfolk as well.

That winter the greatest in the land discussed the burning topics of the Queen's marriage and the succession, whenever two or three of them were gathered together, for solutions could not be shelved any longer. The pock-marks on Elizabeth's face showed how narrowly she had escaped death. None but Dudley could abide the thought of his protectorship, so was it to be Huntingdon or Lady Katherine Grey? None but Dudley could abide the thought of Elizabeth marrying him, so was her consort to be the Archduke Charles, or whom? At one meeting at Arundel House, lasting until the small hours, Norfolk, Howard of Effingham and Arundel attempted to thrash out the problem, but the Queen came to hear of it and was extremely angry.[33] It seems quite likely that she tore out of the Privy Council register pages recording meetings held at Hampton Court while the succession was discussed during her illness, as her successor was to tear pages out of the journals of the House of Commons. If her councillors so forgot their oaths as to discuss matters belonging to her prerogative, it augured ill for January, when Parliament was to meet.

The tocsin was sounded by Alexander Nowell, Dean of St Paul's, in a sermon just before Parliament opened. 'All the Queen's most noble ancestors have commonly had some issue to succeed them, but Her Majesty yet none' and (turning to Elizabeth) 'the want of your marriage and issue is like to prove . . . a plague' no less disastrous than her sister's marriage. He rubbed the point in somewhat pawkily: 'If your parents had been of your mind, where had you been then?' When the Commons made their expected petition for her to marry and settle the succession, she played desperately for time. 'The weight and greatness of this matter might cause in me, being a woman, wanting both wit and memory, some fear to speak, and bashfulness besides, a thing appropriate to my sex.' After beating about the bush she remarked on her illness, which had loomed large in their petition. 'Though God of late seemed to touch me, rather like one that He chastised than one that He punished, and though death possessed almost every joint of me, so as I wished then that the feeble thread of life, which lasted (methought) all too long, might by Cloe's hand have quietly been cut off', her concern had been not for her own life but for her people's safety. They were not to think that she would be neglectful in taking account of their wishes, but she needed time for reflection before making an adequate answer; and she ended by assuring them that 'though after my death you may have many stepdames, yet shall you never have a more natural mother than I mean to be.'

The Lords had presented their own petition for her to 'dispose herself to marry' and to limit the succession. At this Elizabeth was furious and told the deputation of peers that the marks they saw on her face were not wrinkles but pits of smallpox. Though she might be, to some of them, an old maid – she was not quite thirty – God would send her children as he did to St Elizabeth. Time went by and her promise to give a considered reply to the Commons' petition seemed less and less likely to be kept, until at the closing of the sessions on Easter eve, Lord Keeper Bacon read her speech on which she had taken such pains. Again she evaded the issues. She had thought they might decently have stopped wrangling about the succession until they had given her a chance to marry – worrying about other trees blossoming before 'even hope of my fruit had been denied you.' As for her marriage, this was a personal matter and the time was not yet ripe for making a pronouncement. She made them feel they had been intruding on her privacy, trampling on her prerogative, and ended a characteristic speech of 'answers answerless' in which she had deliberately left the position vague, by saying 'I hope I shall die in quiet with *nunc dimittis*, which cannot be without I see some glimpse of your following surety after my graved bones.'[34]

Had her confused and disappointed hearers known it, their debates and petitions had already spurred her into action. Casting about rather frantically for possible ways of escape from the difficult situation, Elizabeth had hit upon a novel solution. When Maitland of Lethington, the Scottish Secretary of State, came to see her three weeks before Parliament was prorogued, she tentatively suggested to him that Mary Queen of Scots might marry Lord Robert Dudley. This scheme for cutting the Gordian knot was proposed in all sincerity, though many then and since have thought it was no more than a sudden whim, a piece of temporizing that could be forgotten once it had served its turn. At all costs she had to prevent Mary from contracting a marriage with a foreign prince, such as Don Carlos, the young Charles IX of France or one of the archdukes, for such would seriously threaten

England's security. At this time Mary's claim to succeed her was far less unacceptable than those of Lady Katherine Grey (who had just produced her second son in the Tower) or of Huntingdon. What better consort for Mary than one whom Elizabeth knew so well? It was, after all, only carrying a stage further the proposal she had made in the autumn for Dudley to be made protector of the realm if anything should happen to her. If Mary married Dudley, Elizabeth would then be prepared to endorse her claim to the English succession, and such would solve at a stroke not merely immediate but the main long-term problems. The deafening parliamentary chorus would then be silenced, the Privy Council would cease arguing and her fear of being rushed into an unsuitable marriage herself would evaporate. The price she would have to pay was almost intolerable – no less than losing her favourite to her rival; but perhaps, if she could be freed from the strain of having to face the conundrum of the succession, she could manage to live without Dudley at her side. The sacrifice would be enormous, but the benefits would be inestimable. The fact that she was fully prepared to let Lord Robert marry Mary, and that the initiative came from her, shows more clearly than anything else that by March 1563 she had realized that she could not marry him herself. For Dudley to reign with Mary in Scotland and he, or his issue, to succeed her in England was the next best thing.[35]

For the moment Elizabeth was only planting an idea in Maitland's mind and she hoped that in due course a firm proposal would come from Scotland. At present no one, certainly not Dudley or Mary, was to share this secret. Negotiations would, she well knew, be fraught with difficulties. Maitland thought it was too improbable for words and treated it at first as a facetious joke. He was so slow to move that in August she sent secret instructions to Randolph, her ambassador in Edinburgh, requiring him as opportunity served, 'by indirect speeches' to suggest as Mary's husband 'some person of noble birth within our realm, having condition and qualities meet for the same'. Lord Robert's name was not, at this stage, divulged, and though these instructions were in Cecil's hand, Elizabeth herself added the words 'yea, perchance such as she [Mary] could hardly think we would agree unto.' Not until March 1564, a full twelve-month after the meeting with Maitland, did Randolph say in so many words that Lord Robert was the intended candidate, and Maitland let him know that Mary had said she 'could have no misliking of him of whom the report was so good and by her good sister was so recommended.' Elizabeth was fit now and Parliament still in prorogation, so there was no urgency to come to a hasty conclusion, but to make Dudley more acceptable in Mary's sight, at Michaelmas 1564 she created him Earl of Leicester with a grand flourish and showered him with grants of crown lands.[36]

AS GOOD
A COURAGE AS EVER
MY FATHER HAD

IN the evening of her life, Sir Robert Cecil who was as much at sea with his sovereign's foibles, inconsistencies and indecision as his father had been in the heyday of her reign, summed up Elizabeth's character in an apothegm: she was 'more than a man, and (in troth) sometimes less than a woman'. But in the mid-1560s she seemed the height of enigma. Her attitude to marriage and to the succession, her relations with Mary Queen of Scots and her relationship with Leicester, and her dealings with Parliament, Council and with foreign powers were unpredictable and defied definition. Policy was in the melting-pot and the Queen was more isolated than at any time in her reign. Could she expect that she could always play everything by ear?

England's intervention in the third French war of religion in 1562 had been a disastrous folly. The loss of Calais still rankled and here seemed a good chance of recovering it, so she had sent Warwick with an expeditionary force to Le Havre, not so much to aid the Huguenots as to oppose the Guise faction. But plague smote the English garrison and those well enough to be invalided home brought the dread disease with them so that for the rest of the century London and the larger towns were never free of the dread epidemic in the summer. Even Warwick was seriously ill. Dudley, who had visited his brother out of compassion on his return from France, realized that he too might become a carrier of the pestilence and sent word to the Queen that he would refrain from attending on her at court, signing himself in that August 1563 'your most bounden, for ever and ever R.D'.[1] For Elizabeth to have escaped smallpox the year before only to have become a victim of 'the sweating sickness' would have indeed been regarded as divine judgement. Yet England's war in France as Condé's ally did not bring only plague and an ignominious peace, for it led to further misunderstandings with Mary Queen of Scots.

Just before England had declared war, preparations were in full swing for a meeting between the two Queens at Nottingham. The tilts had been set up and all 'lusty young knights' were warned to attend the feats of arms, while Mary had sent Elizabeth verses in French and Latin, with a token of a heart of diamonds.[2] The coming of war meant the postponement of the meeting, rather vaguely to some date between the beginning of June and the end of August of the year following at York. In turn that meeting had to be cancelled. Elizabeth renewed the invitation to Mary in the spring of 1564, hoping that their long delayed meeting might take place that summer, during which Mary should at last ratify the Treaty of Edinburgh, disowning her old pretensions to the throne of England, and perhaps be swept off her feet by Dudley; such developments would enable Elizabeth to regard – if not actually to nominate – Mary as her eventual successor. All this was wishful thinking on Elizabeth's part, for Mary had no desire for a meeting at this juncture. Ignorant of his character and physique she was seriously contemplating a marriage with Don Carlos, and when that came to naught through Philip II's lack of interest, her mind turned to young Darnley. Maitland had already whispered to her the suggestion that she should marry Lord Robert, but she had found the idea of a passed-on favourite too bizarre.

Throughout that summer and autumn Elizabeth still fervently hoped that Dudley might cut the Gordian knot by marrying Mary, and to make him the more eligible a suitor she created him Earl of Leicester on Michaelmas day at St James's Palace. The investiture was timed to coincide with the arrival in London of Mary's special ambassador, Sir James Melville. Shortly before Michaelmas, in the garden at Whitehall, Queen and envoy had their first meeting. After a deliberate show of displeasure at Mary's letter, which she tore up, together with her own reply as it was 'too gentle', she asked Melville how his mistress had reacted to the secret suggestion of being Dudley's wife. He answered 'She thought little or nothing thereof', but expected commissioners from both countries shortly to discuss all matters of importance between the two sovereigns. If we are to believe the substance of Sir James's memoirs, she told him that he and his Queen underestimated Lord Robert, the very man she esteemed 'as her brother and best friend, whom she could have herself married, had she ever minded to have taken a husband. But being determined to end her life in virginity, she wished that the Queen her sister might marry him, as meetest of all other with whom she would find in her heart to declare her second person.' Dudley's creation as Baron Denbigh and Earl of Leicester was an impressive ceremony, with the heralds present and the peers in their parliament robes. Old Winchester, the Lord Treasurer, who had hoped to be excused attendance, was not given leave of absence, for the Queen wanted all the highest of the land to witness the event. Her cousin Hunsdon passed the mantle to her, and as she placed it round the shoulders of the kneeling Dudley she could not help herself tickling his neck. When he had left the chamber she asked Melville what he thought of the new Earl of Leicester. The Scot paid a courtly compliment, but she saw through him; 'Yet you like better of yonder lad (pointing to my Lord Darnley, who as nearest prince of the blood did bear the sword of honour that day before her). My answer', recalled Melville, 'was that no woman of spirit would make choice of such a man, who resembled a woman, than a man. For he was handsome, beardless and lady-faced.' It was all Melville could do to avoid blushing, as he had a secret commission from Mary to see Darnley's mother, Lady Lennox, while he was in London. This bore out Bedford's warning that Melville was not a man to be trusted, yet Elizabeth rather took to him and thoroughly enjoyed the challenge of dealing with a man of such sharp wits.[3]

During Melville's stay, she saw him frequently, putting on a different dress for each audience, showing off and fishing for compliments – asking whether she or Mary had the finer hair or the better complexion, who was the more accomplished player on the virginals, the better dancer, the more proficient linguist. Sir James did his best: 'She was the finest Queen in England and mine the finest Queen in Scotland.' Which was the taller? Mary, said Melville. 'Then she is too high,' rejoined Elizabeth, 'for I myself am neither too high or too low.' On one occasion she took him to her bed-chamber and took from a small cabinet various pictures wrapped in paper. Within the little parcel labelled 'My Lord's picture' was a miniature of Leicester, which she was at first reluctant to show him; then she took it out and kissed it. Melville wanted to take it to Mary, but Elizabeth said it was the only picture she had of him. (And yet, protested her visitor, she also had the original.) Elizabeth would not part with it, nor with a ruby as big as a tennis ball, which he suggested might form a suitable gift for his Queen; but *all* her possessions would one day be Mary's if she followed her counsel. The hint was plain enough. Before Melville left Elizabeth had sent instructions to Bedford and Randolph, her commissioners for treating with Scotland, stating that if Mary would marry Leicester, whom she herself 'favours and loves as her brother', she would make her cousin her heir.[4]

While in London Melville made enquiries to see whether the Spanish proposals for a match between Mary and Don Carlos were likely to be revived before his mistress played her next card – to pursue a courtship with Darnley, the goal for which the boy's mother had been intriguing for months. Already, before Melville's arrival, the Earl of Lennox had been given reluctant permission by Elizabeth to go into Scotland, ostensibly to attend to various problems connected with his Scottish estates. In Edinburgh he distributed largesse, Mary herself receiving jewels, a clock and a fine looking-glass; 'his cheer is great and his household many' and as a result 'there is a marvellous goodliking' of his son. Before this report reached London came rumours from as far afield as Avignon that 'there is a privy practice between Lennox and Queen Mary to marry his son. They fear that she is inclined to this offer of Lennox's and take it to be concluded.'

But Elizabeth refused to take the portents seriously and still insisted on her own solution to Mary's matrimonial affairs. In November Bedford and Randolph met Maitland and Murray at Berwick to negotiate terms under which the match with Leicester might come about, but these discussions never got off the ground. Much as Maitland favoured Leicester, he and Murray could not be convinced that Elizabeth was being straightforward, and said that if their Queen in forsaking her friends' counsel and following Elizabeth's should be deceived 'her folly were great and much dishonour to her sister.' Six weeks later, at his mistress's prompting, Cecil was still arguing the case for a Mary-Leicester marriage very forcibly and at great length in a letter to Murray and Maitland: Dudley had been raised to 'the first degree in honour of a prince' and was in every way meet to become consort in Scotland. With his person would go the establishment of Mary's title to the English throne, but he must warn them that Elizabeth would 'never willingly consent' to any other of her subjects becoming Mary's husband. After further talk with his sovereign the Secretary added a final paragraph:

You both know how tickle a matter it is for princes to be provoked to determine of their successors – *Durus enim est sermo* – and such as nature scantily sometime will bear it for her own children with patience or without jealousy. . . . Let not your negotiations, full of terms of friendship and love, be converted to a matter of bargain and purchase; so as though in the outward face it appear a device to conciliate these two Queens and countries by perpetual amity, in the unwrapping thereof there be not found any other intention but to compass at my sovereign's hand a kingdom and crown, which if it be sought for, may be sooner lost than gotten . . .[5]

Though Mary continued to talk equivocally with Randolph, the English ambassador in Edinburgh, her demand that Darnley might join his father in Scotland was a sure sign that the door for further negotiations on the Leicester match had been firmly closed. Elizabeth at first refused to let Darnley go. When the request came in mid-December she was ill – those about her 'feared a flux', but it was nothing more serious than a persistent attack of diarrhoea, which 'somewhat weakened her'. Lady

Lennox gave assurances that Darnley would be gone to his father and back within the month, but Elizabeth knew too much to believe so improbable a tale. Royal permission was certainly needed for such a mission, or the consequences could be very serious for all concerned. And then, unpredictably, Elizabeth gave way, enabling the youth to reach Edinburgh on 13 February. 'There is a suspicion that the [Darnley] match has been arranged with the connivance of some of the great people here', reported the Spanish ambassador. Indeed, Darnley's success was due almost entirely to Leicester, who had begun to fear that Mary might be taking Elizabeth's suggestion about himself seriously; he had no wish to be banished to Scotland while there was still promise of a royal match at home and he secretly let Mary know that the scheme was merely to prevent her marrying someone else, such as the Archduke Charles. Under these circumstances it is very remarkable that Elizabeth gave in to his special pleading and let Darnley travel to his fate, but then, Leicester had a way with him and could get his sudden schemes adopted where cautious statesmen failed.[6]

Almost at once she regretted her decision. On 15 March Randolph delivered her ultimatum to Mary: if she would marry Leicester, then Mary's title to the English succession would be favoured, except that she would postpone holding a full enquiry into her cousin's claim until she 'be married herself or be determined not to marry.' Mary 'wept her fill' at hearing these words and knew she could expect no further accommodation from 'her dear sister', as she was head over heels in love with Darnley, 'the lustiest and best-proportioned long man' she had ever seen, and made up her mind to marry him. She asked Maitland to seek Elizabeth's approval and he, in an aside, suggested a third Englishman, as an alternative to both Darnley and Leicester – the Duke of Norfolk – a proposal which came to nothing at the time, but was to be revived in years to come with perilous consequences. Elizabeth at once summoned her Council on 1 May to sign a full declaration, warning Mary of the consequences of taking Darnley as her husband:

The Queen finding the intended marriage of Queen Mary with Lord Darnley strange, has committed the same to certain of her Council, who with one assent thought that it would be unmeet and directly prejudicial to the sincere amity between both the Queens. They desire to say and to offer Queen Mary a free election of any other of the nobility in the whole realm or any other place.[7]

Leicester's name was significantly absent from the members who signed the declaration. Elizabeth sent Throgmorton to Edinburgh to do what he could to prevent the marriage from taking place and, following the suggestion of the Privy Council, she empowered him to allow Mary to choose *any other* Englishman *except* Darnley. But the day he arrived there Darnley was created Earl of Ross, for which title he swore fealty as a Scottish peer, defying his sovereign in Whitehall. It was a useless exercise for Elizabeth to command him and his father to return to court on their allegiance, but in a pique she shut his mother in the Tower on 28 June. A month later Darnley was proclaimed King and next day Mary married him.

Mary's marriage emphasized as never before Elizabeth's own single state and the lack of any settled plan for the succession. Once she had decided that she could not marry Leicester, she had turned, in desperation almost, to the scheme for making a match with the Archduke Charles, which Cecil and Norfolk never tired of advocating, and the old negotiations with the Empire were reopened apparently in earnest in the summer of 1564. Cecil, as worried as anyone about the succession problem and the isolation of England in a hostile Europe, saw that a Hapsburg marriage could strengthen the old Spanish alliance, the cornerstone of English overseas trade, and nullify the Franco-Scottish menace, quite apart from the considerable diplomatic advantages of increasing England's standing in Europe. Since Charles was a younger son there was on the face of it little danger of England becoming the junior partner in the marriage alliance, as had happened so disastrously with Queen Mary's marriage to Philip of Spain and with Mary Queen of Scots' marriage to Francis of France. Elizabeth's agent in Germany, Christopher Mundt, apparently thought the election of Maximilian II as Holy Roman Emperor an appropriate time for renewing negotiations, which

could form a postscript to messages of condolence on the death of
the old emperor, Ferdinand I, the father of Maximilian and the
Archdukes Ferdinand and Charles. In fact it was nearly a year
before these messages of sympathy and congratulations on the
emperor's accession were received. An excuse was found for
sending a special envoy to England in the spring of 1565 for returning Ferdinand's insignia of the Garter to Windsor, which
would serve as a cloak for Adam Zwetkovich's main mission.
Archduke and Emperor were not blind to the difficulties. 'You
may be certain that our ... brother regards this marriage with
other eyes than he did last year, and although he would be again
prepared to woo the illustrious Queen if he had clear indications
of her intentions, he would not, as on the last occasion, suffer himself to be led by the nose', wrote the Emperor in an *aide memoire*
for Zwetkovich. On Whitsunday 1565 the envoy dined with the
Privy Council after attending service and subsequently saw
Elizabeth. She asked him, 'Are you sure the Archduke will come?'
and then blushed, when he told her of his 'great desire to see her.'
'They tell me,' she continued, 'that public opinion is that the
marriage will certainly take place.' The ambassador was delighted
and said that Charles was the only possible candidate consistent
with her dignity, as the ages of other eligible princes were quite
unsuitable. Then Elizabeth said in a flash: 'I have never said
hitherto to anybody that I would not marry the Earl of Leicester',
as if determined to pour cold water on these discussions. She also
questioned Zwetkovich if he knew whether Leicester was oppos-
ing the match. Quite the contrary, he replied; he was dealing
very favourably with the affair and in his despatch to Vienna he
described the Earl as 'the most important originator and warmest
advocate' of the proposals. But she knew that Leicester had by no
means given up his ambition to marry her.[8]

Zwetkovich listened patiently to her protestations of purity.
'If she had been resolved to die a maid and did not the crown of
England compel her to marry to the profit of England, she would
verily abide by her purpose. She would fain vindicate herself ...
against all the slander that had been cast at her' and she hoped the
House of Hapsburg would find she 'had all the time acted in all

matters with due decorum and attention.' The envoy accepted this awkward challenge and reported to the Emperor that he had made 'diligent enquiries concerning the maiden honour and integrity of the Queen, and have found that she has truly and verily been praised and extolled for her virginal and royal honour, and that nothing can be said against her; and all the aspersions against her are but the spawn of envy and malice and hatred.' Indeed, in his judgement Leicester was a 'virtuous, pious, courteous and highly moral man, whom the Queen loves as a sister in all maidenly honour, in most chaste and honest love', and there was 'no hope for him' on the score of becoming her husband.[9]

While the Imperial envoy was at Whitehall, the court jester gave Elizabeth some matrimonial advice: 'She should not take the King of France, for he was but a boy and a babe; but she should take the Archduke Charles, and then he was sure that she would have a baby boy.' The Queen laughingly translated the joke into Italian so Zwetkovich could understand, and the incident gives the impression of having been a put-up job. There had, indeed, been secret talks for some while with a rival suitor in mind, Charles IX of France, just fifteen years old. The proposal came in the first place from Katherine de Medicis in November 1564, and was taken up with alacrity by Paul de Foix, the French ambassador in London. Elizabeth no more than flirted with the idea and after the scheme was dead and buried she laughed about such an incongruous union, remarking that everyone would say she was marrying her son, even as they had said of her sister Mary that Philip was marrying his grandmother. She had told de Foix how honoured she was by the King's proposal, young though he was. There would be no difficulty with her subjects, 'for I am assured that they would assent to my wishes and they have more than once requested me to marry according to my inclinations.' Of course they would really prefer her to marry an Englishman, but the only possible candidate was Arundel, who 'is further from it than the east from the west; and as for the Earl of Leicester, I have always loved his virtues, but the aspiration to greatness and honour which is in me could not suffer him as a companion and a husband.' For the moment she relished the idea of a rival suitor, not so much to keep the Hapsburgs on their toes as to prolong the negotiations. But Leicester's double-dealing was of a different order, for he was intriguing with de Foix to bring the match with the Archduke to an abrupt conclusion so that the field would be free for him. On the failure of this improbable scheme for marriage with Charles IX, the French ambassador was told to favour Leicester's own suit, as the surest way of stopping an Anglo-Imperial alliance; and so de Foix went all out to persuade Elizabeth to smile on the Earl's advances. But she had seen through them both and said politely that she was still undecided whom she should wed, and the very idea of marriage for her was 'as if some-one were tearing my heart from my body, so averse am I to it by nature.'[10]

By high summer relations between Elizabeth and Leicester were no longer those of devoted brother and sister. While the Austrian negotiations proceeded slowly, with much discussion of pre-liminary articles, including the size of a dowry which Charles might bring, Queen and favourite behaved bitterly towards one another. Her pique at failing to stop Darnley's marriage had much to do with it and she blamed Leicester for persuading her to allow him to go into Scotland. The death of her old faithful, Kate Ashley, whom she had known from her earliest years, left her low in spirits, lonely and querulous. This was a very different woman from the overconfident Queen who had enjoyed leading Sir James Melville such a merry dance the previous autumn. She turned for solace to the company of Thomas Heneage, a courtier already with his foot firmly on the ladder of preferment. He was handsome, full of charm, and, as with the Dudley of the earliest days of the reign, flirtation with him was in Elizabeth's eyes quite harmless since he was already married. In a huff Leicester made indiscreet advances to the beautiful Lettice Knollys, Viscountess Hereford, and a cousin of the Queen's, and this made her furious. 'The Queen seemed to be much offended with the Earl of Leices-ter', noted Cecil in his diary that August, 'and so she wrote an obscure sentence in a book at Windsor.' Behind so enigmatic an entry there was a flaming row. She rated him to his face: 'If you think to rule here, I will take a course to see you forthcoming. I will have here but one mistress and no master', and she said it for all the court to hear. She was sorry for the time she had lost on him, the years that the locusts had eaten, and to make him smart the more Heneage had pride of place at the twelfth night festivities.[11]

Despairing of the Queen's waning interest in the Archduke Charles, Cecil privately summarized the pros and cons of his and Leicester's suits. Everything favoured Charles, assuming various points to safeguard England's interests were assured, and most important in his view 'no Prince ever had less alliance than the Queen of England hath; nor any prince ever had more cause to have friendship and power to assist her estate.' The Secretary's corresponding 'reasons against the Earl of Leicester' were not unjust:

Nothing is increased by marriage of him, either in riches, estimation, power. It will be thought that the slanderous speeches of the Queen with the Earl have been true. He shall study nothing but to enhance his own particular friends to wealth, to offices, to lands, and to offend others. He is infamed by the death of his wife. He is far in debt. He is like to prove unkind, or jealous of the Queen's Majesty.

Not a nail that Cecil did not drive home. In his estimation Leicester had always been the essential trouble-maker at court, and he was like to remain a danger so long as the Queen was single.[12]

The old feud between the Earl and the Duke of Norfolk, never quiescent for long, had broken out in earnest. There had been that unseemly incident in the tennis court in front of the Queen. Leicester 'being hot and sweating took the Queen's napkin out of her hand and wiped his face, which the Duke seeing, said that he was too saucy and swore he would lay his racket upon his face; whereupon rose a great trouble and the Queen offended sore with the Duke.' Their old animosity was now intensified by the return to court of Thomas Radcliffe, Earl of Sussex, who had been for five years Lord Lieutenant in Ireland. His mother had been a Howard and he remained very close to the Duke. A much stronger personality, he took over from Norfolk the lead in the

campaign against the *parvenu* adventurer Leicester. 'There arose
very grievous quarrels in the court, which was divided into
factions and part taking,' wrote Camden, 'and the earls [of
Leicester and Sussex] if at any time they went abroad accompanied
with them great trains of followers with swords and bucklers.' It
was an unhealthy flashback to the fifteenth century. Sussex was
firmly behind Cecil and Norfolk for pressing forward with the
Hapsburg negotiations, for bringing Leicester to heel and making
the Queen see reason. 'My lord of Norfolk loveth my lord of
Sussex earnestly', wrote Cecil with affection, 'and so all that
stock of the Howards seem to join in friendship together.' As 1565
drew to a close there was 'a great controversy' between Norfolk
and Leicester and a 'budget full of petty inventions' about their
enmity went the rounds. Norfolk was peeved that as Elizabeth's
sole duke and the Queen's cousin, she should not have taken him
into her confidence, while the mercurial Leicester seemed bent on
ruining everything.[13]

By the end of November Leicester was again in high favour
with his sovereign and was supremely confident. He apparently
voiced his arrogant ambitions to Cecil, asking him to throw overboard the Hapsburg negotiations on the ground that Elizabeth 'is
not so well disposed to any one as to myself.' Before Christmas
the Duke spoke out to Elizabeth in the plainest terms about the
desperate need for her to marry, settle the succession and pacify
factions within the court and kingdom. In advocating her marriage to the Archduke he said he acted as a spokesman for 'all the
principal people in the realm who loved her and whose feelings
on the subject he well knew.' Those of her councillors who were
advising her to marry Leicester were only doing so because they
imagined that was where her heart lay, 'not because they really
thought the match would be beneficial to the country, or good
for her own dignity.' The Queen thanked him rather gracefully
for these timely words of wisdom, but said she could make no
firm promises; and when the Duke saw Leicester the same day he
reminded him that he had promised to drop his suit for good and
it was with that assurance that the negotiations with Vienna had
been reopened. Yet Leicester abandoned nothing. A day or so

later the French ambassador, utterly foxed by her irresolution, was writing that the Earl had urged her to decide upon marriage by Christmas, though she had asked him to wait until Candlemas.[14]

After Christmas, when Norfolk returned to court, he was angered to find Leicester as conceited as ever. He told him that he would stop at nothing in forcing him to abandon his unseemly pretensions to Elizabeth's hand. Each mustered their forces and to emphasize the divisions at court the favourite's henchmen started to wear blue and Norfolk's supporters yellow. 'I am told Leicester began it, so as to know who were his friends,' wrote de Silva, 'and the adherents of the Duke did the same in consequence of some disagreements they had with them about the aid of the Duke and his friends had given to the Archduke's match.' The Earl of Arundel intervened to try and keep the peace, and there was some kind of reconciliation. They gave the outward appearance of being on very good terms with each other during the festivities following their joint investiture as knights of the French order of St Michael by the French ambassador in the great closet at White-hall Palace. But further troubles flared up only too easily and the Duke repeated his warnings to Leicester in a more friendly tone. He knew, he said, that Elizabeth did not intend to marry him, so nothing could come of his scheming, and he would be blamed by all his countrymen for any further delays in the negotiations with the Archduke, thereby earning much odium. Why did he not, then join with the rest in promoting the Hapsburg marriage? Leicester answered that he would indeed follow this advice if he could so arrange matters that Elizabeth should not think he was neglecting his own suit out of distaste for her, as this 'might cause her womanlike to undo him.' The Council debated whether they should approach Her Majesty on this burning topic individually or collectively, and Sussex lobbied de Silva, who undertook to use his own influence with the Queen. When the ambassador had an audience with her at Candlemas she spoke warmly of Leicester's unselfishness in urging her to marry for the sake of her country, of herself, and even of himself, for he was blamed for her single state.[15]

In May Thomas Dannett was despatched to Augsburg and Vienna to continue discussions with Maximilian II. On the religious question he reported that the Emperor 'seems not to be hard, but looks that the religion his brother was brought up in should be permitted him. . . . Something must be winked at by the Queen', the envoy suggested and for his own part made a show of being broad-minded by accompanying the Archduke to devotions. He sent, as requested, a full report on Charles's appearance and qualities for Elizabeth to consider. He was courteous, affable, liberal, wise and of a good memory; whether he could speak a word of English was not divulged. An attack of smallpox had not disfigured him, and he was 'of a sanguine complexion and, for a man, beautiful and well faced, well shaped, small in the waist and well and broad-breasted; he seems in his clothes well thighed and well legged.' Since he stooped a little, some might say he was round-shouldered, but in the saddle he sat as straight as any man alive. Dannett's flattering portrait certainly aroused interest in England, but Elizabeth would not know whether she could seriously pursue the project until she had set eyes on the man.[16]

Was there no piercing the labyrinth of her diplomacy, no settling of the confusion of her emotions? At the end of June she was jolted by news of the birth of Mary's son. The alleged aside to her ladies-in-waiting on hearing the tidings – 'that the Queen of Scots was mother of a fair son, while she was but a barren stock' – is probably an invention of Sir James Melville, for the Spanish ambassador, who was far better informed of court gossip than the Scot, reported that Elizabeth 'seemed very glad of the birth of the infant.' Whatever her immediate response to the news, the fact remained that she was a spinster still, while Mary had a male heir. Not long afterwards Leicester rationalized his own equivocal position to the French ambassador by telling him, 'I really believe that the Queen never will marry. I have known her since she was eight years of age, better than any man in the world. From that time she has always invariably declared that she would remain unmarried.' (Had he believed what he said it is absurd that he should have wasted the best years of his own life courting her.) As an afterthought, to boost his self-esteem, he said that if she were now to change her mind he undoubtedly would be her choice, 'for I am as high in her favour as ever.' Leicester could never grasp the fact that Amy Robsart's death, which made him free to marry, prevented him from ever marrying Elizabeth; but whatever his failings he had pertinacity and singleness of purpose. At this time, too, according to Camden, Dr Robert Huicke, the Queen's principal physician, was dissuading her from matrimony, 'for I wot not womanish impotency', but the tale is on the face of it improbable. It would have been incredible for Huicke, a divorcee, to have remained in her confidence until his death after imparting advice that made nonsense of her diplomacy, and that his words should then have leaked to the gossips would have made matters ten times worse.[17]

On 2 October the Parliament which had been prorogued for the last three years reassembled at Westminster. Elizabeth was apprehensive, as she knew full well that the Commons would pounce on the questions of her marriage and the settlement of the succession, as well as attempt to tinker with religion, but she could not delay holding a sessions any longer as she needed new taxes to be voted to meet the ever-growing drain on her resources, weakened by the war in France and the expedition against Shane O'Neil in Ireland. In the spring of 1566 she had set down her reflexions on the costs of government. 'Although God hath blessed us with a kingdom of great happiness for people and riches, yet ... we do not receive so much in that behalf for our subsidy and customs as our progenitors did 300 years past, when the charges of government all manner of ways was not a third in comparison with ours at this day.' Living off the crown estate she had nothing more for her own personal expenditure than her progenitors, out of which she was expected to rule her realm in peace and war.[18] The Commons had gone home in 1563 with a firm promise that she would answer their petition about marriage and the succession, but now she was determined they should meddle no further in these very personal affairs. She faced, indeed, a three-pronged attack – from her Council and from the Lords as well as from the lower house – and it would need all her courage and political cunning to ride the storm. The week Parliament assembled, broadsheets were distributed in London criticizing the Queen for not allowing the succession to be discussed. Trouble began at the Council table in her own presence, for Norfolk was put up by his colleagues to broach the delicate topic with a prepared piece, so she might collect her thoughts and have some statement ready when the Commons got their teeth into the problem. The Duke reminded her as tactfully as he could of the Commons petition, still unanswered, surveyed recent political developments in Scotland and Europe which aggravated the English succession question and begged her to allow such weighty matters to be discussed openly and frankly in both Houses. It was a bad beginning and she flew at him in a temper. Of all her subjects her privy councillors knew she had governed well, but the matter of the succession was her private affair which she would delegate to no one. Who succeeded to her throne was her business, not Parliament's, not even her Council's, and she had no wish to be 'buried alive' by making the fatal mistake of naming her successor. She recalled all the comings and goings to her at Hatfield in the last year of her sister's reign, by those worshipping the rising sun, and she wanted no such journeyings in her time. And marriage? They knew all about her treating with the Archduke and an alliance with him was not far off. Without waiting for comment she swept out of the council chamber.[19]

In the Commons various members took the line that they should refuse to vote the subsidy until the succession had been settled. 'Go to the Queen,' said one, 'and let her know our intention, which we have in command from all the towns and people of this kingdom, whose deputies we are.' During this debate members even came to blows, and as no member of the government could give the House a satisfactory assurance, a loyal message was sent, via the Council, that redress of the realm's grievances should precede the voting of supplies. Elizabeth poured out her heart to the Spanish ambassador, who seemed to her the only man in London with any sympathy for her. 'She did not know what these devils wanted', she cursed – in fact she knew very definitely that they were bent on weakening her prerogative. Then it was the turn of the Lords, who sent a deputation to her, headed by old Winchester, the Lord Treasurer, and she rated them severely. The Commons were rebels and none of them would have dared to have behaved in this way under her father. 'My lords, do whatever you wish. As for me, I shall do no otherwise than pleases me. Your bills can have no force without my assent and authority.' She would consult the best lawyers about the succession, but Parliament was too feeble-minded a body to deal with such a matter.

Following this rebuff, the Lords agreed next day to join with the Commons in presenting a united front and as Winchester was vacillating, Norfolk became the spokesman. De Silva, the Spanish ambassador, pieced together an account of this remarkable audience:

The Queen was so angry that she addressed hard words to the Duke of Norfolk, whom she called traitor or conspirator, or other words of similar flavour. He replied that he never thought to have to ask her pardon for having offended her thus. Subsequently they tell me the Queen asserted that she addressed no such words to the Duke. The Earls of Leicester and Pembroke, the Marquess of Northampton and the Lord Chamberlain spoke to her on the matter, and Pembroke remarked to her that it was not right to treat the Duke badly, since he and the others were only doing what was fitting for the good of the country, and advising her what was best for her, and if she did not think fit to adopt the advice, it was still their duty to offer it. She told him he talked like a swaggering soldier, and said to Leicester that she had thought if all the world abandoned her he would not have done so, to which he answered that he would die at her feet; and she said that had nothing to do with the matter. She said that Northampton was of no account, and he had better talk about the arguments used to enable him to get married again, when he had a wife living, instead of mincing words with her. With this she left them, and had resolved to order them to be considered under arrest in their houses. This she has not done, but she has commanded them [Leicester and Pembroke] not to appear before her.[20]

The sessions had become a fiasco, business was at a standstill, the subsidy shelved and, as Winchester had told her earlier, they might all just as well go home. In the end, as a desperate attempt to scotch the affair and end her appalling isolation, she decided to address thirty members from each House on 5 November, to nip a further joint petition in the bud. The Speaker of the Commons was not himself to attend on her instructions, for *she* was to be the sole speaker. In her carefully prepared speech she began by dwelling on her 'mere Englishry':

Was I not born in the realm? Were my parents born in any foreign country? Is there any cause I should alienate myself from being careful over this country? Is not my kingdom here? Whom have I oppressed? Whom have I enriched to other's harm? What turmoil have I made in this Commonwealth that I should be suspected to have no regard to the same? How have I governed since my reign? I will be tried by envy itself. I need not to use many words, for my deeds do try me.

She would never go back on her word, and so she repeated her old undertaking:

I will marry as soon as I can conveniently, if God take not him away with whom I mind to marry, or myself, or else some other great let happen. I can say no more, except the party were present. And I hope to have children, otherwise I would never marry.

In their petition on the succession, she went on, nothing was said about her own safety:

A strange thing that the foot should direct the head in so weighty a cause; which cause hath been so diligently weighed by us, for that it toucheth us more than them. I am sure there was not one of them that ever was a second person, as I have been, and have tasted of the practices against my sister – who, I were to God were alive again. I had great occasions to hearken [at that time] to their motions, of whom some of them are of the [present] Common House. But when friends fall out, truth doth appear, according to the old proverb; and were it not for my honour, their knavery should be known. There were occasions at that time I stood in danger of my life, my sister was so incensed against me; I did differ from her in religion, and I was sought for divers ways. And so shall never be my successor.

Before she finished she lashed out at the bishops and pitied them for their lack of foresight. Then came her winning peroration:

As for my own part, I care not for death; for all men are mortal. And though I be a woman, yet I have as good a courage, answerable to my place, as ever my father had. I am your anointed Queen. I will never be by violence constrained to do anything. I thank God I am endued with such qualities that if I were turned out of the realm in my petticoat, I were able to live in any place in Christendom.

They must realize the present time was not propitious for her to make a declaration about her successor, but:

as soon as there may be a convenient time, and that it may be done with least peril unto you – although never without great danger unto me – I will deal therein for your safety, and offer it to you as your Prince and head without request; for it is monstrous that the feet should direct the head.[21]

She directed her speech to be reported to both Houses. The peers, somewhat cowed, accepted the position, but the Commons could not leave well alone, and in defiance of a further royal order proceeded to debate the succession anew. Elizabeth sent for Mr Speaker and told him that any member still not satisfied with her answer could come and explain himself before the Council – a dire threat. There was a move to present a further petition, but instead they sent her a message asking 'leave to confer upon the liberties of the House'. Suddenly she relented, for the subsidy bill had not proceeded beyond the first reading, and first cancelled the prohibition about their discussing the succession and then, when that did not bring them to reason, on 27 November she went the length of remitting the third payment of the subsidy. This concession indeed worked miracles. They got on with the taxation measure without any more ado, but with one vital proviso – they decided to incorporate in the preamble to the bill the Queen's promise to marry and to settle the succession 'in such convenient time as Your Highness, with the advice of your Council and assent of your realm, should think most meet.' This was a revolutionary step and, had it been successful, would have been the equivalent to the much later practice of 'tacking' money bills. When the draft text of this preamble was shown to her, Elizabeth scrawled a furious minute on these 'lewd practices':

... I know no reason why my private answers to the realm should serve for a prologue to a subsidies-book. Neither yet do I understand why such audacity should be used to make without my licence an act of my words ... I will say no more at this time; but if these fellows were well answered, and paid with lawful coin, there would be fewer counterfeits among them.

This was sufficient to bring them to heel and the preamble as finally phrased was a harmless statement.

Before Parliament was dissolved the Commons turned to religion and a private member brought in a bill to confirm the revised Articles of Religion, but with clauses which would effectively sweep from their benefices any Marian clergy who would not conform. Other private bills, which taken together formed a Puritan programme for the reform of the Church, were also read but not proceeded with. When the bill for the uniformity of doctrine went to the Lords, Elizabeth pounced and the Lord Keeper was forced into revealing that the Queen had stopped its progress. The Puritans in the Commons got their own back by the clever tactics of holding up essential legislation in the form of a portmanteau act to continue in force various statutes that would otherwise have expired at the end of the year. Instead of a dissolution before Christmas it was not until 2 January that Elizabeth came to Parliament for the closing ceremony. After listening for two solid hours to Speaker Onslow she had her own say. She could not bear to let them leave for their homes 'without that my admonition may show your harms and cause you shun unseen perils.' She had always taken her people's love to be more staunch than even the feeling she had to be great, and this alone had lightened her heavy burden:

Let this my discipline stand you in stead of sorer strokes, never to tempt too far a prince's patience; and let my comfort pluck up your dismayed spirit, and cause you think that, in hope that your following behaviours shall make amends for past actions, you return with your prince's grace; whose care for you, doubt you not to be such as she shall not need a remembrancer for your weal.

She was thankful she would never have to face this same collection of trouble-makers again. Time and again they had pressed her, in 1563 and now in 1566, and they thought they were winning the duel, but with as good a courage as ever her father had she had stood alone against their onslaught on her prerogative and outwitted them. She would be in no hurry to summon another Parliament.[22]

For Elizabeth there was no escape from undertaking to pursue the Hapsburg negotiations, to the bitter end, if need be. A portrait of the Archduke was not enough and she was still horrified at the thought of her councillors and envoys discussing her marriage with a man she had never seen. 'I think it would be best for both of us if we could meet', she told him. 'Who knows whether the choice that other eyes have made would please?' She appreciated that Charles might lose face if she turned him down and suggested he might come incognito, as member of a special delegation; if they felt mutually attracted, then preliminaries could be embodied in a binding treaty, if not the delegation could return to Germany, with no one who was not in the secret any the wiser. But there was no hope of the Archduke coming even incognito while there was such fundamental disagreement on the religious question. The Emperor was not at all happy about what Elizabeth euphemistically called Charles's 'dowry of 60,000 scudi', and thought she was trying something on. 'It is the future *wife* who provides the husband a dowry and gives the husband the wedding gift', he pontificated, though he later agreed that it was reasonable for Charles to be endowed with an income from imperial funds. There was not much to choose between Vienna and Whitehall in spinning out the preliminaries. Feeling sore at being pressed so hard by Parliament and Council for her own tardiness, Elizabeth delighted in rapping the Emperor Maximilian's knuckles – though in unimpeachable Latin:

It appears to me somewhat strange, Your Majesty, that five months should have elapsed without my receiving any tidings. I wrote in reference to Your Majesty that I was being fooled, or at least that there were many irons in the fire, so strongly did I suspect that I was being scorned, or being lured on in the expectation of something better.

Maximilian, in a private note to his brother, commented on the

habit of 'our illustrious Queen' picking up and then discarding
the threads of matrimonial diplomacy, 'for she seems to regard it
as profitable to create delays somewhere or somehow in order to
gain an advantage – and this we have some time suspected on the
logic of the facts.'23

At last at midsummer 1567, the Earl of Sussex, one of the chief
supporters of the marriage, left for Germany, ostensibly to invest
the Emperor with the Garter, but he also took with him a portrait
of the Queen. Sussex was to explain that it was not possible for
Elizabeth to allow the exercise of any but the established religion,
yet since there was 'a general toleration therein used to divers
subjects living otherwise quietly', the Archduke would be given
a certain latitude for his private devotions; some compromise was
envisaged perhaps not much different from the privilege which
Queen Henrietta Maria enjoyed in the following century. Yet
when detailed negotiations in Vienna began, this assurance seemed
to Charles and his brother to be far too vague. The Archduke told
Maximilian that the religious articles offered by Sussex were anathema to him, not merely for 'the sake of my Christian conscience, but also because of the marked contemptuous attitude
adopted [in England] towards the true Catholic and apostolic
religion in which I, by the Grace of God, was brought up.' He
asked that Elizabeth should permit him his own private chapel for
mass, with his own chaplains, while he would agree to accompany
her to public Anglican worship. 'Exhaustive conferences' failed to
reconcile their fundamental disagreements, so in October Sussex
sent Henry Cobham home asking for further guidance. 24

The Council were fairly evenly divided on the question
whether further concessions should be offered to the Archduke,
and tempers were raised. Leicester, for one, worked feverishly on
Protestant passions, so that Bishop Jewel harangued the multitude
at St Paul's Cross to have no traffic with idolatry. It was said that
Leicester had suborned Lord North, who accompanied Sussex on
his mission, to act as his eyes and ears and to do all he could to
'hinder the negotiations privily' by saying Elizabeth had no intention of marriage. Cecil, by contrast, desperately wanted the
match to go forward and felt that just a little more exertion would

sway Her Majesty. She asked her councillors their opinions to
help her to make up her own mind, but in the event, with Sussex
in Vienna and Norfolk ill in the country, Cecil missed his two
chief supporters. Norfolk sent his views in writing. He counselled the Secretary to stand by the marriage at all costs, allowing
the Archduke the terms which he had demanded. There was, he
wrote, no prince of Charles's standing or understanding who would
yield any further upon uncertainty. His was a most reasonable
request, and if in the end negotiations foundered on other grounds
than religion, Charles would not have thrown away his principles. The danger of his being allowed his private Roman
Catholic chapel was very small compared with the danger of an
unsettled succession. Not all 'earnest Protestants' were like
Leicester and his men who were 'making religion a cloak for every
shower ... naming one thing and minding another.' To the
Queen the Duke wrote more guardedly: there was a risk of the
Archduke as her consort becoming 'an open maintainer of papistry', which would clearly endanger the unity of the realm, and
'England can bear no more changes in religion – it hath been
bowed so far that if it should be bent again it would break.' That
said, it was important not to let the Archduke be frightened off.
'If this, then, should not take place, what present hope is there of
any other? as delay of Your Majesty's marriage is almost an un-
doing of your realm.'[25]

Leicester's party won the day in November 1567, though the
matrimonial troubles of Mary Queen of Scots (which we are
about to consider) were probably the deciding factor with Elizabeth herself. She told Sussex that she was still keen to invite
Charles to England and during his stay she would of course allow
him to worship privately according to his faith, though she hoped
that on this score she might succeed in persuading him to give
way. Two days afterwards she added a stringent rider, telling
Sussex to make it abundantly clear that there was not the slightest
chance if the Archduke did come to see her, that he could persuade
her to change her mind. Sussex replied that an *impasse* had been
reached, so he speedily invested the Emperor with the Garter and
left for home, utterly despondent that Elizabeth had finally closed

the door. Florid messages still passed between Queen and Archduke for another three years, with Charles underlining the reverence and adoration he felt for her, but the issue which had
dragged on for seven years was now buried for all time. She felt
no less relieved at the outcome than the Archduke.[26]

While the last act of Elizabeth's serio-comic drama with the
Archduke was being drawn out, Mary's matrimonial adventures
were ending in high tragedy. After a brief honeymoon period of
passionate love, King Darnley disappointed her. He went to
pieces as a worthless drunkard and the Edinburgh of Knox and
the Covenanters stood aghast. It was useless for Mary to turn to
her husband for advice on any of the pressing problems of the day,
and so she turned more and more for guidance to her able Italian
secretary, David Rizzio, who had originally come to Holyrood-
house as one of her court singers but rose steadily in favour until
he possessed her confidence. Darnley soon had cause to be jealous
of this upstart and plotted with three peers, Lords Morton,
Lindsay and Ruthven, to put him out of the way. On 9 March
1566 Morton marched a band of retainers into the palace and took
over the gates. Darnley's suite was immediately below Mary's and
at the hour appointed he left his rooms with Ruthven by the
private staircase leading to the Queen's apartments. They found
Rizzio taking supper with Mary in a little room next door to her
bedchamber. Darnley clasped his wife round the waist, while
Ruthven demanded the Italian's instant dismissal on the score that
he was an evil adviser who had caused a rift between husband and
wife. Mary's servants tried to drive Ruthven away, but in came a
posse of Morton's men who dragged the favourite outside, killed
him on the threshold of the royal bedchamber and left his body
near the door of the audience chamber. It was a miracle that the
murder did not cause Mary to have a miscarriage, for she was six
months pregnant.

   The birth of a prince did nothing to heal the breach between
Mary and Darnley. 'The disagreement between the Queen and
her husband', reported Bedford in August, 'continues, or rather
increases', and in the same letter he remarked on the danger of the

Earl of Bothwell. James Hepburn, Earl of Bothwell, the man who
now stood at Mary's right hand, had already earned the reputation of being irresistible to women. He had recently married and
Mary had herself signed the marriage contract, given his young
bride the dazzling dress of cloth of silver she wore on the day, and
provided the wedding breakfast. But everyone knew Bothwell
was a feckless adventurer, trusting to his prowess with women
and his great physical strength to get his way, and Elizabeth's concern was all the greater since the Earl was as great an Anglophobe
as could be found in Scotland. Rizzio's murder and its aftermath
so weakened the reputation of Mary and her court in Europe that
Elizabeth sensed the immediate danger to England had passed; not
even the birth of a prince could reinstate Mary. She still harped on
her hereditary right, 'as has lately been maintained in Parliament
... albeit we are not of mind to press our good sister further than
shall come of her own good pleasure.' Elizabeth graciously declined her invitation to visit Edinburgh for Prince James's
christening, though she sent a gold font, specially made – and if
the baby had outgrown it, she might keep it for the next child.
The time was most certainly not propitious for a general enquiry
into Mary's claim to the English succession, but nothing would be
done, wrote Elizabeth to her, that was prejudicial to her rights. In
the meantime she would do well to confirm the Treaty of Edinburgh of 1560. She sent representatives to attend the christening
on 15 December, but Darnley, the child's father, absented himself.

Darnley became ill – it was most probably syphilis – and lay
low at his father's residence in Glasgow. Mary visited him and,
after some kind of reconciliation, removed him to Kirk o'Field,
his father's tumble-down home outside Edinburgh, so he could
be near her and be properly nursed. Here he was murdered, when
the house was blown up on 10 February. A week later this alarming news reached Elizabeth, with a cartoon showing the stages of
the crime, and she sent Lady Howard and Lord Cecil to break the
news to Lady Lennox who was still in the Tower. All the mother's
scheming had ended in tragedy and the news so weakened her
that Elizabeth sent her own physician to attend her. For months to
come each report from Edinburgh was more alarming than the

last. When Elizabeth learnt that after a token week of mourning, Mary had gone to stay with Lord Seton, whose other guests included Bothwell, she was dumbfounded; it could not be so, she said. Placards were nailed to the Tolbooth in the Scottish capital, complete with portraits of 'Bothwell the murderer' and the words 'The Queen was an assenting party'. Soon the populace of Edinburgh, inflamed by Knox, would cry out 'Burn the whore' as Mary passed by. The stature of the monarchy in Scotland had never been brought so low.

Elizabeth looked back to the slanders she had endured at the time of Amy Robsart's death and reflected that Mary would have to run a far more hazardous gauntlet of abuse. On 24 February she wrote her own words of remonstrance, which she sent up by Henry Killigrew:

My ears have been so astounded, my mind so disturbed, my heart so shocked at the news of the abominable murder of your late husband, that even yet I can scarcely rally my spirits to write to you; and however I would express my sympathy in your sorrow for his loss, so, to tell you plainly what I think, my grief is more for you than for him.

Oh, madam, I should ill fulfil the part either of a faithful cousin or an affectionate friend, if I were to content myself with saying pleasant things to you and make no effort to preserve your honour. I cannot but tell you what all the world is thinking. Men say that, instead of seizing the murderers, you are looking through your fingers while they escape; that you will not punish those who have done you so great a service, as though the thing would never have taken place had not the doers of it been assured of impunity.

For myself, I beg you to believe that I would not harbour such a thought for all the wealth of the world, nor would I entertain in my heart so ill a guest, or think so badly of any prince that breathes. Far less could I so think of you, to whom I desire all imaginable good, and all blessings which you yourself would wish for. For this very reason I exhort, I advise, I implore you deeply to consider of the matter – at once, if it be the nearest friend you have, to lay your hands upon the man who has been guilty of the crime – to let no interest, no persuasion, keep you from proving to everyone that you are a noble princess and a loyal wife. I do not write thus earnestly because I doubt you, but for the love I bear towards you. You may have wiser councillors than I am – I can well believe it – but even Our Lord, as I remember, had a Judas among the twelve: while I am sure that you have no friend more true than I, and my affection may stand you in as good stead as the subtle wit of others.[27]

Bothwell's trial was a fiasco; Mary waved him on his way and welcomed him with open arms on his return with a verdict of 'not guilty'. Elizabeth continued adamant that the murderers of Darnley must be brought to justice, and that if, as rumour had it, Mary was contemplating marrying Bothwell, then this union must be prevented at all costs. As always it was vital for Elizabeth to prevent any return of French influence in Scotland that might even in a minor way revive the 'auld alliance'. The Privy Council fully discussed the situation on 25 April and further warnings were sent to Mary via Bedford, who was to make enquiries about the likelihood of the infant prince being brought in safety to England. At this juncture Elizabeth could do no more than wait upon events, for the future was so uncertain. On 15 May, just twelve days after Lady Bothwell had been frightened into obtaining a dubious divorce, Mary was married to the Earl at 4 o'clock in the morning by the Bishop of Orkney, according to Protestant rites. It could not be so, exclaimed Elizabeth; yet it was. The confederate lords, who had taken a bond before Mary's marriage to Bothwell to set her at liberty and defend her and her son, now gathered their forces. Mary escaped with Bothwell from Holyrood to Borthwick, but soon had to retire to Dunbar. Only a few nobles declared for them and came with their retainers to face the confederates at Carberry Hill on 15 June. Before battle was begun there were abortive discussions about a proposed single combat between Bothwell and a champion from the lords. Meanwhile Mary's little army melted away and, after seeing Bothwell safely from the field, she surrendered, to be taken in disgrace to Edinburgh and from thence to Lochleven Castle. On 24 July Mary abdicated in favour of her infant son and appointed her halfbrother, the Earl of Murray, as Regent. Five days later James VI was crowned King of Scotland in Stirling Castle.

Elizabeth could not but accept the *coup d'état*. She sent Sir Nicholas Throgmorton with letters for Mary and for the lords, which in effect laid down what she regarded as the basis for a settlement. To Mary she again expressed her astonishment that Bothwell and his 'men of notorious evil name' should have been favoured as they had, reiterated her old warnings about the fatal mistake of marrying Bothwell and saw her now as 'a person desperate to recover her honour'. Yet her unjust imprisonment had altered the situation, and she could not allow her cousin 'being by God's ordinance the prince and sovereign, to be in subjection to them that by virtue and law are subjected to her.' Elizabeth would do her utmost to restore her to liberty, to see that Darnley's murderers were punished and to ensure the safety of James, who might well be put in the care of his grandmother, Lady Lennox, in England. To the Scottish lords Elizabeth made it plain that she would assist them only once Mary were released. In a later message to Throgmorton she warned them that if they so much as laid a finger on the head of their sovereign lady, she would revenge the deed for an example to all posterity; they must never forget they were subject to the higher powers, and to show the extent of her displeasure at their grand rebellion she specifically forbade Throgmorton to be present at James's coronation. Murray, Mary's stepbrother, who had been in England to discuss plans with the government, became Regent for the young Prince and in due course the Scottish Parliament pronounced on Mary's guilt and confirmed the new regime. There was much talk of Mary earnestly wishing to come to England. Such was an alarming suggestion for Elizabeth, 'not without great discommodities to us', but at least it would be a less dangerous course than for her to seek refuge in France.[28]

After eight months of Lochleven Mary succeeded in escaping to Hamilton, where she rallied her supporters and prepared for battle. She sent her servant John Beton south with letters for Elizabeth and for the Cardinal of Guise imploring aid against her rebellious subjects. The English Queen at once ordered her ambassador in Paris, Sir Henry Norris, to go to the French King and require him 'to forbear sending any power of men of war to Scotland', for she could not countenance French intervention. To Mary she wrote words of rejoicing at her freedom, tempered with regrets that her association with Bothwell, 'that unhappy rogue', had lost her friends whom she now so sorely needed. Mary must remember the adage that 'those who have two strings to one bow may shoot strongly, but they rarely shoot straight', meaning that if she looked for aid from England she must not intrigue for French support. She would certainly help Mary recover her throne, providing no aid came from France. But before this letter could be delivered Mary's supporters were utterly routed by Murray at Langside, and as she was cut off from reaching Dumbarton, where she hoped to find a passage to France, Mary crossed the Solway and on 16 May 1568, landed in England, where she was destined to spend the rest of her unhappy life.

Elizabeth at once summoned the Privy Council to discuss how the fugitive Queen of Scots was to be treated, for the situation posed delicate problems fraught with ramifications of international diplomacy. For the next sixteen years, indeed, the question of Mary's future remained the key question in English politics. The Spanish ambassador with his ear to the ground knew the initial difficulties well enough:

I think they must be somewhat embarrassed as this Queen has always shown good will to the Queen of Scots and the Council, or a majority of it, has been opposed to her and lean to the side of the Regent and his government. If the Queen has her way now they will be obliged to treat the Queen of Scots as a sovereign, which will offend those who forced her to abdicate, so that, although these people are glad enough to have her in their hands, they have many things to consider. If they keep her in prison it will probably scandalize all neighbouring princes, and if she remain free and able to communicate with her friends, great suspicions will be aroused. In any case, it is certain that two women will not agree very long together.

There was a deep division of opinion. Cecil felt certain that in this crisis Elizabeth would be far better disposed to the Scottish Queen than statecraft warranted. When she was still a captive at Lochleven Elizabeth had faithfully promised to assist her, yet assistance courted danger. Letters came thick and fast from Mary: 'Considering the great trust which I have in you, I am persuaded you will assist me to recover my authority. I hope you will send for me immediately.' Her cousin's first reactions were to do just that; after all, the freemasonry of monarchy, that mutual regard of sovereigns ordained to rule under divine right, demanded more than words of sisterly affection. As Arundel remarked, 'one that has a crown can hardly persuade another to leave her crown because her subjects will not obey. It may be a new doctrine in Scotland, but it is not good to be taught in England.' She summoned another Council meeting at which Leicester and Norfolk, who had been absent from the first, were now asked for their views; it seems that she turned to them to support a more lenient policy than that proposed by Cecil, but in the event it was the Secretary's views which prevailed. The possible courses open to her were to return Mary to Scotland as a prisoner; to support her with an army to regain her kingdom; to allow her to move on to the continent; or to keep her where she was under surveillance. The first would have been an utter breach of faith with Mary, and would have resulted in a life sentence, if not execution; the second was out of the question and would have overturned the Treaty of Edinburgh; the third was too dangerous, for when last in France Mary had persistently claimed to be Queen of England. Mary, perforce, would have to remain in England, but she could not be brought to court until she had been cleared of the serious charges against her. Undoubtedly her presence would encourage Catholics and other dissidents to rally to her cause and it would be expedient for her to be kept in isolation, for the moment under Lord Scrope, Warden of the West Marches and Governor of Carlisle. He was in London at this time, but was at once sent home, accompanied by Sir Francis Knollys, vice-chamberlain of the household, whose presence would serve two purposes; such a high-ranking household official would show that Mary was being treated with the respect she deserved, yet Knollys' Puritan sympathies would counteract any favouritism Mary might receive from Scrope on the score of her religion. Elizabeth ordered Lady Scrope, then at Bolton Castle, to attend on Mary 'and treat her with all honour.' Yet Bolton Castle in Wensleydale was a stately home in bleak country, with the highest walls of any residence in the kingdom. Escape was barely possible. Had Mary

escaped from Lochleven to come to this? Knollys wrote: 'We
have a charge to see that she escapes not, and yet we have no
authority to abridge her nor detain her as a prisoner.' For Mary it
was a matter of splitting hairs.[29]

She pleaded again and again with Elizabeth 'to come in person
and lay my complaints before you to justify myself. . . . I therefore beg you soon to see and speak to me, and speedily replace me
in the rank to which God called me and in which respect all
princes are bound mutually to assist each other.' And again, more
forcefully on 4 June, 'Answer me without delay, decidedly and in
writing, if it is agreeable to you that I should come to you immediately and without ceremony.' If she, Mary's chief friend,
refused, she asked leave to apply to other sovereigns for aid against
her rebellious subjects, 'for thank Heaven I am not destitute of
good friends and neighbours in my just cause.' Elizabeth replied:

There is not a creature living who more longs to hear your justification than myself; nor one who would lend more willing ear to any
answer which will clear your honour. But I cannot sacrifice my own
reputation on your account. To tell you the plain truth, I am already
thought to be more willing to defend your cause than to open my eyes
to see the things of which your subjects accuse you. Did you but know
who the persons are by whom I am warned to be on my guard, you
would not think that I could afford to neglect these warnings. And
now, seeing that you are pleased to commit yourself to my protection,
you may assure yourself that I will take care both of your life and
honour, that neither yourself nor your nearest relatives could be more
concerned for your interests. On the word of a prince I promise you
that, neither your subjects, nor any advice which I may receive from
my own councillors, shall move me to ask anything of you which may
endanger you or touch your honour.

Does it seem strange to you that you are not allowed to see me? I entreat you to put yourself in my place. When you are acquitted of this
crime I will receive you with all honour: till that is done I may not; but
afterwards, I swear by God, that I shall never see person with better
will, and among all earthly pleasures I will hold this to be the first. . . .
God be with you in all your good actions, and deliver you from those
who bear you malice.[30]

Mary could not believe what she read and wept bitterly.

Elizabeth was being forced by events into the role of arbiter between Mary and her subjects, and after many discussions with the Queen and the Regent's envoys both agreed to accept her mediation as the only *modus vivendi*. Before the end of June Murray had sent to London copies of the collection of letters and ballads from Mary to Bothwell which had been found in 'a little coffer of silver and gilt' under Bothwell's bed. There was strong presumption that these 'casket letters' were genuine and if such were the case they proved Mary's guilt in Darnley's death up to the hilt. The English Queen had been persuaded by Cecil that her only real justification to the courts of Europe for keeping Mary under restraint was on the grounds of her alleged complicity in her husband's murder ('vehement presumption' was the favourite phrase). To keep Mary at close quarters because she had preferred a claim to the English throne would not have been accepted as a legitimate reason by the Kings of France or Spain, or the Emperor, and would have provoked serious diplomatic complications – war even. Mary was subsequently removed to Tutbury in the custody of the Earl of Shrewsbury, who was to 'treat her with the honour and reverence due to a princess of the blood royal', a far kinder jailer than Bedingfield had been to Elizabeth at Woodstock. Meanwhile plans were made for holding an impartial commission of enquiry into Mary's conduct, but throughout England, especially in the north country, the laws against Catholic recusants were ordered to be rigorously enforced. The difficult situation upset the hallowed routine of court, for Elizabeth limited her summer progress to the home counties, 'for she is careful to keep near at hand when troubles and disturbances exist in adjacent counties.'[31]

In early October there opened in York the conference at which Mary's fate was expected to be settled. Elizabeth was represented by three commissioners, the Duke of Norfolk, his friend Sussex and Sir Ralph Sadler, an official with great experience of the border country. They were to act neither as accusers, nor as judges who would pronounce sentence; instead they were first to hear the charges brought by Mary's delegates against Murray, and then to hear the rival charges of the infant James's commissioners, led by Murray and Morton, against Mary. The Scottish Queen's future would depend on the findings of Elizabeth's commissioners, and their instructions included advice on how she might return to her throne 'without danger of relapse into misgovernment'. Mary herself would not appear before the tribunal, for she would never acknowledge its authority to investigate her case, but she agreed to be represented by Lord Herries and by John Leslie, Bishop of Ross, who had succeeded Rizzio as her confidential secretary for the last months of her reign.

There were endless precedural difficulties and Norfolk, predicting a lengthy sessions, was anxious to postpone for as long as possible the 'terrors of accusation' against Mary. The Regent was loath to bring forward his most telling evidence until he was quite certain how Elizabeth would act if Mary's guilt in Darnley's murder were established. 'I am sent to learn your accusations,' said Norfolk, 'but neither will I, nor the Queen my mistress, give out any sentence upon your accusation.' According to Melville, the Duke secretly advised Murray that the next time he was called on to submit his case, he should ask for a written undertaking from Elizabeth that she would immediately give a sentence, 'otherwise that you will not open your pack.' This advice the Regent followed and his request was forwarded to Whitehall for Elizabeth to 'aid and maintain them in this accusation if she found Mary guilty.' If, on the other hand, they accused Mary and Elizabeth's support was not forthcoming, their lives would be in danger. But the Queen of England could only give a general assurance that 'her promise would be abundantly sufficient', so Murray held back. Once Elizabeth had unimpeachable evidence of Mary's guilt she would publish the facts and, as a result, all pressure from foreign courts for her to free Mary would cease. But now at York stalemate was being reached.

Norfolk had been shown copies of the casket letters and assumed them to be genuine, 'the matter contained in them being such as could hardly be invented or devised by any other than' Mary. The letters, he wrote 'do discover such inordinate love between her and Bothwell, her loathsomeness and abhoring of her husband that was murdered, in such sort as every good and godly man cannot but detest and abhor the same.' As with all conferences, it was the unofficial talks which counted, and the Duke benignly had a word with everyone of importance. Three days after being shown the casket letters he went hawking with Maitland of Lethington to Cawood, down by the River Ouse, and on the way the Scot suggested that the only way of finding a solution would be for Norfolk to marry Mary, who would thereupon be restored to her throne and in the fullness of time she, or her heir, would reign in England as well as Scotland. Such a match would restore Mary to honour and carry to its logical conclusions the Anglo-Scottish alliance, in which the Duke had laboured so successfully in 1560. Norfolk no more than brooded on the idea. He can hardly have relished the idea of marrying a woman he had never seen who was, according to the evidence he had just read, both a murderess and an adulteress, and he knew well enough the clause in his commission from Elizabeth which stated that anyone with whom Mary contracted a marriage, or anyone advising a match, 'should be *ipso facto* adjudged as traitors and shall suffer death.' But word went round the delegates at York, and the Bishop of Ross called early one morning, before anyone else was about, to be assured of the goodwill the Duke bore his mistress. On 16 October Norfolk reported that the conference 'is the doubtfullest and dangeroust [cause] that ever I dealt in; if you saw and heard the constant affirming of both sides, not without great stoutness, you would wonder!' The same day the Queen sent orders to York to adjourn the hearing, for she had decided, she said, to submit the points Norfolk had raised to a full Privy Council. Everyone at York expected proceedings to be reopened later in the year, but Elizabeth knew enough already to suspect that her cousin had been showing undue partiality to Mary. She had chosen him for his 'fidelity and circumspection' and he had undertaken 'not to lean to the one party or the other'; yet he was abusing the confidence she had placed in him. Elizabeth indeed smelt danger. Rumours that he was contemplating marriage with Mary were being whispered at court and the Queen heard about it from the French ambassador, if not from other sources, before the end of the month. As a result she ordered the conference to be resumed at Westminster, under her nose, before a new body of commissioners, which included most of her Council. It was an extremely worrying time for her. The seizure of Alva's treasure ships when they took refuge in English ports brought the country to the brink of war with Spain, and her heart was heavy with the death of her cousin, Lady Knollys, 'whom she loved better than all the women in the world.' And now her cousin of Norfolk had deserted her.[32]

The new sessions opened in the Star Chamber on 25 November. Ross made his protest that his sovereign was not to be treated judicially 'in respect she is a free princess with an imperial crown given her of God', and then withdrew. The Regent for his part presented four articles about the authority of the English commissioners to pronounce on Mary's guilt, to which he demanded answers, and was told it would be for Elizabeth alone to act on their findings; if guilty Mary would either be delivered to Murray or kept in England. Next day in a dramatic scene the accusation against Mary was delivered – to Murray's chagrin; as Bothwell was the chief executor of Darnley's murder, 'so she was of the foreknowledge' and a maintainer of evil-doers. After much shilly-shallying, eleven days later the casket letters were produced, and sworn to by Morton as authentic, to support the accusation.[33] Ross had been to see Elizabeth, to deliver Mary's protest that her commissioners were not empowered to answer the charges, brought by a procedure that she would never acknowledge as legal, and that the only possible solution would be for his Queen to come before Elizabeth and answer for herself; the dignity of a sovereign required nothing less. After she had called her own commissioners together at Hampton Court to go over the ground, she then wrote to Mary herself, congratulating her on so skilled a servant as the Bishop of Ross, yet advising her most earnestly to answer the charges so that she would be delivered by the justification of her innocence. She indeed had the wolf by the ears. With the evidence before her no power on earth could deny Elizabeth the right to keep Mary under strict custody. She could never agree to meet Mary, but at least she refused to rule out the possibility of ultimately supporting her restoration, for she utterly despised the Regent Murray, who even now was angling for English money in return for promises he would never keep.

During the Westminster Conference and its aftermath there were many secret meetings between English and Scottish politicians, with offers of help and promises undertaken, and Norfolk, now thoroughly discredited with Elizabeth for apparent double-dealing, was approached on various occasions about becoming Mary's husband. Elizabeth asked him to his face about the rumours and when he denied them she suggested that, though now he might hate the idea of such a marriage, perhaps in the future he could be persuaded to change his mind if it were shown to be for the benefit of the realm and the safety of his own Queen. She was indeed weighing him in the balance. He answered with astonishment that 'no reason could move him to like her that hath been a competitor to the crown; and if Her Majesty would move him thereto he will rather be committed to the Tower, for he meant never to marry with such a person, where he could not be sure of his pillow' – an allusion to Darnley's end. But such hints as these played on the Duke's ambition and persuaded him to take the idea seriously. By the opening of 1569 he had determined when opportunity served, and Mary was again a free woman, to marry her, and for all his protestations to the contrary he would never give up this extraordinary ambition. She was a Queen and marriage with him would provide him with a throne: the temptation became irresistible. The schemings of those involved in this project provoked the most serious crisis that Elizabeth had to face, and her surmounting of it was the turning-point of her reign.

MANIFEST DANGER

1569, the year of conspiracy and revolt, began with an attempt by Leicester and Norfolk to dislodge Cecil from the position of dominance he had held since Elizabeth's accession, continued with a series of intrigues involving some of the greatest in the land, and culminated in the rebellion in the north. This succession of plots and counterplots, some bringing the threat of foreign intervention in England and all connected with Mary Queen of Scots, was a direct challenge to Elizabeth and her whole system of government. She was in 'manifest danger', such as she had not experienced since the spring of 1554.

The attempt to remove Cecil was made simply because his opponents could not in the context of the Tudor constitution criticize the Queen herself. As there was no official 'opposition' in the modern sense, it was the duty of those who opposed official policy to intrigue, and Cecil as Secretary was the principal instrument of policies which were becoming increasingly unpopular. No minister of later days could have stayed in office in the face of such unpopularity, but ministers who retained Elizabeth's confidence could only be removed by backstairs methods, and the success of such intrigues depended entirely on how the Queen herself reacted. 'Many did rise against his fortune, who were more hot in envying him than able to follow him, detracting his praises, disgracing his service and plotting his danger', wrote a biographer of Cecil in his own lifetime.[1] Elizabeth recognized the manœuvre for what it was, an attempted *coup* against her.

The seizure in Plymouth Sound of the Spanish ships with £85,000 treasure aboard in November 1568 had provoked a serious commercial crisis with Spain and the Netherlands and brought England to the brink of war. English property in the Netherlands was seized in retaliation and an embargo on trading was imposed – economic sanctions which brought the ports to a standstill. As the situation became blacker Cecil's unpopularity grew. Other critics were alarmed at the growing estrangement from Spain on political grounds, because they feared that England would be drawn into an alliance with her old enemy, France. In the country at large the severity with which the laws against Catholic recusants were being enforced, following Mary's flight, was laid at Cecil's door, and in the Council itself he had few friends. Leicester regarded him as the man who had prevented him from becoming Elizabeth's consort; Norfolk saw him as the sworn enemy of Mary Queen of Scots, whom he was now bent on marrying; Pembroke and Northampton disliked his Protestantism as evinced in his partiality for the Suffolk claim and in his supporting the Huguenots in France and the rebels in the Netherlands; while Arundel, Northumberland and Westmorland, all staunch Catholics, looked for his dismissal as the first step in a grand design for the restoration of the old faith. Together they made an incongruous, though formidable team. 'Although Cecil thinks he has them all under his heel,' wrote de Spes who was in the secret, 'he will find few or none of them stand by him.'[2]

The plan was a time-honoured one. Cecil was to be charged in the Council chamber with being an evil adviser and, once in the Tower, 'means to undo him would not be far to seek.' But Elizabeth saw straws in the wind and, sensing danger, summoned a Council meeting at which she would be present. Her suspicions were confirmed when Cecil's opponents severally made excuses for their absence, and she grasped an opportunity of dealing with them informally on Ash Wednesday. A group of them were in her chamber before supper when she went out of the way to rebuke Leicester for the unbusinesslike attitude of the Council. This provoked the Earl to launch a vigorous attack on Cecil whom so many people thought was ruining the country, and at this the Queen cast aside her mask, praising the Secretary warmly and making a great tirade against Leicester. Sharp comments came from some of the others present. Norfolk told Northampton,

'You see, my lord, how the Earl of Leicester is favoured so long as he supports the Secretary, but now that for good reasons he takes an opposed position, she frowns on him and wants to send him to the Tower.' 'No, no he will not go alone', Northampton replied. So their plans misfired and Elizabeth's handling of the affair should have brought home to her rebel councillors that she was not prepared to sacrifice Cecil and that if they were bent on a change of policies they would need a change of Queen. Though murmurings against Cecil continued, the clique was too dismayed by Elizabeth's attitude to act swiftly and by Easter the move to replace him had petered out, but in the aftermath of Ash Wednesday other distinct, yet simultaneous, schemes were being launched, no less far-reaching in their consequences to Queen and country.[3]

Leicester now put his weight behind the project, brought forward by Maitland of Lethington, for Norfolk to marry Mary as the only realistic solution to the Scottish problem, in which he was supported by Pembroke and Throgmorton. Mary's abdication was to be revoked, Darnley's murder conveniently forgotten, and a divorce from Bothwell obtained, so that after marriage with the Duke she would be restored to her throne, ratify at long last the Treaty of Edinburgh and be pronounced as Elizabeth's heir. The curtain could be rung down on the great drama of matrimonial manœuvres with Hapsburg dukes and French princes, and Dudley himself would achieve his ambition of being Elizabeth's consort. After discreet pondering Norfolk was prepared 'to sacrifice himself' in this way for his own sovereign's benefit. On paper it looked a tidy scheme, but the drawbacks were Cecil's preference for the Suffolk line and Elizabeth's increasing aversion to Mary. For the moment, however, Leicester felt confident he could sway the Council and force a decision on the Queen.[4]

There were other plans afoot which also hinged on a marriage between Mary and the Duke. Arundel and Lumley devised a desperate design, with the full support of Northumberland and Westmorland, for liberating Mary and enthroning her in Elizabeth's stead; this was to be achieved through Spanish aid and lead to the restoration of Roman Catholicism. Mary also had her own schemes, negotiated by the Bishop of Ross with both sets of

English conspirators and with the Scots, which varied from month to month, but in every case her first requirement was to be free and she grasped at the idea of marrying Norfolk as an essential means to achieve this. She told Leicester she would in all things follow Elizabeth's advice, but at once began courting Norfolk by proxy.[5]

Throughout that summer Elizabeth sensed something was afoot and regarded the usual faces at court with growing unease. The undercurrent of discontent was unmistakable. Already in June someone proposed to her a 'general association' for her protection, considering 'the perilous state of the time'. The common bond which subjects of every degree owed her should lead them to associate themselves 'at all times and places to defend the Queen Majesty's most royal person and the common peace of the realm', thus enabling loyal Englishmen 'to withstand any foreign or domestical attempt.' The writer saw the greatest danger in the Catholic recusants and the proposed association was in his view as much a defence of the Protestant religion as a defence of the Queen. Nothing came of the association (the idea was to be revived and put into force in October 1584), but the fact that it could be proposed and considered in detail in June 1569 indicates the political climate. Though ignorant of the identity of the conspirators and of the scope of their plans, the Queen took precautions by ordering systematic musters of the militia in each shire and requiring the Council in the North to take special heed of the state of the north, which she rightly regarded as the most vulnerable quarter. Norfolk had raised the problem of Mary's marriage at a meeting of a quorum of the Privy Council in Cecil's absence, when those present agreed to his proposal that the Scottish Queen should be set at liberty on condition she married an Englishman, and he now hoped Leicester would confront Elizabeth with this resolution; the French ambassador was sure she dare not oppose it. Yet to Norfolk's dismay Leicester did nothing.[6]

The signs were not propitious. Elizabeth, he heard, 'had been out of quiet', and then some of the women at court babbled their hearsay – that the arrangements with Mary had already been concluded. The Queen taxed Leicester with daring to proceed with these plans without first consulting her, but he more or less satisfied her there was nothing in these tales, though her attitude was sufficient warning to tread warily. Time and again he insisted to the Duke that only he, Leicester, could successfully raise this topic with his sovereign. She at last took the initiative by asking Norfolk when he joined her in the garden at Richmond what news her cousin had to tell her. He mumbled that he knew of nothing. 'No,' she cried out, 'You come from London and can tell no news of a marriage?' But instead of speaking out, Norfolk excused himself. Nothing had come into the open before Elizabeth left Richmond for her summer progress. She gave the Duke another chance of being straightforward with her at Sir William More's house at Loseley, near Guildford, and in mid-August, at Farnham, called him to her dinner-table, but once again he remained tongue-tied, partly from timidity, partly from fear of upsetting Leicester's plans, and at the end of the meal the Queen gave him a nip, saying 'that she would wish me to take good head to my pillow' (an allusion to their interview the previous December). 'I was so abashed at Her Majesty's speech,' the Duke later confessed, 'but I thought it not fit time nor place there to trouble her.' Elizabeth had given him three chances of making a clean breast of the whole affair, which he had rejected, and she had every reason for feeling he had forfeited her confidence. He left the progress at Southampton, feeling he had committed himself too deeply to Mary's cause to withdraw, and back in London approved a plan for Northumberland and Leonard Dacre to rescue Mary from Wingfield once he should give the signal. From Northumberland came the proud message that 'the whole of the north' was at his devotion, while from Pembroke, still with the court on progress, came the suggestion that the Queen dare not refuse her permission to the marriage for there was not a person about her who would dare to give her contrary advice.[7]

That same day, however, Hunsdon wrote to Elizabeth speaking out most strongly against so dangerous a proposal and forthwith she summoned the Duke to come to her. Before he had time to obey, Leicester had taken to his bed with a feigned sickness at Titchfield and when the Queen came to his bedside, anxious and full of sympathy, he revealed to her the detailed plans for the Norfolk-Mary marriage. His own loyalty, he assured her, was never in question, yet he craved her forgiveness. Later that day in the gallery at Titchfield she rated the Duke, charging him on his allegiance 'to deal no further with the Scottish cause.' She knew that in the current political unrest the projected marriage would be disastrous for her; within four months of it taking place, she said, *she* would have been in the Tower. The six-week delay in bringing their plans to her notice had made Leicester, Norfolk and their supporters appear as a body of whispering conspirators who would never come into the open, though had they moved speedily in July there might have been some chance of forcing the marriage scheme on Elizabeth. After ten miserable days at Titchfield, where Leicester treated him with cold disdain and the other courtiers followed suit, the Duke left for London, but there were too many rumours for his own peace of mind. Elizabeth feared that his withdrawal from court was the prologue to a general rising, uniting under one banner all the opponents of her regime. Already, her most formidable enemies, the religious malcontents in the north under Northumberland and the political malcontents in the ranks of the Privy Council, were in alliance and civil war seemed possible. In this manifest danger Elizabeth swiftly made her dispositions. She closed the ports, alerted the militia, and sent Huntingdon to supersede Shrewsbury as custodian of Mary, with orders for her removal from Wingfield to Tutbury. She herself would move to Windsor Castle, prepared to stand a siege if necessary. Meanwhile she still hoped she could call Norfolk's bluff and required Leicester and Cecil to write a joint letter to him, ordering him to repair to Windsor and submit. He wrote that he was not well enough to travel – Elizabeth's excuse to her sister from Hatfield at the time of Wyatt's revolt – but hoped to be at Windsor by 26 September. Other messages reached the Duke, including a warning note from Leicester that it was likely he would be sent to the Tower, and with failing courage he rode off that night to his country residence, Kenninghall Palace, feeling home was the only safe place.

The Queen did not realize this was a retreat in fear, but took it as an open act of defiance, the signal for revolt. 'All the whole court hung in suspense and fear lest he should break forth into rebellion', wrote Camden; and it was determined if he did so, forthwith to put the Queen of Scots to death. But Norfolk was indeed ruined 'by his own pusillanimity'; instead of taking the field and rallying his many supporters, he lay low, terrified that he had become 'a suspected person', and saw the shadow of the Tower, as he wrote to Elizabeth, 'which is too great a terror for a true man.' She commanded him on his allegiance to submit, telling him she never intended 'to minister anything to you but as you should in truth deserve', and when he still disobeyed telling him to come straightway, in a litter if need be, in the custody of Edward Fitzgarret. At last he listened to reason, and left home to throw himself onto his royal cousin's mercy, to all intents a prisoner, on 1 October. But before he left he despatched a messenger to the northern earls at Topcliffe to call off their projected rising, 'for if they did, it should cost him his head'; he specially asked his brother-in-law of Westmorland to remain loyal, even if Northumberland should rise. But for the Earls, the Duke's withdrawal to Kenninghall had been the signal for which they had awaited all summer, an overt action which the later message could not effectively cancel. They had brought the partisan hopes of their supporters to fever-heat, and their rising planned for 6 October, though postponed was not cancelled.[8]

The Percys, Nevilles and Dacres ruled a patriarchal society and could count on their tenantry in the Palatinate of Durham and the North Riding of Yorkshire to follow them with blind devotion once they were ready to strike their blow for the old religion and Mary's right to the succession. 'He is a rare bird,' said Sussex, the Lord President at York, when the standard was finally raised, 'that hath not some of his [kin] with the two Earls, or in his heart, wisheth not well to the cause they pretend.' As Sadler noted, 'if the father came to us with ten men, his son goes to the rebels with twenty.' Throughout the summer they had been preparing for battle, holding meetings 'to allure the gentlemen', right under Sussex's nose. There was overwhelming sympathy for Mary and men told tales of their fathers' bravery in the Pilgrimage of

Grace, which had so seriously threatened the monarchy of Henry VIII.

Because of his friendship with the Duke, Sussex was under a cloud in September, and both Queen and Secretary thought he knew more of Norfolk's plans than they did and felt he was not acting vigorously enough against the dissidents; were he to side with the Earls the north would indeed be lost. He did his best to assure the Queen that despite his affection for Norfolk, whom he was sure was an innocent conspirator, this high personal regard counted as nothing beside his devotion to his sovereign, 'for he had always hitched his staff at her door.' He wished he could come to London to justify himself, rather than write, and there was indeed talk of recalling him for examination, but the rapid development of events made it imperative for Elizabeth to pin her faith on him, and he did not disappoint her. He was above all calm, refusing to believe the thousand rumours, and wanted to treat the problem in his own way without interference from court. He called the Earls of Northumberland and Westmorland to York on 9 October to require their help in ending rumours and sent them home to be on hand to deal with any hotheads. 'I trust the fire is spent with the smoke', he told Cecil – 'a great bruit of an intended rebellion, the cause of which is yet unknown and which I think is now at an end.' Any premature action on his part would make the dying embers flare up; he knew the men he was dealing with and realized that those at Windsor could not possibly grasp the intricacies of the local problems. Elizabeth was aghast at his complacency and his underestimating of the gravity of the situation and feared he was treating the Earls with far more sympathy than they deserved. She decided she would deal with them as she had dealt with the Duke and on 24 October she ordered Sussex to send for them at once and in her name summon them to court. At the same time, so doubtful was she of Sussex's loyalty, that she asked other members of the Council in the North to report individually on the situation.

Sussex told Elizabeth that his Council was unanimous that it was best to postpone an examination of the cause of the recent disaffection and to delay sending for the Earls until dead of winter, but since she had come to different conclusions he would do as she had bidden. The causes of the present discontents, he reported, were various and confused – 'some specially respect the Duke of Norfolk, some the Scottish Queen, some religion and some, perhaps, all three.' Sir George Bowes and the other leading members of the Council in the North made similar observations:

Upon the first bruit of a marriage between the Duke of Norfolk and the Scottish Queen, the papists much rejoiced and imagined that religion would be altered, and thereby took encouragement to speak liberally against the Protestants. . . . In the nick thereof, news came that the Duke had left the court and gone into Norfolk, and that thereupon the Earls of Northumberland and Westmorland had caused their servants to take up their horses and be in readiness . . . When the Duke returned to court it was bruited that the confederants in their assembly asked that religion should be the cause of their stir, upon which point it was said they disagreed, and so departed.

All at York agreed that the best policy for avoiding further troubles was to turn as blind an eye as possible to recent events. But the Queen at Windsor could not share Sussex's calm, and forced him into employing tactics which he knew to be fundamentally wrong.⁹

The Earls feared that if they submitted, as Norfolk had done, they would like him be sent to the Tower. At first both excused their attendance at York and then Sussex sent them a *pursuivant*, charging them on their allegiance to report to him. Northumberland promised to come in a day or so, when his business was settled, but Westmorland stoutly refused to obey: 'I dare not come where my enemies are, without bringing such a force to protect me as might be misliked; therefore I think it better to stay at home and use myself as an obedient subject.' His wife had stiffened his resolution and warned him against putting his head in a noose. The Lord President had now to write again, setting down what he had proposed to tell them in person, namely to repair to court on their allegiance. They were to beware of the counsel 'of such as would show you honey and deliver you poison, and stand, as noblemen, upon your honour and truth, for it will stand by you.' They were not to be scared of their own shadows but to submit with humility to the Queen's clemency, otherwise a show of wilful disobedience might provoke her into acting with extremity. But while Sussex's messenger, who carried this letter, was still at Topcliffe, Northumberland's home, towards midnight on 9 November, he heard the bells of the church ring backwards, as the signal to raise the standard of revolt. Northumberland rode south to Brancepeth to join Westmorland and found him at a council of war with the Sheriff of Yorkshire, Richard Norton, and his sons, the Markenfields, Tempests and Swinburnes who had assembled with bands of armed retainers. They discussed whether they should flee the realm, fight to the finish or submit. A letter from Sussex gave them one final chance before proclaiming them as outlaws, yet when they were about to return to their homes Lady Westmorland, Norfolk's sister Jane, swayed them into action. In tears she goaded them: 'We and our country were shamed for ever, that now in the end we should seek holes to creep into.' This was decisive and next day, to show their hand, the Earls rode off to Durham, stormed the cathedral, tore up the prayer-book and English bible and attended mass. After eleven years of peace England was plunged into civil war.

Whatever their earlier hesitations and disagreements, the rebels now made plain that they rose in defence of the Catholic faith, for the religious issue was the only one that could command widespread support; the Earls could hide their own disobedience to their sovereign under the cloak of religion, though in all their edicts they maintained they were acting as true and faithful subjects of the crown. When they went in solemn procession to mass in Ripon Cathedral the Earls' men bore on their backs crusaders' crosses to show they had armed themselves for a holy war, and followed the cross, borne by old Sheriff Norton, with the banner of the five wounds of Christ and the words *In hoc signo vinces*. In the Earls' first proclamation they stated that they and others of the ancient nobility were charged to determine 'to whom of mere right the true succession of the crown appertaineth', but their proclamation at Ripon, addressed to all members of the old Catholic religion, had nothing in it about Norfolk or Mary. It ran:

Forasmuch as divers evil-disposed persons about the Queen's Majesty have, by their subtle and crafty dealings to advance themselves, overcome in this our realm the true and Catholic religion towards God and by the same abused the Queen, disordered the realm and now lastly seek and procure the destruction of the nobility, we therefore have gathered ourselves together to resist by force, and the rather by the help of God and you good people, to see redress of those things amiss, with restoring of all ancient customs and liberties to God's Church and his whole realm.[10]

The rebels' proclamation underlined the manifest danger to the Queen personally and tore to shreds the unity of her kingdom. Glib phrases about rescuing the Crown from evil advisers and restoring ancient liberties had been the stock in trade of English rebels for centuries. There was no comfort for her in the reports that men from the Palatinate and north Yorkshire were flocking to the Earls in their thousands, a near feudal tenantry, knowing no prince but a Percy or a Neville, regarding their liege lord with more awe than their anointed Queen. She, who had never travelled further than the southern Midlands, was amazed at the persistence of inbred loyalties:

> A potent vassalage to fight
> In Percy's and in Neville's right.

She cursed as she heard that Sussex, with a gravely depleted militia, had not attempted to stop the rebel army's progress south and now pinned her faith in Hunsdon's main army, which had been hastily collected from the midland shires to oppose them. By 24 November they were at Selby, within striking distance of Tutbury, and in London the chance of their rescuing Mary Queen of Scots seemed very great. The rebels now had Hartlepool in their hands, at which Alva might disembark his Spanish troops. The papists were predicting that Alva would be in London with Spanish troops by Candlemas and force Elizabeth to hear mass in St Paul's Cathedral. She ordered Mary to be removed for greater security to Coventry and prayed for cousin Hunsdon's success.

Overnight on 25 November there was a complete *bouleversement*, for at Tadcaster the Earls decided they must turn back; the way to the south was blocked by Hunsdon, news reached them of supporting armies led by Clinton and by Warwick, and the only course left was a strategic retreat to give battle on their own ground. The heart was taken out of the rebellion at this withdrawal, and as the Earls rode north their army dwindled in the face of wintry weather and internal strife, until they reached Brancepeth, broken and dispirited, on the last day of the month. Though Westmorland succeeded in taking Barnard Castle, largely through the garrison's treachery, the rebellion was petering out. In Durham, at mid-December, the Earls decided to flee while there was still time and with a few horsemen rode across the Pennines to the Dacre fortress of Naworth and from there into Scotland.

All was not quite over, for Leonard Dacre, who had been in London when the rebellion broke and subsequently returned north to render mild assistance to Lord Scrope in the West March, now embarked on a private war by seizing Graystoke Castle and fortifying Naworth with an army collected from the rank-riders of the Borders. Elizabeth could have no peace of mind until he was captured and early in February ordered Hunsdon to seize him. He found Naworth too well defended to justify an attack and moved his army on, intending to join Scrope at Carlisle, but Dacre followed him, to fight a brave action by the banks of the River Cleth on 19 February. He gave 'the proudest charge upon my shot that ever I saw', Hunsdon reported, but the day ended in his flight to Scotland, leaving behind him three hundred dead and many prisoners. When Elizabeth read Hunsdon's account of his victory over Dacre she dictated a warm letter of thanks, adding her own postscript:

I doubt much my Harry, whether that the victory were given me, more joyed me, or that you were by God appointed the instrument of my glory; and I assure you that for my country's good the first might suffice, but for my heart's contentation the second pleased me. . . . And that you may not think that you have done nothing for your profit, though you have done much for honour, I intend to make this journey somewhat to increase your livelihood, that you may not say to yourself, *perditur quod factum est ingrato*. Your loving kinswoman, Elizabeth R.

This was no idle promise, though Hunsdon who had set his heart on 'picking a salad' from Percy lands subsequently refused to take Northumberland to York for execution himself.[11]

In February with Hunsdon's victory, Elizabeth issued a declaration on the rebellion, surveying the developments in church and state since her accession, portraying herself as 'the natural father over her children' and bluntly pointing to the 'manifest danger' of the past months. The Queen also celebrated the suppression of the rebellion in verse:

> The doubt of future foes exiles my present joy,
> And Wit me warns to shun such snares as threaten my annoy,
> For falsehood now doth flow, and subjects' faith doth ebb
> Which would not be if Reason ruled, or Wisdom move the web,
> But clouds of toys untried to cloak aspiring minds,
> Which turn to rain of late repent by course of changed winds.
> The top of hope supposed, the root of ruth will be,
> And fruitless all their grafted guiles, as ye shall shortly see.
> Those dazzled eyes with pride, which great ambition blinds,
> Shall be unsealed by worthy wights, whose foresight falsehood blinds.
> The daughter of debate, that eke discord doth sow,
> Shall reap no gain where former rule hath taught still peace to grow.
> No foreign banish'd wight shall anchor in this port;
> Our realm it brooks no stranger's force, let them elsewhere resort;
> Our rusty sword, with rest, shall first his edge employ,
> To poll their tops that seek such change, and gape for joy.

She was merciless in her revenge. Sussex had sent the Privy Council his proposals about punishment, suggesting the execution of a handful of insurgents as an example and imprisoning those captives with lands to escheat to the crown, but the Queen commanded much harsher reprisals to be made, and as a result some seven hundred and fifty rebels were executed according to martial law, while a further sixty awaited special sessions at Durham, York and Carlisle. 'You may not execute any that hath freehold, nor noted wealthy, for so is the Queen's Majesty's pleasure', Sussex told his henchman, Sir George Bowes – in other words pardons and reprieves were only to go to those who could afford them; at least the fines and forfeitures would help reduce the heavy bill for suppressing the revolt. Over two thousand of the smaller fry who had followed the Earls paid a fine according to their means and, providing they took the oath of allegiance, were pardoned, but the poorest were in danger of the scaffold. The vast estates of the two Earls, of Dacre, the Nortons, Swinburne and Tempest became forfeit to the crown and while some properties, such as Raby, were retained for strategic reasons, most of these lands were parcelled out by grants and leases to Hunsdon and his followers. This redistribution of property in the north country was much more extensive than the leases and sales of monastic estates of the previous generation and brought to the area a class of landlords who broke the old particularism. Parallel to these upheavals, the court of high commission in the province of York and the church courts in each diocese were active in seeking out offenders, so that hundreds of the clergy were deprived of their benefices. The north country was never the same again.[12]

Despite his share of blame for provoking the northern rebellion, Elizabeth found she could not charge Norfolk with high treason. That her own cousin and the head of her nobility should have behaved as he had done was the greatest blow she had suffered. She called him 'traitor', and when Cecil sent her extracts from the Treasons Statute of Edward III's reign to show he was innocent of such a crime, an interpretation with which the Council agreed, she was almost beside herself. She cried out that she could cut off his head of her own authority, and then appeared to faint. Certainly, in the existing state of politics he was too dangerous a subject to be freed from the Tower, for he had trafficked 'with the daughter of discord'. A forceful pamphlet by Walsingham, then ambassador in Paris, and later to play a key role in bringing Mary to her execution, covered the ground very fully. The fact that Mary was a Guise through and through – 'a race that is both enemy to God and the common quiet of Europe' – an ardent Catholic, and a competitor of Elizabeth for the throne, spelt danger and discord. The proposals linking Mary with Norfolk could be no love match, for they had never set eyes on each other, and he could hardly credit it that a man of religious principles, who respected worldly honour and regarded his own safety, would want to marry the Scottish idolatress for any but *political* reasons. Both partners in furthering their ambitions had plunged the country into civil war, 'for the thirst of a kingdom can never be quenched until it hath hazarded the uttermost trial.' Elizabeth could clearly not countenance the Duke's release, but she did not know how to deal with him any more than she knew how to deal with Mary.[13]

A new twist to the whole affair came with the publication of the bull *Regnans in Excelsis*, by which Pope Pius V deposed Elizabeth and absolved her Catholic subjects from allegiance to her. Rome moved in a mysterious way, and tardily. Had the bull arrived to coincide with the rebellion in the previous November it might have brought many waverers to the northern earls and stiffened the resistance of those who gave up the fight after Tadcaster. But its publication by John Felton at the gates of the Bishop of London's palace in St Paul's in May, three months after Dacre's flight, was an anachronism. More than the rebellion itself, the bull provoked a spate of penal legislation against Roman Catholics which was to be rigorously enforced, and turned every practising papist into a traitor. For the Queen Pope Pius's action was a piece of insufferable insolence. 'Deprived of her pretended right to the realm', indeed! 'A heretic and an abettor of heretics', without dominion, dignity and privilege whatsoever, a price was put on her head and for her Catholic subjects the strain of having to choose between sovereign and pope was intolerable. Not a few became fugitives, joining those rebels who had escaped from justice in England to the continent; for all of the faith who continued to obey the Queen were liable to sentence of anathema.

At midsummer Norfolk had made a fulsome submission in writing, craving the Queen's forgiveness for his offence in following the will-o'-the-wisp of the match with Mary, to which he had been persuaded 'for Your Highness benefit and surety', and vowing 'never to deal in that cause of marriage of the Queen of Scots, nor in any other cause belonging to her, but as Your Majesty shall command me.' He hoped that his statement would persuade her to release him. Only a few of the Duke's most trusted intimates knew that the draft of this submission had been conned by Mary herself! Walsingham, for one, was highly sceptical of the document, for Norfolk had written nothing to show that he now misliked Mary, her title or her claim to the English throne; he could also argue that such a marriage might still be in Elizabeth's interests, and he could always maintain that this very renunciation of her was void if they had a prior contract – 'which excuse would be well liked in such a case of conscience of marriage, or of weighty commodity as a crown.' In the event, because of the Duke's ill health and the danger from the plague to which all inmates of the Tower were liable, he was allowed to continue his confinement in his own residence, Howard House, formerly the Charterhouse. Here before long he became trapped in the snares of the Florentine financier Roberto Ridolfi, the man from whom Felton had obtained copies of the papal bull.[14]

Ridolfi concluded from the events of 1569 that the English were too inexperienced to plan their own revolutions. By nature an inveterate plotter, he was thick with the Spanish ambassador, the Bishop of Ross and others with schemes for rescuing Mary Queen of Scots. Her only hope was in a concerted rising of her English friends, strongly aided by money and arms from the Catholic powers. Ridolfi was convinced that every other Englishman was an ardent Catholic at heart who would fervently take arms in obedience to the Pope and reckoned that as many as thirty-three peers of the realm could be counted on, who could muster between them 39,000 men. He drafted letters in Norfolk's name to Pius V, the Duke of Alva and Philip of Spain to support their holy cause, and though the Duke shrank from signing them, he gave his verbal assent. Spain was to provide an experienced general commanding an army of six thousand trained soldiers who would land at Harwich, merge with an English force raised by the Duke and his friends, rescue Mary, capture Elizabeth and take the capital. With his letters allegedly from Norfolk and authority from Mary, Ridolfi went to Brussels, Madrid and Rome to canvass potential allies, but Alva thought the proposals foolhardy. Fighting a hard campaign against William of Orange he had neither men nor money to spare for so doubtful an enterprise; and he predicted that failure would increase the plight of the English Catholics and almost certainly provoke Elizabeth into executing Mary. Alva wrote to Philip, warning him off the scheme: Queen

Elizabeth 'being dead (naturally or otherwise) or else a prisoner, there will be an opportunity which we must not allow to escape.' But the initiative must come from the Catholics in England; only when they had shown they were capable of achieving their *coup* should Spain send aid. But Ridolfi with his ciphered messages, babbling his way across Europe, failed to appreciate that realist statesmen thought his grand design a piece of wishful thinking. His cipher was not even fool-proof, and others of his team were recklessly careless.

Ignorant of the web of intrigue being spun by Ridolfi, Elizabeth was again seriously considering whether Mary's restoration to Scotland might not be the way out of the dilemma. She knew that so long as Mary remained on English soil she would be the centre and soul of opposition to her. The sympathy Mary was winning from stout Englishmen was alarming, and the pressure from France and Spain for obtaining her release was increasing; indeed, the Duke of Anjou, whom Elizabeth was beginning to court, warned her that unless she took steps to restore Mary to her proper dignity and meanwhile treated her 'in a kind and honourable manner, he should send forces openly to her assistance.' The complications of Scottish politics had increased by the assassination of the Regent Murray in January 1570, and before she could begin fresh negotiations she decided to send Sussex to harry the Borders and beyond, as a reprisal for raids into England by fugitives from the rebel army of the northern earls. Sussex's men sacked fortresses, burnt villages and slew with a new vengeance on this, the last of a long series of punitive expeditions from the Marches that stretched to remote times. That accomplished, Elizabeth again put to her Council the question of Mary. Most councillors, led by Cecil, opted for unstinted support of the infant James's party, which meant sending more English money to Edinburgh; but Elizabeth preferred a new attempt at negotiations with Mary, through the Bishop of Ross. James was to be sent to England as a hostage to be educated for kingship away from rival factions and the influence of the Kirk. At long last Mary was prepared to renounce her claim to the throne of England in favour of Elizabeth and her issue – 'her lawful issue', insisted the other, whereat Elizabeth growled to Cecil, 'she may, peradventure, measure other folk's dispositions by her own actions.' But when the commissioners of the infant James arrived in February 1571, stalemate was soon reached and they excused themselves by saying they had no powers to sign a treaty without first calling a Parliament in Edinburgh. Before further progress could be made came the *dénouement* of the Ridolfi plot, which changed the entire situation.[15]

A messenger of the Bishop of Ross, Charles Bailly, had been searched at Dover and found to be carrying letters from Ridolfi, which Bailly had himself put into cipher. We need not concern ourselves with the complicated by-plots of the intrigue, but after many weeks in the Tower Bailly broke down and gave his interrogators the broad outlines of the conspiracy, stating that the numbers '30' and '40', the addressees of the letters he brought, each stood for an English peer. Ross was now examined, told a pack of lies and was placed under house arrest, while reports began coming in from agents in the European capitals of a widespread plot, involving foreign troops, that had as its object Elizabeth's deposition and Mary's enthronement. Then a messenger carrying a bag from Howard House to Lawrence Bannister in Shropshire became suspicious, because of its weight and provenance, and found inside French gold and a letter in cipher that were intended for Mary's supporters in Scotland. Norfolk's secretaries were examined and threatened with the rack and on 7 September the Duke was escorted back to the Tower. A letter from Mary to him, found under the mat 'towards my lord's bed-chamber, where the map of England doth hang', once deciphered, was enough to hang a man. Never before had investigations into a case of high treason been conducted with such thoroughness, or given rise to such volumes of paper. When enough had been wrung from the Duke, his servants and accomplices, he would go for trial before his peers. The only individual to escape examination was the arch-conspirator Ridolfi, who learnt of the collapse of his grand design in Brussels, where he was pitied for his foolhardy incompetence alike by Spanish and by English émigrés.

On hearing of the Duke's rearrest Mary burst out that all she had tried to do was to regain her rightful crown and 'those who said that she had done more were false villains and lied in their throats'; as for Norfolk, he was Elizabeth's subject, and for him she had 'nothing to say'. To save his skin Ross eventually told his interrogators everything he knew, revealing all that happened since his conversations with Norfolk at the York Conference three years past. His statements proved the Duke's guilt to the hilt and incriminated a host of others, including Lords Arundel, Lumley, Southampton and Cobham, and the Spanish ambassador. The Bishop felt relieved to have confessed so fully, for Mary, he said, was not fit to have another husband, for she had poisoned her first (Francis II), consented to the murder of the second (Darnley), married the murderer (Bothwell) and then led him out to the field of battle that he too might be murdered. Such a betrayal – even by 'the solicitor of a lawfully deposed Queen' – astounded the judicious Dr Wilson, to whom these confidences were made. 'Lord, what a people are these;' he wrote to Cecil, 'what a Queen, and what an ambassador!' Ross was given leave to write to Mary, advising her that it had been incumbent on him to reveal everything, and regretting they had 'ever meddled with such things.' Mary would not believe that he had betrayed her and burst out to her custodian, Shrewsbury, that he was 'a flayed and fearful priest', whose admissions could only have been extracted by the rack and the thumbscrew. The hand of the letter to her was indeed Esau's, 'but the voice was Jacob's.'[16]

For Elizabeth the manifest danger was past, now that the Ridolfi conspiracy had been unravelled, but she could take little comfort in the details of the examinations and confessions of those in the Tower, for they showed how many of her nobles had been involved in Norfolk's schemings to a greater or lesser degree. As she looked round the court, as she eyed the bearded figures at her council table, whom could she trust beside Burghley, the faithful secretary she had at long last raised to the peerage in February? Already Lumley was locked in the Marshalsea Prison, Southampton, another zealous Catholic, was in custody at Cecil House and Arundel was under house arrest. Cobham was soon to be arrested and the young Earl of Oxford, about to become Burghley's son-in-law, was behaving as irresponsibly as ever. At least one of

Derby's sons and a stepson of Shrewsbury were in the plot, while over the water and north of the border were others intriguing for all they were worth. She could not easily forget Leicester's share as the unauthorized broker in bringing Norfolk and Mary together in the summer of 1569, and now there were tales, by no means unfounded, that Sir Christopher Hatton, a rising favourite, was uncertain in his loyalties. Apart from Burghley she could only rely upon Bacon, Knollys, Sadler and Hunsdon among her inner circle of councillors and none of these was popular, least of all Burghley. Since Norfolk was connected by descent or marriage with the whole body of the ancient nobility, there were moments when she doubted whether they would in fact find him guilty when he went before them. She had already moved into White-hall for Christmas by the time the law officers had finished preparing their case, and she felt that a state trial in Westminster Hall, so near at hand, would cast a gloom over the traditional festivities.

She need not have worried about the outcome of the state trial, for at the end of the long day's hearing on 16 January, without equivocation every peer present found the Duke guilty of high treason. After sentence he wrote to her abjectly repenting and asking that she might look tenderly over his children and step-children. She sent a message next day agreeing to his suggestion that Burghley should become their guardian, and this care of hers 'for my poor unfortunate brats' moved him deeply. Elizabeth signed his death warrant on 9 February, but next day cancelled it, as she professed 'a great mislike that the Duke should die'. Indeed she could not make up her mind whether or not to allow the law to take its course. One day, as Burghley told Walsingham with feeling, mindful of her own peril, she was determined that justice should be done, yet the next, when she considered Norfolk's 'nearness of blood, of his superiority of honour she stayeth.' Until now no peer of the realm in her reign had suffered on Tower Hill and she desperately wanted to show clemency to her cousin. She looked back to her own days in the Tower, 'much suspected' and to the affair with Seymour, earlier still, which had cost him his head, even as Norfolk's courtship of Mary by proxy had brought him the sentence of traitor.[17]

When Parliament assembled on 8 May member after member demanded Norfolk's speedy execution and Mary's own trial. He was 'a roaring lion' and she 'a monstrous and huge dragon' who would plague the realm so long as there was breath left in either of them. As their names had been tragically linked together in love, so should their persons suffer together as attainted. A Clytemnestra, who had killed her husband and committed adultery, Mary was convicted by the evidence of Norfolk's trial of treachery by the laws of England and must suffer as those laws required. Elizabeth, said one member, should 'cut off her head and make no more ado about her.' And had she so acted then men would have thought her fully justified. 'You saith she [Mary] is a Queen's daughter and therefore ought to be spared. Nay then, argued Thomas Norton, 'spare the Queen's Majesty that is a King's daughter and our own Queen.'[18]

Then at last Burghley persuaded Elizabeth that sentence against the Duke could be delayed no longer. 'The adverse party must needs increase when they see justice forbear against the principal and him spared to set up the mark', he had written, and he knew that unless he got his own way over Norfolk, there would be little hope of persuading the Queen to come to grips with the problem of Mary. She could not hold out indefinitely against the logic of statecraft and at last, after five months' procrastination, she signed the warrant. For years to come her cousin's death would gnaw at her conscience and she would lay the blame for it on Burghley. Norfolk's blood made Parliament clamour the more mercilessly for Mary's. So long as she lived 'the manifest danger' to Elizabeth remained. 'If you strike not at the root,' thundered John Knox in Edinburgh, 'the branches that appear to be broke will bud again', and the bishops in Westminster, drawing on St Paul as well as the old testament, set out to persuade their Queen that it was her inescapable Christian duty to administer justice severely and uprightly; she 'must needs offend in conscience before God if she do not punish' Mary according to the full terror of her offence. But Elizabeth stopped Parliament single-handed from proceeding against Mary by a bill of attainder, and instead a measure was brought in depriving her of her pretended title to the throne, declaring anyone who suggested her claim in any way to be guilty of treason and making her liable to trial by the peers of the realm if she plotted further against the Queen. The bill 'concerning Mary, daughter of James the Fifth, late King of Scotland, called the Queen of Scots' passed both Houses, yet the detailed drafting and the fiery debates had been in vain, for on the last day of the sessions, four weeks after Norfolk's execution, Elizabeth vetoed this effort at her own preservation.[19]

She had reigned for nearly fourteen years and was still single and had deliberately left the problem of her succession still in the air. She was at odds with her Council, with both Houses of Parliament and with Convocation, and the unity she had striven for in religion had been shattered. England was still isolated, without an ally in Christendom, a negligible country, weak, poor and divided against itself. Had Elizabeth died in 1572 she would have gone down in history as an unremarkable failure, who had broken faith with all who had put their trust in her at the joyous moment of her accession and had been proved by events to be incapable of living up to the promise expected of her father's daughter. But there was soon a new spirit abroad and it stemmed from the sovereign herself.

8

'LA PLUS FINE
FEMME DU MONDE'

A SUDDEN, serious illness in April 1572 brought home to the
Queen and those around her the gravity of all the unresolved
problems. Elizabeth thought her trouble due to something she had
eaten, but it was most probably a fit of colic, complicated by
fever. She said she felt certain she was going to die and for three
nights Leicester and Burghley kept vigil at her bedside, watching
the thread of this one life, on which a kingdom depended, so near
to snapping. The sins of her procrastinations and indecisions would
plague her subjects after she had been called to her fathers, unless
she could be made to see reason. Ten years ago at Hampton
Court they had waited anxiously for her recovery from smallpox
and known the settlement of the succession could be delayed no
longer, yet a whole decade had come and gone with nothing
achieved, despite weighty arguments in Council, loyal addresses
from Parliament and a small fortune spent on special embassies.
Now, with the danger past, she was as affectionate towards
Leicester as she had ever been and even said she was contemplating marrying him.[1]

Certainly Elizabeth had been thinking seriously about marriage
for some time. Half-heartedly she had picked up the threads of the
old Hapsburg negotiations, partly to make sure that no further
developments were possible, partly to advertise the fact that she
was not averse to marriage with a suitable prince. She sent Sir
Henry Cobham to tell the Emperor that she had been unable
until now to give a considered reply to the Archduke Charles's
last proposition, because of 'frequent illness' and the wars in

France and Flanders. If Charles would at last come over to see her, he would be very welcome and they might try together to find some way out of the religious difficulties. The Emperor Maximilian was taken aback at the revival of this long dormant suit and replied that his brother Charles, not imagining that Elizabeth would have delayed answering his proposal for three whole years if she were serious about him, had turned his thoughts to another princess 'with whom there could be no disputes on the subject of religion', namely his niece the Duchess of Bavaria. For his part Charles was full of regrets that Elizabeth had not accepted him at the proper time and hoped she would always look on him as a brother. She at least knew where she stood; though according to one report she felt so greatly insulted – she, the Queen of England, rejected for a mere duchess – that she vowed had she been a man to have challenged the Holy Roman Emperor to a duel. Charles's wedding and the marriage of Charles IX of France to Elizabeth of Austria the same year again rubbed in her spinsterhood.[2]

To end her unenviable isolation in a hostile Europe Elizabeth sorely needed to come to an understanding with France. Estrangement from Spain had reached the danger-point. Spanish reprisals for her seizure of the treasure ships in 1568 were still in force and there was little sign of preparedness to negotiate a settlement that would restore England's trade to its traditional markets, and in the last days of 1571 her expulsion of de Spes, the Spanish ambassador, for his share in the Ridolfi plot, aggravated the situation. Meanwhile had come the astonishing news of Don John of Austria's resounding victory over the Turkish fleet at Lepanto and the discomforting tidings of the Marians' seizure of Edinburgh, leading to the death of Lennox. Puritans such as Walsingham urged the Queen to advance the gospel, in the face of Catholic aggression on every side, by aiding the French Huguenots and giving open assistance to Louis of Nassau and William of Orange in their fight to throw off the Spanish yoke in Holland and Zeeland, but she was too much of a realist. She would subsidize the Huguenots underhand to keep the French civil wars going only so long as a divided France suited her policy, but she would not court disaster by embarking on a costly and bloody crusade to advance Dutch

Calvinism. Elizabeth wanted peace in the Low Countries, so that England's trade could prosper as of old, and she viewed with alarm the prospect of French intervention, which Count Louis of Nassau eagerly invited, for it would be no less menacing to her than French domination in Scotland. She saw herself cast in the blessed role of peacemaker and aimed at mediation, to hold the balance of power in north-west Europe, but she was still not yet strong enough to dictate terms to Hapsburg and Valois, or force Spanish, Flemings and Dutch to settle their differences. Yet there was one trump card she could play in the great diplomatic game and that was her marriageability.

Round about Christmas 1570 when Fénélon, the French ambassador, paid her a visit he found her much more attractively dressed than usual, and she began talking about Charles IX's wedding. Fénélon said he was sorry he could not congratulate her on her own marriage and she parried by admitting how much she regretted not thinking in time about her want of posterity; if she did take a husband, it should only be one from a royal house, of rank suitable to hers. Taking the hint, the ambassador suggested that the only possible candidate was the Duke of Anjou, brother of the French King, as 'the most accomplished prince in the world and the only person worthy of marrying her'. Elizabeth understood that Henry of Anjou was in love with the Princess of Cleves, though she knew all about his excellent qualities. 'But I am an old woman and am ashamed to talk about a husband, were it not for the sake of an heir. In the past I have been courted by some who would rather marry the kingdom than marry the Queen, as generally happens with the great, who marry without seeing one another.' She and Fénélon were continually bantering in this style for many more private audiences before proposals were properly launched. Katherine de Medici had come to the conclusion that she did not intend to marry and, looking for a suitable bride for Anjou, had wondered whether Elizabeth might name a female successor to whom he could be betrothed; the suggestion was a ridiculous one, but it had made Elizabeth think she might like Anjou for herself. She understood he had been brought up by a man 'not averse to the Protestant religion'.[3]

The only thing she said she worried about was Anjou's age. Fénélon assured her 'he bore himself already like a man.' 'Yet he will always be younger than me', she commented; and Leicester, who was with them, added with a smile 'So much the better for you.' Fénélon's advice was that any queen or princess who yearned for true wedded happiness with an ever faithful consort should turn to the House of Valois, but this was too much for Elizabeth's sense of fun and she replied that tales of Madame d'Estampes and Madame de Valentinois made her worry whether the man who honoured her as a queen would also love her as a woman. The arrival of Cardinal Châtillon at that moment with draft articles for a marriage treaty between Elizabeth and Anjou called the meeting to order. For France the prospect of such a match was indeed alluring and Charles IX was not overdoing the compliment when he referred to Elizabeth as '*la plus fine femme du monde*.' The scheming Katherine de Medici would gladly have found any suitable niche for Henry of Anjou away from France, but to have found him a kingdom would have been incredible luck – so incredible, with Elizabeth's past record of courtships, she could not believe she was in earnest.[4]

There is no doubt that Elizabeth initially intended to use the marriage negotiations as a diplomatic exercise, to be protracted for as long as possible and abandoned in due course, though if in the end of the affair she were actually to fall in love with Anjou that would be different. In the early 1570s she still gave the strong impression of being very fond of suitors and most averse to husbands, and the more she learnt about Anjou the less promising it all seemed, for the Duke was ultra-Catholic in his sympathies and had been far too friendly with the Guises. At the English court there was a good deal of idle chatter about Anjou, some of it instigated by Leicester. What a pity, said one of her ladies in waiting that Monsieur were not a year or so older; but Elizabeth reprimanded her: 'He is 20 now and may be rated at 25 for his intellect and physique.' The Lord Chamberlain told a *risqué* story about Anjou visiting Rouen to see a beautiful Flemish girl, but the Queen minded this far less than suggestions of incompatibility on the score of age. She privately asked two of her most faithful

ladies for their free opinion on the proposed match and Lady
Clinton commended the project, saying she must not be put off
by Monsieur's youth, 'for he was virtuous and Her Majesty was
better calculated to please him than any other princess in the
world.' Unwittingly, Lady Cobham was less tactful, for while
approving of the marriage she added a rider that 'those marriages
were always the happiest when the parties were the same age, or
near about it, but that here there was a great inequality.' 'Nonsense!' broke in the Queen. 'There are but ten years difference
between us' – it was, of course, nearer twenty! She quizzed
Norris, the retiring ambassador in Paris, very closely on the
Duke's appearance and, well-satisfied that he was handsome, tried
to hatch a scheme for him to pay a flying visit to England incognito. She would arrange to be on progress in Kent and he could
easily slip across from France by the morning tide and, if they
took an unfavourable view of each other, he need not prolong
his stay but return the same night. Anjou was not prepared to fall
in with these plans, so Elizabeth had to be content with two recent
portraits. Some hasty words of the Duke's, that he would never
dream of marrying the Queen of England 'for she was not only an
old creature, but had a sore leg', were duly reported to her and
she was exceedingly cross, until after too long an interval Katherine de Medici proffered an apology.[5]

By mid-February 1571, Leicester was writing to Sir Francis
Walsingham, the new ambassador in Paris: 'I perceive Her
Majesty more bent to marry than heretofore she hath been.'
Elizabeth herself told Walsingham, after a long rigmarole about
her natural preference for the single life and the many occasions
on which she had been pressed by suitors, even in her father's
reign, that she 'thankfully accepted' Anjou's offer and instructed
him to put forward the marriage treaty of Philip and Mary as the
basis for discussion. 'She could not prevent his exercising that form
of religion in England which was prohibited by the laws of the
realm', but hoped for some modus vivendi. This was hardly an
encouragement for a Roman Catholic no less staunch in his
belief than the Archduke Charles. Burghley, reluctant to drop
the Hapsburgs for the Valois, had initially opposed opening

negotiations with the chance of success so slender, but by now he had convinced himself of the importance of the marriage. 'If I be not much deceived,' he wrote to Walsingham, 'Her Majesty is earnest in this' and he warned him to play down the religious differences in order to keep discussion open. Burghley, whose only way to justify a change of mind was to set down a lengthy memorandum, had concluded that Elizabeth would now marry for 'the benefit of her realm and to content her subjects.' There would be the strong possibility of children and the people would still hope the crown would remain in King Henry's noble line, and it followed that 'the curious and dangerous question of the succession would in the minds of quiet subjects, be, as it were, buried – a happy funeral for all England.' There would be difficulties enough, but England would be insured against a civil war and immune from the crusades of Catholic powers.[6]

In April 1571 Guido Cavalcanti, Katherine de Medici's Italian agent, came over with a formal offer of Anjou's hand. In a cloak and dagger manner he was stopped as he landed at Dover and taken under guard to Burghley's London house for secret talks before he was allowed to go to the French embassy. The terms demanded by the French were that Anjou should be crowned King the day after the wedding and rule jointly with Elizabeth, he should be granted an income of £60,000 a year and be allowed with all his household the free exercise of the Catholic religion. There was the precedent of Philip's joint rule with Mary to allow for Anjou's coronation, and the income, too, Elizabeth was prepared to sanction, but the religious articles were out of the question. This was the point at which the negotiations with Archduke Charles had foundered in 1567 and in the intervening years so much had happened to harden her against Rome; Anjou's supreme pontiff had deposed her for heresy and had tarred her Catholic subjects with the brush of treason. Could not the French see the impossibility of her giving way to their demands? She might perhaps excuse a consort from attending Anglican services in public, but wider concessions were out of the question. Reluctant to end the affair, she flirted with the idea of converting Anjou, as Helena had converted Constantine, and continued to woo him

with words and presents, sending him a stag she had shot while
hunting in Oatlands Park and imploring him to visit her. It is
clear that if the French were obstinate on the religious issue, she
was equally obstinate in not being prepared to commit herself to
marry someone she had never seen. For the remainder of 1571 it
was assumed that the most that could be salvaged from the negotiations would be a defensive alliance between the two countries. It
was Leicester's view of the Anjou match that Elizabeth had 'some
desire to marry, but it was very cold and that she persuaded herself
it was rather behooveful she should marry, than that she had any
will of herself to marry.' It was left to Sir Thomas Smith to give
the *coup de grâce* to the marriage project in the early days of the
new year, for when Katherine de Medici said that her obstinate
son insisted on openly practising his religion, with all its ceremonies, if he came over as Elizabeth's husband, Smith burst out,
'Why, Madame, then he may require also the four orders of
friars, monks, canons, pilgrimages, pardons, oil and cream,
reliques and all such trumperies', which was utterly absurd. Only
two days later Katherine invited discussion on an Anglo-French
league and, as a substitute for Anjou, put forward the name of her
younger son, the Duke of Alençon, 'a much less scrupulous
fellow'. For the next ten years the possibility of Elizabeth actually
marrying Alençon was to be touch and go.[7]

But already a new star was in the ascendant. Elizabeth had first set
eyes on Christopher Hatton as a young lawyer at a masque given
at Gray's Inn in 1564 and found a place for him in her corps of
Gentlemen Pensioners, a personal bodyguard whose duties were
largely ceremonial. A well-proportioned figure, an exquisite
dancer and a man of 'modest sweetness of manner' it was but
natural that he should flourish in the hot-house atmosphere of the
court. He was thirty-one before the Queen's favours towards him
began provoking just such slanders as Leicester's conduct had
stimulated a dozen years earlier. One scurrilous attack on Elizabeth (albeit by a papist who had made a half-hearted attempt to
assassinate Burghley) mentioned her *penchant* for dancers and said
that Hatton 'had more recourse unto Her Majesty in her Privy

Chamber than reason would suffer if she were so virtuous and well inclined as some noiseth her.' Later that same year, 1572, his appointment as Captain of the Gentlemen Pensioners, in succession to Sir Francis Knollys, did nothing to scotch the gossips. His position as favourite was vulnerable, too, from rivals. Leicester, thoroughly put out, offered to introduce Elizabeth to a dancing-master whose agility would make Hatton seem leaden-footed, but the Queen would not be drawn. 'Pish,' she is supposed to have snubbed the Earl, 'I will not see your man – it is his *trade*.' The advent at court of young Oxford made Hatton intensely jealous for a season as Elizabeth 'delighteth more in his personage and his dancing and valiantness than any other.' But Oxford was married to Burghley's daughter while Hatton was a bachelor who believed himself to be passionately in love with his Queen.[8]

In May 1573 he had a serious complaint of the kidneys and Elizabeth not only visited his bedside daily but insisted, when he was well enough to travel, on his going for a cure to Spa in the Low Countries, under the care of her physician, Dr Julio. While away from court he penned a series of remarkable letters to her. Leaving her was a grief and never again would illness or fear of death persuade him to absent himself from her side for a single day. Away from her, 'I lack that I live by ... To serve you is heaven, but to lack you is more than hell's torment.' Only the opportunity of putting his thoughts about her on paper made her absence bearable·

I will wash away the faults of these letters with the drops from your poor Lydds and so inclose them. Would God I were with you but for one hour. My wits are overwrought with thoughts. I find myself amazed. Bear with me, my most dear sweet Lady. Passion overcometh me. I can write no more. Love me; for I love you ...

From Antwerp he bemoaned that it was twelve days since he 'saw the brightness of that Sun that giveth light unto my sense and soul.' He would have her live for ever and pleaded with her 'to love some man, to show yourself thankful for God his high labour in you. I am too far off to hear your answer to this salutation; I know it would be full of virtue and great wisdom, but I fear for some part thereof I should have but small thanks.' Despite the distance between them she must never forget 'your Lidds that are so often bathed with tears for your sake. A more wise man may seek you, but a more faithful and worthy can never have you.'[9]

What are we to make of these effusive pledges of love, these lines so charged with high personal emotion? Addressed to any ordinary woman they could only be regarded as 'love letters'; but written by a subject to the Queen herself, they fall into another category. Such could not be the currency of mere mortal affections. Elizabeth fed on admiration, demanded the choicest flattery of the men around her and needed as a woman to be quickened by ardent protestations of unswerving devotion from those she favoured most. It is all much larger than life-size, fanciful, brimming over with the superlatives of a chivalry of long ago. This brand of court gallantry, first practised by Dudley, first found its verbal expression in Hatton's prose and would reach a climax in the lyrics of Raleigh. 'In the highly artificial atmosphere in which Elizabeth and her admirers moved,' writes one who has examined the depth of her relationship with Christopher Hatton, the letters are 'no more than unusually exaggerated specimens of an epistolary style which her vanity had made customary and indeed compulsory.'[10] Twenty years on and she was to be 'Fair Gloriana', a nymph-like shepherdess, an ageless fairy-tale figure at a time when most women of her age were grandmothers and she was a wrinkled and bewigged spinster. The nicknames which she gave her courtiers were an essential part of this fantasy. Burghley was her Spirit, Walsingham her Moor and Sir Walter Raleigh a punning 'Water'. Since Leicester was 'Eyes', it followed that Hatton was 'Lids' – Gog and Magog of the presence chamber, each embodying part of the Latin tag she was so fond of quoting – *video et taceo* ('I see, but I keep silence'). Leicester's eyes symbolized her own omnipresence and Hatton's lids represented her own understanding in turning a blind eye, perhaps even in an occasional wink. Both favourites childishly carried their pet names a stage further by using crude symbols in their private letters to Elizabeth, as if cocking a snook at high heraldry, Leicester drawing his 'eyes' as two circles, each surmounted by a squiggle for an

eyebrow, and Hatton sketching two triangles for 'lids'. It was all
in the spirit of intimate family jokes in an age which revelled in
puns.

Another letter of Hatton's at this time, when he was jealous of
Oxford ('The Boar', because of the Earl's crest), refers to his other
pet name, 'The Sheep' or 'Your Mutton.'. His mistress should
reserve her most gracious favour 'to the Sheep – he hath no tooth
to bite; where the Boar's tusk may both rase and tear.' He signed
this not from 'Lids' nor with a drawing of a sheep, but with a
triangular hat, crossed through with an X ('Hat–Ten'). and to
conclude there was a pun on E.R., for in his valediction he was
'Your Slave and EveR your own.'[11]

Now it was Oxford, later it was Raleigh, of whom Hatton was
jealous, but considering their rivalry for the Queen's attentions,
Leicester and Hatton remained down the years remarkably
friendly. Of all the favourites Hatton alone stayed single, devoted
to her person to the end, though at one time he had seriously contemplated marriage with the Countess of Shrewsbury's daughter,
Lady Elizabeth Cavendish. He wept when he was out of favour,
went off to sulk in the country, hoping for her to send a jewel as a
love token, or a message by friend Heneage that all was forgiven
and he was restored to her 'blessed favour'. Lover's tiffs, teasings,
retributions, reconciliation made a regular cycle of their emotional
attachments – which one would expect at a masculine court ruled
by an imperious woman. After one such falling-out Hatton sent
Elizabeth an expensive jewel in the form of a true love's knot, 'the
kind she most loves, and she thinks cannot be undone'. But by
then Hatton knew she would never marry him, or anyone else, as
Leicester had long ago discovered.[12]

Early in 1572 Elizabeth's relations with France were still bedevilled
by the position of Mary Queen of Scots, and there was considerable feeling at the French court that Mary's future should be safeguarded by the treaty under discussion. Until the details of Mary's
complicity in the Ridolfi plot were publicized, Charles IX renewed his protests about the treatment to which she was subjected. But Elizabeth defended herself by her reading from French

Of person rare strong limbes & manly shape,
by nature framed to serue on sea & lande
of Frindshipp firm in good state & ill happe
in peace hedde and in ware skill great boulde ha
on horse on fote in perill or in playe
none coulde excel though many did asaye

A subiecte true to Kinge & seruaunt greate
frind to Gods truth enimye to romes decea
sumptuose abroad for honnor of the lande
temperate at home yet keepte great state &
and gaue more mouthes more meate
then some aduaunst one higher stips to st
yet agaynst native reason & iust lawes
his blood was spilt iustles wthout iust cau

Omnium dilecta Deo, tibi militat æther
Et conjurati Venerunt ad classica venti.

...R THE KINGDOME I HAVE BEENE YOVR QVEENE IN ·S· P · O · R · NOW FOR
...NEITHER WILL I BID YOV GOE AND FIGHT, BVT COIE AND T...Y
...TH OF THE LORDE· FOR WHAT AR TEES PROVD PHILISTINE S TH...
...EWLY THE HOST OF THE LIVIŊ GOD· IT MAY BE THEY WILL CHALL...
...A WOMAN SO NA I CHARGE ...E NOVLL ·BOL THAT...
...E BREATH IS IN THEIRE NOSTRELLS ANDIE G...D DOT...

history. Charles should recall that the French shut up the wives of three kings in a row – the spouses of Lewis Huttin, Philip the Long and Charles the Fair, so there was nothing new, certainly nothing outrageous in Mary's 'honourable custody ... for the safeguard of the realm and mine own security, and that by the example of the French which incarcerated Chilferic in a monastery, Charles of Lorraine in a deep dungeon, and the Duke of Milan into an iron grate to secure their estates.' When news of Mary's intrigues with Ridolfi, the Papacy and Spain reached France Charles IX threw up his hands in despair, 'Ah, the poor fool will never cease until she lose her head. ... I meant to help, but if she will not be helped *je ne puis mais*.' Indeed, at that moment a further letter of Mary's asking for Alva's aid in Scotland had been seized.

.At last, on 19 April, the Treaty of Blois was signed by which England and France undertook to come to each other's aid in case of attack and each promised not to assist the other's enemies. Elizabeth had wanted the clause promising mutual aid against attack by a third party to be extended by the words 'even if attacked on religious grounds'. Not surprisingly this was too much for Charles IX, who feared this would gratuitously incite his Catholic subjects to further intrigues and bloodshed, but he did give Elizabeth a confidential assurance on this very point by covering letter. The French at last recognized the *status quo* in Scotland and, by implication, agreed not to intervene any further on Mary's behalf. The treaty was a remarkable diplomatic triumph for Elizabeth and for the first time in the reign England had an ally.[13]

The way was open for exploring the possibilities of marriage with Alençon. Reports on the Duke came in thick and fast both from Clinton, sent to Paris for the ratification of the Treaty of Blois, and from Walsingham. In religion he was 'easily to be reduced to the knowledge of the truth' but his appearance was disquietening, for his face was badly scarred by smallpox, he had a nose so large that it was out of all proportion to other features and he was almost a dwarf. Walsingham could not believe that his Queen could possibly contemplate marriage with such a person:

'The gentleman sure is void of any good favour, besides the blemish of small-pox . . . I hardly think that there will ever grow any liking.' Moreover he was three years younger than his brother Anjou, and this made the difference in age really alarming. Elizabeth at first asked what compensation she could expect for the injury to his face, hinting broadly at the return of Calais. Fénélon denied that Alençon's face presented an insuperable difficulty even to one 'with such a delicate eye as she'; in any case all the pock marks would be discreetly hidden by a beard in a year or two. He knew a doctor in London who had a simple remedy for smallpox scars and the man was sent to France to try his luck on the royal patient, apparently without much success. All hinged on what Elizabeth thought of the Duke when she saw him, and he could write a wonderful love letter. Alençon had hopefully sent M. Le Mole as a personal envoy, to prepare the way for his own courting as much as to discuss a marriage treaty, and though he was no more than a lad, the Queen took to him instantly and had him sumptuously entertained. It was a hopeful beginning, yet chance of real progress[14] was dashed by news from France of the Massacre of St Bartholomew.

The shedding of so much Huguenot blood in Paris and the larger cities, resulting from Katherine de Medici's plot for the assassination of the Huguenot leader Coligny, spread alarm and despondency in England. Protestant refugees came in boatloads to the south-coast ports with tales of horror and Englishmen by the hundred vowed they would go to La Rochelle to fight for their brother Christians. Elizabeth had enjoyed a happy few days in Leicester's domain, with entertainment at Warwick and Kenilworth, until the spell was broken by the news from France. She moved on to Woodstock and after keeping the French ambassador waiting for three days received him coldly, concerned to learn the official version of the massacre. She had not, as some have said, put her court into mourning, for the last thing she wanted was to break with France and the French were no less anxious to maintain the recent alliance. For a show she ordered the navy to put to sea and caused eight thousand men to be sent to reinforce Sir Humphrey Gilbert's band of 'volunteers' who had been posted to

Zeeland in July to counter French influence there. Puritans longed for her to expel Fénélon and forget all idea of a match with Alençon, but she could not risk acting with such imprudent disdain. So the negotiations continued, but at a slower pace and in greater secrecy, until the christening of the French princess gave the opportunity for a real *rapprochement*; Elizabeth agreed to stand godmother, just to show she was not as much of a heretic as they all made out, though she would not risk Leicester losing his life by going to Paris to represent her at the ceremony and despatched the Earl of Worcester in his place, who in the event came to no personal harm even if pirates plundered the christening gift he had brought. More significant was the raging demand to put the Queen of Scots to death as a sacrificial victim for the Huguenots slaughtered in Paris. Fortunately for Elizabeth, Parliament had been prorogued before St Bartholomew's Day, so there was less opportunity for Puritan pressure on her. Yet even before she had received the ambassador at Woodstock she secretly sent Henry Killigrew to Scotland with an offer to surrender Mary to the Regent and Council, 'to proceed with her by way of justice, so as neither that realm nor this should be dangered by her hereafter.' She dare not accept responsibility for Mary's death, now or later, and very earnestly hoped the Scots would execute her without more ado. But the Regent Mar had his price, demanding that she send three thousand English troops to keep public order during the execution and that afterwards she would continue to pay the Scots the sum she had been annually spending on Mary. Nothing became of these negotiations partly through Mar's own death, partly because Elizabeth could not risk her complicity in the plot becoming known, but Killigrew's mission shows how she was trying to turn the Massacre of St Bartholomew to advantage by sending Mary to her death.[15]

The following spring, however, she sent Sir William Drury with troops and a siege train to assist Morton, the new Regent, in forcing the Marians in Edinburgh Castle to surrender. Technically her assistance to Morton violated the Treaty of Blois, but Charles IX with another civil war tearing France apart was in no position to make an effective protest and the alliance survived.

This action in Edinburgh in May 1573 was to be the last occasion on which any Scots would fight for Mary Stuart and for six years the internal affairs of the northern kingdom were of small moment to Elizabeth.

At the same time she strengthened herself by re-establishing normal relations with Spain, broken since the end of 1568. On an impulse in March 1572 she had expelled Count la Marck's bands of privateers, 'the Sea Beggars' which had used English ports as bases for attacking Spanish shipping in the narrow seas. Her motives for this remain bewildering, and she can hardly have predicted the results of her action. After a month's aimless cruising la Marck seized Brill in south Holland, giving the Beggars a base in their own territory, and marking the real beginning of the revolt of the Netherlands. Elizabeth employed 'all correct means' to allow Protestant refugees in England and well-wishers among her own subjects to pass over to the Netherlands to fight against Spanish repression, but at the same time she repeatedly offered to mediate between Philip and his rebellious subjects. She knew that if it were to be a fight to the finish it would prove an enormous struggle for each side and what she wanted was not the Netherlands in revolt, but the Netherlands restored to their old privileges at peace. Her expulsion of the Sea Beggars, whatever its consequences, did much to lessen Anglo-Spanish tension and in due course feelers were put out which led to a renewal of discussions. Trade was resumed in 1573 and the following year the Convention of Bristol settled the complicated series of claims and counter-claims stemming from 1568, while each country undertook to expel the rebels of the other. Alva, Philip's Governor of the Netherlands, knew that even if Elizabeth broke faith with him and encouraged traitors like Orange, there was 'a great difference between open action and underhand'.[16] This accommodation with the Spanish Netherlands, which English statesmen lovingly called the old intercourse with Burgundy, coming on top of the Anglo-French entente, gave Elizabeth five years of peace and security such as she had not experienced since her accession. The internal troubles of her neighbours France, the Netherlands and, to a lesser extent, Scotland, gave her abundant source for satisfaction, and she would fish in these troubled waters as opportunity served. While they suffered their turmoils England could develop her unity, strength and national consciousness.

Despite defensive alliances and commercial conventions, Elizabeth often remarked at this time that a husband and children would be 'most strong bulwarks', and she fondly read and reread Alençon's protestations of love. She hinted to him that he might dart across the Channel and come in strict secrecy to the water gate of Greenwich Palace where she would receive him in person and alone. So romantic a meeting strongly appealed to the Duke, but as luck would have it he was then incarcerated together with Henry of Navarre at Vincennes for plotting with Huguenot leaders. His mother enquired whether in these circumstances Elizabeth still favoured proceeding with a marriage treaty, and she answered that she could not now think badly of a prince who had such a high opinion of her; 'but I must tell you quite frankly that I will not take a husband with irons on his feet.' Alençon was released soon afterwards, but the approaching death of Charles IX prevented the new negotiations with the Duke from developing.[17]

The Duke of Anjou who had so discourteously courted her – 'the old woman with the sore leg' – in 1571, and allowed himself to be elected King of Poland, succeeded to the throne of France in 1574 as Henry III, and his younger brother Alençon now inherited the title of Anjou (though to avoid confusion we will continue to call him Alençon). In the festivities at the French court to mark the new accession Katherine de Medici dressed up two female dwarfs in English costume to mimic Elizabeth and also mocked her father's memory. When she heard of this from Lord North, she took it in very bad part and got her own back by intriguing with Alençon's partisans who were struggling to release him from his mother's control, to pursue his career as a *mauvais sujet*. At length the Queen Mother of France apologized, saying that had Lord North's French been better he would have understood that the buffoonery was not nearly as insulting as he imagined. Soon Henry married Louise of Lorraine but his bride 'lacked presence and majesty' as well as beauty; indeed, Elizabeth's special envoy at the French court went out of his way to assure her that 'there is more beauty in Your Majesty's little finger than there is in any one lady' there, 'or in them all'. Soon he reported that the royal bride had taken to sea-bathing at Dieppe to promote conception, while by other letters came news of the birth of a female monster with two heads at Vincenza, because, it was hinted, the mother had left child-bearing until too late in life. As she read the reports from abroad, Elizabeth's mind was always being diverted to thoughts of marriage and children, romantic dreams which ended in nightmares. And Alençon, irresponsible little fool, was now indiscriminately paying court to the sister of Henry of Navarre and the daughter of Philip of Spain.[18]

When Alva had been replaced as Governor of the Netherlands by the milder Requesens, Elizabeth tried hard to mediate between him and William of Orange, on the basis of a return to traditional liberties. She blamed William for continuing what she now regarded as an unnecessary war for the sake of a religious toleration she could not understand. She desperately wanted a peaceful settlement, honourable to both sides, and could never bring herself to countenance rebellious subjects against their lawful sovereign. William's Calvinism was just as repugnant to her as his rebelliousness, a point of view which Walsingham never grasped and Burghley had reluctantly to admit, and she was determined to hold the reins of policy herself. She was so distressed at her inability to mediate at this time that she had a series of sleepless nights and even beat 'one or two of her ladies in waiting'. In August 1575 she openly proclaimed the Prince of Orange as a rebel and later threatened that she would aid Philip to restore the province of Holland to his obedience. In fact Elizabeth was free for the first time from pressing problems and could luxuriate in procrastination, to the dismay of her councillors. As Sir Thomas Smith, her Secretary of State, complained:

This irresolution doth weary and kill her ministers, destroy her actions and overcome all good designs and counsels – no letters touching Ireland, although read and allowed by Her Majesty, yet can I get signed. I wait whilst I neither have eyes to see or legs to stand upon. And yet these delays grieve me more and will not let me sleep in the night.... For private matters and suits I have the same success. They increase daily. Yea nor nay can I get, and as I hear Her Majesty hath forbidden Mr Hatton and my Lord Leicester to move suits . . .

It was not that she was tired or unhappy; her natural instinct was to wait upon events and allow letters to answer themselves.[19] When the crucial moment came she knew how to act vigorously and independently.

In the interval between Requesens's death and the arrival of his successor, Don John of Austria, in the Netherlands in 1576, the Spanish army mutinied for lack of pay, sacking Antwerp in their fury and sending tremors throughout Europe. The States General concluded a treaty with Holland and Zeeland, known as the Pacification of Ghent, which recognized William of Orange as Stadtholder of those two provinces. William appealed to Elizabeth to mediate with Philip of Spain for the confirmation of the Pacification and also asked her for a loan. Now she acted with promptitude and firmness, despatching Sir John Smith to Madrid and Edward Horsey to Don John, threatening to aid the States General with money and men if they refused to recognize the settlement. Indeed, she had already sent the States £20,000 for immediate needs, with promise of further supplies. As a result of her intervention, Don John accepted the States' terms by his 'Perpetual Edict', and she had achieved the settlement she wanted: a united Netherlands, self-governing, with the liberties they had enjoyed under the Emperor Charles V, still under Spanish sovereignty but free from the tyranny of a Spanish army. This achievement has been termed 'the high water-mark' of Elizabeth's entire foreign policy.[20] When, shortly after his arrival in Brussels, Don John met Fulke Greville, he asked if he could look at a portrait of his Queen, and gazing at it, the victor of Lepanto envied her 'for her virtues and mighty puissant state'. Unlike his master in the Escorial, Elizabeth knew instinctively when to throw aside her mask of irresolution and direct affairs.[21]

She appeared to have put Alençon out of her mind and gave the impression of becoming an embittered old maid, and when Mary Shelton, one of the ladies of her Privy Chamber, at this time married a Mr Scudamore without her leave, she let fly at the unfortunate girl, dealing 'liberal both in blows and words' so that 'no one ever bought her husband more dearly.' Her godson, Sir John Harington, tells the tale that 'she did often ask the ladies around her chamber if they loved to think of marriage, and the wise ones did conceal well their liking thereto, knowing the Queen's judgement in the matter.' A less wise virgin, Kate Arundel, said she had thought much about marriage, and if her father would give his consent she would wed the man she loved. 'You seem honest, i' faith,' said Elizabeth, 'I will sue for you to your father' (Sir Robert Arundel), and kept her promise. When the Queen told Kate that the match would have her father's blessing, the girl was overjoyed. 'I shall be happy, and please your Grace.' 'So thou shalt; but not to be a fool and marry', Elizabeth chided her. 'I have [thy father's] consent given to me, and I vow thou shalt never get it in thy possession. So go to thy business. I see thou art a bold one, to own thy foolishness so readily.' It was a bitter trick to have played, a dog in the manger attitude to matrimony, all tears, pain and resentment.

It was to young Harington that she sent a copy of her speech to Parliament in 1576, to ponder in his hours of leisure, in which she confessed her dislike of marriage:

If I were a milkmaid with a pail on my arm, whereby my private person might be little set by, I would not forsake that poor and single state to match with the greatest monarch. Not that I do condemn the double knot, or judge amiss of such as, forced by necessity, cannot dispose themselves to another life; but wish that none were drawn to change but such as cannot keep honest limits.

Yet for the sake of her realm she would dispose herself towards matrimony if the conditions were favourable. In 1576 they were not, but by 1578 she had decided they were.[22]

Don John's Perpetual Edict was misnamed. There were no satisfactory guarantees that Holland and Zeeland would enjoy liberty of worship and William of Orange cold-shouldered the new Governor. Don John had his own ambitions, for once the Netherlands had been pacified he intended embarking his troops for an invasion of England, where he would rescue and marry Mary Queen of Scots and oust Elizabeth from her throne. When the Queen of England caught wind of these plans she countered by insisting to the States General that the Spanish soldiers should be sent home by the land route and in a panic Don John seized Namur in July 1577. Again Elizabeth acted swiftly, offering the States a loan of £100,000 and promising to send troops if the Duke of Guise came to Don John's aid, as was feared. Soon war was renewed in all its horrors in this cockpit of the reformation, and with the arrival of Alexander Farnese, Prince of Parma, with a Spanish army, Protestant princes offered further aid. Elizabeth agreed to loan money on the security of her own jewels to enable John Casimir of the Palatinate to bring in a force of eleven thousand German and Swiss mercenaries, providing her name was not divulged. Whatever the Puritan hotheads said, she could not risk openly challenging Spain to war. In the cold war of the later sixteenth century, which countries were giving foreign aid to which counted as the greatest of diplomatic secrets. At this point Philip sent Bernardino de Mendoza to England as his ambassador, the first resident since the expulsion of de Spes in 1571, with full instructions to convince Elizabeth of his friendship towards her and his profound hope that she would not countenance any help being sent from England to prolong the rebellion.

Of more significance, the Catholics of Artois and Hainault turned for help to the Duke of Alençon. Katherine de Medici and Henry III were delighted to have the adventurer away from France and what could be more suitable for him than to carve a French duchy out of the southern Netherlands. He became elected to the high-sounding office of 'Defender of Belgic liberty against the Spanish tyrant' and for England the prospect of French conquests of the Low Countries became far more alarming than continuing Spanish domination. To her councillors' surprise, consternation even, Elizabeth decided on controlling Alençon – something his mother and brother had never succeeded in achieving – by the expedient of reviving the marriage project, and he quickly warmed to the idea, for she was in a position to provide him with money for his troops as well as to bestow on him a consort's crown.

After Christmas 1578 Alençon sent over Jean de Simier to court Elizabeth by proxy and she almost gave the impression of being swept off her feet by his typically French gallantry that made Leicester's attentions seem heavy-handed by comparison, and Hatton *gauche*. A frog he would a-wooing go, and her court had never seen the like. Simier, her 'Monkey', as she nicknamed him, made her feel she really was '*la plus fine femme du monde*', and she fell in love with the idea of love. He was a ladies' man, no doubt about it; 'a most choice courtier, exquisitely skilled in love toys, pleasant conceits and court dalliances', as the chronicler puts it, and with his entourage of frisky fellows livened up the staid routine of Whitehall and Richmond. Who but Simier would have raided her bedchamber to pilfer her nightcap, that he might send an illicit love token to Alençon? For Elizabeth it was a revelation to be wooed in this way – even by proxy. Not surprising, then, that Leicester was very much put out by these antics, while Hatton was in tears. They thought Simier was being far too amorous and Leicester accused him of making use of 'love potions and other unlawful arts' to entice her to Alençon. When one of her ladies spoke up for Leicester, she railed at her, 'Dost thou think me so unlike myself and unmindful of my royal majesty that I would prefer my servant whom I myself have raised, before the greatest prince of Christendom, in the honour of a husband?' She revelled in this fantastic game of love, was loath to be out of Simier's company and would have not a word of criticism of his behaviour. 'He has shown himself faithful to his master, is sage and discreet beyond his years in the conduct of the case', she told Sir Amyas Paulet, her ambassador in Paris, adding the snub, 'we wish we had such a servant of whom we could make such good use.' And if she called her Monkey's conduct discreet, what then was indiscretion?[23]

After several weeks of Simier's amours Elizabeth suddenly awoke to the fact that Alençon was being painfully slow in coming to pay his own devotions. If he really wanted to lay himself at her feet, as he professed, then he should delay no more. She rubbed into Paulet that a voyage to England could hardly be less embarrassing for Alençon than his late campaign in the Low Countries. If her suitor (she slyly thought of his pock marks and his height) 'had to deal with a princess that had either some defect of body, or some other notable defect of nature' then there would be excuse for his tardiness; but considering the gifts the Creator had bestowed on her, 'which we do ascribe to the Giver and not glory in them as proceeding from ourselves (being no fit trumpet to set our own praises), we may in true course of modesty think ourselves worthy of as great a prince as Monsieur is.' But the French, suspicious that months had been spent nibbling at the clauses of the draft marriage treaty, wanted a definite answer: would she, yea or nay, accept his hand? Elizabeth made her standard retort that she could not commit herself to a marriage with a stranger she had never met and insisted that the outstanding points in the treaty should be left to personal discussion between the two of them. At last Alençon was ready to come and awaited a passport, signed by the Queen, to permit him to enter the realm.[24]

That Elizabeth, after years of shilly-shallying, now wanted the Duke at court was too much for Leicester, who retired to his bed at Wanstead with a diplomatic illness. She came to visit him, to be certain his condition was not serious, and while he was still away sulking a member of the sovereign's guard fired on Simier in the grounds of Greenwich Palace. There had been a scare three weeks before when the royal barge carrying the Queen, Simier, Hatton and Leicester down the Thames to Greenwich had been shot at from a small boat. Many thought the intended victim was Simier, but Elizabeth was prepared to accept the story that the weapon had gone off accidentally and she subsequently pardoned the man concerned as well as granting her wounded bargeman a disability pension of £6 a year. But the later attack Simier regarded in a different light. Knowing the Earl's aversion to the Alençon match, which at last seemed a possibility, Simier jumped to the conclusion that the attempt on his life in Greenwich Palace gardens had been plotted by Leicester, and fearful as much for his own safety as for the success of the negotiations, he brought out the sharpest weapon in his armoury. With a flair for winning confidences and a nose for distinguishing idle gossip from uncanny truth, Simier had succeeded in uncovering the secret of the year, which had been so well kept that even Elizabeth knew nothing of it. Leicester was married. In September 1578 he had actually taken Lettice Knollys, widow of the Earl of Essex, as his wife twice over, for her father, Sir Francis Knollys, treasurer of the household and a cousin of the Queen, insisted on a second ceremony which he could himself witness, fearing that Leicester might otherwise throw her overboard, as he had disavowed Douglas, Lady Sheffield. There had been rumours enough of the Earl's trifling with Lettice Knollys, but nothing to suggest they had become man and wife.[25]

Simier's revelation hurt Elizabeth more than anything since Norfolk's treachery. Her master of the horse married, indeed! This was worse than Amy Robsart's death, worse than the bastard son born to Lady Sheffield. Her own Robin, to whom she had just lent £15,000 she could ill afford,[26] whose protestations of adoring love she had always regarded as sincere, had deliberately deceived her. *Video sed taceo*: she could condone a flirtation that had come to her notice, but she could never forgive him for contracting a marriage without her leave. Here he was, posing as a lone, forlorn widower, counselling her very strongly against plighting her troth to Alençon, while he was in fact a married man himself. In a burst of anger she ordered him to be sent to the Tower, and he would have gone, had it not been for the persuasive reasoning of Sussex, who despite his own abiding dislike of Leicester knew that the Queen must be prevented from striking an angry blow that would do untold harm to her own dignity. Instead of the Tower of London the Earl was lodged in an isolated tower in Greenwich Park and it was announced at court that he was taking physic and would see no one. After a few days he retired to his house at Wanstead, debarred from the Queen's presence until her fury had abated. It was fortunate for him that her mind was distracted by the arrival of Alençon.

She at last saw 'her frog' at Greenwich on 17 August and her first impressions were most favourable. She had feared the worst about his face and his physique, but need not have worried. He was a prince of the House of Valois, a young romantic and ardent wooer, and he had very considerable sex appeal. Such qualities more than balanced oddities of appearance; even the tilt of his strange nose and his tiny hands had a wayward handsomeness about them. Her womanly vanity was satisfied that a princely suitor had at last come in person; others had sent messages, deputations and presents ever since her accession, but Alençon was the first to plead his own passionate cause. What transpired at Greenwich during his twelve-day stay is conjectural, for as the Duke had arrived incognito, ambassadors, whose despatches might have produced choice tittle-tattle, were not invited to the palace to meet him; so Mendoza merely referred to the visit he was supposed to know nothing about as 'a love dalliance'. Alençon followed the resident Simier's advice and left England fairly convinced he had won her heart and that she meant every word of her promises of eternal love. Once over his sea-sickness, he sent her passionate letters from Boulogne with a gift of a 'little flower of gold, with a frog thereon, and therein Mounseer his physiognomy, and a little pearl pendant'.[27]

Protestant horror at the Massacre of St Bartholomew's was still fervent seven years afterwards, and the latent, age-old prejudice against France, that would in the next century find an apposite slogan in 'No Popery and no wooden shoes', flared up. Had Elizabeth forgotten Calais and the treachery of the Guises, the fires of Smithfield and the perfidy of Mary Queen of Scots? In August, perhaps while Alençon was at Greenwich, the Puritan John Stubbs, whose sister had married the prophesying Cartwright, gave vent to the fears of half the nation in a forceful tract against the match, *The Discovery of a Gaping Gulf Whereunto England is like to be swallowed by another French Marriage if the Lord forbid not the Bans by letting Her Majesty see the sin and Punishment thereof.* As the title suggests, Stubbs did not pull his punches. The Queen was too old to be contemplating marriage, and was at the most dangerous age of all for child-bearing, as her most faithful physicians could tell her; and as for Alençon he was not merely a cunning French debauchee but 'the old serpent himself in the form of a man come a second time to seduce the English Eve and to ruin the English paradise'. Here is 'an imp of the crown of France to marry with the crowned nymph of England', and his manner of courting, by paying Elizabeth a personal visit *incognito* was highly deplorable – 'an unmanlike, unprince-like, French kind of wooing'. Under the guise of his private chapel the Roman mass would be restored in the land, idolatry would flourish and the word of God be silenced.

About the time that Stubbs's tract was published, Elizabeth received a long letter from Sir Philip Sidney in politer terms speaking out against the marriage on behalf of all English Protestants, 'your chief, if not your sole strength'. 'How the hearts of your people will be galled, if not aliened' if this marriage should come about. The Duke's parentage, religion, nationality and personal qualities made him a most unsuitable suitor, and 'the very common people know that he is the son of a Jezebel of our age', a phrase that in another context would have delighted Elizabeth. From the pulpits came virulent phrases about the daughter of God being corrupted by the son of Antichrist, and to silence this criticism Elizabeth issued a proclamation on 27 September, to be read by the bishops to all their clergy, defending herself and the character of the Duke at length, while a preacher at Paul's Cross praised the achievements of the government and assured the multitude that their Queen would live and die in Christ. Stubbs's *Gaping Gulf* had been castigated in the proclamation as a lewd, seditious book, showing true regard neither for the realm nor for the Queen and all copies were to be seized and burnt. Author, printer and publisher were speedily sent for trial and sentenced under a statute of Philip and Mary to lose their right hands and undergo imprisonment. Elizabeth pardoned the printer, but Stubbs and his publisher, William Page, had to endure the barbarity of a law which even a common law judge thought illegal. Long afterwards William Camden remembered standing in the crowd at Westminster to see the sentences carried out by a cleaver and mallet. As soon as Stubbs's right hand was off he 'took off his hat with the left and cried aloud "God Save the Queen".' Then he fainted and was taken off to the Tower where he spent the next eighteen months. The publisher, Page, was made of sterner stuff and lifting up his bleeding arm told the crowd 'I left there a true Englishman's hand.' Elizabeth's popularity was at a very low ebb.[28]

Did the Queen really want to marry Alençon in 1579, assuming the religious and constitutional knots could be undone, and, if so, did she really expect still to bear children? While Alençon was twenty-three, she was exactly twice as old, and forty-six was a difficult age. Her emotional instability was never so marked as in the middle and last acts of her protracted courtship with the Duke; she loved him, she loved him not; she would marry him straightway, she lost all interest in the negotiations; she desperately wanted a baby, she dare not face the shock of consummation and the dangers of childbirth. All the signs are that at forty-six she was reaching, had perhaps even reached, the menopause. At any time in the last fifteen years news of Leicester's marriage would have wounded her womanly pride deeply, but coming now, at this crucial time in her life, it tore at her affections. Since Leicester had deserted her, Alençon gave her what she knew was her last chance of fulfilling herself as a woman and she accepted his advances with relief.

Burghley had not the slightest doubt about her ability to become a mother, as he penned in a memorandum for his eyes alone in March 1579:

Considering the proportion of her body, having no impediment of smallness in stature, of largeness in body, nor no sickness, nor lack of natural functions in those things that properly belong to the procreation of children, but contrariwise [and this is significant] by judgement of physicians that know her estate in those things and by the opinion of women, being most acquainted with her Majesty's body in such things as properly appertain, to show probability of her aptness to have children, even at this day.

Many women even older and with a less suitable physique had given birth to healthy babies, and without impairing their own constitutions. The best medical opinion, Burghley noted, gave her as much as another six years in which to bear children: moreover sexual relations and the processes of conception and childbearing, far from endangering her health would improve her general condition;

and to this end were to be remembered the likelihood of Her Majesty's pains in her cheeks and face to come only of lack of the use of marriage, a thing meeter by physicians to be advocated to Her Majesty than to be set down.[29]

Sussex, Leicester and Walsingham, though they did not write elaborate memoranda on the topic, were no less certain than him that Elizabeth was capable of bearing children. For them to have kept up an elaborate and prolonged pretence to the Queen herself on this delicate matter is one thing – and Sussex was too simple and bluff a fellow to have tried it – but they could hardly have refused to have faced the facts realistically in their strictly private correspondence if marriage and issue had been quite out of the question. The frank opinion of Burghley, arrived at through discussion with the Queen's physicians, makes nonsense of all the hearsay of those on the fringe of affairs and of the tales woven by later generations that Elizabeth was barren.[30] Some historians have thought her conduct in courtship could only be explained rationally on the supposition that she had a physical defect precluding hopes of issue but all the evidence points the other way.[31] In 1579 Elizabeth was convinced that a marriage with Alençon could be fruitful and desperately wanted it to take place. Leicester's marriage to Lettice Knollys had finally erased any lingering doubts she may have had about him and the shock of Leicester's infidelity had driven her at forty-six into Alençon's arms.

Had she been a free agent she would have accepted Alençon's proposal without more ado, but outbursts such as Stubbs's *Gaping Gulf* made her uneasy; she was always sensitive to public opinion, and instead of giving way to her heart she turned to her Council for advice. While nothing was settled she decided once again to prorogue Parliament. Assuming the Council gave her the support she needed and expected (for they had been urging her to marry since her accession), she would do it and share the responsibility with them. Having put the question, she knew there would be a division of opinion, but she expected that Burghley, the great protagonist of the match, would carry the day. So the Council debated the issue on 7 October, from 8 a.m. to 7 p.m., 'without stirring from the room, having sent the clerks away.' The pros and cons of the marriage as it affected domestic politics and international affairs were threshed out and every aspect of the affair was considered at length, except the Queen's personal feelings. At the end of the day Burghley found himself in a minority, for of the twelve present seven were against the marriage, including, as expected, Leicester and Hatton; but the Lord Treasurer managed to persuade them to give an open verdict and with Leicester and two others went to tell her that they could make no positive recommendations until they knew her own mind. Burghley as foreman of the jury even suggested to her that she should ask each of the twelve present, and the absentees, his opinion individually.[32]

She had been expecting a resolution warmly welcoming the match, not an 'answerless answer', which came as a calculated insult to her, and she told them so quite frankly, 'not without shedding of many tears'. She rued her decision to allow them to meddle in her affairs and later in the day she recalled the four senior councillors for a painful audience. Elizabeth marvelled 'that any person would think so slenderly of her as that she would not for God's cause, for herself, her surety and her people, have so strait a regard thereto as none ought to make such a doubt as, for it, to forbear marriage and to have the crown settled in her child.' The Council, wise after the event, worded an appropriate message of unanimous assent to the marriage 'if so it shall please her'. This was hardly encouragement, and she more or less told them so; if they could do no better than that, she did not think it meet to tell them whether or not she would take Monsieur as her consort. In November, according to Mendoza, she again told her Council she was determined to wed and they 'need say nothing more to her about it, but should at once discuss what was necessary for carrying it out.' A quorum of councillors, excluding Leicester, talked terms with Simier, but Elizabeth made him agree to a moratorium of two months in the marriage treaty during which she would attempt to gain popular support for the match. By then, in effect, she had decided to proceed no further. Soon Simier, as well as Alençon, had left England and she lost all interest in them both.[33]

Alençon's campaign in the Netherlands was not threatening England's security, yet Elizabeth needed to be assured of the friendship of France more than ever. As the decade opened estrangement from Spain was growing. Drake's successful maraud-ing in the new world could not indefinitely be overlooked by Philip II because it was 'beyond the line' and Spanish aid for the rebels in Ireland was undisguised. Alva's swift conquest of Portu-gal, following the death of the old Cardinal King, added a fine navy and important dockyards to the maritime power of Spain, still enjoying the reputation conferred by the Battle of Lepanto. The Most Catholic King might at any time send an invading force to England under a papal banner to complete the work begun by the Jesuit missionaries, rescue Mary Queen of Scots and depose Elizabeth. France was England's present help in trouble and to cement the alliance begun at Blois in 1572 Elizabeth had perforce to lead Alençon by the nose, tempting him anew with the prospects of her hand and waste money on his swashbuckling forays against Parma. What she envisaged was a rounded offen-sive and defensive league with France, as security against Spain, and to achieve this she would carry her flirtation with her Frog to absurd lengths. In February 1580 Mendoza reported a discus-sion he overheard on the vexed marriage negotiations, in which she quizzed Burghley and Archbishop Sandys of York:

My Lord [Archbishop], here I am between Scylla and Charybdis. Alençon has agreed to all the terms I sent him and he is asking me to tell him when I want him to come and marry me. If I do not marry him, I do not know whether he will remain friendly with me; and if I do, I shall not be able to govern the country with the freedom and security I have hitherto enjoyed.

Sandys tactfully said everyone would be delighted with her decision, whatever it was; but Burghley advised her to marry Alençon if she wanted to, 'and no harm could come to the country', and if she was lukewarm she should undeceive him at once. 'That', retorted the Queen, 'is not the opinion of the rest of the Council, but that I should keep him in correspondence.' Such, indeed, was her policy – to keep Alençon on a string, for as long as she dared, and then to reject him, without endangering relations with France. This weaving of an elaborate Penelope's web was a tricky business and as she was to be chief actor in the drama, in a role that still had an immense personal appeal for her, she would brook no interference from her Council, whether from the Burghley or the Leicester faction.[34]

After further calculated procrastinations the threads of negotiation were taken up again in November 1580. Four months before, Burghley had told the French that once their civil war was over the marriage articles could be settled in a day, and that Elizabeth was 'positively distraught with her love for the Duke', but now that peace had been signed between the warring parties in France, she was again playing for time, even though she publicly urged that she wanted everything settled before she was too old to bear children. She was still very moody. In March Ann Vavasour, one of her maids of honour and a girl by all accounts with a reputation for promiscuity, gave birth to a son in the palace, vowing in labour that the Earl of Oxford was the child's father. On the evening of her delivery Elizabeth had Ann removed to the Tower, furious at young Oxford's illicit love and her maid of honour's easy compliance.[35]

She went down to Deptford on 4 April to honour Drake, who had returned home in the late autumn from his remarkable voyage round the world in *The Pelican*, now aptly renamed *The Golden Hind*, 'fraught with gold, silver, silk and precious stones'. Elizabeth's own share of the booty, as a private investor in the voyage, was in the region of £160,000 – as much as a normal Parliamentary grant – since each of the backers enjoyed a return of 4,700 per cent. The chests of rich booty plundered from the *Cacafuego* had been sent to the Tower as Elizabeth had steadily refused to listen to Mendoza's pleadings that these prize goods should be restored to Spain. So Drake's investiture aboard *The Golden Hind* was rather more than a domestic event, and the Queen planned to make as much political capital from it as she could. She slyly told him that she had a gilded sword to strike off his head for turning pirate, and then handed the sword to the Seigneur de Marchaumont, who was Alençon's special agent in London, asking him to perform the ceremony for her, which he gladly did. This alone foreshadowed an Anglo-French league against Spain. While she was boarding Drake's ship, one of the

Queen's purple and gold garters had slipped down, and de Marchaumont had claimed it as lawful prize, intending to send it as a keepsake to Alençon. Elizabeth asked for it back, 'as she had nothing else with which to keep her stocking up', promising to surrender it to him on returning to the palace. So the garter followed the nightcap and the other trophies pocketed by Simier. Drake's present to her on this great day was an ornament of diamonds, and some said it was in the shape of a frog. 'This and all other signs seem to indicate a real intention to effect the marriage', wrote Mendoza in alarm.[36]

A fortnight later the French commissioners for arranging the marriage treaty arrived in England, a great concourse of notables led by the Prince Dauphin, for Elizabeth insisted the mission should include princes of the highest rank. The entertainment of five hundred Frenchmen at court for several weeks posed many problems. Feeling was running so high that the Queen feared some ugly incident might be sparked off by a Protestant hothead or a Francophobe – something more akin to the Massacre of St Bartholomew's than a stray shot at Simier – and so she issued a proclamation calling on all her subjects to show special honour to the distinguished visitors and forbidding anyone to draw a weapon or provoke a quarrel on pain of death. She was determined to impress them with *fêtes galantes*, and for the occasion a special banqueting-house was constructed of wood and canvas in the gardens of Whitehall, 332 feet long and nearly as broad, with the canvas walls painted outside to resemble stonework, and with ninety-two windows. The inside was 'most cunningly painted' with impressions of the heavens, while great baskets of bespangled greenery and green-grocery decked out the roof like a harvest festival.[37]

Alençon himself was marooned in the Netherlands, but his absence suited the Queen remarkably well. The highlight of the festivities was a Triumph in the tiltyard on 15 May, where the set piece was the 'Fortress of Perfect Beauty', which was assailed by Desire and his foster children, courtiers led by Philip Sidney – an incongruous role for one who had been so outspoken against the marriage in its earliest days. Cannons were fired with scented powder and toilet water for ammunition, and there were frolics with 'pretty scaling-ladders and then footmen threw flowers and such fancies against the walls with all sort devices as might seem fit shot for Desire.' This elaborate pageant, with its enormous cast in dazzling costumes, was an allegory on the royal courtship. In vain did messengers address the Queen herself at intervals in the battle asking her to surrender her perfect beauty to virtuous desire. An angel spoke for the defenders of her maidenly citadel: 'Sir Knights, if in besieging the sun you understood what you had undertaken, you would destroy a common blessing for a private benefit ... Will you subdue the sun? ... We are content to enjoy the light, you to eclipse it.' Long into the evening the performance lasted, until the challengers gave up the unequal struggle. Virtue was too strong for Desire, and the Fortress of Perfect Beauty was 'to be reserved for the eye of the whole world.'38

The message cannot have been lost on the French embassy, yet the significance of the two months' merrymaking, the splendid dinners and costly pageantry cannot have been lost on the rest of the diplomatic corps. The marriage negotiations might founder yet again, but here was the firm foundation of an *entente cordiale*, much more far-reaching than the Treaty of Blois, a power to challenge the might of Spain. Protracted discussions on the marriage treaty made little progress, even though the form of wedding service to be followed was agreed upon. At the end of it all Elizabeth made it quite plain that whatever document the commissioners signed, the application of its clauses would depend on a definite agreement between Alençon and herself. The affair was as much in the air as it ever had been.

Would Alençon still return to woo her in person, and if he came would he succeed? Mendoza, the Spanish ambassador, was offering a hundred to one that the nuptials would never take place. To encourage her suitor Elizabeth complied with his urgent request for funds, sending him £30,000, which helped him to pay his troops after forcing Parma to raise the siege of Cambrai. After putting his soldiers in winter quarters, he finally arrived at the end of October and was most warmly received. A week or so of listening to her Frog's ardent protestations and she declared he

was 'the most deserving and constant of all her lovers', and
counted on being able to prolong the preliminaries. To appease
Protestant critics she even persuaded him to accompany her to St
Paul's Cathedral and gave him a kiss in front of the congregation
as a reward. The climax of their affair was a scene in the gallery at
Whitehall on her accession day, celebrated this year with especial
pomp. She told the French ambassador he could write to Paris
with the news 'that the Duke of Alençon shall be my husband',
and then turning to her suitor 'kissed him on the mouth, drawing
a ring from her own hand and giving it to him as a pledge', while
Alençon gave her a ring of his in return. Then she called her principal courtiers and the other ambassadors from the presence
chamber out to the gallery and repeated her pledge. The Duke
was 'extremely overjoyed', Burghley praised the Lord that his
Queen had at last got to the point, Leicester fretted and Hatton
was in tears. Londoners reckoned the marriage was 'as good as
accomplished' and there were bonfires in Antwerp when the
news arrived.[39]

Few realized that the Queen's performance in the gallery at
Whitehall was no more than a clever piece of acting, carefully
premeditated and rehearsed. The story goes that the same evening
her ladies, prompted by Leicester and Hatton, 'wailed and by
laying terrors before her did so vex her mind with argument'
against marriage that she had a sleepless night. The following
morning she sent for the Duke and told him that two more such
nights and she would be in the grave, but in the long silent
watches, torn between her duty as a Queen and her feelings as a
woman, she had decided to sacrifice her own happiness for the
welfare of her people, though her great affection for him was un-
diminished. When he later asked leave to depart the court she
bade him stay – she would marry him, she said, at a more propitious moment, but at present her own feelings were too disturbed.
So Alençon obediently and hopefully stayed on for another three
months, fêted, courted and slow to realize he had outstayed his
welcome. The 'wailings' of her women certainly had something
to do with her uneasiness, but they did not now quite suddenly
'terrify her from marrying' as Camden suggests. Elizabeth used

their warnings on the perils of childbirth as an excuse for jilting her Frog, but in fact her mind had been made up eighteen months earlier, when she saw the deep opposition of her Council.[40]

She was now eager to be rid of him and suggested to Burghley and Leicester that he might be bribed to go. Leicester thought £200,000 would be an appropriate sum, but she was angry at the idea of wasting so much money. No, she would neither marry Alençon, nor would she give him another sou, and told him so to his face; then later she relented a little and said her warm affection for him remained, so she would for ever be a sister to him. As the new year opened she stiffened herself once more and said marriage was still possible, but she could not agree to it unless both Calais and Le Havre were handed over to be garrisoned by her soldiers, and as the tail end of the negotiations dragged on everybody became more and more irritable, with Sussex and Leicester coming to blows in the council chamber. When she heard that the commissioners from Flanders had gone to Alençon in London to expedite his return, she sent for them and hammered home their lack of manners: 'You shoemakers, carpenters and heretics, how dare you speak in such terms to a man of royal blood like the Duke of Alençon. I would have you know that when you approach him or me, you are in the presence of the two greatest princes in Christendom.' But at least they were trying to persuade him to leave England. At one time she sent for Simier, by now no longer the Duke's agent, but a personal envoy of the French King to spy on her, and he agreed that a marriage with Alençon would now be absurd. Poor Simier had a narrow escape from assassination in a plot hatched by a French rival in which Leicester's name was again linked, and when Elizabeth heard of it she told the Earl he was 'a murderous poltroon' and deserved to be hanged.[41]

At last, on 1 February, the Queen left London with the Duke on the first stage of his return journey to the Netherlands and at Canterbury she wept diplomatic tears when she bade him farewell and told him she would be unhappy until he came back to her. He took with him £10,000 in cash with a firm promise of £50,000 more and finally went aboard *The Discovery* at

Sandwich, attended by Leicester, Hunsdon and other peers who were to escort him to Antwerp. But for the bad weather she would have gone right to the coast with him. Glad as she was to be free from his embarrassing company she soon appeared to regret his absence; without Alençon, she protested to Leicester, she could not live an hour longer and counted the days until he was due to return in two months. Each kept the suit alive on paper by writing passionate letters. She would give a million pounds to see her Frog swimming once more in the Thames instead of in the murky marshes of the Low Countries. Elizabeth had 'danced for very joy' when his departure had at last seemed certain, but now she was melancholy and wrote verses in the style of Petrarch 'On Monsieur's Departure':[42]

> I grieve, yet dare not show my discontent;
>   I love, and yet am forced to seem to hate;
> I dote, but dare not what I meant;
>   I seem stark mute, yet inwardly do prate.
> I am, and am not – freeze, and yet I burn,
> Since from myself my other self I turn.

There are more lines in a similar vein. She could not 'rid him' from her thoughts and asked for some 'gentler passion' to possess her. The affair had gone on for far too long and her emotions were always being blunted by harsh political considerations. 'For her own mind, what that really was' (wrote an Englishman well-versed in diplomacy, long after her death) 'I must leave as a thing doubly inscrutable, both as she was a queen and a woman.'[43] Elizabeth had been in love with the idea of love for so long, until in the late summer of 1579 she most certainly wanted to marry Alençon and but for the opposition of Leicester, Hatton and their friends would have done so. Thereafter, though she still regarded the Duke tenderly, as the man she might have wedded, she knew marriage was now impossible, whatever pretences she kept up. The match was too unpopular in England and the shock of her discovering that killed it, while all the time she was ageing and appreciated that a childless marriage would be really disastrous. Better by far to remain a virgin Queen than become a motherless wife, like her sister. Alençon was certainly fulfilling her hopes of him in the diplomatic field, and his very existence postponed her day of reckoning with Spain. Her decision to reject him recovered her lost popularity in England and with her people's faith in her restored she could gamble still on the succession. She wept not for Alençon's leaving her, but for her own lost chances of love, marriage and children, for by February 1582 she was approaching her forty-ninth birthday, and the ending of her lengthy courtship was sad because she knew it would be the last. During its stages she had changed from being 'la plus fine femme du monde' to an old maid. When Alençon died of a fever in June 1584 no one at first dared tell her the dread tidings, but she put her court in mourning and continued to observe the anniversary of his death; he had served nobly in fighting her battles in the Netherlands and she had also for a season been in love with him.[44]

THE SPLENDIFEROUS
PLANET

No sovereign has had so many allegorical names applied to her, from 'Deborah' in the earliest weeks of the reign to 'Oriana' in her last decade, but to her courtiers Elizabeth was 'The Sun Queen'. She shone, giving 'the common blessing' of light and the warmth of her rays promoted growth; she dazzled, and at times burnt with a fiery intensity. 'Many make suit to have the twinkling of one beam of the splendiferous planet', and those not in her presence lived in a shadow. Hatton, with special appreciation of the Queen, longed when away from court to see again 'the brightness of that sun that giveth light unto my sense and soul'. Unaffectedly, her godson Harington used the 'sun' motif to depict her temperament: 'When she smiled, it was a pure sunshine that everyone did choose to bask in if they could'; but he went on to add that the storm clouds could gather without warning, and then 'the thunder fell in wondrous manner on all alike.' The set speech of the angel in the triumph devised for the French embassy in 1581 dwelt on the theme and the poets – Raleigh, Spenser, Shakespeare – developed it. We shall meet with similar allusions. The portrait of Elizabeth standing on the map of the world was probably painted with this in mind.[1]

The setting for royalty was the court, a hybrid amalgam of councillors, civil servants and household officials, surrounding the sovereign, moving with her from palace to palace and progressing with her in the summer months as she toured the less far-flung regions of her realm. It was essentially a masculine society, including the greatest in the land, yet Elizabeth succeeded in dominating it, fascinating them all and persuading most that they must be at least a little in love with her. The greater part of the reign she had not merely one favourite, but three or four and even in his prime Leicester ranked no higher than *primus inter pares*. Servants of the crown were entitled to board and lodging at court but, whatever their status, their wives could not of right share this privilege, and though exceptions were made to this rule out of favour, the rule itself remained.

Elizabeth had an instinctive love of crowds, of the bustle of people around her, and a feeling for great activity and so life at court became one long crowd scene, with herself holding the centre of the stage. She was one of those people who are able to command any gathering without apparent effort and accordingly she relished an audience, as it showed her at her best. It was when she kept to her private apartments, solitary and uncommunicative, that ministers worried, for they knew she was either ailing or was deeply upset; a few days of thunder were better than twilight. She was the sovereign source of power and her patents the passport to wealth, and so men turned to her, eager to wear her livery and fell under her imperious spell. She shone, a radiant blaze of diamonds, and her whole court glittered. Did she not spend £405 a year on spangles, to turn out her menials in proper show as well as to brighten up her own wigs? Noblemen who might have been trouble-makers in their own demesnes, far from the capital, were enticed to court to kiss her hand in fealty, given a job to do and kept under view, fluttering like moths around a candle and encouraged, as Sir John Neale puts it, in 'spending their wealth on the relatively harmless but prodigal ways of court.' The attractions of court and capital were self-evident and irresistible – the shops in Cheapside, the masques in the banqueting hall, the performances in the tiltyard and the opportunity of being at the centre of power. Lads from the provinces came not so much to the City of London to seek their fortune as to apprentice themselves at court in the Queen's service. With her extensive patronage through grants of offices, privileges and estates, it was the privy chamber at Whitehall, the luxurious world beyond magic casements, not the streets of London, that were paved with gold.[2]

It was not easy for a woman to maintain discipline among such a concourse of men. They itched to draw their swords on the slightest provocation and the higher their rank the quicker they were to take offence that their honour had been called in question. The naturally high-spirited could be diverted to the tiltyard and the chase to let off steam, and in fact the marshal of the household kept the peace so effectively that its coroner had surprisingly little to do. There were brawls and unseemly incidents, many threats of violence but little violence itself, and though factions formed of men in the livery of a Leicester or an Essex, they caused no real trouble at court. Elizabeth impressed on all that brute force would lead nowhere. Being a woman she could smooth their rough manners into courtly ways, tame their masculinity and allow them the privilege of participating in the idyll of the Queen, the masque of Fair Oriana, who was a woman as well as a ruler, and a virgin to boot. It may seem fantastic to us, yet these tactics succeeded. There is a further point. The reformation had ended the cult of Our Lady in England, which in the high middle ages had been deeply rooted and strong enough to claim so many churches dedicated to St Mary the Virgin, promote the foundation of numerous guilds and chantries with her as patron and bring as many pilgrims to the shrine of Walsingham as to Becket's tomb at Canterbury. A kindred devotion to spotless maidenhood had featured in the old ideal of chivalry. Deprived of their devotions to the Virgin Queen of Heaven, many now found an emotional outlet in paying a special kind of homage to the Virgin Queen of England, secular but with a powerful streak of romantic mysticism. How otherwise, it is asked, can we account for the 'emotional response amounting almost to worship which the name and idea of Elizabeth inspired in the men of her time'. Without these she would hardly have given her name to an age.[3]

For the Queen's officers of state attendance at court was obligatory, unless they obtained leave of absence. Many kept terms like lawyers or dons, and sought permission to join their wives and families out of town at Christmas, Easter and during the summer progress. Such leave was a privilege, not a right. Too prolonged or too frequent absences were impolitic; the courtier

who spurned the Sun's rays was indeed badly placed for further
preferment, and not a little denigration and whispering against
him went on behind his back by those intriguing to step into his
shoes. When Cecil returned from the north, where he had been
negotiating the Treaty of Edinburgh in the summer of 1560, he
found himself much out of favour simply because of the malicious
stories told against him in his absence. Norfolk hated a courtier's
life, yet dared not risk too long a sojourn in East Anglia. Even
those employed on the Queen's business found their characters
were being blackened and knew that their own nominees for
places of profit were bound to be at a disadvantage, compared
with those whose patrons were on hand in the audience chamber.
'I pray you to stand fast for your poor absent friends against
calumnators', wrote Leicester to Walsingham, from the Netherlands, and while he was away Whitgift, Cobham and Buckhurst,
all opponents of the Earl, were made privy councillors, through
Burghley's influence; the Lord Treasurer could not have pulled
this off had Leicester been at court.[4]

The Queen's personal female attendants numbered no more
than eighteen – four gentlewomen of the bedchamber, eight
gentlewomen of the privy chamber, all of them ladies of rank, and
six young maids of honour, whose ambitious parents hoped they
would have their chances in the marriage market improved
through attendance at the finest of all finishing schools. These
were the standard-bearers of the regiment of women who saw to
the Queen's wardrobe and toilette, her food and her creature
comforts in the private apartments and in whose company she
spent most of the day. There is no evidence that she ever seriously
discussed political questions with them, though individual courtiers did attempt to bring pressure on them, for instance during
the courtship with Alençon, or when they were asked to promote
suits for offices and rewards. With her ladies she talked about religion and philosophy, pulled to pieces preachers and other per-
sonalities and listened intently to court gossip. This was her family
circle. She took an absorbing interest in her young maids of
honour, dressed usually in white, expected to be privy to their
secrets, teased them, often cruelly, about their love affairs, but if

all went happily ever after, became godmother to their children.
Woe betide the courtier who took liberties with her maids! Both
Raleigh and Oxford went to the Tower for the flagrant seduction
of Elizabeth Throgmorton and Ann Vavasour and late in the
reign Leicester's son Robert was banished from court for daring
to kiss Mistress Cavendish. High-spirited though the court was,
and despite the slanders about her relations with a Leicester, a
Hatton and an Essex, Elizabeth tried to preserve a moral tone
which showed up the licentiousness of most of the European
courts.

She acquired a vast family of godchildren – over a hundred of
them. This readiness to stand sponsor was just as marked in the
early years of the reign when her own marriage seemed likely as
in her later years of spinsterhood. In 1560-1 she stood godmother
to as many as nine infants baptized in the Chapel Royal, among
them the offspring of Lords Cobham, Berkeley, Montague,
Mountjoy and Sheffield, of Garter King and of Secretary Cecil.
Next year the babies she sponsored were all children of com-
moners, among them the offspring of Atkins the scrivener. On
every occasion she made payments to the nurses and midwives,
which did not vary with the rank of the parents.[5]

Elizabeth inherited fourteen principal residences in London and
southern England, ranging in size from Whitehall Palace, which
sprawled over twenty-four acres to become the largest palace in
Christendom, to Woodstock Manor. Greenwich, her birthplace,
remained her favourite home. Five palaces were recent additions
to the royal patrimony, the most modern of which was Protector
Somerset's house in the Strand, still unfinished when he overreached himself. Wolsey's magnificent residences at Whitehall,
known in his day as York House, and at Hampton Court had
come to the crown on his disgrace. St James's was a windfall of
the reformation, when the inmates of the house originally founded
for leprous women were pensioned off to increase the size of
Whitehall, while in the Surrey countryside the stone from
Merton Abbey had provided the foundations of her father's
splendid folly at Nonsuch. These acquisitions more than com-

pensated the crown for the effective loss of residential quarters at Westminster Palace, which had never been rebuilt following a great fire twenty years before she was born. Her grandfather's palace of Richmond, named after his Yorkshire honour, had replaced the medieval house at Kew, also gutted by fire. Compared with these modern buildings the royal quarters at Windsor Castle, Eltham in Kent and at the Tower of London were unhygienic and uncomfortable. The more distant royal manors such as Oatlands near Weybridge, Woodstock, and even Hatfield, were in comparison little more than overgrown hunting-lodges, and Elizabeth used them as centres from which to follow the chase and as key points in her progresses. Hers was a goodly inheritance and she did not attempt to increase it; in fact she spent less proportionately on the upkeep of her residences than any sovereign since Edward II.

Though there were significant variations between one palace and another, most were arranged on the following plan. Since most of them were for easy communications built on the riverside, there was always the danger of flooding and so the royal apartments were placed on the first floor. The apartments were approached by a staircase leading on to a gallery, which became a busy thoroughfare when the Queen was in residence; here the importunate suitors waited, praying for the opportunity of pressing their claims to her patronage. Beyond a curtained door was the presence chamber, where audiences were given. This led in turn to the privy chamber and withdrawing room where Her Majesty usually fed, and to the royal bedchamber. The hall where she would feed in state on red-letter days, and the chapel were both on the ground floor, though her pew generally took the form of a gallery in the west end, to save unnecessary steps. The rest of the ground floor was given over to the complex of administrative and domestic offices, stores and quarters for the minor grades.[6]

All the palaces had their own privy gardens, and like a good mistress of the house Elizabeth would now and then pick blooms herself for arranging in her apartments. But at Whitehall the flower gardens were too small to provide all the decorations and so flowers and herbs were sent by river from Hampton Court and Greenwich, and masses of ivy and young birches were brought from the Queen's woods at Chislehurst and Farnborough. On special occasions evergreens and herbs were tied to the gates and railings of Whitehall, while throughout the summer window boxes and white wicker baskets full of flowers were hung round the courtyards. In winter she made do with artificial flowers and the scent of musk.[7]

To see to the needs of the Queen and her following there was an enormous domestic staff, organized by departments – the Robes, the Beds and the Laundry; the Pantry, the Buttery, the Bottles, the Ewery and the Pitcher-House; the Kitchen, the Boiling House and the Bakehouse; the Larder, the Acatary, the Poultry, the Pastry and the Confectionery; the Spicery, the Waifery, the Woodyard and many more. Among the more miscellaneous tradesmen on the palace payroll were two clockmakers, an armourer, an arrowhead maker, a bucketmaker, an engraver of stones, a locksmith, wheelwrights, a feather-dresser, ratcatchers and crowkeepers and, to keep the air sweet, an arranger of herbs and distiller of sweet waters.[8]

The Queen's ceremonial guard comprised fifty gentlemen pensioners under their captain, with a standard-bearer, all in their distinctive uniforms. More onerous duties fell to the yeomen of the guard, numbering two hundred men, with less splendid livery and only 16d. a day. With the development of the 'progress' and the continuing popularity of the hunt, Leicester's own department as master of the horse grew in size, and by the middle of the reign the royal mews contained 273 horses looked after by a staff of 128, quite apart from the studs at Marlborough and elsewhere. Besides sixty-four grooms there were four coachmen, six littermen, sixteen footmen, the chief avenor (who saw to the fodder), saddlers, bitmakers, farriers and the yeoman of the stirrup. In the kennels separate staffs tended the packs of harriers, buck hounds, hart hounds, otter hounds and mastiffs. William Scarlett, master of the barge, headed a crew of forty-two watermen in the royal livery, and his flotilla of barges and pinnaces was kept trim by a team of shipwrights.

The 'below-stairs' staff which saw to the domestic arrangements of the palace came under the control of the Lord Steward, who was aided by the treasurer of the household and the controller. Of Elizabeth's successive stewards, Arundel, Pembroke, Lincoln, Leicester and Hunsdon, only the last effectively administered the department himself, and for most of the reign the real power behind the scenes was Sir Francis Knollys, who succeeded old Sir Thomas Parry as treasurer in 1570. Knollys, a staunch Puritan, was balanced by his controller, Sir James Crofts, a Catholic and a pensioner of Philip II. Henry VIII's reforms of the household by the Eltham Ordinances, which laid down precisely the duties and privileges of officials of every grade, were still the rule, yet much was winked at. In 1561 Elizabeth signed fresh ordinances which specified allowances at table and listed menus, yet these, too, were frequently disregarded, for although she herself ate and drank in conspicuous moderation she ignored the requirements about fast days, ordering a full menu for every day of the week. Much more serious was the practice of courtiers and ladies in waiting absenting themselves from the Queen's board, to dine privately in their rooms on food specially prepared for them in the privy kitchen, and so the 'diets' served in hall in empty places were appropriated by servants, and by servants' servants. There was much waste and frequent pilfering by scores of boys lurking outside the kitchens, and because there was so much food to spare the palace always attracted an army of beggars, until the rigorous legislation of 1597.

Parliament in 1563 allocated an annual sum of £40,027. 4s. 2¼d. to the cofferer of the household for the Queen's domestic expenses, which was a far from generous sum since at no time after 1547 had costs been running at so low a figure, though men argued that there was as yet no consort to feed, no separate establishment for princesses or a queen dowager to be maintained. With the fall in the value of money it became impossible to run the household on so tight a budget; by 1573 expenses had reached £49,000, and soon Elizabeth had to dig even deeper into her own pocket. When we read the menus of the feasts given in honour of distinguished foreign visitors – who thought the Englishmen's reputation for gluttony not undeserved – and tot up the free daily diets served for the 1,500 courtiers and retainers in this large establishment of its kind in the world, it seems amazing that it was not costing more than twice that sum. The cautious Burghley regularly lectured the Queen on the necessity of keeping to the parliamentary grant, and every few years advocated a series of economies, thanks to which she never had to go cap in hand to the Commons for an increased grant. One reform, introduced in 1575, was to send royal agents direct to France to purchase supplies of wine, which saved a substantial amount but upset the London vintners who lost their profit. Another was having a private royal brewery for producing the 2,500 tuns of ale and beer consumed in a year. The first brewhouse, on the site of Syon monastery, was not a success as 'the water there did not hold the like relish the London brew did', so another was established at Puddle Dock, but the strength and flavour of the beer caused constant criticism. Eventually a brewer was found who agreed to supply the court at 2s. 6d. a tun less than the current market price.[9]

Much more successful was the reform of the ancient system of purveyance. Purveyors had gone out from the various household departments to the shires to buy up corn, cattle and all other items required, depleting the local market and driving hard bargains. These purveyors were regarded as 'hurtful to many, odious to all' and the Queen herself branded them 'harpies'. Though they were her officials they took their cut in all the deals they made and kept the farmers and merchants waiting for their money. One purveyor of the Acatary was granted a lease of rich pasture at Tottenham Court for fattening cattle before slaughter, but had herded the royal beasts in a tiny area, using most of the land for his own stock. Similar abuses were widespread and such men as Knollys and Crofts were reluctant to see the system reformed since they, too, had their pickings. After years of worrying over the problem and after being thwarted by Leicester, who in his last days had a vested interest as Lord Steward in keeping things as they were, Burghley succeeded finally in arranging separate long-term contracts in each of the counties, which was to the mutual advantage of crown and subjects. This contract system saved Elizabeth £19,000 a year, and the parts of England most distant from the capital, which had hitherto escaped very lightly, now bore their fair share of the burden of purveyance. That saving of £19,000 shows the kind of profits which the 'harpies' had been making.

When Burghley was gone, Elizabeth assumed the mantle of reformer herself. Richard Brown, clerk controller of the household, noted down her stormy interview with him about increased costs: 'Why was £40,000 not enough to live on?' she thundered, and the man politely reminded her of price increases and to prove his point prepared tables showing comparative costs at her accession and forty years later, with bread, beer, wood, coal and wax costing £12,000 a year more than of old. 'And shall I suffer this?' she asked him, when shown the papers:

> Did I not tell you, Brown, what you would find? I was never in all my government so royally with numbers of noblemen and ladies attended upon as in the beginning of my reign. . . . I will not suffer this dishonourable spoil and increase that no prince ever before me did, to the offence of God and the great grievance of my loving subjects, who I understand daily complain and not without cause, that there is increase daily of carriage and provisions taken from them at low prices and wastefully spent within my court to some of their undoings. . . . I will end as I began, with my subject's love. It is no marvel that these grievances were complained of in Parliament.

She told poor Brown to remind her to send for the treasurer, controller and others to have it out with them, but it was too late; she died before she could get to grips with the accounts.

The bulk of the food supplies were handled by two separate departments, the Acatary and the Poultry and the traditional responsibilities of each, though somewhat illogical, were rigorously respected; for instance while sheep fell to the lot of the Acatary, lambs were in the Poultry's province. In one year Elizabeth's court consumed 1,240 oxen, 8,200 sheep, 13,260 lambs, 2,330 calves, 760 steers, 53 boars, 310 pigs, 560 flitches of bacon and 33,024 chickens, besides a great deal of other poultry and game. Turkey was almost as rare a treat (seven dozen birds a year) as swan (six dozen), but the menus sometimes offered a game course provided by such birds as heron, bustard, mullard, snipe, ram-runner, lapwing, mew, brew, stint and godwit, as well as the more orthodox quail, lark and woodcock; pheasants and partridge were rarely served and grouse not at all. In season venison was a common dish, being provided from the royal parks and forests. The court used 60,000 lb. of butter a year, which on the estimated 1,500 mouths to feed, works out at 40 lb. per person.[10]

For all the fuss made about fast days, statutorily endured on Wednesdays and Fridays for the undoubted blessing of employing the fishermen of England and thereby training a vigorous naval reserve, the court did not set a good example. Too little fish was eaten, partly, we know, from choice, but also because of difficulties in obtaining supplies; the purveyor of sea fish at Rye, in Sussex, was so notoriously slack in paying his bills that fishermen boycotted him and other officials exercising their right to have first pickings of the fish sold at Billingsgate were unpopular with the Fishmongers Company of London. Moreover, keeping very large quantities of perishable sea fish fit for consumption raised problems only solved in more recent times. Neither the salted dried 'stockfish' brought in by the Iceland boats to Bristol and Hull, nor the herrings smoked at Yarmouth were regarded as very appetizing fare for courtiers, though for the lower orders these were a staple of everyday diet. Fresh water fish was a simpler commodity and during the reign special ponds were made at Southwark on the bankside and at Staines, near Windsor, which were kept well stocked. Elizabeth enjoyed imported sturgeon and salmon sent down by the Governor of Berwick on Tweed.[11]

The pressing problem of solvency made her increasingly avaricious. By the 1590s it was noted 'There is now no one at court but gives her [presents] at certain feasts, as on her birthday, her coronation day and on such occasions; and when they cannot give her anything, she gladly takes a dozen angels.' There had always been the traditional exchange of presents on New Year's Day and the higher the post a courtier held, the more lavish the Queen expected the gift to be. Her laundress offered an embroidered handkerchief, Smyth, the dustman, two bolts of cambric and her chief physician a magnum of toilet water and some candied ginger, but those nearest to her knew that nothing less than gold or precious stones would do. A penurious young man might compose a pretty verse flattering Oriana's beauty, but he could not hope to get away with this the next year. It was different for a scholar and Roger Ascham's death was due to a chill he caught in December 1568, sitting up all night to finish a poem to the Queen. At Greenwich on New Year's Day 1587, Hatton proffered a coronet and also a carcanet, or ornamented collar of gold, garnished with sparks of diamonds, with enamelled links, pendants of other jewels and fifteen gold buttons set with seed pearls and the words 'Tu decus omne tuis'. Heneage gave her a gold pomander and chain set with pearls, Leicester a rich purse and a brooch and Essex a 'fair jewel of gold like a rainbow'. Blanche Parry had brought her a serpent's tongue made of rubies and gold, Lord Admiral Howard a collar of gold like half-moons, while Drake delighted her with a fan of red and white feathers, splendidly jewelled, which opened to show her own portrait. Not all the gifts were so fine. Lord Lumley's book of psalms in Latin was only marginally suitable, but the pearls from the Countess of Oxford were marked as 'very mean'. Careful accounts were kept of these gifts and the entries there show how much gilt plate – her invariable present – the Queen gave in return. Leicester's due was one hundred ounces a year, five times more than the dustman; the maids of honour ten ounces and the mistress of the maids 13¾. Perhaps Leicester's most startling gift of all to her was a 'very fair jewel of gold, being a clock fully furnished with small diamonds and rubies; about the same are six bigger diamonds pointed, a pendant of gold diamonds and rubies, very small, and upon each side a lozenge diamond and an apple of gold, enamelled green and russet'.[12]

A very careful check was kept on all these jewels and fineries and detailed notes were made of even the most minor losses. It was formally recorded, for instance, that on All Hallows Day 1566 'Her Majesty wore a gown of black velvet embroidered and set with certain buttons of gold and diamonds, at what time one of the said diamonds fell from the button and was lost off her highness' back' and this statement was signed by Ladies Knollys, Stafford, Carew and Blanche Parry, a formidable defence against her searching questions. A little later she lost a diamond from a gold clasp on her 'gown of cloth of gold with roses and honeysuckle' at Greenwich. Every item was rigorously accounted for. In 1600, when she needed money so badly to meet increasing expenses at court and the costs of the wars in the Netherlands and Ireland, she looked through her jewel house, weeding out items that could be realized. First there was the 'coarse rubbish', such as broken chains of the Order of the Garter, old trenchers, dog-collars, dagger-blades, toasting-forks and useless knick-knacks, which she sent to the mint for melting down and using for gold and silver coins. Marketable items she sold to John van Hesse and other merchants for £9,393; these included her father's last great seal, bracelets of gold enamelled with green with the inscription '*Dieu et mon Droit*', crucifixes, the head of John the Baptist on a charger in gold and agate, a sapphire of incredible size 'in the shape of a heart, with a hole in it', one hundred garters of Venice gold, a whistle of gold King Henry had used at sea, and 'two pair of spectacles garnished with gold and a bracelet'; one wonders to which of the Tudors these last had belonged.[13]

Elizabeth maintained separate 'wardrobes' at Whitehall, Hampton Court, Windsor and the Tower, the last clearly the place to which she consigned clothes she would never wear again but could not bear to part with. Her portraits and the descriptions of ambassadors and others have familiarized her formal appearance in all her glory, especially in the elaborate farthingales in the French style, using some twenty yards of material, which came in with the Eighties and were worn with long stomachers and tiers of ruffs. Sumptuary laws checked extravagance, laying down the style and fabric to be worn by ladies in each rank of society, but the Queen herself spurned the homespun and indulged in expensive fineries unchecked. This was the great age of Italian silks and satins, and the colours were marvellous, not only rich crimson cloth of gold or masareene blue, but delicate shades like 'straw-coloured embroidered in silver and gold', dove-colour embellished with orange touches, tawnies and russets. It was in the second year of her reign that Mistress Montague, her silkwoman, gave her her first pair of knitted silk stockings, which so captivated her that she said she would henceforth wear nothing but silk. To show off her own person to best advantage she kept her gentlewomen in black velvet gowns (at least she never gave them anything other than black velvet), and dressed the vestal maids of honour in white. Inventories of her wardrobe reveal how heavily jewelled most of her dresses were; one had a thousand seed pearls on it, another a diamond for every day in the year.[14]

Even in old age she could startle the beholder, as a Frenchman, with an eye for fashion, relates:

She was strangely attired in a dress of silver cloth, white and crimson (or 'silver gauze', as they call it). This dress had slashed sleeves, lined with red taffeta and was girt about with other little sleeves that hung down to the ground, which she was for ever twisting and untwisting. She kept the front of her dress open and one could see the whole of her bosom, and passing low, and often she would open the front of this robe with her hands, as if she were too hot. The collar of the robe was very high, and the lining of the inner part all adorned with little pendants of rubies and pearls, very many, but quite small. She had also a chain of rubies and pearls about her neck. On her head she wore a garland of the same material and beneath it a great reddish-coloured wig, with a great number of spangles of gold and silver, and hanging down over her forehead some pearls. On either side of her ears hung two great curls of hair, almost down to the shoulders and within the collar of her robe, spangled as the top of her head.

For his next audience she wore black taffeta, bound with gold lace and lined with scarlet, over a white damask petticoat, opened in the front so that her navel was visible! No wonder the Puritans anatomized the abuses of high fashion, and what a change from the young princess whose modest appearance had earned such praise from Roger Ascham. But the truth was that Sieur de Maisse, Henri IV's special envoy, was absolutely fascinated by her, which was what she had intended. Another remarked that in going to chapel her bosom was uncovered, 'as all the English ladies have it till they marry.' He saw no impropriety in her dress, and noted the great dignity with which she bore herself.

What also impressed de Maisse was palace etiquette:

> When the Queen is served, a great table is set in the presence chamber near the Queen's throne. The cloth being laid, a gentleman and a lady come in, walking from the end of the room with the course and make three reverences, the one by the door, the next in the middle of the chamber, the third by the table. Then they set down the course and the lady tastes the food. [As a precaution against poisoning.] The guards bring in the meal in the same manner then the lady tastes the food with a piece of bread and gives it to the guards. Such food as she wanted was taken into the privy chamber.

The food by French standards was 'neither very sumptuous nor delicate', but the ritual of serving it he thought superb.[15]

It was foreign visitors to court who remarked on this ceremonial that had grown up around her and hardened in the last decade of the reign; her own courtiers had become so used to it that they did not regard it as noteworthy. A German writer reports how she would go to chapel on an ordinary Sunday morning in as much state as if she were opening Parliament. The presence chamber was crowded with notables waiting to form into a great procession in ascending order of precedence. At length came the Knights of the Garter, followed by the Lord Keeper, with the great seal of England in a red silk purse; and then preceded by sceptre and sword of state came Elizabeth herself, followed by her ladies in waiting and maids of honour. As she walked slowly along the rushes she would pause to speak to an ambassador in his own tongue, or to have a friendly word with a humble subject among the crowd of onlookers, and as she passed everybody went down on both knees. If, as often happened, the crowd broke into shouts of 'Long Live Queen Elizabeth', she would turn round as she reached the ante-chapel to say 'I thank you all my good people.' She knew when to relax strait-laced rules, maybe out of kindness to let an old petitioner sit on a stool by her throne as she questioned him in the presence chamber, for she was no slave to empty formality. Yet occasions of state demanded dignified ceremony, otherwise the court would not be a court, and at such times she was a stickler for etiquette. At a reception for the Lord Mayor in 1582, a young blade 'being more bold than well-mannered, did stand upon the carpet of the cloth of estate and did almost lean upon the cushions' where she was sitting in majesty, so she reprimanded the Lord Chamberlain and his gentlemen ushers for allowing such disorders.[16]

Every day of the year thirteen poor men at the palace gates were given 5d. apiece by the almoner's staff. The Queen's 'privy alms', or casual gifts to needy folk whom she came across on progress, averaged £240 a year. Almsgiving reached its peak in holy week, for in addition to the Maundy Money there were extraordinary distributions of alms to the poor on Maundy Thursday, Good Friday and Easter Day, totalling some £130. On Maundy Thursday she herself took part in the traditional ceremony at which she presented to as many poor old women as she had years a purse each, with as many pennies, and a further 20s. in token payment for the gown the Queen was wearing. Originally the gown had gone to the most needy person present, but to save having to make an invidious choice, or draw lots like the soldiers at the cross, she decided to give each pauper a further gift. The antiquary William Lambarde who watched the royal maundy being distributed at Greenwich in 1573, when Elizabeth was thirty-nine, wrote an account of it. The thirty-nine pauper women were arranged on benches in two lines in the Great Hall, where the floor was specially carpeted and by each place was a cushion for Her Majesty to kneel upon as she washed the women's feet, to commemorate Christ's washing his disciples' feet on the first Maundy Thursday. The yeoman of the laundry entered bearing a silver basin of warm water and sweet herbs, and one by one washed each person, wiped their feet on his towel, made the sign of the cross above the toes and kissed them. Next the sub-almoner in a similar manner washed all thirty-nine pairs of feet and when he had finished the almoner did the same. These preliminaries over, Elizabeth came into the hall attended by thirty-nine gentlemen, each with towel and basin, and the service began. After the gospel for the day, the Queen began her long task and a different gentleman waited by each pauper while she washed, dried, crossed and kissed the feet as the three officials had done. This over, she went down the ranks distributing to each woman four yards of broadcloth, to make into a gown, and a pair of shoes. Next she gave each a wooden platter with Lenten fare – half a salmon, half a ling, six red herrings and two small loaves – and an issue of claret. The gentlemen in waiting surrendered their aprons and towels and these, too, were given away; and then the Treasurer of the Chamber came with thirty-nine small white purses, each containing 39*d*., and a red leather purse with 20*s*. 'for the redemption of Her Majesty's gown'.[17]

As 'God's creature' by divine right, stemming from the anointing at her coronation, Elizabeth touched for the King's Evil, following the traditional rite, but with the words of this office Englished and the prayers pruned of their most Catholic phrases. It was enough for her that her father had touched for the Evil, and she would follow him. Puritans scoffed at the alleged efficacy of 'her mere superstitious touch' to cure cases of scrofula, but increasingly from the middle of the reign she touched both at Whitehall and on progress.[18]

Elizabeth's was still an itinerant court in the old tradition, transferring from one residence to another at irregular dates in the calendar. Early in August 1559, for instance, Elizabeth left Greenwich for nearby Eltham Palace for a three-day stay and then moved on to Nonsuch in Surrey. After six nights there she transferred to Hampton Court, breaking her journey at Richmond, though not sleeping there, and she remained at Hampton Court until the end of October, when she moved to Whitehall. Because of poor roads, travelling from palace to palace was less easy in winter, and much of the delight of the twelve days of Christmas for the household staff lay in the fact that the court was settled. At other times removals might be ordered, or cancelled, at short notice, routes or destinations might be changed without warning, and as supplies for the court and fodder for the great number of horses had been laid in at various stages of the journey well in advance, there was much waste. There is a pleasant tale about one of her carters, who, on being told of yet another change of plans – the third that day – slapped his thighs and said 'Now I see that the Queen is a woman, as well as my wife.' From a window overlooking the courtyard Elizabeth overheard him and called out 'What a villain is this!' throwing down to him three angels.[19]

But Elizabeth was not merely travelling from palace to palace as an essential exercise in domestic economy, nor was she compulsively for ever on the move like Alice's Red Queen. She developed the summer progress, her annual holiday, as a piece of statecraft, as it enabled her to put into practice two of the wisest maxims of royal governance – for her to get to know her realm, and for her to show herself to her people. In our age of television and newspapers with mass circulations, eager to give space to the releases of the palace press officials, it is hard for us to imagine what subjects thought of a sovereign they prayed for Sunday by Sunday but had never seen. For her to restrict the circulation of false likenesses and attempt to secure that only authorized portraits were reproduced for sale was one thing, but it was a minor advantage compared with taking her whole court on tour of the provinces, truly for her subjects 'the greatest show on earth', and townsmen, where civic receptions were held, could actually hear her speak. Nothing did so much to strengthen the average Englishman's bonds of affection to his sovereign as catching sight of her as she rode by with her great train of followers, so that her progresses about her kingdom each summer, when London was really unhealthy in the heat, became legendary.

If her officials lived most of the year at her expense, so that Whitehall Palace became in effect the largest hotel in the world, she expected to be entertained in return by the richest of them during her summer progress. Not that it saved her any money, for Burghley patiently worked out sums to show her that progresses added over £1,000 to her annual charges, with bread costing 1d. a loaf more in the country than at court. She refused to listen to his plea that some courtiers should be left behind – a release from a tedious duty which they would have welcomed – because she saw the importance of putting on a show, though she did at last agree to reduce the numbers of servants in her train. Many misconceived her passion for holidays away from the capital and the least charitable told scurrilous tales that 'she never goeth in progress but to be delivered of one of Leicester's children.'[20]

By now fewer fittings for the royal suite travelled with the court than in medieval times, but there was still a great deal of baggage and the Queen invariably took her own bed and bedding with her. Many ill-founded myths have been perpetuated about the houses, and even the rooms, in which Elizabeth is reputed to have slept on her tours of southern England and the Midlands, but wherever she slept it was always in her own bed, lovingly transported by the groom of the wardrobe of beds. This was in keeping with a tradition that would be kept up by her immediate successors and even Queen Victoria less than a century ago had her own bed sent by train, on the few occasions on which she visited her son at Sandringham. No longer did a royal chaplain carry a portable altar on a sumpter mule, but the royal clerk of the market was always in her entourage, holding sessions in each parish through which she passed to check weights and measures against his standards to ensure that wicked grocers and others were not cheating her purveyors. If the weather seriously interfered with progress, the presence in her train of the master of the royal tents, hales and pavilions ensured that the Queen would never be utterly stranded for the night; in fact there is no evidence that she ever slept under canvas, but quite often the tents were set up for a picnic meal.[21]

Off she went, riding side-saddle or in a coach, with Leicester, as master of the horse, holding her bridle as they approached a town or crossed a county boundary, to be ready for a seemingly endless series of welcoming addresses from mayors and lords lieutenants. Before her rode a noble bearing a sword and all round her were members of her bodyguard of henchmen; behind came other officers of state, household officials and menials, comprising a train that often exceeded five hundred persons. They made a glorious sight, bringing a blaze of colour to the countryside as they noisily wended their way across England at three miles an hour, and humble folk would come out of their cottages to stare in amazement and cheer; perhaps it was the only chance many of them had had of seeing their Queen and they could not expect another. De Spes, the Spanish ambassador in 1568, so much more appreciative of Elizabeth's incredible popularity than his predecessor de Feria had been ten years back, wrote about her reception in Berkshire:

She was received everywhere with great acclamations and signs of joy, as is customary in this country, whereat she was exceedingly pleased and told me so, giving me to understand how beloved she was by her subjects and how highly she esteemed this, together with the fact that they were peaceful and contented whilst her neighbours on all sides are in such trouble. (She attributed it all to God's miraculous goodness.) She would order her carriage sometimes to be taken where the crowd seemed thickest, and stood up and thanked the people.

She loved crowds, but knew what so many of the great forgot – that they were made up of individuals – so by deft touches she had a friendly word with as many as she could, purchasing unswerving loyalty with a smile, the wave of a hand, a nod of acknowledgement. This was part of the business of being a crowned head and Elizabeth performed it extremely well. How bored she must have been with the turgid phrases of loyal addresses, the weak rhymes of the versifiers, ambling rustic manners and the lack of polish in the ceremonial of so many provincial city fathers, yet she suppressed her yawns and her temper, and was very gracious. The temptation to be offhand when she was tired and too much time had been lost already was very great. When Serjeant Bendloes, coming to pay his respects to the passing monarch in Huntingdonshire, said to the royal coachman: 'Stay they cart, good fellow, stay they cart, that I may speak to the Queen', it seemed so incongruous that she laughed 'as she had been tickled', but saved the poor man from utter ridicule by giving him her hand to kiss. After four days at Elvetham she could have been excused from not prolonging her departure any further, yet when a farewell 'Come Again' was sung to her at the park gates, she stopped her coach to hear it right through, though the rain was heavy.[22]

The route of the progress was carefully planned in advance by the Lord Chamberlain, once the Queen had made known her intentions about dates and the direction in which she wished to

travel; but the final itinerary would sometimes bear little re-
semblance to the original scheme, for Elizabeth kept changing her
mind and first-hand reports from the provinces suggested alterna-
tives, so that the proposed route 'hath changed every five hours'.
Hopefully the Chamberlain would prepare the 'gestes', or table
of lodgings appointed for each night, which would be published
at court and copies were then sent to mayors and lords lieutenants
with orders for them to provide adequate supplies of food, fuel
and fodder and to certify that their areas were free from infection.
Gentlemen ushers of the chamber went down to inspect the
lodgings available and the Queen's waymaker surveyed the condition of the roads which would be pounded by the 220 carts of the
advance baggage train before the Queen's own carriage passed.
The rate of advance was slow, no more than twelve miles a day,
and bad weather could seriously upset the timetable. In reality to
send the court on tour in this way was a very formidable undertaking and, however detailed the arrangements, too many things
could go wrong. When Elizabeth reached Bristol in 1574 she
gave a prayer of thanksgiving for 'preserving me in this long and
dangerous journey' and every man and woman in her train must
have added their own heartfelt 'Amen'.[23]

While the itinerary was still in draft, in the face of rumours and
information gleaned by backstairs enquiries, most of those in
danger of having to play host began to make excuses – the house
was too small, the ways were foul, there was illness about, there
was insufficient time for proper preparations. Nearly all were too
proud to hint that the bill would ruin them, and the case put up by
the Marquess of Winchester that a royal visit would involve
'more charge than the constitution of Basing may well bear', was
a feeble one, coming from the grandson of a Lord Treasurer.
Archbishop Parker, faced with entertaining the court at Canterbury, agreed reluctantly to put up the Queen, the Treasurer, the
Chamberlain, Leicester and a few other notables, provided they
brought their own furnishings, but since his house was 'of an
evil air, hanging upon the church and having no prospect to look
on the people' – an artful suggestion that – Elizabeth might really
prefer to lodge at her own palace at St Augustine's, while her

courtiers could be wished on the canons in the close. Once it was
clear that the Queen was going to come, the next line of defence
was to try and ensure it would be a short visit; the Earl of Bedford
pleaded with Burghley in 1572 to 'help that Her Majesty's tarrying be not above two nights and a day' when she was coming to
Woburn Abbey. There was intriguing with the Lord Chamberlain to alter the route, the gentlemen ushers were offered bribes
and Leicester would try and use his influence to protect a friend;
indeed the Earl earned a sharp reproof from Lady Norris for
persuading Elizabeth against staying at Rycote, when the family
really wanted her to come. At great houses supplies were laid in,
special ovens built, carpenters kept busy, musicians hired, additional plate, hangings and Turkey carpets borrowed and the place
'made sweet against the Queen's coming'. Though certain
charges for food and drink could with luck be recouped from the
cofferer of the household, the host's total charges for entertaining
the whole itinerant court were very burdensome. Each of Elizabeth's visits to Theobalds cost Burghley 'two or three thousand
pounds'; her stay at Canterbury, which the Archbishop failed to
dissuade her from, made him £2,000 the poorer, and the charge
of her visit to Harefield brought a similar bill to Lord Keeper
Egerton. His predecessor, Lord Keeper Bacon, was fortunate to
escape with a short royal descent on Gorhambury in 1577, which
cost him only £577. Friends, neighbours and dependents were
expected to rally round with gifts in kind to shed some of the
burden. Egerton was able to exert considerable pressure, as Lord
Keeper, to extract donations for the feasts at Harefield in 1602.
The Lord Mayor of London provided a pipe of sack, sturgeon,
gulls, partridges and pheasants; Sir Francis Carew sent apricots,
plums and 'preserved oranges'; Walter Cope gave a Banbury
Cake, cheeses and cherry wine; and his own chaplain two sugar
loaves. Fellow peers sent sixty-seven bucks and twelve stags.
Apart from the costs, the honoured role of playing host to the
Queen was fraught with anxiety. As that great interpreter of
Elizabethan England, Sir Edmund Chambers, has neatly put it:

You probably got knighted, if you were not a knight already, which
cost you some fees, and you received some sugared royal compliments

on the excellence of your entertainment and the appropriateness of your 'devices'. But you had wrestled for a month with poulterers and with poets. You had avoided your house, and made yourself uncomfortable in a neighbouring lodge. You had seen your trim gardens and terraces encamped upon by a locust-swarm of all the tag-rag and bobtail that follows a court. And with your knowledge of that queer streak in the Tudor blood, you had been on tenterhooks all the time lest at some real or fancied dislike the royal countenance might become clouded and the compliments give way to a bitter jest or open railing.

At the end of it all the home park would resemble a fairground, crops in neighbouring fields be trampled down, you would count the silver to see what the hangers-on had pilfered and gloomily inspect the alleged damage to borrowed tapestries.[24]

Entertainment of Her Majesty involved much more than board and lodging, for she expected her hosts to provide amusements, and there was competition amongst the wealthiest to see who could stage the most lavish spectacles in her honour, with water festivals, firework displays, elaborate mimes and pageants, with poems by those prolific versifiers William Churchyard and George Gascoigne, which were subsequently published as mementoes. In these dramatic performances, Elizabeth was flattered as 'the beauteous Queen of Second Troy', 'the Fairy Queen', 'Diana', 'Sweet Cynthia' and 'the Shepherdess'. The preparations for her three-day stay as guest of Hertford at Elvetham included an army of labourers digging a great pond in the shape of a half-moon, with three islands, capped by buildings representing a fortress, a ship and a snail, as the setting for an imaginative 'triumph'. It was also incumbent on the host to give her costly presents 'even then at her departure'. Lord Keeper Puckering was prodigal in his gifts when she came to his house at Kew in 1595, presenting her with a fan with diamonds set in the handle, a jewelled nosegay, valued at £400, a pair of virginals and some clothes. Occasionally the gifts were below standard, and the Queen did not hide her displeasure. She had hoped that Lord Admiral Nottingham would take the hint she had dropped and give her 'his rich hangings of all the fights with the Spanish Armada in '88', but instead he gave her some items of clothing. Palace officials also expected rewards as a matter of course, when the time came for the court to move on, and quite often this was a payment for nothing more than preventing things from going wrong – a form of blackmail that no one dared reform.[25]

The assignment of accommodation in the houses visited was always a ticklish problem. In a large, modern residence, like Burghley's Theobalds (to which Elizabeth was much attached), matters were reasonably simple. Burghley's dining room became her privy chamber, his vine chamber served as her withdrawing room, the tower room became the Lord Chamberlain's apartment, and so on. Any nobleman's house was a miniature palace, with its main chambers and suites of rooms largely modelled on domestic arrangements at court, so where the Queen and the most eminent in her train should lodge was fairly obvious, and it was lower down the ranks that trouble really began. Apart from travelling, a progress was unpopular with courtiers as a whole since many with comfortable quarters at Whitehall knew they would have to rough it in the shires. Sir Henry Lee was not going to put up with a tent on the progress to Hampshire in 1591: 'I am old,' he wrote, 'and come now evil away with the inconveniences of progress. I followed Her Majesty until my man returned and told me he could get neither fit lodging for me nor room for my horse.' Some complained about having to accept accommodation beneath their dignity, others bickered about the claims of rival rank and office, and in cramped quarters the best of friends became uneasy bedfellows. The Queen's favourites were as touchy as anyone on this score and when, during the visit to Archbishop Whitgift's palace at Croydon, Lord Howard of Effingham, then Chamberlain, allowed Raleigh to occupy the lodgings set aside for Hatton, there was a fearful scene, with Elizabeth losing her temper with Howard. Lesser fry had to make do with out-houses, village inns and tents in the grounds.[26]

A summer progress was the norm in the first half of the reign, which the Queen only cancelled in a serious crisis, as during the French war in 1562, or when the plague was prevalent, as in the first great visitation in 1563. If the political situation was uncertain, making it unwise for her to go far from the capital (as in

1568, with Mary's escape to England), she journeyed no further than the home counties; otherwise she travelled considerable distances over ten or more weeks. In 1560 and again in 1569 she went to Southampton, in 1564 to Cambridge and two years later to Oxford; in 1572 she first ventured into the Midland shires, while the next summer she spent more quietly in Kent and Sussex. 1574 saw her as far west as Bristol and in the longest of all progresses the following year she visited Worcester, had a three-week stay with Leicester at Kenilworth, and went on to Lady Essex at Chartley, a few miles north-east of Stafford and the most northerly point in the realm she ever reached. The last of her major progresses was the visit to East Anglia in 1578, for the next year she was too occupied entertaining the French embassy and with the coming of the Eighties the darkening international situation kept her at home. To everyone's surprise she set out again in 1591, for Hampshire, where the Earl of Hertford fêted her at Elvetham and next summer returned to Oxford; she was still on the move in the home counties in the last three summers of her reign.

Subjects who saw her rarely, or not at all, envied the good fortune of Londoners in having the Queen in their parish for the major part of the year. At one time she had hoped to extend her 1575 progress by visiting Shrewsbury, Ludlow, the seat of the Council of Wales and the Marches, and even in crossing into the principality, as befitted Henry Tudor's grandaughter, but none of this could be fitted in. Again, her plans to visit York, headquarters of the Council in the North, in 1584, had to be abandoned. Twice it seemed certain she would visit Wiltshire, but on each occasion fresh arrangements were made, while the citizens of Leicester were warned in four different years to expect their sovereign, but each time were disappointed.

The climax of her progresses was her visit to the Earl of Leicester at Kenilworth in the hot July of 1575, where on her arrival the clock on Caesar's Tower was deliberately stopped to prolong the fantasy of a midsummernight's dream. Thanks to Sir Henry Killigrew, Leicester had secured the services of an Italian who was an expert in fireworks displays; the man had wanted to have live dogs, cats and birds sent in orbit in a fiery dragon and discharged, but he wisely adopted a more modest plan – even so there was 'blaze of burning darts flying to and fro, gleams of stars coruscant, streams and hails of fiery sparks, lightning of wild fire a'water and a'land.' In Kenilworth Castle there were great banquets, masques, performances of the Coventry Hock Tuesday play and other dramatics; out of doors there was hunting and bear-baiting, and an awkward half-hour at the end of a chase was filled with an improvised dialogue between a savage, dressed in moss ('the Wodwose', a folk hero of yore) and Echo. Leicester's crowning achievement was an ambitious water pageant, 'The Delivery of the Lady of the Lake', in which Proteus rode on a dolphin ('The dolphin was conveyed upon a boat, so that the oars seemed to be his fins; within the which dolphin a consort of music was secretly played'). The Earl had other entertainments in reserve in case Elizabeth prolonged her stay even further.[27]

Provincial cities could not attempt to imitate pageantry on the scale which London had put on for the coronation, nor could they afford the costly spectacles devised for Leicester, yet within their limits each managed something characteristic and memorable. While resting in her lodgings after arrival at one city, it was suggested to Elizabeth that 'if it were her pleasure at any time to take the air abroad, there were devices to be seen to pleasure Her Majesty.' How disappointed they would have been had she kept to her chambers! Bristol, as second port in the kingdom, staged a naval battle, with the destruction of the Fortress of Feeble Policy, and Norwich, home of the new draperies, put on an exhibition of children knitting and spinning. 'I have laid up in my head such good will, as I shall never forget Norwich', said Elizabeth, on bidding farewell to the citizens, who long remembered her kindness to the schoolmaster who had been so shy at having to make a Latin speech. At Warwick she similarly befriended the recorder, who had been shaking in his shoes. 'It was told me that you would be afraid to look upon me or to speak boldly, but you were not so afraid of me as I was of you.'

Entertainment with a greater intellectual stiffening was provided by the universities. In August 1564 Elizabeth took up her residence at King's College, Cambridge and between the heavy series of orations, disputations on such homely themes as 'monarchy is the best form of government', the banquets and divine service, saw three plays produced in the chapel – the *Aulularia* of Plautus, which lasted three hours, a modern version of *Dido*, also in Latin, both of which proved an utter bore to the fidgety courtiers, like Norfolk, who had forgotten their classics, and to everyone's relief a modern comedy in English by Nicholas Udall. One afternoon there was a long debate between doctors of divinity on the motion 'Scripture has greater authority than the Church' at the end of which Elizabeth was entreated to say something herself in Latin. She at first refused, coyly suggesting that a speech in her native tongue might be more appropriate, but Cecil, the Chancellor of the University, reminded her that at a formal gathering, the University could only be addressed in Latin; three words, he hinted, would suffice. She floored them all by speaking six hundred on the subject of diligent study. They expected her after this to watch a Latin translation of a Sophocles tragedy in the evening, but she had had quite enough. Her absence from the play disappointed a group of young men who had worked up a masque to be added as an epilogue to the main production, so they trailed her to Hinchinbrook, her next halt, and she allowed them to perform it for her in the hall. Their masque was in fact a burlesque on the Roman mass, and one of the characters appeared as a dog bearing the host in his mouth. The Queen was so offended at this undergraduate prank in the worst possible taste that she left in the middle of the performance. Cambridge Protestantism indeed![28]

Oxford behaved itself in 1566 and so earned a return visit. She thought very highly of an English play, *Palamon and Arcite* by Richard Edwardes, master of the children of her Chapel Royal, which was performed in Christ Church Hall. Though a wall near the entrance to the stage collapsed, killing three people, in the course of the performance, the show went on. For this production she had loaned some clothes that had belonged to Queen Mary and part of a gown of purple velvet was somehow lost.[29]

After a more strenuous week of civic and academic receptions and entertainments at Oxford in September 1592, where the plays produced for her were described by a Cambridge man as 'but meanly performed', Elizabeth made for Rycote with a reduced train, to enjoy a quiet weekend with the Norrises. She had often revisited the house since her journey to Woodstock in disgrace in 1554, when Lord Williams of Thame had befriended her, as it always gave her real pleasure to be in the company of Williams' daughter Lady Norris, whom she nicknamed 'the Crow', from her dark colouring. Lord Norris welcomed her with an apt little speech; they were a depleted family for such an occasion, as four of their sons were at the wars, which 'hath so often affrighted the Crow, my wife, that her heart hath been as her feathers.' Next day the hosts put on their own miniature pageant, while the Queen was in the gardens, musicians playing. First came in a servant dressed as an 'Irish lackey', shouting 'News out of Ireland', bearing a charming letter from son John, President of Munster, marked 'I fly only for my sovereign', and wrapped inside was a gold dart set with diamonds; for 'darts' were Irish weapons. He was followed by a man in the rig of a Flemish skipper who brought a similar greeting from son Thomas, serving in Flanders, marked 'I open only for you'. His gift was a gold key, the symbol of Ostend, the key to Flanders. Lastly arrived a lad in the costume of a French page, purporting to have just landed from Brittany; he brought three letters from the two Norris boys fighting in the English force in the 'War against the Three Henries'. The first was a mock love letter to a local lass 'Mistress Squeamish', which had everyone in fits of laughter, but the other two were touchingly loyal epistles containing offerings of other jewelled miniatures – a sword and a truncheon. Elizabeth was overjoyed at this performance. Old Norris, putting on a solemn face told her that, while he was glad his sons had remembered their duties, he regretted that their sister Katherine, the wife of the Governor of Jersey, had forgotten hers, but then she might be excused, for she was a woman, and he hoped the Queen would take that reflexion in good part. Next day, as she was leaving, came a message from Jersey, with Katherine's apology for her tardiness and a daisy of gold set with rubies. These four soldier sons were all to lose their lives in her service before the Nineties were out, two dying from wounds in Ireland, one from wounds in Holland and the last killed in action in France.* Elizabeth remembered that visit when news came of the first son's death and wrote to Lady Norris the most poignant of her letters: 'My own Crow, harm not yourself for bootless help, but show a good example to your dolorous yoke-fellow.'[30]

In the last years of her life her chief ministers tried to stop her from overtaxing herself by what they regarded as unnecessary travel, but she was determined not to stay put in London. Did she not deserve a change of scene and air? Against their advice in 1600, she had gone to Nonsuch, and after a few days decided to go on her travels. 'The lords are very sorry for it, but Her Majesty bids the old stay behind and the young and able to go with her. She had just cause to be offended that at her remove . . . she was so poorly attended, for I never saw so small a train.' In those latter days her obstinacy and indecision were as marked as ever, and she displayed all the impatience of the proverbial back-seat driver. On a whim she would decide to alter course and pay a surprise visit to a favoured courtier, and this sudden change of plan would euphemistically be called 'a by-progress', with which the unsuspecting host and the more placid household officials coped as best they could. At the turn of the century her ministers racked their brains to find enough to amuse her in or near London; they arranged for her to go a-maying at Highgate and she so enjoyed it that the next year she attended the May Day revels at Lewisham. 'All is to entertain the time; and win her to stay here if may be' – it was Christmas 1602 – and the plan worked, for at the last minute she decided to cancel her intended removal to Richmond, even though most of the carriages were already on their way.[31]

If she wanted a change from Whitehall, then a day visit to a courtier's house within easy reach was so much easier and cheaper for everybody than removal to another royal residence and the entertainment provided could be just as enjoyable as a specially staged triumph. We catch a glimpse of Elizabeth right at

*A fifth son, Sir Edward Norris, must have been present at Rycote in 1592.

the end, paying a call on Sir Robert Sydney at Penshurst, where the host wrote:

She seemed most pleased at what we did to please her. My son made her a fair speech, to which she did give most gracious reply. The women did dance before her, whilst the cornets did salute from the gallery, and she did vouchsafe to eat two morsels of rich comfit cake, and drank a small cordial from a gold cup. She had a marvelous suit of velvet borne by four of her first women attendants in rich apparel; two ushers did go before, and at going upstairs she called for a staff, and was much wearied in walking about the house, and said she wished to come another day. Six drums and trumpets waited in the court and sounded at her approach and departure. My wife ... did wear a goodly stuff of the bravest cut and fashion, with an under body of silver and loops. The Queen was much in commendation of our appearances, and smiled at the ladies, who in their dances came up to the step on which the seat was fixed, to make their obeisance, and so fell back into their order again. The younger Markham did several gallant feats on a horse before the gate, leaping down and kissing his sword, then mounting swiftly on the saddle, and passed a lance with much skill. The day well nigh spent, the Queen went and tasted a small beverage that was set out in divers rooms where she might pass, and then in much order was attended to her palace ...[32]

The last reception on the grand scale was that given by Lord Keeper Egerton at Harefield in August 1602. Elizabeth had driven there from a modest gathering at Harlington in Middlesex, where her host, Sir Ambrose Coppinger 'because he had been a Master of Arts entertained her himself with a Latin oration.' As she came through the gates of Harefield Place she was met near the dairy house by two rustic characters, a bailiff and a dairymaid, who acted a welcoming dialogue: 'The Mistress of this fair company, though she know the way to all men's hearts, yet she knows the way to few men's homes,' said Bailiff to Joan, 'except she love them very well, I can tell you!' And after much bantering the girl presented a jewelled rake and fork to the Queen, 'the best housewife in all this company'. There was more to come when she reached the steps of the house, where a chair had been set for her to listen to the dialogue of 'Place' and 'Time', the former in 'a parti-coloured robe, like a brick house', and Time with an hour-glass, stopped. 'The great that we are to entertain', said Time, 'doth fill all places with her divine virtues, as the Sun fills the world with the light of his beams. But say, poor Place, in what manner dids't thou entertain the Sun?' 'I received his glory and was filled with it'; we can almost see the Queen's lips forming a smile of satisfaction. On the Monday Lady Elizabeth Walsingham gave her 'a robe of rainbows' – a nice touch, as it *had* rained on St Swithin's Day – and later there was a masque in which the satyrs chided the nymphs (played by boys) for being too venal. At an appropriate break in the weather a sailor ran a lottery, and all the ladies from Queen to 'country wench' drew verse poesies from his lottery box, but it had been carefully arranged that Elizabeth, her ladies in waiting and maids of honour should all be successful in the draw and win money prizes. At the end of her stay Time and Place reappeared (the latter now in black, to mourn her going) and presented her with a jewelled anchor, since 'This harbour is too little for you and you will hoist sail and be gone.'[33]

From the sublime to the ridiculous, Elizabeth moved from Harefield to Burnham in Buckinghamshire, the home of Sir William Clarke, whose frugal entertainment 'pleased nobody, but gave occasion to have his miserliness and vanity spread far and wide.' A peer who was present remarked that Clarke provided neither 'meat nor money to any of the progressers. The house Her Majesty has at commandment and his grass the guards' horses eat, and this is all.' Queen and courtiers were relieved to move on to the royal palace of Oatlands.[34]

The court was essentially the fount of government, but turning aside from the audiences and council meetings, the reading of despatches, perusal of accounts and the other ever-increasing paperwork of the palace which demanded so large a share of the Queen's waking hours, there is the question of how she, and those about her, spent their leisure. For exercise she regularly followed the chase even in her sixties and sometimes shot with the cross bow, but royal tennis was not a woman's sport. For solitude she had libraries at Whitehall and Windsor, in the charge of a keeper paid at 6s. 8d. a day, and here she would read, translate and write occasional verse. But the personal interests in which she led the court to leave its mark on the age were music, the drama and the tilt, and in her patronage of these activities she was her father's daughter through and through. This gave her court another dimension and heightened her own image. The chivalry of the tiltyard, the triumphs of the madrigalists and the nationalist upsurge of Shakespeare's history plays in a very remarkable way all paid the same homage to Elizabeth in the unique role of her people's Queen.

She inherited King Henry's musical taste and ability, and but for very real enthusiasm for singing at court *The Triumphs of Oriana* would never have been written, the 'fa-lals' would have sounded hollow. Elizabeth's early promise as a musician was in terms of more than courtly praise, and she had lessons on the virginals from Christopher Tye, her brother's 'music lecturer'. When years afterwards, Tye was playing the organ at service in the Chapel Royal she sent a verger to the organ loft with the reproof that he played out of tune; his retort, that the man should tell the Queen it was her ears that were out of tune is clearly apocryphal. On her musical establishment she spent no less than £1,574 a year. Apart from the gentlemen and children of the chapel there were over sixty instrumentalists – seventeen trumpeters, seven players of the viols, seven flautists, six performers on the sackbutts and three drummers, augmented later in the reign by two harpists and three virginal players.[35]

Musicians were highly favoured in various ways. Tye, rector of Doddington in Cambridgeshire, the richest living by half in all England, was frequently allowed to absent himself from his cure of souls, to Bishop Cox's dismay, in order to be at court. Elizabeth well rewarded the genius of Thomas Tallis and William Byrd by granting them jointly the monopoly of publishing all vocal and instrumental music, and even the ruled 'manuscript' paper. Byrd, that giant of English polyphony, with his settings of the communion service and his Latin motets written for the Queen's chapel, was at heart a recusant, but so long as Elizabeth was on the throne he never faced prosecution. She looked after Anne, the widow of Richard Farrant in 1583, by granting her property in Yorkshire, at Wootton in Oxfordshire and at Islington in the suburbs of London. William Treasorer, who was repairer of the organs at Whitehall and maker of the Queen's instruments, was rewarded with a licence – more valuable than it sounds – to export ashes and old shoes, 'in recompense of making a rare musical instrument for our chamber, such as we have not heard the like before'. Under her patronage new skills were developed. She gave one of her trumpeters, George Langdale, the monopoly of making trumpets and sackbutts, 'whereof he hath been the first deviser and maker within this our realm.'36

Reminiscing in old age Elizabeth told a visitor that she had 'composed measures and music and had played them herself and danced them.' Though no copies can at present be traced, she actually published two compositions in 1578 – 'two little anthems or things in metre of Her Majesty'; let us hope that copies may yet come to light in a cathedral library. We are on surer ground with her own playing, though a later age was so convinced of her mastery of the virginals that the name was unhistorically traced to the 'Virgin Queen', whereas virginals were known by that name, being instruments for young ladies, before her birth. She arranged for Sir James Melville to be given the chance of eavesdropping on her playing when he came to Whitehall as Mary's envoy in 1564. Lord Hundson took him to a gallery from which he could hear her practising, quite alone, and then, tip-toeing beyond the curtained door, he stood behind her 'a pretty space hearing her play excellently well. But she left off immediately, so soon as she turned her about and saw me, and came forward, seeming to strike me with her hand, alleging she used not to play before men, but when she was solitary, to shun melancholy.' What was he doing there? He apologized; it was unpardonable to intrude, but 'I heard such melody as ravished me', and he could not but admit her playing was far superior to his own Queen's. Another ambassador talked with her about music on Christmas Eve 1597, as they listened to the spinet, probably in the same room at Whitehall that Melville had entered. 'She told me that she loved music greatly and that she was having a pavane played. I answered that she was a very good judge and had the reputation of being a mistress in the art. She told me' (and her modesty – or was it her delight in understatement? – had grown with the years) 'She told me she had meddled with it divers times and still took great pleasure in it.'[37]

The pavane and the other dances still drew her from her chair and a few months before her death she was dancing with the Duke of Nevers. Dancing had become an essential accomplishment of the courtier, as Hatton's rise to fame had made abundantly clear, and as the steps became more complicated a number of dancing schools opened in London, doing brisk business. There were soon so many of these academies, many of them 'conducted by persons unqualified both by their knowledge and their morals', some using Italian or French names, that Elizabeth was persuaded to clamp down on them. She was particularly anxious to suppress those who, 'under the pretence of good exercise, entice the young to exercise lewd behaviour', and in 1574 she appointed Richard Frythe, and two others, 'well known to the nobility and others of credit', to be the sole teachers of dancing in London and the suburbs.[38]

The masque, originally a masked dance with miming, had developed until it was something akin to modern ballet. Professionally staged by the master of the Queen's revels, with set pieces and elaborate costumes, the performance was interspersed with songs and spoken verses and at the end those in the audience were expected to take to the floor as well. There were usually performances at court during the twelve days of Christmas, on Shrove Tuesday and at Midsummer, and to stage a special masque was now the normal way of honouring a notable embassy or celebrating a society wedding. Elaborate plans were made for three nights of masques for the abortive meeting between Elizabeth and Mary Queen of Scots in 1562 at Nottingham Castle, in the course of which 'Discord' and 'False Report' were to be imprisoned, 'Friendship' was to enter the hall on an elephant and 'Peace' in a chariot, and then the English and Scots, led by their two Queens, would dance together into the night. What under her father had been 'masking after the manner of Italy' had taken firm roots and developed under Elizabeth specifically English characteristics.

.The eight 'court interluders' who played a scene in the intervals of a masque, were not very active at court beyond the first two years of the reign, but the Children of the Chapel, noted as much for their acting in the great chamber as for their sweet singing in the choir, went from strength to strength, being most in demand for palace productions at Whitehall and Windsor and also for appearing in dramatic companies in London. Yet the popularity of the boy players under their talented master, William Hunnis, brought the whole future of English drama under attack. The Puritans had seen nothing wrong with a masque in which cardinals, bishops and abbots were lampooned as crows, asses and wolves, but once the subject matter of the drama was broadened they branded all as 'bawdy fables'. 'The play' was for Puritans nothing less than pagan idolatry and the productions staged at their Queen's court were especially sinful because they began at the late hour of 10 o'clock, sometimes took place on the Lord's day and, much worse, had boys playing female roles. But Elizabeth was not going to give up her boy players. 'Plays will never be suppressed while Her Majesty's unfledged minions flaunt it in silks and satins. They had as well been at their popish service in the devil's garb', ruffed and surpliced in the Chapel Royal, thundered one Puritan pamphlet in 1568. The dramatic companies under the patronage of Leicester, Sussex and other peers were also under fire, and had the Puritan city fathers had their way there would not have been a single playhouse in London or the suburbs and no one would ever again take up the 'base trade of a mercenary interlude player'. It was Elizabeth's active support, politically and financially, that saved the drama, as it saved church music, from being sacrificed for narrow Calvinistic principles. So strong was the opposition that nothing less than the Queen's patronage would have sufficed to keep the theatre alive and to nurture it. It was an essential part of her mission in treading the *via media* to see that the chill wind of the reformation did not drive the renaissance from England.[39]

She formed her own dramatic company, 'Queen Elizabeth's

Men' in 1583, by selecting twelve of the best actors from the
existing companies, under Leicester, Sussex and Oxford. They
did not confine their performances to court, but toured the
country, playing as far afield as Bristol and Shrewsbury, and the
City of London was forced to give them a playhouse. This made
it plain that the Queen considered the drama as something absolutely vital. Others followed her lead and in 1585 Howard formed
the Lord Admiral's Company, led by Edward Alleyn and financed
by his stepfather-in-law, Philip Henslowe, which gave Christopher Marlowe the opportunity of proving his worth. The same
year the 'Lord Chamberlain's Men' were instituted, though it was
not until 1594, under Hunsdon's reorganization of the company
after the plague, that it became important, for then it was firmly
linked with the genius of William Shakespeare. But for the Queen,
the theatres would have closed, as the Long Parliament was to
close them, and the world would never have known the contents
of the First Folio.

Among the twelve original members of the Queen's company
was Richard Tarleton, the first great English comedian. Ugly, with
a flat nose and a squint, he had merely to show his face, like a
Robey or Chaplin, to have the audience in fits of laughter. A
natural clown, he could also sing and fence superbly and his brilliant extempore wit coined the word 'Tarletonizing'. Elizabeth
was absolutely delighted with his performing. A scribbled note, in
1585, when Sussex was Lord Chamberlain, catches the brilliance
of this star of the command performances:

How Tarleton played God Luz with a flitch of bacon at his back, and
how the Queen bade them take away the knave for making her to
laugh so excessively, as he fought with her little dog, Perrico de Faldas,
with his sword and long staff, and bade the Queen take off her mastick;
and she calling to the Lord Chamberlain to do his office to bring a
charger and to take him away, Tarleton answered:

> Oh, Thomas, Thomas, with your white rod
> Be not so saucy to correct a God.[40]

Not for nothing did Tarleton regard himself as the idol of the court.

After Tarleton's death the Queen's Men were never quite the
same, but the Lord Chamberlain's Men gave court and capital the

greatest series of plays to be written in the whole of history, _Titus Andronicus, Hamlet, The Taming of the Shrew, Love's Labours Lost, Romeo and Juliet_ and the rest. We see Elizabeth seated on a high throne, 'so beautiful to my old sight as ever I saw her' – mastick or no mastick – with her darling Essex next to her, for the first performance of _A Comedy of Errors_ and five months later as guest of honour at the début of _A Midsummer Night's Dream_, performed for the wedding of the Earl of Derby and Lady Elizabeth Vere. In the winter of 1601–2 no fewer than ten new plays were performed at court – a wonderful testimony to her own vigorous interest in the drama in her last days.[41]

There were tiltyards for jousting at Greenwich, Hampton Court and Whitehall, the last on the west side, enlarged and enclosed by Elizabeth in 1561, with a high gallery for spectators. Jousts covered three forms of knightly prowess – the tilts, in which horsemen used blunted spears; the tourney, in which they used swords; and the barriers in which the assailants fought on foot, alternately with pike and sword. The simpler exercise of the barriers could take place by torchlight and was even held indoors, in the banqueting house. Mock jousting also featured in court masques, such as a fight at the barriers between amazons and knights in 1579, and escapades with hobby horses and, no doubt, much extempore clowning. As the reign developed the principal tilt came to be held on accession day. Seeded champions would issue their challenges a few days before, to fight for a jewel, usually given by the Queen. Archery contests apart, this was the only form of organized sport in Tudor England and great crowds – 'many thousands' – came to watch the event, which began at noon. One who saw the accession tilt in 1584 remarked that anyone could get a seat in one of the stands by paying 12_d_. As champions, wearing their distinctive colours, brought their horses into the arena, trumpets sounded; their servants seeing to the horses and helping them to mount:

were disguised like savages, or like Irishmen, with their hair hanging down to the girdle like women; others had horses' manes on their heads, some came driving in a carriage, the horses being equipped like elephants, some carriages were drawn by men, others appeared to move by themselves; altogether the carriages had a very odd appearance. Some gentlemen had their horses with them and mounted in full armour directly from the carriage. There were some who showed very good horsemanship and were also in fine attire. The manner of the combat each had settled before entering the lists. The costs amounted to several thousand pounds each. When a gentleman with his servant approached the barrier, on horseback or in a carriage, he stopped at the foot of the staircase leading to the Queen's room, while one of his servants in pompous attire of a special pattern mounted the steps and addressed the Queen in well-composed verses, or with a ludicrous speech, making her and her ladies laugh. When the speech was ended, he in the name of his lord offered to the Queen a costly present, which was accepted and permission given to take part in the tournament. In fact, however, they made sure of permission before preparing for the combat. Now always two by two rode against each other, breaking lances across the beam. On this day not only many fine lords were seen, but also beautiful ladies, not only in the royal suite, but likewise in the company of the gentlemen of the nobility and the citizens. The fête lasted until 5 p.m.

On that day Oxford and Arundel were the victors. They were expected to present their shields with mottoed emblems to be hung in the Shield Gallery down by the Thames, overlooking the privy stairs.[42]

On other occasions the tiltyard was used for bear-baiting and even bull-fighting. Sometimes Elizabeth watched a single dog take on three bears and in May 1600 'commanded the bears, the bull and the ape to be baited.' She had no leanings towards re-forming the cruelty of the age. Other animals were kept behind wooden bars in the royal menagerie at the Tower of London, where the king of beasts gave his name to the Lion Tower.[43]

Life at court was a strange mixture of old traditions and recent innovations, and the changes Elizabeth had introduced were the more readily accepted because she was a woman. In her palaces grandiloquent luxury alternated with acute discomfort. There were countless tapestries for the walls but not nearly enough carpets for the floors; there were impressive thrones yet not a single comfortable chair; heating and ventilation were equally inadequate and there was no bathroom, although Greenwich

Palace did boast a water closet which had been invented by Sir John Harington for fun. For all the pressures on her purse Elizabeth succeeded in maintaining a dazzling spectacle, for she knew that the reputations of sovereigns at home and abroad largely hinged on the courts they kept, and hers would stand comparison with any in Europe.

THE DAUGHTER OF
DEBATE

MARY Queen of Scots by her very presence as Elizabeth's prisoner sowed discord in the realm which the Catholic powers were at last in a position to exploit with the coming of the seminary priests. In Madrid, Paris and Rome plans were being laid for 'the Enterprise of England', a crusade under the banner of the counter reformation, aiming at Elizabeth's death, Mary's release to reign in her stead and the restoration of Catholicism, and it was Mary's active encouragement of these conspiracies that sent her to her death. Tyrannicide became, if not exactly an article of faith, a most laudable undertaking and the early 1580s passed in a succession of plots against the Queen's person. This was the heyday of Walsingham's spies, the years of the rack and thumbscrew, with Mary subjected to greater restrictions and whole weeks of near hysteria in the House of Commons. 'These hellhounds,' wrote Thomas Digges, MP for Southampton, of the Jesuit missionaries, 'cladding themselves with the glorious name of Jesus and such wretched souls as they bewitch with their wicked doctrine, are indeed the only dangerous persons to Her Majesty.' A single well-aimed bullet would be enough to plunge England in civil war.

Leicester was fearfully concerned at Elizabeth's insistence that 'the increase of Papists in her realm can be no danger to her'; she was too merciful towards them, steadfastly refusing to regard her Catholic subjects *ipso facto* as traitors. Delighting in crowds, she took too few precautions for her personal safety and it was left to Burghley to frame regulations that, for instance, prevented her from accepting gifts of perfumed gloves and sleeves from strangers, through which poison might cunningly be administered, unless the scent 'be corrected by some other fume.' When she had stomach upsets and headaches men jumped to unwarranted conclusions, and Hatton once noted with relief that her sickness had been traced to the strange practice of eating cereal for breakfast – 'a concoction of barley sodden with sugar and water, all made exceedingly thick with bread' – which lost her her dinner and supper, but not her life. Elizabeth herself remained outwardly very calm, followed her normal routine and said repeatedly she would rely on the armour of God's providence. Returning from Hampton Court to Whitehall in November 1583, crowds of her subjects knelt by the wayside, imploring her to take due care of her person, wishing her 'a thousand blessings and that the evil-disposed who meant to harm her might be discovered and punished as they deserved.' She thanked them warmly for their love but refused to be cut off from her people, however great the dangers. Only once do we hear of her being afraid, when she was reported to be so 'overcome by a shock of fear' on her way to chapel that she had to return to her apartments, but the source of this tale is a tainted one. Nothing between her accession and the defeat of the Armada increased her popularity so much as being the intended victim of assassins.[1]

The arrival of Campion and Parsons in June 1580 was, however, a serious threat to the peace of the realm. Campion, the one really attractive figure among the products of Douai, who would have been President of St John's, if not a bishop, had not Rome called him, made many converts. On landing he had addressed an open letter to the Privy Council declaring that he had returned home to preach the gospel and save men's souls, not to meddle in politics, but the distinction was one which was alien to the age. He preached in London and toured the shires, a hunted man. In a panic the Council drafted plans to segregate known recusants, to keep them under supervision, and a lengthy proclamation was issued appealing to Englishmen to stand fast in their allegiance to the Queen, 'free from the bondage of the Roman tyranny'. Countless rumours stemming from English fugitives in Flanders and France had it that the Catholic powers had agreed on a joint invasion to 'dispose

of the crown and of the possessions of the subjects of the realm at
their pleasure', and an effective piece of government propaganda
was needed to close the ranks so that 'by God's goodness these attempts are likely to be frustrate.' The Jesuits were inevitably regarded as the shock troops of the Enterprise and the government
were uneasy until Edmund Campion was in custody. There is
good reason for accepting that Elizabeth had a secret interview
with him at Leicester's house and disputed the arguments in his
Ten Reasons against the Anglican Church; this was not their first
meeting, for she had been impressed with his scholarship on her
visit to Oxford in 1566. Undoubtedly considerable efforts were
made to persuade him to retract but the alleged promise of the
Queen, that if he conformed she would reward him well, even to
the extent of the see of Canterbury, has little enough foundation.
He had asked for a public disputation, on the lines so dear to Oxford theologians, and this was granted him, if only to show people
that the government was going out of its way to be fair. For four
sessions in the chapel of the Tower he faced the Dean of St Paul's
and the Dean of Windsor, displaying his abundant learning and
his ignorance of political realities. Burghley and others wanted
him tried on the issue of religion, and the drastic law of 1581 had
already come into effect, but Elizabeth insisted that the indictment
be within the scope of the old treasons statute, namely 'for conspiring to compass the death of the Queen and raise sedition
within the realm.' The verdict, as Campion knew, was a foregone
conclusion and he went to Tyburn on 1 December to provide
the Enterprise with a martyr.[2]

While Campion was still at large, Parliament had been framing
more draconic legislation against the Catholics, much more severe,
in fact, than the Queen was prepared to allow. In its earliest stages
the bill 'to retain the Queen's Majesty's subjects in their due
obedience' prescribed the death penalty for those who converted
any subject to the Church of Rome, but she insisted that conversion by itself was not a treasonable act and accordingly it was
amended to conversion accompanied by withdrawal of allegiance
from her. Elizabeth's moderating hand has also been traced in the
removal of the clauses in the draft bill which, for instance, forbade

lawyers found guilty of recusancy from practising and required schoolmasters to subscribe to the Articles of Religion in addition to the existing statutory subscription to the Oath of Supremacy. In the face of the Jesuit missionaries and disturbing rumours from abroad, the Commons were panicking, and it speaks volumes for the Queen's calmness and sense of moderation that she had the rigours of the bill toned down. The act in its final form was quite fierce enough. A fine of £66. 13s. 4d. (200 marks) was laid on any priest celebrating mass, with imprisonment until the sum was paid, and those found hearing mass were fined one hundred marks and sent to prison for a year. The penalty for being absent from Anglican services had remained at one shilling a Sunday since 1559 but now a further sum of £20 a month, a staggering fine, was imposed on all recusants aged sixteen or over, and the weekly shilling was still due. Anyone whose recusancy persisted for a whole year was required to enter into bonds for his good behaviour in the sum of £200 until such time as he conformed. These financial provisions, apparently the suggestion of Aylmer, Bishop of London, no doubt appealed to the Queen. Recusants were to be taxed out of existence, yet in the first year of operations total fines reached only £909 and by 1587 little more than double that sum was collected.[3]

After fifteen years of captivity it was small wonder that Mary clutched at straws. She complained with bitter tears of her 'hard usage' from Elizabeth, the lack of respect paid to her, a Queen, subjected to a myriad of indignities and confined in uncomfortable, even unhealthy, conditions. The house at Sheffield was so bad that she could not 'much longer endure it without manifest danger of my death', for hers was a 'poor, languishing, sickly body'. Later she condemned Tutbury as being cold, damp and draughty. Elizabeth sent her own physicians to attend her, anxious at times for the world to know her prisoner was not neglected, though hoping that a natural death might bring an end without high tragedy. To get through the day Mary wrote letter after letter, read, and busied herself with embroidery. At one stage she asked for some poodles to be sent from France, 'for except in reading and working, I take pleasure solely in all the little animals

I can obtain'; she kept pigeons and red partridges, caged, like herself, as 'it is an amusement for a prisoner.'[4]

In a long, violent letter to Elizabeth in November 1582 Mary gave a catalogue of all her sufferings and demanded 'satisfaction before I die, so that all differences between us being settled, my disembodied soul may not be compelled to utter its complaints before God.' She wanted her liberty and an accommodation with her son. Elizabeth was not unmoved and set in train negotiations with Scotland, sending in turn Beale and Mildmay to Sheffield to discuss possibilities of concluding a treaty for Mary's release. But anxious as Elizabeth was to find a solution, she knew that there could be no alternative to keeping Mary as a state prisoner. As Henry III of France put it, 'I do not believe that so long as Elizabeth lives she will ever be set at liberty.' For his part, James VI, when freed from the tutelage of Lennox or Arran, was unwilling to compromise his own future; to share the throne of Scotland with his mother would be bad enough, but to have her block his path to Whitehall would be intolerable. There could be no comfort in her release for Elizabeth; how the papists would rejoice and the Jesuits plot if she stayed freely in England, and if she went to the continent it would be even more dangerous. To release her now would make nonsense of all the old justifications for fifteen years of captivity, even though she might agree to waive her claim to the throne of England. The worst feature of any negotiations with Mary, as Walsingham noted, was 'the small trust that may be given to her to keep her promises', and she was never so deep in intrigue with those plotting to rescue her as when she solemnly maintained she would 'rather die in captivity with honour than run away with shame.' Meanwhile, between the storms, she and Elizabeth kept up the pretences of pleasantry by exchanging gifts, wigs, rings, miniatures and the like. Fate had prevented them from meeting: 'Would to God she could talk with her for two hours' sobbed Mary.[5]

There was a new face at court at the end of 1581 which helped Elizabeth to bear more easily the strains of the last days of Alençon's courtship. Walter Raleigh, a west country-man with a good record of service in the Irish wars, was nearly twenty years younger than the Queen. Most probably he was introduced to court by Sussex, now nearing his end, but still the authority on Ireland. Tall, handsome and 'damnable proud', he 'had gotten the Queen's ear in a trice . . . and the truth is she took him for a kind of oracle, which nettled them all.' His rise was so meteoric that later generations felt it needed such an incident as throwing his cloak in the mire for Elizabeth to walk upon to account for his instant favour at court. There is a much truer ring about the line Raleigh reputedly scratched with a diamond on a window pane (which Fuller, the originator of the cloak story, also records):

'Fain would I climb, yet fear I to fall'

to which Elizabeth added:

'If thy heart fail thee, climb not at all'.

Truth was, the adventurer needed little encouragement, and history does not need the cloak. His was a many-sided genius, which the Queen recognized instantly, a man of outstanding brilliance that attracted her on quite a different level from Leicester or Hatton. Soon he was her 'Water' and she could not bear to be out of his company. She leased him Durham House, granted him a valuable monopoly in connexion with the sale of sweet wines and knighted him. He had 'wit', in the Elizabethan sense of the term. 'When will you cease to be a beggar?' she asked him. 'When you cease to be a benefactress', was his apt reply. Through the Hakluyts and his stepbrother, Sir Humphrey Gilbert, Raleigh became irrevocably attracted to the idea of sending expeditions to North America to plant settlers and secured a royal charter to protect their interests. Elizabeth refused to let her favourite go on the voyage but gave her patronage to the Roanoke project by accepting Raleigh's suggestion that the colony should in her honour be named Virginia.[6]

Hatton could pen a passionate letter as well as dance exquisitely, but Raleigh had the edge on him, for he could communicate his adventurous spirit in matchless verse. For everyone else at court

Elizabeth was the sun, but for Raleigh alone she was the moon –
Cynthia the cold, chaste moon:

> My thoughts are winged with hopes, my lips with love,
> Mount love, unto the Moon's clearest night,
> And say, as she doth in the heaven's move,
> On earth so wanes and waxeth my delight,
> 　　And whisper this but softly in her ears
> 　　Hope oft doth hang the head and trust shed tears.

Cynthia was 'dear Empress' of his heart, 'The merit of true
passion'. This Queen, now past her fiftieth year, was the mistress
he would devotedly serve:

> A saint of such perfection
> As all desire, but none deserve
> A place in her affection.

She could not cease being a benefactress, so all the court were importunate beggars; he alone from higher motives offered love.

> Those eyes which set my fancy on a fire,
> Those crisped hairs, which hold my heart in chains,
> Those dainty hands, which conquered my desire,
> That wit, which of my thoughts doth hold the reins!
>
> Those eyes for clearness do the stars surpass,
> Those hairs obscure the brightness of the sun,
> Those hands more white than ever ivory was,
> That wit even to the skies hath glory won!
>
> O eyes that pierce our hearts without remorse,
> O hairs of right that wear a royal crown,
> Of hands that conquer more than Caesar's force,
> Of wit that turns huge kingdoms upside down!
>
> Then Love be judge, what heart may thee withstand?
> Such eyes, such hair, such wit, and such a hand!

Hatton, in despair that a younger suitor should supplant him, sent
the Queen, through Heneage's agency new love tokens to charm
Raleigh from her thoughts; there was a miniature gold bucket and
a costly 'fish prison', both playful allusions to 'Water', which
prompted her to send word that 'the Water and the courtiers
therein do content her nothing so well as her Sheep.' But Raleigh,

young still and single, could outmatch his rivals. At Christmas
1584, in the interval of parliamentry wrangling about measures
for her safety, she flirted with him openly, teasing him about a
smut on his face, that she was going to remove with her own
handkerchief; 'she was said to love this gentleman now beyond
all others.' Fascination, intense interest, but not love. She needed
his adoration, but could not love him and doubted, for all his protestations, whether his affections were as strong as his verses made
out. Raleigh was not content to be a passive worshipper of his
Moon goddess and as the months and years went by became sadly
disillusioned. For ten years he held the stage at court, to be
banished from it as soon as he found real happiness in a woman
who could reciprocate his love. The bitterness of it all comes out
harshly in his later poems, for he had seen through the tinsel and
beyond the masked expression; sunshine and moonhaze had
vanished like his own tobacco smoke.

> Say to the Court it glows
> And shines like rotten wood.[7]

Pius V's bull of 1570 had made Elizabeth's assassination lawful in
the eyes of his Church, but Gregory XIII went much further and
encouraged it. Two English nobles had asked the papal nuncio at
Madrid whether they would incur mortal sin by attempting the
deed and received from the Cardinal Secretary at the Vatican the
unequivocal answer: 'Since that guilty woman of England' causes
so much injury to the Faith, 'there is no doubt whatsoever who
sends her out of the world with the pious intention of doing God's
service not only does not sin but gains merit.' One such was John
Somerville of Edstone in Warwickshire, who had fallen under the
spell of a priest living with his wife's parents, Edward and Mary
Arden, and became infected with a 'frantic humour' to go on a
pilgrimage to court in October 1583, where he would 'shoot the
Queen with a dag', or pistol, as he wanted 'to see her head set
upon a pole, for she was a serpent and viper.' He had scarcely set
out when he assaulted passers-by and boasted to them of his design, so that he was soon in the Tower, where he gratuitously involved his wife, her parents, other relations and the priest by his

confession. After his trial he strangled himself in his cell. Some have dismissed Somerville as a madman, but it seems he was no more than a simple soul who took the Catholic hierarchy at their word. There were perfectly sane Roman Catholics, like Jeffrey Leede in Essex, who declared Elizabeth would not live half a year more.[8]

In this decade of plots and counter plots Sir Francis Walsingham came into his own. Modern scholarship, including the longest biography on any Elizabethan, has not altered the broad lines of the vignette of Walsingham given in Camden's obituary notice of him:

A man exceeding wise and industrious, having discharged very honourable embassies, a most sharp maintainer of the purer religion, a most diligent searcher of hidden secrets, who knew excellent well how to win men's minds unto him and to apply them to his own uses, insomuch as in subtlety and officious service he surpassed the Queen's expectation, and the Papists accused him as a cunning workman in complotting his business ...

For seventeen years he was Principal Secretary of State and for most of that time he had no colleague, though when ill or away on a special mission Lord Treasurer Burghley doubled as secretary. His Puritan fervour was a personal handicap in his embassy at Paris and in his dealings with the Dutch, when Elizabeth required him to pursue a cautious policy instead of devising for her the role of champion of Protestantism. Time and again he lamented her failure to hear the gospel aright and her miserliness to French Huguenots and Dutch Calvinists. Yet this same religious fervour brought him to develop a remarkable intelligence system as the only way of meeting the challenge of militant Catholicism and slaying 'the bosom serpent' Mary.

England in 1582 was still isolated, with an accredited ambassador only in Paris and an agent (paid by the merchants of the Levant Company) in Turkey. England could have done with more 'residents' of the calibre of Sir Richard Shelley, who had settled in Venice on account of his religion, but remained intensely loyal to Elizabeth and played a major part in settling commercial disputes in the Italian states. Only two foreign ambassadors were in London at this time, the French and the Spanish, and Mendoza, the latter, might more accurately have been described as Philip II's ambassador to the captive Queen of Scots than to the Queen of England. To counter this isolation and obtain vital news, Walsingham had placed agents in Spain, France, Flanders and elsewhere, who sent home regular reports of events, shipping and troop movements and advices about the English émigrés. At home he had men to watch the ports, to scrutinize the posts, cipher experts and spies of varying degrees of intelligence and trustworthiness. In the cold war of the early 1580s this was an essential part of the office and work of Principal Secretary, and Walsingham became renowned for his 'certain curiosities and secret ways of intelligence'. Thanks to his system the Throgmorton and Babington plots were cracked and Mary's guilt was proved.[9]

He looked to the north as the most dangerous area, for Henry of Lorraine, Duke of Guise, had sent Esmé Stuart, Seigneur d'Aubigny, to Scotland to ingratiate himself with his young royal cousin, and until the Ruthven raid in August 1582, when the 'English party' captured James's person, there was every need to keep a close watch on the Borders. In May one of Hunsdon's men stopped a servant of Mendoza's, disguised as a tooth-drawer crossing from Scotland into England and carrying letters for Mary and for Guise concealed behind a little looking-glass, specially made for the purpose by his ambassador. These letters were the first real indication that Walsingham had of 'the Enterprise of England'. But soon the Jesuit Holt, who was found at Leith with letters in cipher, said on being cross-questioned that there was 'a purpose in hand by the Pope and divers princes Catholic' to make war on England for Mary's benefit. To help with the problem of ciphers Walsingham won over a member of the French embassy and this Henry Fagot, as he called himself, succeeded in persuading one of the secretaries to send Walsingham copies of all the letters which Mary wrote to his ambassador. It was also Fagot who gave the tip that Francis Throgmorton came frequently to the French embassy, but always at night.[10]

Throgmorton, a Catholic by upbringing, had, like John Somerville, been a student at Hart Hall, Oxford; he was distantly related to Edward Arden who had suffered as a result of Somerville's folly. After a few months at the Inner Temple, where his Catholic-ism was well known, he went abroad on what amounted to a grand tour of conspiracy. He was closely in touch with Sir Francis Englefield, Charles Paget and other leaders of the English fugitives, hobnobbed with Jesuits and Spanish friars and moved self-impor-tantly between Brussels, Madrid, Rome, Paris and Guise's newly-founded seminary at Eu, in Normandy, for English and Irish exiles. In the 'Enterprise' he was determined to play his part, which was to provide local knowledge about harbours and tides and lists of English Catholics with the men, horses and arms at their disposal who would rise for Mary when Guise landed. Throg-morton was also to act as go-between with Mendoza and the French embassy in London, through which all Mary's correspon-dence passed. He returned to London in April 1583. After Fagot's hint Walsingham's spies trailed him for six months before swoop-ing. When they battered at his lodgings in Paul's Wharf, he ran upstairs frantically munching a letter from Mary and somehow he managed to send away a casket of secret correspondence to Men-doza, though enough incriminating papers were left to make cer-tain of his own hand in the treason.

Throgmorton wrote to Mendoza on a playing card, thrown out of his window in the Tower, assuring him he would reveal noth-ing, however grim the tortures, and when first racked he kept his word, but the threat of a second session with the infamous rack-master, Norton, was enough to loosen his tongue. This Walsing-ham had predicted: 'I have seen as resolute a man as Throgmorton stoop, notwithstanding the great show he hath made of Roman resolution. I suppose the grief of the last torture will suffice with-out any extremity of racking to make him more conformable.' He now told of the correspondence between Mary, Guise and Mendoza, of the plans for the invaders to land in Sussex, where Charles Paget and others would be waiting at Arundel, of the aid being given by the Earl of Northumberland, in fact everything he knew, including his own modest role in the scheme, for which he went to Tyburn.[11]

History was repeating itself. Just as the unravelling of the Ridolfi plot in 1571 had brought the expulsion of de Spes, so now the fulsome confessions of Throgmorton forced Mendoza's departure. His continued residence had for long been an absurdity; not once in the last two years had he 'made show to move Her Majesty in anything concerning his master's affairs' and London boys playing at soldiers pelted the haughty Spaniard with stones knowing he would never complain to their elders. He was summoned to the Privy Council and given fifteen days to leave the country for conspiring with Mary, Guise, Northumberland and others. His parting shot was 'as I have apparently failed to please the Queen as a minister of peace, she would in future force me to try to satisfy her in war.' Mendoza was the last Spanish ambassador in London during the reign. Yet Mendoza's departure, Throgmorton's execution and Northumberland's suicide served only to encourage others to take up partnership in the 'Enterprise of England'. An even closer watch was kept on the ports and the border, and Mary's security was looked into anew. The Admiral of Zeeland, acting on Walsingham's advice, intercepted a vessel in the spring of 1584 which was conveying the Jesuit Fr Creighton to Scotland. The priest hastily tore up a letter as the ship was boarded, but made the mistake of throwing the pieces over the windward side, so most were blown back on deck and reassembled, to show Walsingham great developments in the plans for the 'Enterprise'. Soon, however, the third Duke of Guise had problems of his own to face, for with Alençon's death the Protestant Henry of Navarre became heir to the throne of France and Guise now busied himself in consolidating the Catholic factions in France into a league to oppose Henry.[12]

The assassination of William of Orange in July 1584, coming on top of the Throgmorton plot, brought home the perennial perils of Elizabeth's position. William had been an easy target for assassins; in 1582 he had been seriously wounded, but now the attack had been fatal those in England who had dismissed the possibility of a cold-blooded murder of the Queen were forced to think again. It *could* happen here. A friar in Dunkirk predicted that another Burgundian will 'not be wanting to kill that wicked woman' and French priests in Rouen said the feast of St Bartholomew should be solemnized six times a year, for Elizabeth was unchaste, a Jezebel and a heretic. William's death moved Elizabeth profoundly, much more than her letters to his widow would suggest; then and there she came 'to half a resolution' that she must defend Holland and Zeeland against Spain, and feared that open war with Philip could not be avoided much longer.[13]

The tragedy of Orange provoked the Privy Council, at Walsingham's instigation, to devise a novel pledge of allegiance, the Bond of Association, in which all the Queen's faithful subjects would join in a vast voluntary secret society to defend her person and avenge her death. Because there was no precedent for such a bond, the drafting of it, no less than the procedure to be followed, posed problems. In the original draft the signatories bound themselves to serve, obey and defend the Queen 'against all estates, dignities and earthly powers whatsoever and to pursue to utter extermination all that shall attempt' anything against her. As it stood this was an unexceptional exercise in loyalty, but Burghley and Walsingham felt it was insufficient for dealing with Mary if she were not herself an active party to Elizabeth's death – a far from hypothetical situation. Thus they added a solemn undertaking that the signatories would never accept 'any such pretended successor by whom or for whom any such detestable act shall be attempted or committed', and these persons were to be 'prosecuted to the death' by any means. The possibility that Mary would be innocent of any plot against Elizabeth's life was more than the Council was prepared to allow. Not so Elizabeth; for her this was tyrannicide by vengeance, and when Parliament later set about elevating the Association into a statute she made her position clear.

She claimed then to know nothing about the Bond of Association until the first of the series of documents (that signed by privy councillors) was presented to her at Hampton Court on 19 October. No doubt she had more than an inkling of what was afoot and approved in principle of the Bond going the rounds, like a monster testimonial to her popularity. Soon membrane after membrane of parchment, signed by the literate, marked with a cross between witnesses by others, all bearing tags and seals, came down from the shires for presentation at court, eventually from the outposts in North Wales, Cornwall and the North Riding. Mary Queen of Scots, who would willingly sign anything, herself offered to subscribe![14]

Writs had gone out for a new Parliament to deal with the national emergency, and the men sent to Westminster in this first election for a dozen years were intensely loyal – with one astounding exception, as we shall see. Because of its concern for Elizabeth's safety Parliament was excessively hostile to Mary. The Oath of Association had bound subscribers to debar from the throne and to pursue to extremities any claimant to the throne by whom or for whom the assassination of Elizabeth should be attempted, and as it stood it was aimed at James VI little less than at Mary Stuart. A bill was now introduced with the intention of clarifying the position. Mary was still to be subject to the full penalties of the oath, but Elizabeth was to be empowered to except her son. Far from making things clearer the Commons added a fresh uncertainty: those who had signed the Association would be faced with choosing whether to obey its provisions or to abide by statute law. A clause in the bill could not retrospectively change the wording of the solemn bond and it would have been an intolerable business sending revised forms of oath all over the realm for fresh signatures and seals. Argument was protracted and then the Queen sent a message by Hatton. As always she sensed danger when the loyal House, from the best of motives, touched on the thorny problem of the succession; even the Privy Council had made a fearsome mess in the wording of the Bond. Now she told Parliament that their concern for her safety was 'more than her merit', though her strong shield of defence was in God. She did not want any claimant to the succession to be punished without a trial and was adamant that the penalties should not extend to 'the issue of the offender' (James VI) 'unless he was himself implicated in the conspiracies.' Her intervention seemed only to provoke further trouble and she then asked the bill to be put aside until after Christmas. More rapid progress had been made with the bill against Jesuits. All Jesuits, seminary priests and others who had taken Catholic orders since 1559 were to leave the realm within forty days; for those who remained in England or entered the country were punishable as traitors. Laymen who received or helped priests were also accounted traitors, though in the Lords, perhaps at the Queen's instigation, this penalty was reduced to one of felony.[15]

During the debate on the Jesuit bill Dr William Parry, MP for Queenborough, spoke out strongly against it, not he said because he was a favourer of seminaries, but because the measure was 'full of blood, danger, despair, terror or dread to the English subjects of the realm, our brethren, uncles or kinsfolk.' For this outburst the House ordered him to be taken into the Sergeant's custody, causing no little embarrassment since Parry had been at court, still called himself a servant of the crown and had recently been denouncing English Catholic refugees to Burghley. Elizabeth herself examined him and being reasonably satisfied with his explanations recommended his pardon. And then, in mid-February, the Commons were aghast with the news that this same Parry had been plotting to kill the Queen. When Walsingham told her the details of Edward Neville's denunciation, she appeared to remain very calm, but agreed to authorize special prayers to be said throughout the land for her happy delivery. The Commons wanted the traitorous member to suffer an exceptionally cruel form of death, but this Elizabeth refused.[16]

It is difficult to be certain of the extent of Parry's treachery. The renegade Neville's evidence was scarcely worthy of the faith which the judges placed in it. According to him Parry had suggested they should each ride on either side of the Queen's coach as it passed into the park and shoot at her head with pistols; alternatively Parry had ample opportunities at court of meeting with Elizabeth. A story current late in the reign was that he had come to Hampton Court with a knife hidden in his sleeve, but when he was ushered into her presence Elizabeth so frightened him by recounting a dream of the night before in which she had a vein opened that the doctor fainted. We do know, however, that he had received a copy of Cardinal Allen's tract on the honourableness of killing an excommunicated queen and earlier still had been intriguing with Thomas Morgan for a Scottish force to invade England. At one moment Parry was boasting of the crime he had planned, the next he was denying he ever intended to become an assassin – clearly a person as unstable in his mind as in his loyalties. He expected a pardon right to the end, in recognition of his erstwhile services to the government in betraying Catholic secrets, but the feeling against him in the country was too strong for Elizabeth to have intervened even had she so wished, and Parry was executed at Tower Hill on 2 March 1585. The alarming aspect of the Parry plot was this: here was a man almost universally believed to be guilty of treason in the highest degree, who had subscribed to the Oath of Supremacy; and men wondered how many crypto-Catholics there were in the realm in places of responsibility who had taken the Oath of Supremacy and even subscribed to the Association with a grain of salt.[17]

At one point in his trial Parry had said he knew he must suffer death, for he was 'not settled' (that is to say was a Catholic); 'Look into your study and into your new books and you shall find what I mean.' This recent publication was in fact *Leicester's Commonwealth*, which had first appeared on the continent the previous summer and was now circulating so widely in England that the Lords had brought in a bill in December to prevent slanderous libels. Written with singular vituperation by publicists among the English fugitives in these years of violent pamphlet warfare, it blackened Leicester's character on account of his Puritan leanings which, it was asserted, made him champion the claims of his brother-in-law, Huntingdon, to the succession. In the process of besmirching Leicester some of the muck inevitably fouled the Queen's name, as the authors clearly intended it should; by implication the book was a tract in favour of Mary Queen of Scots. The French edition was even worse, for it contained 'a very filthy addition' and Stafford, the ambassador in Paris, was torn between taking the matter up with the French authorities in defence of Elizabeth's honour, or letting it rest, lest drawing such attention to the book should increase sales. 'I know well enough that though the names be left out or the matter coloured, in the French, there be enough that can read the English and know the parties that can take pains to gloss and interpret the text.' Elizabeth spoke out very forcibly in defence of Leicester's honour and noble character, as she had done in the face of earlier detractors.[18]

The revelations of the Parry plot made progress on the bill for the Queen's safety the more urgent. Burghley, worried as ever about a civil war on the demise of the crown, had been drafting clauses to provide for the government of the realm in the emergency of Elizabeth's sudden death and aimed at bridging an interregnum through a grand council of state, vested with full executive power, which would see to the capture and trial of the assassins and recall the last Parliament. But Elizabeth would have none of it. Tidy, paper constitutions, which put the crown imperial into commission, with councillors of state overseeing the succession like a pack of Calvinist elders electing a minister, were more than she could stomach; besides, it would not work, as she had seen with Northumberland's Council in 1553. Burghley and the rest might panic, but she would take her chance on survival, and die in her bed full of years. She must have smiled wryly when the Commons approached her for advice on re-drafting the safety bill, and in the final measure she had her way in all points of significance. If she *were* killed, a commission of privy councillors (not a grand council) was to pursue the guilty, and no more, for the question of a successor was sacrosanct. In the event of a plot against her life, attempted rebellion or invasion by or for a claimant to the throne, commissioners were to sit in judgement after full investigation, so that only the guilty would suffer; the nameless claimant, Mary, would be debarred from the succession, but her heir was not, unless he was a party to the offence. Lastly it was declared that the obligations of subjects under the Bond of Association were to be interpreted according to the provisions of the Act.[19]

Elizabeth grieved that the House should waste so much time on her safety instead of getting down to the subsidy bill, and then they put that on one side while they tampered with religion. There was a pointed discussion when Whitgift came to the Queen to offer the clerical subsidy voted by Convocation, and she praised the clergy's businesslike ways in 'voluntarily and frankly' dealing with supply, while the laity 'must be entreated.' Burghley, who was there, protested that the clergy's offering was a pittance compared with what Parliament would vote and attacked the

Archbishop about the ordination of men of poor intellectual calibre. Elizabeth stood firmly by Whitgift who explained to Burghley that there simply were not enough graduates to go round 13,000 parishes – (the fact is familiar enough today). 'Jesus, thirteen thousand!' added Elizabeth. 'It is not to be looked for.' In fact the Puritan Party, led by Mildmay and Knollys, was reluctant to vote supplies until steps had been taken to reform the Church to their liking. They began by passing a bill for the more reverent observance of Sunday, which the Queen subsequently vetoed, and then drafted bills for suppressing unqualified preachers, for freeing ministers from the obligation to subscribe to the Articles of Religion and for curtailing the powers of bishops in depriving clergy from benefices, all against the Queen's express prohibition. She sent for the Speaker to warn the Commons that there must be no further discussion of church reform, which was the province of Queen and Convocation, and as for those councillors like Mildmay who had disobeyed her strictures, 'we will redress or else uncouncil.' The Puritans were not going to give in so easily and in the end, having received the subsidy bill, she prorogued Parliament. At the closing ceremony she vetoed no fewer than fifteen bills, including the one dear to Burghley, for continuing to observe Wednesday as a second fish day. In her speech she could not but mention the state of the Church and told the bishops that if they did not amend things she would depose the lot of them – a threat which hardly met the Puritans' criticism. She reminded the Commons of her frequent bible reading and reflected that too many were 'overbold with God Almighty, making too many subtle scannings of His blessed will, as lawyers do with human testaments.' It was the differences in religion that had brought peril to her person. She would not emulate Romanists 'nor tolerate new-fangledness. I mean to guide them both by God's holy true rule', for all men were her subjects, whether they had signed the Bond of Association or paid fines for recusancy.[20]

The previous April Sir Ralph Sadler had taken over from Shrewsbury as Mary's custodian. The Earl had longed to be free from his duties and latterly his wife, the brassy Bess of Hardwick, had been spreading disgusting tales about his relations with the royal prisoner, even that he had given her a child. Sadler was only intended as a stop-gap; his loyalty and ability were beyond question, but he was old and Elizabeth felt that Mary's dignity required at least a peer of the realm as her keeper. She hoped Lord St John could be induced to take the post, but he declined and would suffer 'any extremity rather than go.' So Sir Ralph had to stay on for a whole year until relieved by Sir Amyas Paulet, a very strait Puritan, who had been ambassador in Paris. Ever since the days of the Throgmorton plot Mary had been deprived of her correspondence, and her two removals during Sadler's year of office were welcome distractions and widened her horizons a little. First she was taken from Sheffield to Wingfield in Derbyshire and in January 1585 farther south to Tutbury Castle in Staffordshire, where much stricter precautions were taken for her security, with thirty soldiers on the premises wearing swords and daggers. Wherever Mary went in the castle or grounds she was accompanied, and under Paulet an ever closer guard was kept, making her years under Shrewsbury seem lax in retrospect.

Meanwhile the plotters had not been idle. Guise had offered a reward for Elizabeth's murder and there were enough bold spirits among the English Catholic communities in France and Flanders who were convinced they had a mission to do the deed and took their instructions from Thomas Morgan, Mary's agent in Paris. Among these were the members of George Gifford's Catholic Association, founded in 1580 to further the work of the Jesuit missionaries, including Anthony Babington who had not many years since been a page in Shrewsbury's service. Walsingham's spies were everywhere, winning confidences, reporting conversations, deep in counterplots; a Babington, a Savage, or whoever it was would sooner or later be caught in the net, yet Walsingham would not rest until he had landed the biggest fish of all – Mary herself. Elizabeth knew nothing of his masterly schemes until he had completed his self-appointed task. Across the Channel Guise was hopeful, consistently overestimating the strength of militant Catholics in England and always underrating Elizabeth's ability to survive a crisis. What a complete misunderstanding of her personality is betrayed by his verdict that she 'is so timorous of nature that she will be affeared to do anything', and yet he was the one who was destined for the assassin's knife.[21]

In December 1585 Walsingham's men arrested Robert Gifford as he stepped ashore at Rye, with a letter of introduction from Thomas Morgan to Mary. Gifford was a Catholic exile whose parents lived within a few miles of Tutbury and would thus be ideally placed for carrying letters and furthering plans for Mary's escape. He was taken to Walsingham who won him over to help in betraying Mary by means of perfecting a secret channel for correspondence. Gifford accordingly presented his credentials at the French embassy and told Mauvissière he had devised a scheme for conveying letters to and from Mary. The arrangement was that the brewer from Burton who supplied the household at Chartley (to the north of Tutbury, whither Mary had been removed) used beer barrels in which a water-tight container for letters could be slipped through the bung-hole. The ambassador sent a trial letter which she received on 16 January and in due course came her reply, but only after it had been copied and deciphered by Thomas Phelippes, Walsingham's cipher expert who was stationed near Chartley. Soon Phelippes was kept very busy indeed, for Mary, deprived of correspondence for so long, asked to be sent all the letters for her which had been piling up for over two years at the French embassy, ranging from detailed plans for an invasion of England passed on by Morgan, to exhortations from Fr Robert Parsons to be of good cheer. But it was seven months before Walsingham got what he wanted.

Anthony Babington, back in England, was approached by a missionary priest, John Ballard, and persuaded to consider killing Elizabeth; sixty thousand troops were ready over the water, he assured him, to ensure the rescue and accession of Mary and the triumph of the Catholic faith. Babington hesitated about taking so glorious a role, but he talked the matter over with his group of intimates and eventually wrote in July to Mary herself:

Myself, with ten gentlemen and 100 our followers, will undertake the delivery of your royal person from the hands of your enemies. For the dispatch of the usurper (from the obedience of whom we are by the excommunication of her made free) there be six noble gentlemen, all my private friends, who, for the zeal they have to the Catholic cause and Your Majesty's service, will undertake that tragical execution.

Phelippes rubbed his hands when he read that letter and added to his transcript for his master, 'we attend her very heart at the next.'

Babington had asked Mary if she agreed with his proposed order of operations, namely that Elizabeth should not be murdered until Mary was free, but Mary preferred Elizabeth's death to come first. 'The affairs being thus prepared and forces in readiness, both within and without the realm, then shall it be time to set the six gentlemen to work, taking order, upon the accomplishing of their design, I may be suddenly transported out of this place.' Mary had signed her own death warrant by so unequivocally giving her imprimatur to the design. By sending it to Babington Mary had placed herself squarely within the Act of 1585 for the Queen's safety. What a world of difference to the circumspect behaviour of the young Elizabeth at Hatfield at the time of Wyatt's rising, much suspected, yet committing nothing to paper. The letter proper is absolutely genuine, as the most scholarly of Mary's apologists admit, and its authenticity was vouched for by her two secretaries, who wrote it and ciphered it from Mary's own minute. Talk of forgery would scarcely have arisen had not Walsingham had a postscript added asking Babington to reveal the identity of his six companions. This was an error of judgement, for Babington became scared and tried to flee.[22]

Mary was overjoyed at news of the plot. By the next brewer's delivery came a letter from Mendoza, now in Paris, telling her that Philip's 'armada by sea is preparing with the greatest expedition', the finest fleet ever, which would play its part 'in the setting of Your Majesty at liberty.'

Walsingham had kept the entire affair very much in his own hands. After intercepting Mary's reply to Babington he had written to Leicester, in the Netherlands, explaining that he had not told his colleagues, but Elizabeth had heard about it, for he added 'My only fear is that Her Majesty will not use the matter with that secrecy that apperteineth' and asked that his note should be destroyed. By 11 August it had come into the open with the

proclamation for the arrest of Babington and his fellow conspirators, whose names had been supplied by Ballard, the priest, already
in custody. Their identity gave the Queen no little surprise, for an
'alarmingly large number' of them had close connexions with her
court. Edward Abington (or Habington) was the son of her
Under-Treasurer, Chidiock Tichbourne was a servant of Hatton's
and Charles Tilney was the son of Philip Tilney, her fourth cousin,
who had entertained her on progress in Suffolk. The ports were
closed and Elizabeth repaired instinctively to Windsor Castle, as
she had done in the autumn of 1569, yet now the bells rang and
bonfires flared to signal her happy delivery. Tichbourne was taken
in south London, but it was not until 14 August that Babington
and other accomplices were captured after hiding in St John's
Wood. Abington eluded the hue and cry for a month in Worces-
tershire and Edmund Windsor for half a year, but that mattered
little. Enough of the ringleaders were in custody for a mass of
depositions to be taken; Babington himself was cross-questioned
on nine occasions. On 11 August while out hunting near Chartley
Mary's secretaries, Nau and Curll, were sent under arrest to London, while Paulet ordered Mary's immediate removal to Tixall,
which gave an opportunity of going through her papers with a
fine tooth-comb, though for some while no definite move was
made against her.[23]

Elizabeth had ordered Burghley to ensure that nothing should
be said in the trial of the conspirators which would incriminate
Mary – nothing, that is to say, 'that shall be requisite for the maintenance of the indictment.' This order has generally been ascribed
to a fear that if Mary's supporters thought their captive Queen to
be in danger they would attack Elizabeth's person. At this moment,
however, Elizabeth was very emotionally disturbed, overwrought
even, for Walsingham's successful detections had rendered impossible any extension of the procrastinations of eighteen summers
and she knew she would at last be forced to come face to face with
the problem of Mary. Time and again she had shirked the issue,
not because she doubted Mary's guilt in Darnley's murder or
questioned the validity of the casket letters, any more than she
now doubted Mary's complicity in the Babington conspiracy or

thought her letter a forgery, but because Mary was by inheritance and anointing a Queen, ordained to rule, her own kinswoman and the next heir to her throne. In the late Parliament there had been a move to revive proceedings against Mary, dormant since the breakdown of the Westminster Conference in 1568, but Elizabeth had stifled it singlehanded, letting Mary know that her action had been 'not without the great misliking and discontentments of our best devoted subjects.' But now Elizabeth could not escape from the act of Parliament for her own safety which required her to appoint a special tribunal to investigate Mary's part in the plot and pronounce sentence.[24]

Even before the trial of the Babington conspirators she had ordained that sentence, when given, should be the most terrible form of execution possible, that same way of death which she had refused to sanction for Dr Parry, 'considering this matter of horrible treason against Her Majesty's own person hath not been heard of in this kingdom.' Even the suggestion of a protracted execution would not satisfy her. The first seven were cut down after hanging for a very short time, disembowelled and mutilated while still alive, quite the most brutal punishment that the law allowed, but the others were reprieved from this torment on her express orders and were not mutilated until they were dead. Thus Chidiock Tichbourne and the other young Catholic gentlemen, with their attractive-sounding names and the swaggering portraits they had commissioned to honour their future fame, earned their niche in the annals of England.

It was days before Elizabeth could bring herself to order Mary's removal from Chartley. She refused point blank to have her sent to the Tower for trial as the Privy Council wanted and could not decide whether she should be taken to Hertford Castle or to Fotheringhay in Northamptonshire; the first was too near London, the second too far from Windsor. At moments she thought it monstrous to allow even a lawfully-deposed sovereign in the dock and in her disturbed state missed the steadying advice which old Sussex had given in times of crisis almost as much as she missed the comfort of Leicester's presence. She displayed the same irresolution over choosing the additional commissioners who were to be associated with the privy councillors at the trial and cavilled about the actual terms of the commission and the title by which Mary was called in the document, so that Burghley and Walsingham. were driven almost to distraction by her alternate wavering and interference. At last it was settled that the commissioners should begin their work at Fotheringhay on 11 October. William Davison, who had been appointed a secretary of state to take some of the burden of routine business from Walsingham, feared his Queen 'will keep the course as she held with the Duke of Norfolk, which is not to take her (Mary's) life without extreme fear compel her.' Early in September, as a safeguard against the Queen's wavering, the Council advised her to summon Parliament; she did not welcome this suggestion, for a Parliament in session would hamper her own actions and since every House of Commons for the past fifteen years had cried out for Mary's blood, she knew what to expect from the next. But Burghley persuaded her that to involve Parliament in Mary's fate would ease the burden for her and make 'the world abroad better satisfied.' The last Parliament had been prorogued until 15 November, which was too late, but there was no point in their assembling until after the verdict against Mary had been reached. In the end writs went out for a new Parliament to meet on 29 October, but letters were sent to the electors asking for the return of the old members. She was intending to open the sessions in person, as usual, but nearer the time decided she must absent herself, not wishing, as she later remarked, to preside over proceedings against her kinswoman. For all she allowed them to accomplish they might just as well have stayed at home.[25]

To warn Mary of her approaching trial Elizabeth had written to her on 6 October in the most formal terms. To her great and inexorable grief, 'as one void of all remorse or conscience', she had heard that Mary pretended not to be privy to the plot against her. 'As we find by clear and most evident proof that the contrary will be verified', she must present herself before the chief noblemen, councillors and judges appointed to charge her with the crime. 'Living as you do within our protection and therefore subject to the laws of our realm and to such a trial as by us shall be thought most agreeable to our laws', Mary had no cause to take exception to the proceedings. When Mary began by refusing to plead before the commissioners as she would not own their competence to try her, Burghley wrote off to Elizabeth at Windsor saying they intended none the less to proceed. She scribbled a note at midnight agreeing to this but at the same time forbidding them to make any sentence without further conference with her, and Davison, who was with her, hoped in vain this letter would arrive at Fotheringhay too late. Hatton, who displayed here, as at the trial of the Babington conspirators, those qualities which prompted the Queen to appoint him Lord Chancellor in 1587, succeeded in persuading Mary that she would only damage her reputation if she avoided a trial and a formula was found which took account of her 'protest'. The proceedings in the great hall at Fotheringhay went their predicted course, rehearsing all the evidence in justification of a verdict arrived at in advance, as was the invariable practice with state trials, and on 25 October the commissioners reassembled in the Star Chamber to review the case and pronounce Mary as 'an imaginer and compasser of Her Majesty's destruction'. All her skilful advocacy had been in vain. In their verdict they made a point of adding that Mary's guilt was in no sense prejudical to the claims of James VI to the English succession. Elizabeth delayed a formal proclamation of the sentence for another five weeks. The Scottish as well as the French ambassadors had been making some show of intervention to persuade her to stay further proceedings, but Mary in a final desperate gesture had already written to Mendoza in Paris assigning to Philip II her prescriptive right to the throne of England.[26]

Lord Chancellor Bromley reminded Lords and Commons at the opening sessions that Parliament had been summoned not for making laws or voting taxes, but for an extraordinary cause of 'great weight, great peril and dangerous consequence'. In the Commons Hatton opened the case against Mary and then old Sir Ralph Sadler, Mary's ex-keeper, prayed God to influence the Queen 'to take away this most wicked and filthy woman'. Others identified the Queen of Scots as the centre and soul of conspiracy against Protestant England so long as she lived and railed at her for being a Scot by nationality, a Frenchwoman by upbringing, a Guise by blood, a Spaniard in practice, a papist in religion, through and through an enemy of England. One followed another to shout in unison the self-evident truth, that to destroy her would be 'one of the fairest riddances that ever the Church of God had.' With one accord they joined the Lords to petition Elizabeth that Mary must pay the penalty of the law as enacted in 1585, and on 12 November representatives waited on her at Richmond, where she had retreated to be away from the outbursts at Westminster. Elizabeth knew about the petition and must have seen a draft of it, because she asked it to be amended to include a reference to the Bond of Association, and the Speaker duly inserted the words 'Either we must take her life from her without your direction, or else . . .' She wanted to emphasize that the act of 1585 for her safety had sprung from the Association, itself the spontaneous undertaking of thousands of her subjects, for she was going to dwell on it in her reply. Would that she and Mary were milkmaids, then she would willingly have pardoned her on confessing the offence, for she meant no malice, she assured them. The act of 1585 had not been made to trap Mary, but to warn her of the fell dangers of conspiracy, and she could easily have been sent for trial under earlier laws; yet that act had 'laid a hard hand on me and that I must give direction for her death, which cannot but be most grievous.' Then she recalled the Bond of Association, of which she claimed to know nothing till the final documents with their loyal signatures and seals were presented to her; as that Association was 'a perfect argument of your true hearts and great zeals to my safety, so shall my bond be stronger tied to greater cares for all your good.' As for their present petition, she would make answer in due course.

When Hatton reported this to the House of Commons he mentioned a matter which Elizabeth had overlooked in her answer but required him to declare now, namely that she would be glad to spare Mary's execution 'if by any other means to be devised by Her Highness's Great Council of this realm, the safety' of Queen and country could be ensured. This was not at all the attitude they had anticipated, and in the next few days Lords and Commons

agreed that there was no possible alternative to Mary's death.
When another delegation waited on her at Richmond to convey
their final decision she gave a characteristic performance. No one
should accuse her, she said, of dragging things out to make a mere
show of clemency. In her time she had pardoned many rebels and
winked at many treasons and yet, she seemed to argue, they would
prevent her from being merciful to a kinswoman. She had learnt
in the hard school of statecraft:

> I was not simply trained up, nor in my youth spent my time alto-
> gether idly; and yet, when I came to the crown, then entered I first into
> the school of experience, bethinking myself of those things that fitted a
> king – justice, temper, magnanimity, judgement. As for the two latter,
> I will not boast; my sex doth not permit it. But for the two first this
> may I truly say: Among my subjects I never knew a difference of per-
> son, where right was one; nor never to my knowledge preferred for
> favour whom I thought not fit for worth; nor bent my ears to credit a
> tale that first was told me; nor was so rash to corrupt my judgement
> with my censure, before I heard the cause ... We princes cannot hear all
> [causes] ourselves. But this dare I boldly affirm: my verdict ever went
> with the truth of my knowledge.

She was in splendid form and appeared to be working towards a
peroration in which she would regally condemn Mary; and yet
she ended on the proverbial question-mark:

> As for your petition; your judgement I condemn not, neither do I
> mislike your reasons, but pray you to accept my thankfulness, excuse
> my doubtfulness, and take in good part my answer answerless ...

This, and her earlier speech, were rushed into print in a tract
edited by Burghley's son, Robert Cecil, for which Elizabeth herself corrected the prepared text (for she had spoken on both occasions extempore). Translations soon appeared in Latin, French and
other languages and Stow's new edition of *Holinshed's Chronicles* –
the one Shakespeare found so useful – also contained the speeches,
when it appeared in January.[27]

The Council pressed her to authorize proclamation of sentence
against Mary, as the act of 1585 required, but Elizabeth was in no
mood for hasty action, and Burghley in despair feared that sessions

would go down in history as the vain Parliament, or people 'nick-name it a Parliament of Words.' She decided to prorogue Parliament and scribbled a note to Lord Chancellor Bromley for his speech, which the poor man was unable to decipher, for it was so hastily written. Then, on an impulse, she let them sit a further week, and in fact had the Houses adjourned, not prorogued. She at last agreed to issue the proclamation before the Houses rose, but disliked Burghley's wording of it. Though promise of the document was made on the last day of this extraordinary session, it was not published until two days later, on 4 December. Never had Elizabeth acted with quite such uncertainty as in the last three months and if she continued in this way there would be faint chance of her councillors getting her over the final and highest hurdle, to sign the death warrant – and not retract. She was pressed to come to the point after Christmas at Greenwich, but re-iterated that to send Mary to her fate was 'utterly repugnant to her mind'. For some weeks she had been giving a series of audiences to the French and the Scottish ambassadors, who alternately threatened to invade England if she touched a hair of Mary's head and offered guarantees for her good behaviour if only her life would be spared. The Queen heard them out, knowing that she was fully insulated from danger from Scotland through a new treaty and certain that James VI's show of saving his mother was no more than a diplomatic move; the King was too wise to ruin his chances of succeeding Elizabeth in England by an act of rashness, however filial, and the judgement in the Star Chamber and the revised wording of the act of 1585, on which Elizabeth had insisted, brought their rewards. After a further attempt of the Scots to postpone discussions, so they could send a messenger to Edinburgh and back, Elizabeth had had enough. She would *not* give them the extension of eight days they asked, no 'Not another hour.' Christmas festivities, even with Leicester back at court, had been over-shadowed by the crisis, and in the calm before the storm rumours were rife: there had been a new plot to take Elizabeth's life – Mary had escaped from Fotheringhay – London was burning – the Spaniards had landed in Wales and Guise in Sussex – even that Elizabeth was dead. Some hoped that rumours might scare her into coming to the point, but she refused, and as January passed it seemed she would act as she had done with Norfolk.[28]

A warrant had been prepared on Burghley's orders soon after the sentence had been proclaimed and left with Mr Secretary Davison. On 1 February without warning she sent for him to bring the document and, after reading it through, signed it. She asked Davison whether he were not heartily sorry to see it done, and he replied judiciously that since Mary had threatened Elizabeth's life he could not be sorry to see his mistress take an honourable course, preferring the death of the guilty to the slaughter of the innocent. She smiled her approval and ordered him to carry the warrant to the Lord Chancellor's for the great seal to be affixed, 'as secretly as might be' (lest, Davison wrote later, the news becoming public before the execution was done might 'as she pretended, increase her danger'). She asked him on the way to Bromley's office to call in at Walsingham's house, for his colleague was ill, to 'communicate the matter with him, because the grief thereof would go near (as she merrily said) to kill him outright' – a wry touch of humour. The Queen reflected that she had deferred the matter so long 'that the world might see that she had not been violently or maliciously drawn thereto' and said she preferred to have the execution done secretly in the hall of Fotheringhay, instead of openly on the castle green. Davison was about to take his leave, but she called him back and 'fell into some complaint of Sir Amyas Paulet and others that might have eased her of this burden, wishing that Mr Secretary [Walsingham] and I would yet write unto him and Sir Drew Drury to sound their disposition in that behalf.' In other words she wanted them to shoulder her burden by taking the law into their own hands, according to the original intention of the Bond of Association. Leicester and even Archbishop Whitgift had thought poison or a suffocating pillow a not dishonourable way out of the dilemma for her, and a less painful experience for Mary. Now Elizabeth had given her necessary authority for the execution, could not the actual manner of carrying it out be done in a way that would save her from the feeling that she was party to the judicial murder on the world's stage of an anointed queen? When Henry Plantagenet had decided Becket must die and had asked 'Who will rid me of this turbulent priest?' the four knights had immediately known where their duty lay. Thousands of her subjects had freely offered in October 1584 to do what she now hoped Paulet and Drury might arrange, to make amends for cruel necessity.[29]

Davison reported his remarkable interview to Burghley, called as he was bidden on Walsingham and imparted to him the Queen's orders about the letter to Paulet; thence to the Lord Chancellor, who had the warrant sealed at dusk. By then Walsingham's letter to Mary's keeper at Fotheringhay was ready. Davison added his signature and it was despatched. In it they reported the Queen's observations on Paulet's lack of zeal for her service, for he had not 'in all this time ... found some way of shedding the life of the Scots' queen', and how unkindly she had taken it that such loyal servants as he and Drury should fail in their duty, thus casting 'the burden upon her, knowing as you do her indisposition to shed blood, especially of one of that sex and quality, and so near her in blood.' That day the Privy Council met at Greenwich, not directly to discuss Mary, but to require the Archbishop, as censor of publications, to stop the sale and investigate the contents of the new edition of *Holinshed's Chronicles* because it contained 'reports of matters of later years that concern the State and are not therefore meet to be published in this sort.' Clearly, the text of Elizabeth's speeches to the Parliamentary deputation pressing for Mary's execution was the cause of the trouble.[30]

Next morning Elizabeth sent Davison word that he should not go to the Lord Chancellor until he had spoken further with her, so he speedily came to her presence where she asked him whether the warrant had passed the seal. 'What needeth that haste?' she cried when he told her it had, but he denied he had acted any more hastily than she had ordered, and asked if it was still her intention to proceed with the affair. 'But me thinketh', she reflected, 'that it might have been *otherwise* handled for the form', naming a few courtiers who agreed with her. Davison mumbled that the most honourable way was the safest, and quickly left when the Queen went into dinner. The new Secretary was out of his depth, too 'simply practised in court arts' to divine his Queen's intentions, but extremely unnerved by her attitude; in alarm he called on Hatton, fearing that all the blame for the passing of the warrant might be shifted on himself. They went on together to Burghley, who recognized the urgency of the situation and summoned as many privy councillors as were near at hand to a secret meeting the following morning, at which they undertook to take complete responsibility for sending the death warrant to Fotheringhay. We have only Davison's account of the meeting in the Lord Treasurer's chamber at Greenwich. Although the Privy Council register records a meeting there on 3 February, attended by only five councillors, at which a minor piece of business about the Admiralty Court's jurisdiction was transacted, it makes no mention of the larger meeting of ten members, including Leicester and Walsingham (for whom the news that the Queen had signed truly acted as a tonic) to deal with the problem of Mary, even though Beale, the clerk of the Council, was present. Here Burghley covered the familiar ground, read over the warrant and said they must advise on the most expedient means for carrying out the Queen's wishes, for by signing the warrant she had done all that reason or the law allowed. It would be of dangerous consequence if she should fall 'into any new conceit of interrupting or staying the course of justice', so he concluded they must act speedily without further reference to Elizabeth. If she did not know her own mind, they knew theirs. All present swore they would not reveal to her the fact that they were despatching the warrant to Fotheringhay, a mission they instructed their Puritan clerk, Beale, to undertake as speedily and secretly as possible. He also took instructions to the Earl of Kent for overseeing with Shrewsbury the arrangements for the execution, as a result of which Mary went to her death early on 8 February.

The secret was well kept from Elizabeth, yet she can hardly have expected her councillors who had been clamouring for the warrant to be signed for so long to have let it lie dormant. Had she seriously had second thoughts, she could have required the warrant to be cancelled on the 2nd or 3rd of February. Even at this stage she pinned her hopes on Paulet devising an easier means. Davison found her with Raleigh in the privy chamber and she similarly recounted a dream of the night before – that Mary had been executed, 'pretending to be so troubled with the news that, if she had had a sword, she could have run me [Davison] through – but this being delivered in a pleasant and smiling manner, I answered Her Majesty that it was good I was not near her so long as that humour lasted.' Yes, she answered him, she still wanted to go forward with the execution, but still looked for another way. Later, probably it was the Sunday morning, she read Paulet's reply to Walsingham's letter, which threw her in a fury, for he did not mince his words. He rued that he had lived to see this day, in which his sovereign lady required him to do an act 'which God and the law forbiddeth.' He put his life and property at her disposal, if such were the penalty for disobedience, 'But God forbid I should make so foul a shipwreck of my conscience, or leave so great a blot to my posterity, or shed blood without law and warrant.' (Drury took comfort in the fact that Walsingham's letter had only been addressed to Paulet, so could not require an answer from him.) She gibed at the man's 'daintiness', mocked his 'perjury' for refuting the Oath of Association he had taken, and moving into the gallery continued her denunciation, 'blaming the niceness of those precise fellows' who were all words and no action. Whether she was still hoping for a secret end to the affair when a day or so later she complained to Davison of the Council's lack of care for her own safety 'in that it was not already done', or whether she was merely anxious to have Mary dead, is uncertain. Never were her words so cryptic, her behaviour so uncertain as in these days.[31]

When she heard that the sentence had been carried out on 8 February by virtue of her warrant, it was her anger, not her sorrow that counted; the latter may have been assumed, never the former. She first flew at Hatton, disavowing that she had ever intended Mary's death, and blamed the whole Council for abusing the trust she had placed in them. Davison was committed to the Tower and Burghley dare not appear at court, 'finding his bitter burden of Her Majesty's displeasure' increasing with the days; there was a rumour of Elizabeth sending him to the Tower, and there is some evidence that Leicester was intriguing for this to be done. It seemed an age since the Queen had written that charming letter, addressing him as 'Sir Spirit', to cheer him out of his melancholy when he had been oppressed by court factions and out of sorts with gout. Playfully then she had counselled him then to 'Serve God, fear the King and be a good fellow to the rest'; but now his fear of her was different in kind, and he assumed his long reign, now in its thirtieth year, was over. Only just in time, on 6 February, had he acquired a royal grant of the manor of Sevenoaks in Kent. He heard Davison was like to be hanged outright without trial and risked stating his own dissent from those judges who admitted such was within the Queen's prerogative. At the end of March all those ten councillors who had sanctioned the execution were summoned before the Lord Chancellor, Archbishop Whitgift and the two chief justices to justify their action, which they defended on the grounds of Davison's report of Elizabeth's intention to have the warrant sealed and of the importance of safeguarding her person by swiftly sending it to Fotheringhay. Not one of the ten revealed their secret oath to keep Elizabeth ignorant of their decision until the execution had been effected. Meanwhile Davison had been examined by the law officers and subsequently went for trial in the Star Chamber before a special commission from which all the principal councillors were significantly absent, but which included such Catholics as Lumley, Worcester and Sir James Crofts. Davison came as a lamb to the slaughter, 'sick of the palsy' and with his arm in a sling. None of the Queen's remarks made to him about Mary in those remarkable audiences at Greenwich, that featured so fully in his depositions, came out at the trial, and at the end of the day for extreme contempt of his sovereign he was fined ten thousand marks and imprisoned during her pleasure. He indeed was made scapegoat of the whole affair until, after the Armada had been defeated, he was released from the Tower and had his staggering fine remitted; for another twenty years he was still paid his stipend as a Secretary of State but never again served in that or any other office. Burghley after four months of marked disfavour returned to court and his multifarious duties.[32]

In her heart Elizabeth had known that the Queen of Scots must die, for statecraft required it: *salus reipublicae suprema lex* was a maxim that could not go unheeded. Yet 'law' comprised not only 'the law of God' and 'the law of nature' – vague phrases under which Elizabeth could have sheltered as an excuse for doing nothing about Mary, because of the dictates of conscience, the strength of regal cousinage or the weakness of her own sex; it also embraced the statute laws of the realm, which required a formal execution, not a hole-and-corner judicial murder. That she should have sunk to attempting to persuade Paulet and Drury to act underhand is a stain on her character which can never be expunged, however subtle the explanations. A day or so before she had signed the warrant she had written to James VI about his mother; she knew that by saving 'the serpent that poisons me' she would herself be destroyed. 'Transfigure yourself into my position and suppose what you ought to do', she suggested to him. Keep Mary alive, however secure her imprisonment, and the plots would continue as they had done with increasing violence for fifteen years. If she were, as some say, trapped by her councillors' action, she had allowed herself to fall into the trap by making no effort to communicate with Burghley, Walsingham, Hatton or Leicester during that first fateful week in February. Now she was angry that they had been bold enough to take the decision which she had shrunk from and she took her revenge on Burghley and Davison, which showed them where the sovereign power really lay, and this allowed her to face the stormy criticism from foreign courts behind a mask of ignorance. Was it to be wondered at that the Catholic world regarded her in the very same light as the Protestants had looked on Katherine de Medici after St Bartholomew's? From time to time politics (even in modern democracies) demand a scapegoat if the work of government is to be carried out and Secretary Davison was thus sacrificed in the spring of 1587. There was no other way.[33]

James VI hinted rather too broadly that his honour, impugned by his mother's death, could only be salved by Elizabeth proclaiming him her heir and, though she made no declaration, such was the long-term effect of what happened at Fotheringhay. Mary's death even more than the failure of the rebellion of the north, completed the political work of the reformation in England; it was a final declaration that England was a Protestant country with all that this implied and thereafter Catholicism was a hopelessly lost cause. The manner of Mary's end rather than the death itself gnawed at Elizabeth's conscience, though time would put the events of those tense weeks in perspective. To her surprise her popularity at home increased considerably and this enabled her to lead her people through the crisis with Spain. Pope Sixtus V, when news of Mary's execution reached Rome, remarked 'What a valiant woman. She braves the two greatest kings by land and sea . . . It is a pity that Elizabeth and I cannot marry: our children would have ruled the whole world.' In spite of herself she had become the hope of the Protestant world, a role with no attractions for her, and became plunged in a war she detested and which would extend beyond her death.

IN THE MIDST AND
HEAT OF THE BATTLE

'JESUS! Was there ever a prince so smitten by the snares of traitors without the courage or counsel to reply to it? ... For the love of God rouse yourself from this too long sleep.' Such was Elizabeth's reproof in May 1585 to Henry III (who as Duke of Anjou had turned her down) for allowing himself to become enmeshed in the toils of the house of Guise and for refusing to come to the aid of the Netherlands. Similar words might well have been spoken against the Queen herself by Walsingham and the other militant Puritans for tarrying so long over Mary's execution while Catholicism under Philip II, Parma and Guise threatened the very existence of Protestant Europe. In fact the die had been cast eighteen months before Fotheringhay. After years of waiting upon events she stirred herself as Brussels fell, then Antwerp, to send her own army to the Netherlands. She had always abhorred war for its wastefulness and inhumanity and even though she was now an ally of the Dutch Provinces she would pursue one series of negotiations after another to attempt a settlement. With the brief exceptions of the war against the French in Scotland in 1560 and the ill-fated expedition to Le Havre two years later, England had remained at peace with her neighbours; she had clung tenuously to peace with Spain, despite embargoes on trade and the expulsion of ambassadors. But now England was destined to remain at war for the rest of her life and the paradox was that during the long series of drawn battles in the Low Countries and the naval campaigns in Europe and the Americas the country achieved a far greater unity and national consciousness than ever before, and this

SERO SED SERIO

redounded to the Queen's reputation. The war in its early years was popular and helped to heal many of the internal dissensions.[1]

If Alençon's death was a setback, William the Silent's assassination was an incalculable loss to the struggle against Spain. Elizabeth never really appreciated William's true worth until he had gone, and then she realized how much would depend on her. Henry III, to whom the Dutch turned in their hour of need, proved incapable of resolution and in January 1585 Guise signed a secret treaty with Philip II for a Holy League to exclude Henry of Navarre from the French succession. The Pyrenees were no more – Elizabeth's own treaty of Blois was made scrap paper; and Parma's steady advance from the coast threatened the very existence of the United Provinces. The outlook was as dark and uncertain as at any time since her accession, and as if to bring home England's plight Philip seized all English vessels in Spanish waters in May. After weeks of inconclusive negotiations the Dutch sent commissioners to London to offer Elizabeth the sovereignty of their provinces if she would give them the men and money they so desperately needed to keep Parma at bay.

The extent of Elizabeth's commitment in the Netherlands was unmistakably her own decision. Some thought that direct government of the troublesome provinces from London was an admirable solution and to the surprise of some of her councillors she rejected the idea of sovereignty out of hand. As a crowned head she had no alternative. It would have been an unpardonable affront to Philip II, the legitimate ruler, and she knew how she would have felt had he accepted a sovereignty of part of her realm offered by the northern rebels in 1569. Once she accepted sovereignty of Holland and Zeeland the chances of negotiating a peace would be gone for ever and she would find England tied to a costly, endless war. Instead of this she took the Dutch under her protection – a unique constitutional solution to the problem. The first treaty, signed at Greenwich on 3 September, was concerned solely with the relief of Antwerp, whose governor was so sure she would not intervene that he had begun talking terms of surrender with Parma. Four days later the great city fell and the news so alarmed her that those at court were sure she would 'send some great person with great forces, presently for the defence of Holland and Zeeland, or else they will, out of hand, follow Antwerp.' At once she concluded the general treaty of Nonsuch with the Dutch for providing at her own cost an army of 5,100 foot and 1,000 horse under a commander of high rank so long as the war should last. Flushing and Brill were to be handed over to her to be garrisoned by English troops and she would send two civilian members to sit on their Council of State. The costs to her would be crippling.[2]

The Queen had not come to a hasty decision and to show the world that she was acting openly, in the best interests of the Netherlands and not from any desire of territorial gain she published the reasons for her intervention in a Declaration in August, in English, French and Dutch; by the middle of the month she had a copy of it presented to Parma himself. In it she recalled the long series of treaties between England and the Netherlands for mutual protection and defence, underlined the fundamental ties of trade which had been sanctified by the *'Magnus Intercursus'* of Henry Tudor with Burgundy and rehearsed the 'barbarous cruelty of the Spaniards'. Her aim was that the provinces by being brought under her protection should be enabled to enjoy their ancient freedom peaceably, which would ensure the stability of Europe and the security of England. Her declaration was cautiously phrased, yet so far were her ideals from being trimmed to state-craft that the document has even been compared with the American Declaration of Independence. It was a challenge to Spain that, unlike the activities of Drake – and he was now despatched with a fleet to the Azores – could not be ignored. Though Elizabeth would do her utmost to negotiate, sending her army to the Netherlands meant war with Spain on all fronts. Four years before, after the Regent Morton's death, she had told a Scottish ambassador, 'I am more afraid of making a fault in my Latin than of the Kings of Spain, France, Scotland, the whole house of Guise and all their confederates. I have the heart of a man, not of a woman, and I am not afraid of anything.' She was sure her own courage would not let her people down.[3]

Though she professed to be uncertain whom to send as governor-general of her army, there had never for a moment been any doubt in her own mind that she must sacrifice Leicester for this task. Always when there was some special responsibility to be borne she turned to him; in 1562 she had singled him out as Protector if anything should happen to her; in 1588 she would appoint him lieutenant-general for the defence of the realm when invasion seemed imminent. Walsingham and others might hint at the greater military experience of Lord Grey of Wilton for the Netherlands command or give vent to private doubts about Leicester's fitness for a post requiring great circumspection, but for the Queen, 'the nobleman of quality' she had promised to send could mean only one person. Of course she hesitated and prolonged the leave-taking, not that at this stage she thought the Earl was planning to take his wife with him. Elizabeth's own ill health was the reason for postponing his departure. 'I found Her Majesty very desirous to stay me', he told Walsingham:

She makes the cause only the doubtfulness of her own health, by reason of her often disease taking her of late, and this last night worst of all. She used very pitiful words to me of her fear she shall not live and would not have me from her. You can imagine what manner of persuasion this must be to me from her, and therefore I would not say much for any matter, but did comfort her so much as I could, only I did let her know how far I had gone in preparation.

A week later she agreed to his sailing, yet in fact he did not leave England for another twelve weeks. Fortunately the campaign against Parma, mightiest soldier alive, was not waiting on Leicester's arrival. The main army of Englishmen, eager to flash their swords in a righteous cause, had left, so had Sir Philip Sidney, Elizabeth's Governor of Flushing, allies of the volunteer soldiers of fortune, the cream of the nation's manhood, who had been fighting the Spanish since 1569.[4]

Leicester became increasingly reluctant to take on an awkward command with what he regarded as quite insufficient powers, his authority limited by the Dutch Council and by instructions from home. He would as soon have died, he swore, than have his Queen clip his wings thus, and when he finally left England on 9 December he prayed that she would 'never send general again as I am sent – and yet I will do what I can for her and her country.'

On New Year's Day 1586 a delegation arrived at Leicester's lodgings at the Hague to offer him, as Her Majesty's lieutenant, 'the absolute government of the whole provinces of Holland, Zeeland, Friesland and Utrecht', and he was foolish enough to accept the offer. Knowing better than anyone how sensitive Elizabeth was to the question of his authority it was a disastrous act, and made nonsense of the letter and spirit of the royal declaration of the previous August. As soon as she heard she fumed, 'It is sufficient to make me infamous to all princes, having protested the contrary in a book which is translated into divers languages', and she penned a personal reproof in her most forceful vein (to be taken over by Heneage), requiring him to make a public resignation of the office he had been rash enough to assume:

How contemptuously we conceive ourself to have been used by you, you shall by this bearer understand, whom we have expressly sent unto you to charge you withall. We could never have imagined, had we not seen it fall out in experience, that a man raised up by ourself, and extraordinarily favoured by us above any subject of this land, would have in so contemptible a sort broken a commandment, in a course that so greatly toucheth us in honour, whereof, although you have shewed yourself to make but little account, in most undutiful a sort, you may not therefore think that we have so little care of the reparation thereof as we mind to pass so great a wrong in silence unredressed. And therefore, our express pleasure and commandment is, that all delays and excuses laid apart, you do presently, upon the duty of your allegiance, obey and fulfill whatsoever the bearer hereof shall direct you to do in our name: whereof fail you not, as you will answer the contrary at your uttermost peril.

She was furious that he had taken the title 'Excellency'; and yet, he complained, 'when she made me an earl I had that style due to me', telling Walsingham he had declined an even greater title. But unless the title 'His Excellency the Captain General' were abolished he would be recalled. Nearly as serious in Elizabeth's eyes was his scheme to have his wife to join him, playing the great lady 'with such a train of ladies and gentlewoman and such rich coaches ... as Her Majesty had none such.' In a temper she shouted that the very hand which enabled him 'can beat him to the dust.'[5]

Yet the Earl stayed in the Low Countries until November, feebly directing a campaign that was only rescued from ignominy by the heroism of Sir Philip Sidney's mortal wound at Zutphen. Leicester was much moved by his son-in-law's ideal of perfect service and Elizabeth, though she did not care over-much for Sidney, saw that her people had taken him to their heart and gave him a state funeral in St Paul's, an honour not again accorded to a subject until Nelson's obsequies. A national hero made some amends for the burdens of war and the failure of her various projects to bring about peace once the 'cautionary towns' of Brill and Flushing had passed to her control and could be used as bargaining counters. Initially she estimated her army serving with the Dutch would cost £126,000 a year, the equivalent of an entire subsidy, but it was soon obvious that a land campaign was a Moloch, eating up the wealth of England, and since she could not afford to wage an offensive war capable of decisively defeating Parma she knew one campaigning season after another would end at best in stalemate. It was not perfidious conduct to seek terms that were honourable for her Dutch allies, but all Parma wanted was to hold out a hope of peace to give Spain further time for preparing for the invasion of England. Leicester had found it impossible to co-operate with the Dutch, had quarrelled with Prince Maurice of Nassau, their best soldier, had upset Sir John Norris, his ablest lieutenant, and could not abide the English representatives on the Council of State. Moreover he was ill and desperate to be home again.

By June Elizabeth had relented of her anger and wrote tenderly to him: 'Rob, I am afraid you will suppose by my wandering writings that a midsummer moon hath taken large possession of my brains this month, but you must needs take things as they come into my head, though order be left behind me.' At last, in November, he was given leave to return, while Parliament waited for sentence against Mary to be proclaimed. With him at her side once more she forgot about his ill success and stoutly defended him against the Dutch envoys who had pursued him with complaints of utter ingratitude. After a course of the waters at Bath had alleviated his sickness she sent him back to the Netherlands, much against her will, to prevent the fall of Sluys; when despite the gallantry of Sir Roger Williams, the key port fell to Parma, Leicester stayed on with instructions to persuade the Dutch to join in fresh peace negotiations, which he was most reluctant to undertake. In November Lord Willoughby was appointed to succeed him and next month he returned home for good. Elizabeth was vehement against those councillors who felt he should be made to answer for the mismanagement of the campaign; indeed he was now in as high favour as at any time in twenty-five years.[6]

Leicester had taken with him his stepson, Robert Devereux, Earl of Essex, then at eighteen on the threshold of a dazzling career, yearning to win his spurs. At Zutphen, where Sidney was wounded, Essex had his taste of glory and earned his knighthood on the battlefield. Returning to England he became the idol of the court, that marvellous boy who was able to charm the Queen more than any man, perhaps, since Seymour long ago. Essex had inherited the striking black eyes and auburn hair of his mother, Lettice Knollys, whose own grandmother had been Anne Boleyn's sister, and his stepfather was grooming him for the succession. What chance had Raleigh now, or Hatton? Youth, chivalry, birth, wealth, all were on his side, and no one could accuse him of being an upstart or deny his entitlement to swagger. A spoilt child, clearly – insolent, selfish, given to petulant moods – yet a youth of strange magnetism, for whom men would willingly risk their lives.

In the aftermath of Mary's execution, with Leicester at Bath, it was Essex alone who was able to transport Elizabeth from her acute depression to idyllic fields; at times they stayed up till dawn together, playing cards. The Queen, in fact still held the balance. Raleigh could not with justice complain that he was being disregarded, for he had slipped into Hatton's shoes as Captain of the Guard, when the latter went to the woolsack, and he acquired much of the traitor Babington's estates and goods. Some few courtiers might sneer at Raleigh being in 'wonderful declination', but in the great game of preferment and precedence he still landed on ladders at the throw of the dice. There was a stormy scene that summer at North Hall, when Lady Warwick was entertaining the

Queen, for among the other guests was Essex's sister, Dorothy, who had been banished from court for her secret marriage to Sir Thomas Perrot, an enemy of Raleigh's from his days in Ireland. Her presence in the royal party was seen as a calculated insult and Essex, as the girl's brother, for the first time had to stand up to Elizabeth's anger, and blamed it all on 'that knave Raleigh, for whose sake she would grieve me in the eye of the world.' He may not have boxed Raleigh's ears, as some say, but he certainly remonstrated with the Queen, reminding her of what Raleigh 'had been and what he was' and Elizabeth retorted with devastating comments about his mother, Lettice Knollys. 'What comfort can I have,' wrote the Earl, 'to give myself over to the service of a mistress that is in awe of such a man.' (Until the day before those might have been the words of Raleigh complaining of him!) Feeling desperately miserable he fled on impulse to the coast, intending to find a boat to take him to Holland and a hero's grave, when a courtier brought the Queen's command to return forthwith to court. All was forgiven. She would not have him risk his life any further in her service, as she wanted him near her always; and to seal his position at Christmas she made him a Knight of the Garter and appointed him master of the horse on his stepfather's resignation.[7]

Elizabeth's army did not inspire confidence by its performance in the Netherlands, largely because England's military organization remained medieval, and the Musters Act, under which troops were levied, went little farther than the Assize of Arms of 1181. Constitutionally, the Queen had not even the right to send any of the levies to serve outside the realm. Many schemes were suggested to her for forming a standing army, but she simply could not afford it, and Parliament would not listen to such unnecessary extravagance. Small wonder, then, that England's untrained levies from the shires made a poor showing against the regular, professional troops of Parma. The corruption of the commissariat, the abuses of the muster-masters and paymasters, and the system whereby Wart, Shadow and Feeble could take the place of able-bodied men at arms are well-known features of Elizabeth's army, whether the troops were serving on the Borders, in Ireland, the Netherlands or Brittany. That in the face of these difficulties the *esprit de corps* was so high and the disasters not greater is due to the calibre of the officers, many of them young, who served with a patriotism that was largely inspired by devotion to the Queen herself. Take, for instance, this letter from a father proud of his son's 'lusty courage' in volunteering to fight in Ireland: 'I love him the better because he hath chosen rather to take those pains, travails, hazards and dangers upon him for the Queen's Majesty and his country than to give himself to ease and pleasure.' The average young dandy at court in 1586 made the same choice.[8]

By contrast with the army, the navy had been completely reorganized, first by Benjamin Gonson and William Winter and, since 1578, by Sir John Hawkins. He created an entirely new arm in evolving a small, streamlined vessel that was much more seaworthy, easier to handle and able to stay at sea for longer periods than the traditional man-of-war; he also constructed a splendid force of larger vessels with long-range guns, of the type of Grenville's *Revenge*, and modified many of the older ships. By wholesale reform of the dockyards and the system of construction Hawkins, as treasurer of the navy, made the fleet a powerful instrument of war, able to fulfil its traditional role of defending the coast and yet fully capable of undertaking expeditions to harry the Spaniards in their own waters or to intercept the plate fleet. What particularly appealed to Elizabeth was that he achieved all this and still saved her money. It had been a proud moment for her to show the fleet of new warships at anchor in the Thames to Alençon, and at Greenwich Palace there was salt in the air and a smell of pitch. Compared with the forest of masts of the galleons at Cadiz and Lisbon, hers was a small fleet – no more than twenty-five major vessels in 1587 – but all were in first-rate condition. Her potential naval reserve was considerable – merchantmen, fishermen and other craft whose owners were eager to join in a syndicate to plunder beyond the line, to go after pirates, and even in a crisis to defend the realm. Elizabeth's naval expenses in 1570 averaged less than £10,000 a year; by 1586 the figure had increased to £32,000, the next year to £43,000 and in 1588 leapt to

£153,000 – a year in which her revenues, augmented by exceptional measures like forced loans, reached £392,000, and yet £120,000 of this was needed for the army in the Netherlands. Philip II had his American gold and silver, which in time devalued all Europe's currencies, but Elizabeth had to be cheeseparing or she would have gone under. In Spain, France and even the Dutch Provinces it would have seemed incredible for the improvement of harbours to have been financed by a public lottery, yet to such expedients was the Queen of England reduced. The country's wealth had increased, but it seemed nigh impossible for her to tap this new wealth through taxation so that the crown, too, could share in the prosperity. As Bacon was to remark, 'He that shall look into other countries and consider the taxes . . . that are everywhere in use, will find that the Englishman is most master of his own valuation and the least bitten in purse of any nation in Europe.' They were the masters and she suffered for it.[9]

During the dozen or so years before the breach with Spain England's solidarity developed as never before. France and the Netherlands were torn by civil wars, but at home 'the Queen's peace' prevailed. It was she who by some miracle of diplomatic finesse had prolonged the breathing-space, enabling enormous strides to be made in making England as self-sufficient as possible. She granted patents of monopoly for producing essential items like saltpetre and sulphur, encouraged German engineers to prospect for lead, iron and copper, and welcomed Huguenot settlers from Brittany who came over to escape persecution and spread the craft of sailmaking. The state papers and the Council registers give abundant information about the many ways national resources were being exploited, waste eliminated and inventiveness rewarded; the enthusiasm and the vigour were inculcated from above and subjects responded to the challenge. Historians of the last generation have pieced together that a veritable 'industrial revolution' was afoot in the later sixteenth century. Though Elizabeth so disliked coal that the palace still burnt wood, despite the extra cost, there was a marked increase in the production of coal, thanks to developments in mining and drainage. Cloth remained the staple commodity of foreign trade, but the clothing industry was much more diversified than of old and apart from the traditional broadcloths from Wiltshire, Devonshire and the West Riding, each with their own distinctive weights and textures, there was a remarkable output of new draperies from Norwich, the second city of the kingdom, and in Lancashire – momentous innovation – cotton yarn was for the first time being woven with woollen. The range of new fabrics from English looms in the Seventies and Eighties – with outlandish names like 'moccadoes', 'friziadoes', says – made a similar impact on the world to the invention of nylon and other man-made fabrics of our own day. This was the wealth of Elizabethan England.

The great commercial boom of Henry VIII's reign could not last indefinitely, and overseas trade had been depressed for practically the whole of the third quarter of the century. In those years, so like our own, of disappointing trade returns, merchants were persistent in their search for new markets. Laments for 'the vent of cloth' were frequent. Hitherto English trade had been concentrated at Antwerp, the emporium for all Europe, but from the early Sixties, the religious and political upheavals in Philip's dominions threatened that proud city's commercial dominance. In 1564 the merchant adventurers, denied entry to Antwerp for a season, chose Emden as their staple town, and the Anglo-Spanish embargo of 1568–73 turned them first to Hamburg, then to Stade as alternative gateways to continental markets, and soon Antwerp's days were numbered. Instead of sending the bulk of their cargoes to the Scheldt, they adventured to the Baltic, the Mediterranean and beyond. Beginnings of this enterprise had been laid as long ago as 1553 with the incorporation of the Muscovy Company under Sebastian Cabot, with the object of seeking a passage to Old Cathay, which brought England into contact with Russia. Between 1577 and 1581 Elizabeth granted charters to companies trading to Spain and Portugal, to the Baltic ('The Eastland Company') and to Turkey ('The Levant Company'), following concessions won from the Porte in the face of stiff French and Venetian opposition; Raleigh's Virginian Company for settling a colony in the New World ended in disaster, but on the very last day of the century the most famous of all these trading monopolies, the East

India Company, was chartered. Gradually the pattern of trade was completely redrawn. Instead of supplies being purchased in the Netherlands, English ships brought home from Danzig Baltic timber, pitch and tar, while the Levant Company's ships sailed from Constantinople with rare goods formerly bought at the Antwerp spice market. By 1580 the Moors of Barbary were providing Elizabeth with the bulk of the saltpetre needed for the manufacture of gunpowder. Well before the Scheldt was closed in 1585 English merchants, actively encouraged by the Queen, had freed themselves from dependence on Antwerp by forging new commercial links which a naval war would severely strain but fail to break. The design was that London should come to occupy the extraordinary position as a truly international port which Antwerp had enjoyed in its heyday.

Philip II, by contrast, had relied for his wealth on the specie of the New World. From the first, Englishmen had refused to accept the papal dogma that reserved to Spain all territory west of the Azores and north of the Tropic of Capricorn ('The Line') and during the Sixties many had sailed in search of trade, encouraged by the thought that if the Spaniards denied them opportunities of trading they would plunder with impunity. Too often, in those days, when the Spanish ambassador had complained of Englishmen's attacks on the plate fleets, Elizabeth had shrugged her shoulders and said most of the culprits were Scotsmen who spoke English to avoid being known. She had a financial stake in John Hawkins' second voyage of plunder in 1566, undertaken in utter disregard of the prohibitions from Madrid and he proudly told the Spanish vice-admiral in the Caribbean that he sailed 'by order of Elizabeth, Queen of England, whose fleet this is.' Drake's raid on Nombre de Dios in 1572 opened a new chapter in peacetime privateering, and he returned home with £40,000 in the currency of the day, and encouraged the Queen to invest heavily in his voyage round the world, which produced such rich dividends that she knighted 'her pirate', who became and remained a national hero. Such depredations were justified on the grounds of religious fervour and patriotic zeal, and Hakluyt's *Principal Navigations, Voyages and Discoveries of the English Nation* became as popular as Foxe's *Book of Martyrs*. And now, in 1585, the Queen provided £10,000 and lent him two of her ships for his descent on Santo Diego and Cartagena. It was not the loot that counted, as much as the opportunity in peacetime for English seamen to experience authentic naval warfare.[10]

In Madrid and Brussels plans for the Enterprise against England went forward. The Spanish admiral, Santa Cruz, had some years past proposed a combined naval and military expedition, but Philip II had found it too costly in conception. With Elizabeth's open intervention in the Netherlands he decided he could no longer postpone an attack on England until the Provinces had been reduced to Spanish rule, and he would divert from the campaign against the Dutch as many troops as could be spared to cross the Channel under Parma, while a powerful fleet should control the Narrow Seas. 'The Kingdom of England', Philip had written thirty years ago as Mary's consort, 'is and must always remain strong at sea, since on this the safety of the realm depends', and yet his spies reported that Elizabeth was saving money on her fleet. He had never forgiven her for her slight in turning down his proposal of marriage in the first months of the reign, and year by year she had tricked his ambassadors about her attitude to him, to his Church and to his people. She had spurned his well-intentioned advice on government and stopped her ears to his repeated warnings about the dangers of heresy. She had treated his representatives de Feria, de Quadra, de Spes and Mendoza quite ignominiously, and gone against the record of history and long established ties of amity and commerce by transferring her allegiance from the imperial house of Hapsburg to the house of Valois. She had frequently encouraged buccaneers to plunder his plate fleets and for years aided the Dutch in their rebellion against his rule with money and now with her own army. Worst of all this heretic of a sister-in-law had defied the Pope. The King of Spain's patience was exhausted. All the reports he carefully scrutinized in the Escorial left him in no doubt that it was his Christian duty to invade England and depose Elizabeth. Pope Sixtus V who had long been urging vigorous action, blessed the Enterprise, even though he had not subscribed towards its heavy costs, and Philip was at pains to declare his lofty motives: 'God is my witness', he wrote to the Cortes, 'that it was not the desire to gain new kingdoms that guided me, but the zeal for his service and the hope of glorifying the holy faith. For this I have risked everything – my patrimony, the cause of God, the glory of the state and my own honour.' He was convinced that English Catholics – no less than twenty-five thousand of them – would rise as a man to welcome Parma's army of liberation from the Protestant yoke.[11]

First reports of the Spanish preparations reached London in December 1585, as Leicester was leaving for the Netherlands, but it was not until the following midsummer that Elizabeth began to take the threat seriously by ordering lords lieutenant in the shires to muster the militia and arrange for a system of beacons to signal warning of the Armada's approach, from headland to headland. Thanks to Sir John Hawkins' careful administration the navy was in readiness on paper, but the Queen would not have ships unnecessarily in commission, for prolonging the maximum degree of preparedness meant wasting money on victuals and seamen's wages. She as paymaster would insist on dictating grand strategy to her admirals, for if she gave them *carte blanche* her small reserve of treasure would have vanished before the campaign proper opened. To her seamen attack was the best method of defence and in the spring of 1587 she authorized Drake to take four of her ships, with sixteen privately-owned vessels, on an expedition to Spain, in which he swept into Cadiz creating terror and confusion among the shipping concentrated there. He could not risk attempting a further raid up the Tagus to Lisbon, but off the Azores captured the *San Felipe*, a Portuguese galleon, with £140,000 of treasure. The raid to singe the King of Spain's beard had been remarkably successful, for it postponed the date of the Armada's sailing and provided the Queen with £40,000 as her share of the booty, for which she sent Drake her 'princely thanks'. Her admirals wanted to launch repetitive raids like the one on Cadiz, for beards, though singed, could grow again. Elizabeth could not endorse their idea of sea power. For her the navy was, indeed, the wooden walls of England, an offshore defensive system, like a chain of floating fortresses. If Drake and half the fleet were to desert the English Channel for punitive raids far afield, the wooden walls would be seriously weakened; and the oceans were too wide to be certain that the Armada could not elude the fleet sent to intercept them, and then England would be defenceless – 'a town besieged where the walls shall fall flat down to give entry to the enemy.' With the landsman's caution she restrained her captains – forcibly restrained them by keeping them short of supplies; and with her reluctance to force her country to face the supreme test she still hoped she could negotiate with Spain.[12]

At the end of July 1587 she was aghast to learn news of a 'wicked plot' to take Leicester's life now he was back in the Netherlands to try and save Sluys and persuade the Dutch of the virtues of negotiation, and a week later came a false alarm of a great fleet of two hundred sail off the Lizard, which made her put the maritime counties on the alert. On 9 October she again thought danger was imminent and ordered the local vice-admirals to stay all shipping and the lords lieutenant to have their levies at an hour's call. The fleet, fully mobilized, stayed in the Channel until January; by then it was obvious that no Spanish attempt would now be made until at least the late spring and Elizabeth ordered the ships to be reduced to half strength. Naval historians now absolve the Queen from 'the wholesale death of English seamen from starvation' and from cheating survivors of their wages; the fact remains, had she not been parsimonious when her admirals were bent on lavish expenditure there would not have been the money to buy victuals and pay wages for the crucial weeks.[13]

The seers of old had selected 1588 as a year of disaster, for the portents were uncomfortably similar whether one turned to biblical numerology or to the heavens. Philip Melancthon, whose scriptural expertise was beyond reproach, had calculated that the final cycle of history since the Incarnation would end in 1588, just seven times ten years since the end of the last cycle when Luther had defied the Pope. Long before then Regiomontanus of Königsberg, the mathematician on whose astronomical tables Columbus had relied when he sailed to discover America, had predicted for this same year of grace upheavals, lamentations and the ruin of empires – perhaps a final catastrophe for the whole of creation. All over Europe the fortune-tellers were busy as the New Year approached; in England the suppressed edition of *Holinshed's Chronicles* in January 1587 had alluded in awe to these ancient divinations and the Privy Council now forbade the compilers of almanacs to make any reference to the fears in everyone's minds. Elizabeth, with her penchant for astrology, must surely have discussed the portents with one of Dr Dee's disciples, and drawn some terrible inference from the fact that the moon's eclipse coincided with the beginning of her ruling sign 'virgo'. For Dee, on the continent, the year had begun dreadfully, for his boy Michael pierced his eye with a sharp stick.[14]

Drake was itching to be afloat again; he had told a Spaniard in London at Christmas that the next Christmas he would celebrate in Portugal as victor. Hawkins, dismayed at what he considered the Queen's inability to see through Parma's feigned concern to negotiate, looked on a vigorous campaign as the best of all weapons of diplomacy: 'Our profit and best assurance is to seek our peace by a determined and resolute war', he wrote. Parma, who had been digging canals and assembling his flat-bottomed boats ready for the invasion, was worried about the strength of his army and asked his royal uncle for a supporting force of six thousand seasoned soldiers. Elizabeth had given the chief command to Lord Howard of Effingham, with a grand fleet based at Queenborough for the defence of the Thames; from Dover Sir Henry Seymour commanded a light squadron to patrol the Straits, while at Plymouth Drake had thirty ships in readiness for watching the western approaches to the Channel. In May Howard moved his fleet to join Drake's in Plymouth Sound, but Elizabeth refused to allow him to go marauding; his task was to defend the island, not to carry the war into enemy waters.[15]

To meet the extraordinary costs of the fleet and of the militia Elizabeth had again required her wealthier subjects to subscribe to a forced loan, as she had done after the northern rebellion, and this gradually brought in £75,000. The coast towns had been ordered to fit out ships and this 'ship money', one day to be branded a tyrannical demand, was now an exercise in self-help. Had

Parliament been sitting, it would still have taken many weeks for loyally voted supplies to have been collected, and unpopular as Elizabeth's emergency measures were, she was asking of her subjects no less than she was asking of herself. Her own reserve fund – 'chested treasure', as it was called – had sunk in four years from £299,000 to £55,000. Was it surprising that she owed the wages of her troops in the Netherlands and had refused a subsidy to Henry of Navarre? Some £30,000 was raised in the city during March, the Treasurer was anxiously calling in all arrears of crown debts and even while the Armada was in the Channel there was haggling with the London livery companies for a further £26,000.[16]

In March, as Leicester resigned his command in the Netherlands, a new round of peace negotiations opened. Elizabeth had included her controller, Sir James Croft, as one of the commissioners – a shrewd move for he was a pensioner of Philip II, and though there was the risk of him playing her false his presence at Ostend showed Parma that she meant business. As it turned out Croft either misunderstood or deliberately misinterpreted the general's attitude in his report of their discussions so that when he returned to England in August he was imprisoned. Talks went on steadily in fact till the Armada was in the Channel, with both sides 'sewing the fox's skin to the lion's'. Admiral Howard charitably wrote of Croft: 'A good will I think he had, but surely no good workman.' What ended all hope of an accommodation and served as a Spanish declaration of war was the publication of Cardinal William Allen's *Admonition to the Nobility and People of England Concerning the Present Wars*, printed in Antwerp and smuggled over in large quantities in June. Allen, the first English Cardinal since Pole, was the most authoritative of the exiles and he had taken up his pen to remove any doubts which English Catholics may have had about their Queen. He reiterated that Sixtus V had confirmed Pius V's bull concerning her 'illegitimacy, usurpation and inability to the crown of England', for she was a heretic, had committed sacrilege and led an 'abominable life'. It was the bounden duty of all the faithful in England to rise when Parma's army landed 'to help towards the restoring of the Catholic faith and deposing the usurper.' Allen was no mealy-mouthed cleric and Elizabeth, when she read a copy of his pamphlet, was furious at his 'roaring hellish' vituperation; that one of her own subjects should have actually maintained in print that she was a usurper, a tyrant and a heretic was far worse than his blackening her character. But she did not panic, as did many of her Council, into believing that Catholics would accept Allen's words as holy writ and rise up against her. Others were alarmed for her own safety, yet she put on a great show of supreme self-confidence. Admiral Howard could not believe that she had not yet taken special precautions for defending herself against assassination: he sent her two mild salvoes pleading with her to be careful, and when she evaded them he directed a broadside from his inappropriately named flagship, *The Ark*, on 23 June: 'For the love of Jesus Christ, Madam, awaken thoroughly.' What was the point of defeating the Spaniard, he felt, if his Queen should out of false bravado allow herself to be slain. But Allen's *Admonition* convinced her it was time to allow Howard a free hand to put to sea and he soon had other matters on his mind.[17]

In the western approaches Howard heard news that the Spaniards had left Lisbon in May, had been badly tossed by gales and were now refitting in the harbours of the Bay of Biscay. Off he went to destroy them, but after three days the wind veered to the south, so he turned his ships to make for Plymouth, knowing that the same wind would send the Enterprise against England on the final stages of its voyage. On the afternoon of 19 July the Spaniards sighted the Lizard and next dawn they saw the warning beacons on the headlands. Howard brought his fleet out of Plymouth on the 21st to make contact with this imposing enemy 'with lofty towers castle-like, in front like a half-moon' and for over a week there was a running fight up the Channel. Medina Sidonia, who like Nelson was always so terribly seasick, reached Calais with his fleet more or less intact, reasonably confident of making his rendezvous with Parma. Not until the Armada was off Portland Bill, on 23 July, did the order go out for the main army to repel invasion to assemble at Tilbury. By a master-stroke on the evening of the 28th, Howard sent in to Calais Roads eight fireships which brought havoc to the anchored galleons. Camden credits the

Queen with the suggestion of using fireships, but it is hard to believe this. Next day the English closed in to fight the battle of Gravelines, showing their great skill in handling their vessels and proving their superiority in gunnery, and soon those galleons that escaped the fight or avoided running aground on the Flemish sandbanks were driven by gales into the mists of the North Sea and were never to re-enter the Channel. Though Elizabeth's navy had retained the command of the narrow seas, accurate news of the action was long in reaching the Queen. Besides confusion about what had taken place there was, even much later, misunderstanding about the strategic advantages gained. Even if the remnant of the Armada did not return to the Straits, it was widely believed that Parma would still attempt an invasion.[18]

As reports came in of the chase up the Channel right to the narrow straits, she wanted to be in the thick of it, instead of being hedged in at St James's by the guard formed for the defence of her person, and announced she would visit the coast, but Leicester as Lieutenant General politely forbade it. Then, 'not a whit dismayed' at the prospect of danger, she told him she would come to the camp at Tilbury, and he had not the heart to dissuade her but took Mr Rich's house for her a few miles away. She came down by barge on 8 August to inspect the men and let them see her; as she rode through the ranks, wearing the steel corselet found for her, 'like some Amazonian empress', they fell on their knees in prayer. She returned next morning to watch an exercise and then review the troops. With Parma's army across the water the danger seemed very great, and to steel the resolution of the men mustered at Tilbury, whose task was to prevent an advance on London, Elizabeth issued her order of the day, making a speech in the heroic mould that thrilled all who heard it:

My loving people, We have been persuaded by some that are careful of our safety, to take heed how we commit ourselves to armed multitudes, for fear of treachery; but I assure you, I do not desire to live in distrust of my faithful and loving people. Let tyrants fear. I have always so behaved myself that under God, I have placed my chiefest strength and goodwill in the loyal hearts and goodwill of my subjects; and therefore I am come amongst you, as you see, at this time, not for my recreation and disport, but being resolved, in the midst and heat of the battle, to live or die amongst you all; to lay down for God, my kingdom, and for my people, my honour and my blood, even in the dust. I know I have but the body of a weak and feeble woman; but I have the heart and stomach of a King, and a King of England too, and think it foul scorn that Parma or Spain or any Prince of Europe, should dare to invade the borders of my realm; to which, rather than any dishonour should grow by me, I myself will take up arms, I myself will be General, Judge and Rewarder of every one of your virtues in the field.

I know already for your forwardness you have deserved rewards and crowns; and we do assure you, on the word of a Prince, they shall be duly paid you. In the meantime, my Lieutenant General shall be in my stead, than whom never Prince commanded a more noble or worthy subject; not doubting but that by your obedience to my General, by your concord in the camp and your valour in the field, we shall shortly have a famous victory over these enemies of my God, of my Kingdom, and of my People.

The cheers were thunderous. While she was dining with Leicester in his tent came news that Parma was already embarking his troops (a false report as it proved) and was to sail over on the spring tide. There were incredible practical expressions of loyalty. Sir Henry Lee, who had long felt out of things, had come down with ten horses at his own charge to stay by her person; men in a Dorset regiment of militia mustered £500 to be given the chance of forming part of her bodyguard. Among the courtiers serving afloat were Oxford, Northumberland, Charles Blount, surprisingly, Robert Cecil and understandably Raleigh.

Those words, at Tilbury, as Leicester put it, had 'so inflamed the hearts of her poor subjects as I think the weakest person among them is able to match the proudest Spaniard that dares now land in England.' She stayed near the camp for a whole week, convinced that 'in honour she could not return to London, in case there were any likelihood that the enemy should attempt anything.' Once it was clear that Parma dare not risk the crossing, the danger was past and the navy was rapidly demobilized so that by the beginning of September only thirty-four ships out of the grand fleet of 197 remained in commission. Before then Elizabeth had returned triumphantly to London for full-scale celebrations of the victory on which it was far easier to persuade her to spend money than on seamen's victuals; but from Whitehall she issued orders that the abuses in the pay of the men at Tilbury Camp were to be investigated. She had a vague idea of making Leicester her viceroy, as she had during her illness in 1562; in many ways such an appointment would have been no more than continuing his special powers as Lieutenant General of the realm beyond the emergency, but Burghley and Hatton were so opposed to her suggestion that she did not pursue it. Yet Leicester's own entry to London was little less than regal and in the next few days he was constantly in the Queen's company. Both were far from well, and with Essex's grand review in the tiltyard over, Leicester set out by easy stages for Buxton to take the waters. Lady Norris put him up at Rycote in the room usually reserved for Elizabeth, and from here he wrote to her:

I most humbly beseech Your Majesty to pardon your old servant to be thus bold in sending to know how my gracious Lady doth, and what ease of her pain she finds, being the chiefest thing in the world I do pray for, for her to have good health and long life. For my own poor case I continue still your medicine and it amends much better than any other thing that hath been given me. . . . I humbly kiss your foot, from your old lodging at Rycott this Thursday morning, by Your Majesty's most faithful and obedient servant, R. Leycester.

Alas, the Queen's specific could not rid him of his fever and he died within the week. We do not know how the news was broken to her and courtiers were reticent about how she took it, but there is a ring of truth about the report of a Spaniard in London that from sheer grief 'she shut up herself in her chamber alone and refused to speak to anyone, until the Treasurer and other councillors had the doors broken open and entered to see her.'

Her 'sweet Robin' gone – for all his faults the man to whom she had been emotionally tied for thirty years. Death soured the fruits of victory, the Protestant wind had scattered her enemies and snuffed out this precious light to leave her in utter solitude that made her feel her age. Evidence for the strength of their relationship did not come out until after her own death, when among the few especial treasures she had kept in a little casket by her bed was Leicester's note from Rycote, which bore her own docket 'His last letter'.[19]

However low she felt in spirits as a woman, she had as Queen to enter into the public rejoicings of the signal victory, with services of thanksgiving and an accession day of especial pomp. The defeat of the Armada was a decisive battle not in the sense that it brought Philip II to his knees suing for peace, secured overnight the independence of the Dutch Republic or ended for good England's fear of invasion; it was decisive in that it checked the colossus of Spain, which had been growing to unprecedented strength from Lepanto, through the conquest of Portugal to the latest campaigns of Parma in the Netherlands. And because the Enterprise against England had been a holy crusade, the fate of the galleons showed that the counter reformation had reached full tide, no less than it marked the apogee of Spanish prestige; 'those black dogs are profligated and returned home with shame.' Neither Spanish power nor Roman Catholicism would ever be the same again. Who can tell the outcome if the battle of Gravelines had been lost by Howard of Effingham and Parma had been encouraged to attempt a landing at Rochester? A Spanish conquest would have been against all the odds, yet under such circumstances it would have been very possible for a fanatic to have killed the Queen. As it turned out, England's victory was quite naturally interpreted both at home and abroad as divine intervention. God was not, after all, on the side of the big battalions and the lords of the silver mines; and in the aftermath of the action French Huguenots no longer feared that the world for them had ended with St Bartholomew's and Dutch Protestants no more regarded the assassination of William the Silent as the death knell of their struggle. 1588, the year of evil omen, put a new heart into the Protestant cause. Philip had begun his instructions to Medina Sidonia with the invocation, 'As all victories are the gifts of God Almighty and the cause we champion is so exclusively his, we may fairly look for his aid and favour.' And now the God he so piously worshipped in the chapel of the Escorial, the God of Rome, the Inquisition and the Jesuits had withheld his blessings. In

England the crisis had passed and, as Elizabeth had predicted, her Catholic subjects by and large had rejected the doctrines of Cardinal Allen's propaganda; despite papal bulls and the teaching of Jesuit missionaries they had accorded their loyalty to their Queen a higher priority than their loyalty to their Church. Soon to be torn by internal dissensions in the 'archpriest' controversy, recusants had ceased to be a danger to the state.[20]

Deborah had vanquished Sisera; the Supreme Governor had been blest while the Most Catholic King had been cursed from on high. A prayer composed for the Chapel Royal in those critical days, calling on God to scatter his enemies 'and especially regard thy servant Elizabeth', had made plain 'she seeketh not her own honour, but thine' – and yet, no single act of her entire reign increased her fame so much as the defeat of Philip's grand fleet. No longer could her most scathing critics speak of her as mistress of an insignificant island, backward and poor; she was now a mighty prince, the victor of Spain. Not for nothing did the King of Denmark carry round with him her picture in a tablet of gold. The learned wrote triumphant poems in all languages, and in London no fewer than twenty-four ballads were published commemorating the victory; in one of the few which has come down to us Thomas Deloney paraphrased the speech at Tilbury:

> Our gracious Queen
> 　　doth greet you everyone
> And saith 'She will among you be
> 　　in every bitter storm.
> Desiring you
> 　　true English hearts to bear
> To God, to her, and to the land
> 　　wherein you nurséd were.'[21]

To commemorate the victory Elizabeth took the unprecedented step of ordering the Mint to strike a silver medal, bearing on the obverse her bust in profile and on the reverse an ark on the waves. Next year there was a further issue of a slightly larger medal in gold, silver and copper, this time with the Queen's bust in fullface, and on the reverse an island with a flourishing bay tree, immune from the storm which tossed the ships and sea monsters round about. As a personal commemoration – again a unique undertaking – she sat for a special portrait (reproduced here plate 7), which showed her resplendent, her right hand on the globe. Behind her right shoulder is a view of the English galleons, with their St George's crosses, returning proudly from Calais Roads, while on the other side are the Spanish vessels foundering in the storm. To her, the instrument of God's providence, belonged the palm.[22]

Years afterwards Bishop Godfrey Goodman, who was at the time the schoolboy nephew of the Dean of Westminster, vividly remembered catching his glimpse of Elizabeth in the winter of '88:

I did then live at the upper end of the Strand near St Clement's Church, when suddenly there came a report to us (it was in December, much about 5 of the clock at night, very dark) that the Queen was gone to council, and if you will see the Queen you must come quickly. Then we all ran; when the court gates were set open, and no man did hinder us from coming in. Then we came where there was a far greater company than was usually at Lent sermons, and when we had stayed there an hour and that the yard was full, there being a number of torches, the Queen came out in great state. Then we cried: 'God save Your Majesty! God save Your Majesty!' Then the Queen turned to us and said 'God bless you all my good people!' Then we cried again 'God save Your Majesty! God save Your Majesty!' Then the Queen said again unto us, 'You may well have a greater prince, but you shall never have a more loving prince.' and so looking one upon another a while the Queen departed. This wrought such an impression upon us, for shows and pageants are ever best seen by torch-light, that all the way long we did nothing but talk what an admirable Queen she was, and how we would adventure our lives to do her service.[23]

Life was never the same with Leicester gone, yet she put on as brave a face as she could and warmed her chillness of spirit with his stepson, Essex, with Raleigh, with any who could minister to her loneliness. Essex like a spoilt child was quick to take offence if she smiled on any but himself. Sometime that winter she had been so impressed by the performance of Charles Blount, Lord Mountjoy's son, in the tiltyard that to encourage the lad 'she sent him a golden queen from her set of chessmen', which he proudly tied to his arm with a crimson ribbon. Essex was extremely jealous and gibed 'Now I perceive that every fool must have a favour', for which remark Blount challenged him to a duel in Marylebone Park and wounded him in the thigh. 'By God's death!' Elizabeth exclaimed when she heard of it, 'it was fit that someone or other should take him down, and teach him better manners, otherwise there would be no rule with him.' So she forbade them to come to court until they had made it up. A few weeks later there was a violent quarrel between Raleigh and Essex, and the latter issued his challenge. This time the Queen intervened, requiring the Council to forbid the fight. We are almost back to the court of the first year of the reign, with Leicester, Pickering and Arundel, vying for her favour except that by now, however much they praised her virginal beauty, she had turned fifty-five and was not even in love with love.[24]

All eyes were now on France, which vividly showed the perils of a disputed succession. Until the defeat of the Armada Guise and the Catholic League had been carrying all before them. Early in 1588 Elizabeth's ambassador had been pressing Henry of Valois once more to break with the League and ally himself with Henry of Navarre; if he would arrest the Duke and his cardinal brother on a charge of treason she would raise troops for him in Germany, even though the £31,000 she had paid the previous year had been so bad an investment. The French King, however, decided that the only solution would be for Navarre to declare himself a Catholic – wiser advice than appeared at the time and which after years of campaigning Navarre was forced to follow. On 2 May 1588 in the Day of Barricades, at the time when the Armada was leaving Lisbon, the people of Paris had risen for the Guises. The King had slipped through the Duke's fingers, fleeing to Chartres, but all hopes of his making a firm stand were dashed by his Edict of Union in which he vowed to exterminate heresy. By the autumn, with Philip II's plans for a swift conquest of England overthrown, Henry III roused himself as Elizabeth had for so long been urging – he, of whom Guise had said 'this is a King who needs to be frightened', at last struck at his mentor. He had summoned the

Estates General to his court at Blois and here on 23 December he arranged for his bodyguard, the famous forty-five, to murder the Duke and the Cardinal. This was Henry III's moment of triumph: 'At last am I King of France – no more a prisoner and slave', he is said to have remarked, though in fact, far from gaining his independence, he was driven into the arms of Navarre. The Leaguers under the Duke of Mayenne still held Paris and it was while Henry was investing the city the following August that a Jacobin monk murdered this last of the Valois, who before expiring named Navarre as his successor. As a result the theatre of Anglo-Spanish operations was inevitably extended to France, for Elizabeth's loan to Henry IV of £20,000 and a force under Lord Willoughby was soon countered by Parma's advance through Picardy and a further Spanish force in Brittany. For all the naval successes of 1588, Elizabeth was still in the midst and heat of battle.

Ever since September 1588 she had been under pressure from her sea captains to carry the war into enemy territory. Certainly the chance of destroying the galleons which had limped into Biscayan ports for overhaul was an opportunity not to be missed and she was soon convinced that a single mighty swoop on Santander, San Sebastian and the other harbours would eliminate all future danger from Spain and force Philip to sue for peace in the Netherlands. There was also the alluring possibility of establishing from the Azores a blockade of the silver fleets. As it was, Elizabeth's acute shortage of money dictated the nature of this expedition to Portugal, which was to be a joint-stock enterprise for which she at first could undertake to subscribe no more than £20,000 and 'six of her 2nd. sort of ships'. Her reserve fund of 'chested treasure' was fast disappearing and though Parliament had voted two whole subsidies, which would produce £280,000, they had spread the collection of it over four years. Once the Portuguese expedition was regarded as a classic example of the Queen's 'ineptitude in martial affairs', yet in recent times the blame for its failure has been fairly laid on the commanders. Nothing is further from the truth than Raleigh's jibe that had Elizabeth listened more readily to her men of action she would have reduced the King of Spain to 'a King of figs and oranges'. Had she been able to finance the expedition herself, the chances are that the difficulties and disappointments would never have arisen. The delays in sailing were, indeed, largely due to wranglings with the Dutch, whose aid in providing transports for the soldiers she so badly needed. In the end she had perforce to increase her share of the costs to £50,000. London merchants and others who had eagerly come in with Drake and Norris, the respective naval and military commanders, looked for a ready return in plunder and it proved so easy to recruit men that twice the number sailed as had been originally intended, playing havoc with the victualling arrangements.[25]

First and foremost she insisted that the Spanish shipping in the Biscayan ports should be destroyed; that accomplished, the fleet should tackle the shipping in the Tagus and, if conditions were favourable, they were to reinstate Don Antonio, the ex-King of Portugal, who had been in exile in England for the past eight years. Yet instead of following her instructions Drake at the end of April 1589 sacked Coruna, hoping for plunder. Here there was only a single Armada galleon and six other vessels, but a great store of wine which the men laid their hands on proved, literally, fatal. When she heard of the raid Elizabeth sent Drake and Norris a stiff reminder of their fulsome promises that their 'principal action should be to take and distress the King of Spain's navy and ships in ports where they lay; which if ye did not, ye affirmed that ye were content to be reputed traitors.' And now, far from dealing with the vessels in Santander and San Sebastian, they moved on towards Lisbon, but here again Norris disobeyed instructions by landing his troops some forty miles north-west of Lisbon instead of forcing the entrance to the Tagus. Support for Don Antonio proved negligible and many soldiers died like flies before they had sight of Lisbon.

Elizabeth's anger was all the greater because Essex had in flagrant disobedience joined the expedition. Knowing she would refuse his special pleading he had slipped away from court and taken passage in the *Swiftsure* at Falmouth. First she sent Sir Francis Knollys to look for him at Plymouth, then Huntingdon was ordered to secure his return. It was too late, and the peremptory summons for 'immediate repair unto us' took two months to deliver:

Essex, your sudden and undutiful departure from our presence and your place of attendance [as master of the horse] you may easily conceive how offensive it is, and ought to be, unto us. Our great favours bestowed on you without deserts hath drawn you thus to neglect and forget your duty; for other constructions we cannot make of those your strange actions.

When at length he obeyed, she forgave her adventurer readily enough; to have him back safe and sound, his own reputation for valour undimmed by the military disasters, was bliss indeed. Abandoning the attack on Lisbon, Drake took a fleet of corn ships from Hamburg and burnt Vigo, but of a truth England's Armada had fallen flat. Elizabeth chided the joint commanders from going to places 'more from profit than for service' and warned them of the dangers of allowing themselves to be 'transported with an haviour of vainglory, which will obfuscate the eyes of your judgement.' Her thanks to them on their return was icily given – 'as much had been performed by them as true valour and good condition could yield' – for the plunder was valued at a mean £30,000 and for the sake of that paltry sum all chance of wiping out Spanish seapower had gone. Now Philip could recover, and by 1596 was able to send another Armada against England. Instead of achieving a decisive end to the hostilities she was forced back on a continental, defensive war, that was long, costly and the type of campaigning at which the English never excelled. Not until the danger from the Leaguers was over and Henry IV established in his kingdom did she risk another large-scale attack on Spain. To be still in the midst and heat of battle was a bitter disappointment for her.[26]

Early in 1590 Essex secretly married Frances, the widow of Sir Philip Sidney and daughter of old Walsingham, now very near his end. When by the autumn Frances was great with child, Elizabeth had to be told, but Essex did not flinch from telling her himself and behaved with unwonted discretion. To the Queen the fact that he had married at all was a personal affront, made ten times worse by the fact that he had not told her in advance and married so beneath him. Yet by now Elizabeth was becoming hardened to the matrimonial escapades of her favourites and the storm passed quicker than any had anticipated. He pleaded with her to have command of an English army in France and after three refusals he stayed on his knees for two whole hours imploring her to send him to succour Navarre. She gave way in the end, only to change her mind repeatedly, but she condescended to inspect his cavalry at Covent Garden and at length he landed at Dieppe in August 1591 with 3,400 men to supplement the earlier force sent there under Sir Roger Williams. Nothing went right. Walter Devereux, Essex's brother, was killed within the month, Navarre would not think of following the Queen's suggestion that he should slip over to see her at Portsmouth, which peeved her, and yet he seemed reluctant to begin the siege of Rouen. Soon Elizabeth had had enough of this foolery and ordered Essex to return, though through the skilful pleading of Robert Carey, who told her the favourite was resolved 'to retire to some cell in the country', feeling unable to look a man in the face if he could not now retrieve his honour, a reprieve was wheedled out of her, but not for long. Back at court she behaved so slightingly towards him that he could not bear it and wrote a hasty protest: 'I see Your Majesty is constant to ruin me. I do humbly and patiently yield to Your Majesty's will. I appeal to all men that saw my posting from France, or the manner of my coming hither, whether I deserved such a welcome or not.' Then she relented and let him return to the battlefield and he wrote from there telling her he was bent on a piece of gallant service, with the assurance that once this were achieved and his honour redeemed:

no cause but a great action of your own may draw me out of your sight, for the two windows of your privy chamber shall be the poles of my sphere, where, as long as Your Majesty will please to have me, I am fixed and unmoveable. When Your Majesty thinks that heaven too good for me, I will not fall like a star, but be consumed like a vapour by the same Sun that drew me up to such a height. While Your Majesty gives me leave to say I love you, my fortune is as my affection, unmatchable.[27]

Such charming protestations only made her wish to have him back at court; and reason soon backed up emotion, for Rouen was proving a tough nut to crack, sickness was depleting the English army more rapidly than Leaguer bullets, and, above all, the finances of the enterprise were tangled. On Christmas Eve she wrote commanding him to return once he had handed over his command to Sir Roger Williams, bringing with him 'the best sort of the gentlemen there', and this time he speedily obeyed, kissing the hilt of his sword as he stepped aboard the boat to bring him to England.

Elizabeth had been low in spirits, as not a month earlier Christopher Hatton had died. In his last attack of his old kidney trouble she had visited his bedside at Ely Place to comfort him, bringing perhaps those 'cordial broths' of which Fuller speaks and telling him to cease worrying about the £42,000 he owed her on his account as receiver-general of first fruits and tenths. Of a truth, 'her Eyes' was past worrying. She had fished for men's souls with so sweet a bait, as he had put it, 'that no one could escape her network', and she had caught many poor fish – yes, he had been one – 'who little knew what snare was laid for them.' He, alone of her favourites, had stayed a bachelor for her sake, and now the Lord Chancellor of England in his Naboth's vineyard by Hatton Garden took leave of his great fisherman, and would dance no more.[28]

The campaigns in France and the Netherlands were as disappointing as she had feared, and even the removal of Parma by a stray bullet at Rouen did not radically alter the situation. On the defensive again, English men-of-war kept a blockade of the Channel, straining relations with the German ports of the Hanse, the Danes, the Poles and perhaps especially, their Dutch allies, to prevent money from reaching Flanders and corn and naval stores from passing westward to the open seas and Spain. If another major descent on the Peninsula was out of the question there was ample scope for privateering – a method of warfare conducted by subjects at their own expense which greatly commended itself to the Queen. The prince of privateers was George, Earl of Cumberland, who always wore in his hat a glove she had dropped; so much more dignified than the jewelled garter the French ambassador had coveted. She wrote Cumberland playful letters: 'It may seem strange to you that we should once vouchsafe to trouble our thoughts with any care for any person of roguish condition, being always disposed' to chasten the vagabond, but it was her pleasure to wish 'good success in the action now you have in hand.' Yes, she was his partner in the present voyage! In 1591, too, she sent six of her largest vessels under Lord Thomas Howard to the Azores to lie in wait for the plate fleet, but Philip's escort fleet on its way westward to meet the *flota* surprised them and for fifteen hours the *Revenge* under Sir Richard Grenville tried heroically to battle her way through the Spanish squadrons in one of the greatest fights of all naval history. Elizabeth took little comfort in Raleigh's *Report on the Truth of the Fights about the Isles of Azores*, which he had compiled through interviewing the survivors, for she knew the Spaniards took enormous pride in capturing the *Revenge* and thought Grenville's gallantry a crass waste of life. More rewarding was the enterprise launched by Raleigh and his brother for attacking the plate fleet off Panama, for which she provided two ships and Cumberland six. Through her intervention Raleigh was replaced by Frobisher, as commander, being required to return home after sailing some sixty leagues out of port with the fleet. He heard that the silver ships would not sail that year and against all orders made fresh dispositions; sending Frobisher to the Spanish coast with half the ships to act as a blind while Burrough lay off the Azores with the rest. Dispirited, Raleigh doubled back to Plymouth, fearing the Queen's anger on more than one score, yet Burrough made a magnificent prize, the *Madre de Dios*, a huge Portuguese carrack, of 1,600 tons, with her seven decks laden with jewels, spices, drugs, ivory and all the wealth of the Indies, and the Queen secured the lion's share.[29]

Raleigh, whose stock should have been higher than ever after Essex's marriage and Hatton's death, the potential high priest of Elizabeth's affections, whom she had forbidden to take part in a dangerous voyage, had deserted her. Whether he seduced Bess Throgmorton is doubtful; at any rate the Queen behaved as if he had, and was prepared to believe court gossip about his 'brutish offence'. For a whole decade, despite various provocations, her 'dear Water' had been loyal to Cynthia and now, at forty, he had committed the crime of forsaking her for the eldest and plainest of the maids of honour. It was impossible for a favourite to retain her full trust if he were unwise enough to become romantically linked with some other woman – most of all a maid of honour. Both were sent to the Tower, as each should have predicted. He wrote in high courtly fashion to Robert Cecil a letter intended for Elizabeth's own eyes:

My heart was never broken till this day that I hear the Queen goes so far off, whom I have followed so many years with so great love and desire in so many journeys, and am now left behind her in a dark prison, all alone. I that was wont to behold her riding like Alexander, hunting like Diana, walking like Venus, the gentle wind blowing her fair hair about her pure cheeks like a nymph, sometimes playing like Orpheus; behold the sorrow of this would once amiss hath bereaved me of all. Oh love that only strength in misfortune, what is become of thy assurance!

It was all too far-fetched and a little unkind to Bess Throgmorton, but in his desperate position flattery was the only weapon to hand. He was let out on parole only to travel to Dartmouth to stop, rather belatedly, the pilfering of the cargo of the *Madre de Dios*, and tactfully arranged that Elizabeth should be given a far greater share of the plunder than her investment in the voyage warranted, but it did not buy his freedom. Another three months and he and Bess were released from captivity, yet he could never hope to purchase his sovereign's favour.[30]

The spoils of the great carrack for years kept English privateers at sea, but never again was there so great a prize. Philip of Spain, as Elizabeth had feared after the Portugal expedition, had been restoring his power at sea by building new galleons and reorganizing the defence of Central America, and as a result the last voyage of Drake and Hawkins to the Caribbean in 1595–6 was a chapter of disasters. They failed to intercept the treasure ships, quarrelled, and, as Hawkins lay dying, he dictated a legacy of £2,000 to the Queen to salve his conscience for having over-persuaded her to undertake the expedition. Drake found Puerto Rico too heavily defended to attack and Nombre de Dios of famous memory yielded no treasure; soon he was down with dysentery and buried at sea off Porto Bello.

Before Drake's fate was known plans were being laid for a massive combined assault on Cadiz, to sear the flesh rather than singe the beard. Now that Henry IV had established himself in France a new strategy was possible and the way was open for a fresh offensive in the Peninsula, to make the launching of another armada against England impossible. While preparations were going forward, with the utmost secrecy about the destination of the fleet, the Cardinal Archduke Albert of Austria, Philip's Governor of the Netherlands, began a surprise attack on Calais. For a few days Elizabeth was uncertain whether she could afford to answer Henry IV's urgent appeal for aid, but the thought of having an English army again in control of Calais was something she could not resist; never had she given up hope of its return – it was worth to her a score of 'cautionary towns' in the Netherlands. On Good Friday 1596 orders went out to the commissioners of musters to have six thousand men at Dover by the Sunday night, ready to embark under Essex, unquestionably the best lieutenant-general for the enterprise. She had heard the Archduke's artillery from Greenwich and knew the need for haste, yet, as always, she had second thoughts about the soundness of the strategy and of the economics of her decision. On the Wednesday after Easter she sent final orders for the troops to embark and in a note to Essex warned him not to 'peril so fair an army for another prince's town', unless the position were desperate; 'God cover you under His safest wings, and let all peril go without your compass.' But next evening as the transports were ready to leave came news to Dover that Calais had fallen. Calais, in Spanish hands! A safe harbour for another armada; and so tremors were felt in London. The Queen debated whether it were wise now to allow her own fleet to sail for Cadiz, leaving England unguarded, but having decided to press forward with the expedition she rebuked everyone from the Lord Admiral downward for unwonted tardiness. Now Essex and Howard were to be replaced as commanders, then they were reinstated; at one time Elizabeth cancelled the whole expedition, and then she was won round by her commanders at Plymouth into allowing them to proceed – a grand force of 120 sail – and penned her own words of Godspeed to Essex, sending a special prayer she had composed. She rehearsed reasons for the enterprise and 'these being the grounds, Thou that diddest inspire the mind, we humbly beseech with bended knees prosper the work, and with the best forewinds guide the journey, speed the victory and make the return the advancement of Thy fame and surety to the realm, with the least loss of English blood.'[31]

Her prayer was answered. In the early hours of Sunday 20 June Cadiz was surprised; the galleons and other shipping destroyed, the city captured. Essex wanted to hold Cadiz with a garrison as another Calais, a new English outpost on the continent, but this was rejected. The victory of the glorious twentieth of June had been complete. 'Let the army know I care not so much being Queen, as that I am sovereign of such subjects', she wrote to her commanders, but for her the return of the victors was soured by the well-founded feeling that she had been cheated out of far too much of the spoils. Embezzlement was rife; it was known that a great diamond that should have gone to her had been broken up and parcelled out amongst the London jewellers, and her own agent, Sir Anthony Ashley, who had accompanied the voyage to look after her interests was despatched to the Fleet Prison. There was bitter quarrelling between Raleigh and Essex as to which of them was the real hero of the expedition, which forced courtiers to take sides in yet another episode of their personal feud. Essex had wanted to stay in Spanish waters to intercept the treasure fleet, but at a council of war the Lord Admiral and Raleigh had overruled him, and great was the Queen's anger when it was learnt that just two days after the English had left, the galleons from the Indies put into Lisbon for safety. In revenge for the attack on Cadiz, which showed the world how vulnerable Spain was, Philip decided to put another armada collected from ports other than Cadiz to sea that same year. But the preparations were inadequate and the weather unpropitious, so the October gales of the Bay of Biscay took a heavy toll and the survivors made for home as best they could.[32]

The familiar faces at court were growing older and the gaps in the ranks were increasing alarmingly in 1595-6. The passing of Philip, Earl of Arundel, a godson of Philip II, brought her no regrets. Traitor to her for the sake of his conscience, he had died in the Tower in October. Norfolk's eldest son, he had spent the greater part of his adult life in prison, for his youthful promise had been stunted by an ever hardening bigotry. Mindful of her unease over signing his father's death warrant, Elizabeth had refused to have his sentence carried out, but she would not allow his children to visit him in his cell unless he recanted. In December died Henry, Earl of Huntingdon, *facile princeps* of the Suffolk line of the succession so dear to the Puritans, yet as loyal a ruler of the north country as she could have wished for. By the time she heard from the West Indies that Drake, 'her pirate' would never again cheer her at Greenwich or annoy her from Plymouth, Lord Keeper Puckering, a man she much admired, had died. There was a moving little scene in the privy chamber after his successor, Egerton, had been sworn in, for Elizabeth said to him – no doubt in explaining why he was not to have the title 'Lord Chancellor', for none since Hatton had enjoyed that – 'I *began* first with a Lord Keeper, and he was a wise man, I tell you, and I will *end* with a Lord Keeper.' Burghley was quick to intervene: 'God forbid, Madam, I hope you shall bury 4 or 5 more.' 'No,' the Queen answered him, 'this is the last', and burst into tears. The same month her cousin Hunsdon, the Lord Chamberlain, who twenty-six years back had routed the rebels in the north, died and was followed in July by Sir Francis Knollys, treasurer of the household and Essex's grandfather. As the year turned again, a much more personal link with the past was snapped when she lost from her inner circle Blanche Parry, of late so weak and blind, who had been with her since childhood days when Seymour had romped with her, and now she gave orders for her to be buried with the dignity of a baroness. Soon it would be Burghley's turn, and the old man had already prepared for his own succession by securing his son Robert's appointment as Secretary of State, while Essex was at sea. It was hard for a Queen to see her old servants disappear from the scene. Winter was tiring her and after a Council meeting she would nowadays have a lie down.[33]

Anthony Rudde, Bishop of St David's, should have known better than to have preached a Lenten sermon before the Queen at Richmond Palace, on a text from Psalm 90: 'Lord, teach us to number our days that we may apply our hearts unto wisdom.' He zealously reminded her of her age of sixty-three and of the need for repentance; bemused by the mystical numbers he worked up his theme to the startling significance of '7 times 9 for the climacterial year'. The Bishop could see the scowls from his sovereign, and improvised as best he could. The year 1588, he said, was long predicted a dangerous year, yet it had pleased God to preserve her and gave her a famous victory, so 'there was no doubt but that she should pass this year and many more', providing she faithfully kept her divine meditations. Elizabeth rebuked the preacher. He might have 'kept his arithmetic to himself, but I see that the greatest clerks are not always the wisest men.' It was not for this that she had escaped the alleged conspiracy of Dr Lopez to poison her, and now wore from her girdle, where Mary had a rosary, the rich jewel Philip II had given this strange Portuguese physician in earnest of his attempt.[34]

But anyone who doubted her ability to weather the grand climacteric or thought her powers of ruling were failing, should have overheard the tirade she made against the Polish ambassador, who had come to deny England's right of search in the Channel and protest about the ways in which her men-of-war were interfering with neutral states' trade with Spain. Elizabeth was in the presence chamber in her chair of state when the ambassador entered, kissed her hand, walked three paces back and embarked upon his prepared Latin oration about England's infringements of the Law of Nature and the Law of Nations, threatening her that if she did not remedy these troubles, his master, the King of Poland, would. She 'made one of the best answers extempore in Latin, that I ever heard, being much moved to be so challenged in public', wrote Robert Cecil:

Was this the business that your King has sent you about? Surely I can hardly believe that if the King himself were present he would have used such language, for if he should, I must have thought that his being a King, not of many years – and that not by right of blood, but by right of election . . . And as for you, although I perceive you have read many books to fortify your arguments in this case, yet I am apt to believe that you have not lighted upon that chapter that prescribes forms to be observed between Kings and Princes . . . We will appoint some of our council to confer with you, to see upon what grounds this clamour of yours has its foundation, who have shoed yourself rather a herald than an ambassador.

When he had bowed himself out, she said to her courtiers with a twinkle, 'God's death, my lords . . . I have been enforced this day to scour up my old Latin that hath lain long in rusting.' She wished that Essex had been among the lords at her side to hear her, but he had insisted on pursuing martial glory on the Islands Voyage; Cecil, however, took the hint and sent him a brilliant account of the audience.[35]

She found no satisfaction in this war that the young gallants who worshipped Essex delighted in. As she had told her last troublesome Parliament in 1593, when she dismissed it:

> In ambition of glory I have never sought to advance the territories of my land (nor thereby yours). If I have used my forces to keep the enemy from you, I have thereby thought your safety the greater and your danger the less. If you suppose I have done it in fear of the enemy, or in doubt of his revenge, I know his power is not to prevail, nor his force to fear me, having so mighty a Protector on my side.[36]

Peace now seemed as far off as ever and, except with the followers of Essex, the war had become unpopular in England. The economic consequences of the war, including high taxation, the dislocation of foreign trade and the pressing of men for service added to a series of poor harvests and recurrent plague had brought disillusionment. Elizabeth's own popularity, so great in the Armada years, had begun to wane, and some even failed to keep her accession day as a holiday.

THE GREAT LIONESS

THE last half-dozen years of Elizabeth's life, when she had passed the grand climacteric, have often been portrayed as an epilogue to the reign, with a character of their own in which court and country waited in 'melancholy and pensive cogitation' for the sun to set. This was certainly the age of the new men, personified by Robert Cecil, all of whom had been born since she had come to the throne, men with very different concepts of government from their fathers. There was disillusionment about the war and a markedly grasping attitude towards public service; in literary circles there was something of the *fin de siècle*. But if the scene had changed, the same chief character still dominated it. Her powers were very far from failing her and, with her unequalled experience of the arts of government, she was now prepared to make decisions more quickly than at any time. To his own amazement Essex found he could not tame 'the great lioness' and paid for his folly in assuming he could thus challenge the Tudor monarchy at its height. For Elizabeth the epilogue began not a moment before her final illness in February 1603.

She had a bout of illness in the spring of 1596, its symptoms inflammation of the breast and recurrent insomnia, not dissimilar to her final sickness. While Essex was away on the islands voyage she had a more general fever, 'her hands so burning hot, her complaint of distemperature in all parts, with the feeling of a soreness in her body, back and legs.' Perhaps, indeed, the trouble was quiescent throughout the intervening years, but she made light of it, for she hated admitting she was not well and disliked taking medicines. At one time she had 'a desperate ache in her right thumb', but woe betide the courtier who dared to refer to this as gout. She continued to eat and drink sparingly and took more frequent exercise than most women of her years, sometimes hunting on successive days. The slightest hint nowadays that she was a little out of sorts threw her ladies in a panic; she well knew, she told James VI with an eerie chuckle, her funeral had long been prepared.[1]

Her teeth gave her much trouble, as they had even as a baby, but she no longer feared the tooth-drawer. In 1578 when she was enduring a prolonged attack of toothache, which her ordinary doctors could not relieve, the Privy Council consulted 'an outlandish physician'. As the man might have been a traitorous papist, he was not allowed to see the patient, but advised extraction either by surgical instruments or through applying the juice of the herb fenugreek which would loosen the roots so that the decayed tooth could easily be drawn by hand. Elizabeth dreaded the thought of an extraction, but Bishop Aylmer of London offered himself as a guinea pig, for 'although he was an old man and had not many teeth to spare, she should see a practical experiment on himself.' In this way she was persuaded into having the offending tooth removed to her great satisfaction, and in the next ten years lost many more, 'so that one cannot understand her easily when she speaks quickly.' The injudicious use of toothpicks made those yellowish ones that remained uneven.[2]

In these last years she resorted to all kinds of cosmetics to keep alive the charming masquerade of Oriana. Her hair, alas, was in no better shape than her teeth and where once she had tinted her locks, she now wore auburn wigs; her hair, noted the Venetian ambassador, was 'of a light colour never made by nature'. None but her ladies knew the extent to which salves and unguents mended her complexion until Essex burst into her bedchamber at Nonsuch in the autumn of 1599 and found her devoid of artifice. Because of her fame and longevity it was only natural that she should be credited with all kinds of recipes for perfumes and 'cosmetic waters', though we know she imported rose water from the continent in bulk. The use of cosmetics which was part and parcel of the renaissance had its severe critics in Puritans like Philip Stubbes, who had lost his right hand for criticizing Elizabeth's match with Alençon, and had he or any other dared to condemn her own use of 'these seasonable aids to beauty' she would have retorted that any woman had a duty to amend the scars of small-pox, but especially a Queen. The fact that Stubbes and his fellows quoted Calvin as saying 'whosoever do colour their faces or their hair with any unnatural colour, they begin to prognosticate of what colour they shall be in hell', showed how little they deserved to be taken seriously. Always she found the renaissance was on the side of the angels.[3]

Her enemies could not wait for her to die of old age. Plots for taking the Queen's life were still being hatched in Flanders and Spain – harebrain schemes for casting a noxious perfume in her path or burning a strange ball of incense whose sickly smoke would send her into a trance from which she might never awaken. The most fantastic attempt was the one allegedly undertaken by Edward Squier, a rolling stone who had been scrivener, stable lad and then seaman. Captured at sea by the Spaniards in 1595, he had been sent to Seville where by means of the Inquisition and the cunning of an expatriate Jesuit, Richard Walpole, he was per-suaded to assassinate both the Queen and Essex, in praise of holy church. With his knowledge of the Queen's stables he should find it easy to daub poison on the pommel of her saddle and Walpole gave him a recipe for a potent mixture which included opium and mercury water. Through an exchange of prisoners Squier was re-turned to England and found lodgings at Greenwich where he concocted his poison with ingredients purchased from apothe-caries in Paternoster Row and Newgate Market. He tried it on a dog that died, then put the confection in 'a double bladder', wrapped with parchment, and one July day in 1597 went to the Queen's stables, with his hands protected by heavy gloves. Shout-ing 'God Save the Queen', he punctured the bladders with a pin and daubed some of the poison on the velvet-covered pommel of the saddle on the horse caparisoned for Elizabeth's use, 'and soon after Her Majesty rode abroad.' Had he hung about Squier would have discovered that 'the great lioness' was of a tougher breed than the mangy dog, but he fled from Whitehall to get himself taken on as a sailor in Essex's ship on the islands voyage. One evening he smeared some of the poison on the chair, 'under the spar deck where the earl used to dine and sup', and Essex sat there all supper time but without the slightest ill effect. In time Walpole and his fellows, fearing Squier had double-crossed them, apparently informed the authorities by some means and the man was taken, examined and a fulsome confession extracted from him. After a celebrated trial Squier was executed for high treason. In some ways the episode seems too bizarre to have been invented and Edward Squier was a much more likely traitor than Dr Lopez in 1594.[4]

After the triumphs of the attack on Cadiz, the Queen's favourite had become the darling of the adventurers, the younger sons who had found their feet in warfare and looked on soldiering as a glorious profession, and the Earl reciprocated their affection. 'I love them for mine own sake, for I find sweetness in their conversation, strong assistance in their employment and happiness in their friendship. I love them for their virtue's sake and for their greatness of mind.' They were the unacknowledged flower of England. 'If we may have peace, they have purchased it; if we must have war, they have managed it.' Preachers now compared Essex with the greatest generals of all time, his health was drunk in tavern and alehouse and the mob treated him with near idolatry. Herein lay the peril. No other favourite had been popular. Leicester had had his following at court and his Puritan allies, yet he remained even at the peak of his career as a man disdainful of the multitude; Hatton had been a party of one, while Raleigh was distrusted on all sides for his cleverness. But here was Essex courting popularity, expecting to reward his followers from the Queen's patronage; he was slow to see that he was heading for disaster.

Elizabeth was truly fascinated by him, despite his obvious weaknesses, so that when he was absent she was irritable with him for deserting her and jealous of his military triumphs, because they detracted from her own popularity, a fundamental matter on which she had remained acutely sensitive. 'Her people's loves' – the phrase of so many of her speeches – burned with a lesser intensity if Essex stole the limelight, whereas he should have been content with basking in her rays at court. Francis Bacon with his unusual perception saw to the heart of the problem, and told Essex with disarming frankness what his Queen must really think of him – 'a man of a nature not to be ruled, that hath the advantage of my affection, and knoweth it; of an estate not grounded to his greatness; of a popular reputation; of a military dependence.' There could not be, Bacon commented, 'a more dangerous image than this represented to any monarch living, much more to a lady, and of Her Majesty's apprehension.' Unless he behaved as a serious councillor and spurned his easily-won popularity he would be undone and Bacon would have chosen the wrong patron. Better by far to imitate his enemy Robert Cecil, so diligent in his paperwork, than rest on his laurels as victor of Cadiz.[5]

It was largely through a *rapprochement* with Cecil that Essex had won the command for 'the islands voyage' to the Azores in 1597 and off he sailed with the familiar protestation that he would 'strive to be worthy of so high a grace and so blessed a happiness. Be pleased, therefore, most dear Queen, to be ever thus gracious, if not for merit, yet for your own constancy.' The expedition had been undertaken with the usual objectives – to capture the plate fleet and prevent another armada from leaving Spain – yet ended miserably, for there were no prizes and the galleons did sail, though after hovering off the west of England for a week they were forced home by gales without firing a shot. At Ferrol Essex had a mighty quarrel with Raleigh, now restored to the Queen's favour as captain of her guard and allowed to take part in the voyage, and it was Raleigh who first reached England and submitted his own account of the dismal campaign. Howard reported from court that he 'did never see creature receive more comfort than Her Majesty did when she saw by Sir Walter Raleigh's letter' that Essex was safe and sound, and she cried for joy.[6]

Back in 'her safe harbour' he cursed and sulked when she would not gratify his friends with rewards. He made wild promises to them and to try and substantiate these he pressed the Queen mercilessly, but she dug in her heels and refused to have Sir Robert Sidney as Lord Chamberlain or as Lord Warden of the Cinque Ports, simply because he was totally unsuited for either post. Rather than have one of the Earl's nominees as a thorn in her flesh as vice-chamberlain of the household, she decided to keep the office unfilled. Bacon, who had been led to expect one of the plums of the legal profession, was left out in the cold. Essex could get anything for himself, but nothing for his friends, complained one of them. Such a verdict in fact did less than justice to Elizabeth, for the Earl's supporters had their fair share of the pickings of places at court, provided they were fitted for them, and throughout the Queen endeavoured to maintain a balance between Essex's and the Cecils' parties. Neither should have the monopoly of power, for that belonged to her alone. The Earl had increased his own secretariat to deal with this 'patronage' and had his own agents in France and elsewhere supplying him with intelligence, but the whole edifice was but a pack of cards. Elizabeth was hurt that just when he should have been at court he failed to attend Whitehall for the festivities of her accession day in 1597, and she was irritated by his absence from Parliament and Council. Bacon again chided him to 'dissemble, then, like a courtier', following the example of his stepfather Leicester. 'The greatest subject that is or ever was greatest in the prince's favour, in his absence is not missed; and a small discontinuance makes things that were, as if were not, and breeds forgetfulness which gives way to wrath; and the wrath of a prince is as the roaring of a lion.' Yet he still thought he could tame her.[7]

Born into the peerage, Essex could never appreciate Elizabeth's sensitiveness about further creations of peers or wholesale dubbing of knights in the field of battle. In Fuller's phrase she 'honoured her honours by bestowing them sparingly' and during her whole reign created, restored or recognized no more than eighteen titles, and of these only Burghley and Compton belonged to new families. Burghley had been asked in 1589 to draw up a select list of Armada honours, including six earldoms, and Elizabeth had wanted to promote him to a marquisate, which he had probably declined on grounds of expense; and then she had second thoughts about the scheme. In fact between Burghley's elevation in 1572 and her own death she created only three titles; one was the admission of Lord Willoughby to the title on his mother's side, the second was the belated promotion of the Armada admiral, Howard of Effingham, to the earldom of Nottingham in 1597 and the last the elevation of Thomas Howard, Norfolk's second son, as Lord Howard de Walden. After Norfolk's attainder there was no duke and by 1603 the peerage numbered a mere fifty-nine titles. Yet Essex had promised to get Sir Edward Wotton a peerage and the knight had offered £1,000 to a lady to keep him up to it. When he suggested to the Queen that she make Wotton a baron she told him, 'But what shall I do with all these that pretend to titles? I would be willing to call him and one or two more, but to call many I will not; and I am importuned by many of their friends to do it.' Instead of accepting her decision he asked her to let him bear the burden of scrutinizing other claims to her patronage: 'I will not doubt but to find cause to keep them back and let the fault be mine.' This was the very last thing she would allow. He had been furious about the wording of Nottingham's peerage patent which described his brilliant service in 1588 and at the sack of Cadiz in terms which the favourite could not stomach, and he hysterically asked for an enquiry and challenged Howard and his sons to a duel. Very typically Elizabeth had restored the balance by creating him Earl Marshal in December 1597.[8]

The new Earl Marshal became insufferable. Cecil and his father were trying their hardest to put out peace-feelers with Spain so that Elizabeth might join in the treaty which Henry IV was signing with Philip; but Essex was bent on the continuation of the war. Old Burghley said he 'breathed nothing but war, slaughter and blood' and picking up his prayer book turned to Psalm 55: 'Bloodthirsty and deceitful men shall not live out half their days.' The Queen wanted peace, but an honourable one, which safeguarded the Netherlands, and nothing had ever been further from her intentions than war for its own sake, the warped sense of military glory that Essex embodied. His impetuousness reached a new height in July during discussions in Council for selecting a successor to Lord Burgh as Lord Deputy of Ireland strong enough to crush the rebel Tyrone.[9]

The Irish problem had always irritated Elizabeth on two counts: the disunity and disobedience of that kingdom detracted from her own sovereignty and all attempts to resolve the Irish to order had cost a great deal of money. The Hibernian bog swallowed up £2,410,000 from the outbreak of O'Neill's rebellion in the early 1560s to the unconditional surrender by Tyrone within days of her own death, and yet in the best of times the kingdom provided a crown revenue of no more than £5,000. General after general had lost his reputation in attempting to pacify the unhappy country, for 'there is no land in the world of so continual war within himself, nor of so great shedding of Christian blood, nor of so great robbing, spoiling, preying and burning, nor of so great wrongful extortions continually as Ireland.' The country was in effect a vast no-man's-land, like the Scottish border in the worst of years; here were amorphous territorial earldoms and a confusion of petty chieftainships which defied administration from Dublin castle. Shane O'Neill's appeal to the Guises and the Pope had alarmed Sir Henry Sidney, who feared that unless the Queen took firm steps, Ireland would be lost like Calais, and so she had formed the English presidencies of Connaught and Munster to replace the old Anglo-Irish earldoms, and 'adventurers' were encouraged to settle there to wean 'the wild Irish' from their uncivilized ways and to turn them into Protestants. In Munster James Fitzmaurice Fitzgerald had arisen and with papal blessings had formed an international brigade in 1573 to free Ireland from its English yoke. An army had laid Munster waste, but the kingdom was still 'a boisterous sea ... ever to make Her Majesty seasick at their tempestuous ragings.' Now, with promise of Spanish aid, Hugh O'Neill, Earl of Tyrone, the one Irish leader of the century with more than native cunning and bravery, aimed at becoming King of Ireland, and Elizabeth knew the danger was great, the more so since France had come to terms with Spain.[10]

She had proposed that Sir William Knollys, Essex's uncle, should be sent as Lord Deputy, but Essex was determined to have Sir George Carew appointed, for it would suit him to have so ardent a supporter of Cecil away from court. His weak arguments were patiently considered and when it was obvious the Queen would have the last word, he turned his back on her 'as it were in contempt, with a scornful look. She waxing impatient gave him a cuff on the ear and bade him be gone with a vengeance.' He would never learn, and foolishly laid his hand on his sword, but Admiral Nottingham stepped between him and the Queen. Before he marched out of the room he swore in a passion he 'neither could nor would swallow so great an indignity' and would not even have taken it from Henry VIII himself. Away at Wanstead, his temper cooled but his pride would not let him apologize:

Madam, when I think how I have preferred your beauty above all things, and received no pleasure in life but by the increase of your favour towards me, I wonder at myself what cause there could be to make me absent myself one day from you. But when I remembered that Your Majesty hath by the intolerable wrong you have done both me and yourself, not only broken all laws of affection, but done against the honour of your sex, I think all places better than where I am, and all dangers well undertaken, so I might retire myself from the memory of my false, inconstant and beguiling pleasures ... I was never proud, till you sought to make me too base. And now, since my destiny is no better, my despair shall be like my love was, without repentance. ... I must commend my faith to be judged by Him Who judgeth all hearts, since on earth I find no right. Wishing you all comforts and joys in the world and no greater punishment for your wrongs to me, than to know the faith of him you have lost, and the baseness of those you shall keep,

> Your Majesty's most humble servant
> R. Essex.

She desperately wanted him back at court, but it must be on her terms. He must come in person and repent of his rash defiance; there could be no half-way house, no place for an intermediary to reconcile them. 'He hath played long enough upon me and now I mean to play awhile with him and stand as much upon my greatness as he hath upon his stomach.' Yes, they could tell the Earl of Essex she valued herself at as great a price as he values himself.[11]

Immediately she was more concerned about crabbed age than youth, for Burghley lay dying. He offered to resign his offices, but she would not hear of it, knowing he would want to end his days in harness as Treasurer of England and master of the wards, and she came to his bedside to feed 'her Spirit' with a spoon. Theirs had been a remarkable partnership. She had stood by him early in 1569 when the cabal of Norfolk and Leicester had threatened to overthrow him and he had survived her blame for Norfolk's execution and her anger over Mary's death warrant. Elizabeth had disliked his brand of Cambridge Protestantism, but he had mellowed with the years and had been the ideal counterpart to Leicester, just as his son Robert was already proving the necessary corrective to Leicester's stepson. More than any among her servants Burghley had tried to be detached, statesmanlike, though native prejudice made this difficult to achieve and he had not been afraid to admit when he was wrong nor to compromise without being a time-server. No one had worked harder for her, penning endless memoranda and rarely absent from Council. His work shaped the office of Principal Secretary, and if he had become Treasurer too late in life to undertake the administrative reforms so urgently needed, as an elder statesman he was irreplaceable.

Before Burghley's funeral came terrible news from Ireland. The English army under Sir Henry Bagnal marching from Armagh to relieve the Blackwater fort had been utterly routed by Tyrone; it was the worst disaster, some thought, since England lost Calais. Essex hastened to court after two months' absence to proffer advice in Council and offer his services as commander in Ireland. Elizabeth still refused to see him or take notice of his letters, for unless he fully submitted she could not admit him to her presence. Then he became ill – who knows whether it was a diplomatic sickness to which he was prone as much as Leicester had been; and on an impulse she forgave him and to speed his recovery sent one of her doctors to Wanstead. In effect she had yielded to his challenge, and both knew it. As vent for her annoyance she turned to the Earl of Southampton who had fled to Paris when she had discovered his affair with Elizabeth Vernon, a maid of honour, but returned to London to marry her in secret once he learnt she was pregnant. He had left her again for France but was now commanded home.[12]

At the accession day tournament that November Raleigh, as Captain of the Guard, made his come-back at court by equipping a company of men in orange tawny plumes, but the effect was ruined by Essex marching into the tiltyard a private army two thousand strong all in identical plumage. This display of childish vanity annoyed the Queen little less than it exasperated Raleigh and she closed the proceedings much earlier than usual. In Council, as a year earlier, Essex was so highly critical of every name suggested for the Irish command, that Elizabeth eventually decided to cut short the endless arguments by sending him there himself. This was, in a way, what both of them wanted. The Queen knew the situation required a forceful leader, respected and experienced in campaigning to deal with Tyrone and decided to take Essex at his word. The Earl was quick to accept the challenge to his military prowess and glad to be escaping from court; 'methinks it is the fairer choice to command armies than humours.' There was another factor, too, for in January had appeared John Hayward's *First Part of the Life and Reign of Henry IV*, which dealt at length with the deposition of Richard II, and Elizabeth regarded it as more of a tract for the times than straight history because of its extravagant dedication to Essex. At times she even professed to think that Hayward was not the real author, but was sheltering 'some more mischievous person'. There was 'much descanting about the book and many exceptions are taken, especially to the epistle' of dedication. Who other than Essex would advocate the Queen's deposition? Let him be gone, then, and see to the deposition of Tyrone, while the ill-fated Hayward was tried in the Star Chamber and sent indefinitely to prison. Essex left for Ireland on 27 March 1599, with an enormous army of 16,000 foot and 1,300 horse, but the Queen had tied him with detailed instructions and had vetoed his appointment of Southampton as general of horse. As he left there were brisk sales of the new ballad 'London's loath to depart'.[13]

From the very outset Essex disobeyed the letter of his instructions. He was to confer no knighthoods except for especial valour, yet at once indiscriminately dubbed many captains; he was to march into Ulster against Tyrone forthwith, yet he did nothing except waste the wages of his men. Elizabeth was disturbed by his reports during that summer and chided him by every post to embark upon the campaign with vigour and cease interpreting her orders according to whim. 'We must deal plain with you and that [war] council, that it were more proper for them to leave troubling themselves with instructing us by what rules our power and their obedience are limited.' She began to fear that 'your purpose is *not* to end the war', and a declaration signed by all his captains advising against the invasion of Ulster, which he forwarded, shocked her: that men of such slender judgement should question the strategy of war was an unpardonable affront. She asked Francis Bacon in confidence what he thought of the proceedings in Ireland and he answered frankly,

Madam, if you had my Lord of Essex here with a white staff in his hand, as my Lord of Leicester had, and continued him still about you for society to yourself, and for an honour and ornament to your attendance and Court in the eyes of your people, and in the eyes of foreign ambassadors, then were he in his right element. For to discontent him as you do, and yet to put arms and power into his hands, may be a kind of temptation to make him prove cumbersome and unruly. And therefore if you would send for him, and satisfy him with honour here near you, if your affairs – which I am not acquainted with – will permit it, I think were the best way.

It seemed to Essex from the tone of the Queen's letters that Cecil and his henchmen were bent on his overthrow. In Dublin Castle he and Southampton talked of marching an army on London, but Blount restrained them from so foolhardy an act, though what he did was scarcely more sensible. Instead of attacking Tyrone, he made a truce with him and in direct disobedience to Elizabeth's latest orders, prohibiting his return under any circumstances, he left Ireland on 24 September in a blind fury. Four days later he reached Nonsuch Palace at 10 a.m. and rushed upstairs in his riding boots to Her Majesty's apartments. He did not even stop to wash the mud of his travels from his hands and face. Through the presence chamber he strode and through the privy chamber, pushing aside the astonished pages, grooms and ladies in waiting, until he reached that holy of holies, his sovereign's bedchamber. Elizabeth had only just risen from bed and had scarcely begun to dress, so the Earl thus saw her as no male subject had ever seen her before, stripped of the trappings of regality and bare of the artifice of womanhood. Here she was without her wig and her rouge, without her great ruff and her jewels, looking (but for her beautiful hands) a rather ugly woman of sixty-six. He knelt to kiss her hand and almost at once left to change from his riding clothes, fully confident he could win through by sheer charm. Did she, one wonders, in her surprise think of administering another box on the ears? For sceptre and crown would come tumbling down should this rash fellow destroy the public image of Gloriana.[14]

Later that morning she gave him a lengthy audience in private, in which he explained his conduct of the campaign. She dined alone while the Lord Deputy ate in the hall of state, with courtiers plucking his sleeve as he passed to learn the latest news from Ireland, though Cecil and Raleigh kept aloof. In the afternoon Elizabeth sent for him to answer her searching questions. Why had he returned without permission, leaving Ireland in so hazardous a state? What did he mean by daring to dub scores of knights? Why was Tyrone the rebel enjoying a truce instead of licking his wounds? She barely listened to his excuses but dismissed him to confer with Cecil and a few others, and at 10 p.m., twelve hours since he had stormed her bedchamber, she ordered him to be confined to his lodging. Next day he faced a three-hour grilling from the lords of the Council.

Knowing his desperate appeal to her had failed, Essex feared the Tower, but it was her pleasure to send him to York House in the custody of the Lord Keeper. Soon he became ill, from worry, lack of sleep and nourishment and Lady Essex petitioned in vain to be allowed to visit her husband. At the end of November the Star Chamber was crowded for the Lord Keeper's end of term speech in which he enlarged on sedition in general and Essex's disobedience in particular. Other judges and councillors followed with their declarations making abundant justification for the Earl being kept in custody. Soon his household was dispersed and as his health deteriorated further through acute depression, he prepared to meet a natural death. As so often, another's illness touched a responsive chord in Elizabeth and she ordered that eight of the best doctors should look after him and allowed his countess to be with him, though to the Queen's annoyance he was prayed for in London churches. Between them, medicine and intercession effected his recovery and after Christmas plans were made for his trial, though these were cancelled on his penning a fulsome submission. Mountjoy was sent as his successor to deal with Tyrone, but Essex remained a prisoner in his own house. In May he attempted another appeal:

Before all letters written in his hand be banished, or he that sends this enjoins himself eternal silence, be pleased, I humbly beseech Your Majesty, to read over these humble lines. At sundry times I received these words as your own, 'that you meant to correct and not to ruin', since which time, when I languished in four months' sickness, forfeited almost all that I was able to engage, felt the very pangs of death upon me, and saw my poor reputation not suffered to die with me, but buried and I alive, I yet kissed your fair correcting hand and was confident in your royal word; for I said to myself, 'Between my ruin and my Sovereign's favour there is no mean, and if she bestow favour again, she gives it with all things that in this world I either need or desire.' But now that the length of my troubles and the increase of your indignation have made all men so afraid of me as my own poor state is ruined, and my friends and servants like to die in prison, because I cannot help myself with my own, I not only feel the weight of your indignation and am subject to their malicious informations that first envied me your favour, and now hate me out of custom; but, as if I were thrown into a corner like a dead carcase, I am gnawed and torn by the basest creatures upon earth. The prating tavern haunter speaks of me what he lists; they print me and make me speak to the world and shortly they will play me upon the stage. The least of these is worse than death, but this is not the worst of my destiny; for you, who have protected from scorn and infamy all to whom you once avowed favour but Essex, and never repented of any gracious assurance you had given till now, have now in this eight months of my close imprisonment, rejected my letters and refused to hear of me, which to traitors you never did. What remains is only to beseech you to conclude my punishment, my misery and my life altogether, that I may go to my Saviour who had paid Himself a ransom for me, and whom, methinks, I still hear calling me out of this unkind world in which I have lived too long, and once thought myself too happy.

This moved her deeply, and though she could not bring herself to write to him, she remarked that her intention was to make him know himself and his duty, but that done she would again have him in her service, and her words were duly reported to Essex House.[15]

Next month he attended on the judges at York House to hear his censure for the mismanagement of the Irish campaign; the Queen had spared him the rigours of a trial in the Star Chamber. In turn, Egerton, Coke and Bacon presented an unanswerable case and for his defence the Earl knelt humbly and protested a loyal and unblemished heart. At the end of the long day each judge delivered his separate censure, each spoke tenderly of the Queen's mercy; he was to remain confined in Essex House until it should please Her Majesty to release him and meanwhile he was deprived of executing any of his offices. She kept him waiting another twelve weeks before she set him free and he gave out that he would spend his days in retirement. What worried him now was not his life but his debts, amounting to some £16,000, and the trouble was that the principal source of his income, the lease of the duties on sweet wines, expired at Michaelmas and if Elizabeth were not to renew it he would be undone. He wrote with a new urgency: 'Haste paper to that unhappy presence, whence only unhappy I am banished. Kiss that fair correcting hand . . . Say thou comest from shaming, languishing, despairing SX.' She sighed when Lady Scrope spoke up for him, and said 'Indeed, it is so'. He wrote again bluntly pointing out that his creditors were hungry and spelling out how desperately he needed the renewal of the wine lease. It was no good his signing himself 'Your Majesty's humblest, faithfullest and more than most devoted vassal'; she knew at last he had been beaten, and as he grovelled she decided to teach him a lesson he would never forget. She would *not* renew his lease, neither would she bestow it on some other person; she would keep it in her own hands and if he mended himself to her liking he could have it back in due course. She had put down the mighty from his seat; he who had dared to court her people's favours had forfeited hers.[16]

Essex could not believe his star had fallen. Cut off from the presence chamber, he believed the wildest rumours and overreached himself. Harington, who visited him, was much disturbed by the state of his mind as he uttered 'strange words bordering on such strange designs', that he quickly left. The Queen's 'conditions were as crooked as her carcase', he swore. Megalomania and fast approaching bankruptcy drove him to a final gamble; in which young adventurers and cronies from past campaigns eagerly joined. They planned to take the Tower, the city and the court and wring from the aged Queen Essex's right to be Lord Protector of the realm. As a manifesto for their designs they bribed the players at *The Globe* to put on *Richard II* for the night of Saturday 7 February; they would rescue the Queen from Cecil and her other evil advisers, but if the need arose, they would not shrink from shedding her blood. Elizabeth at Whitehall, less than a mile from Essex House, waited and then issued her summons through the Council for him to repair to court. He was too far committed now to put his head in a different noose. On the Sunday morning the Lord Keeper, Sir William Knollys and others came down the Strand to reason with him, but were made prisoners, while the mob shouted 'Kill them, kill them.' His followers advised an immediate attack on the court but he rode off to the city to see the mayor and sheriffs, shouting 'For the Queen! For the Queen! A plot is laid for my life.' Close behind came a herald sent by Cecil with a proclamation which denounced him as a traitor. In Whitehall Palace Elizabeth took the news very calmly, as barricades were erected and the Lord Admiral collected a little army to lead on Essex House. He that had placed her in the seat of Kings would preserve her in it, she said by way of grace and enjoyed a good dinner; and was curious to venture out in person 'to see what any rebel of them durst do against her', but Cecil insisted on her staying within. Soon it was all over. London, Elizabeth's city, that she had wooed and won in the first weeks of her reign, had remained intensely loyal to her. Apprentices might cheer my lord of Essex but the citizens would not fight for him against her. Next day, after the Earl had spent an uneasy night locked up in Lambeth Palace, the Queen gave an audience to the French ambassador and told him 'a senseless ingrate had at last revealed what had long been in his mind.'

The verdict of his peers was a foregone conclusion, but would Elizabeth sign his death warrant? Captain Thomas Lee had a madcap scheme to break into the privy chamber at Whitehall while she was alone at supper on the Thursday night and 'pin her up' until she signed an order for his master's release, but he was arrested lurking at the door. Essex's own confession, in which he implicated his sister and so many of his friends, convicted him far more deeply in her eyes than his trial, for he admitted England was not big enough to hold both Elizabeth and himself; the Queen, he said, could not be safe so long as he lived upon the earth. She signed the warrant on the late afternoon of Shrove Tuesday, though apparently she delayed sending it to the Tower until after attending the Shrovetide play. Perhaps she waited to give him the chance of begging for his life, but he realized how hopeless his case was and spared her the anguish of having to reconsider it. On Ash Wednesday 1601, in his thirty-fourth year, the only man she had really cared for since Hatton's death went out into the courtyard of the Tower to his private execution.[17]

London ballads, always a helpful index to what approximated to public opinion, came down heavily for the Queen and the *status quo*. There were a few verses with nostalgic sighs for Essex, but they circulated in manuscript and none dared to publish them until the new reign:

> Count him not like Campion,
>> (those traitrous men), or Babington;
> Not like the Earl of Westmorland
>> By whom a number were undone.
> He never yet hurt mother's son –
>> His quarrell still maintained the right;
> For which the tears my cheeks down run
>> When I think on his last Goodnight.

But there was one ballad, the lines so heavily revised that it is scarcely legible, never apparently printed, which celebrated the defeat of Essex as a fable of 'the great lioness' and 'the huge great camel'. Such was the basic situation; for all his imagined power, the Earl had no chance against so weighty an opponent. Not the mightiest of camels could hope to tame the king of beasts.[18]

The self-destruction of Essex eliminated the opposition to Cecil, who in the last remaining years of the reign had more influence than any minister since Northumberland through his accumulation of offices for himself and the wide patronage he dispensed to hench-men. Elizabeth had always balanced one faction at court against another, but now found her councillors men of one political complexion instead of members of a coalition. Cecil now paid for Essex having been so popular a figure and was dubbed 'Robin with the bloody heart' and 'a Machiavel with a crooked back'.

> Little Cecil trips up and down
> He rides both Court and Crown

went the political satire, but Robin's authority was much less than absolute, for it was limited first by the Queen herself and secondly was not bound to endure beyond the Queen's life. Cecil had, per-force, to look over his shoulder, as his father had done in 1557, without utterly compromising himself. 'The Queen indeed is my sovereign,' he had written, 'and I am her creature. I may not least deceive her.' He had discussions about the future in London with the Master of Gray and others sent down from Edinburgh, but was too competent and cautious to be driven by blind ambition as Essex had been. James VI had been prepared to send an embassy to deal with the Earl if need be, but dare not risk breaking with Elizabeth; to intrigue with Essex was too big a gamble when so splendid an inheritance was involved. He instructed the Earl of Mar and the Abbott of Kinloss 'to dally with the present guiders of the court' and walk warily 'betwixt these two precipices of the Queen and the people, who now appear to be in contrary terms.' Elizabeth was cold with his envoys; it was not for authorizing such dubious whisperings behind her back that she had warmly congratulated him on escaping from the Gowrie conspiracy. There were some who spread tales that the King of Scots had been heavily committed to Essex's challenge and he was loud in his denials, which Elizabeth fully accepted; perhaps she even thought him unnecessarily sensitive on that point. With relish she told him of the Earl's débâcle – 'that being utterly extirpated in 12 hours which was in hatching divers years.' But if Essex had lost his wine licence James still enjoyed his English pension and, he felt sure, retained Elizabeth's favour, for she still spoke of him as one for 'whom since your cradle I have ever had tender care.' To the end she still wrote to him in obscure sentences, knowing he would catch the right nuances, while Cecil conducted his correspondence in cipher. 'Let not shades deceive you, which may take away best substance from you, when they can turn but to dust or smoke', she told him in her near illegible scribble, and with fond wishes asked him to scan her words 'as becometh best a King.' James VI could interpret this in only one way, and rejoiced that the succession was still his.[19]

The lioness aged, but she had changed little with the years, and within a month of Essex's execution snarled at young Pembroke for falling victim to the occupational hazard of a courtier, seducing a maid of honour. Pembroke, who a few days before had succeeded his father, had thoroughly disappointed his Queen. Close observers had commented on 'his cold and weak manner of pursuing Her Majesty's favour, having had so good steps to lead him unto it.' He lacked spirit and courage where Elizabeth was concerned and 'is a melancholy young man', and yet he entered on a passionate affair with Mary Fitton, two years his senior, who was as like as not Shakespeare's Dark Lady of the Sonnets. She 'would put off her head tire and tuck up her clothes and take a large white cloak and march as though she had been a man' to meet Pembroke out of court. The secret of the maid of honour's pregnancy was somehow kept from the Queen right until she was delivered of a still-born son, whom Pembroke admitted to be his. As punishment Elizabeth sent him to the Fleet Prison, but after a month allowed him to continue his confinement at his own house on the score of illness. Sir Edward Fitton, veteran of Irish affairs, hoped in vain that correction would bring home to him his clear duty to marry Mary, 'as good a gentlewoman as my lord, though the dignity of honour be greater only in him, which has beguiled her.' The Earl had other plans and would have nothing to do with the girl, so he was banished from court and did not reappear in Elizabeth's lifetime. His last service to her was the melancholy one of bearing the great banner at her funeral.[20]

That autumn there was talk of another marriage, for the Emperor of Muscovy, Boris Godunov, had sent an ambassador with gifts of sables and hawks to prospect in England for a wife for his son, in preference to marrying him off to a daughter of the Holy Roman Emperor. At first Elizabeth had thought the Earl of Derby's daughter might suit him, until she discovered that the Russian prince was far too young for her; she could never forget the pointed remarks about differences of age when Alençon had been her suitor. If she had a princess of her own blood, she wrote to Muscovy, she would have given her blessing to such a match, and proceeded for the last time in her life to defend her spinsterhood:

... it hath pleased Almighty God to dispose our mind as it could never give way to those affections which might have been the means to raise an issue of our own person – a matter whereof we have no cause for our own mind to be sorry, but only because we perceive how infinitely our people would have been comforted to be assured to have been left to no other's rule than such as should be derived from ourselves.

Inevitably in these days the succession was on her mind.[21]

When she opened Parliament at the end of October, exceptionally few members saluted her with the customary 'God Save Your Majesty', and on leaving the Lords no one obeyed the gentlemen ushers calling to make room for her to pass. She was losing her popularity with members, but had she lost her touch? The reason for the sessions was the granting of further heavy taxation to meet the costs of the war with Spain and the rebellion in Ireland, but the Commons instead of discussing the terms of the subsidy turned at once to the grievance of monopolies. In granting the Speaker's petition for free speech Elizabeth had certainly not intended that this should extend to a matter so closely touching her prerogative, though she half expected there would be an onslaught on the system, once a useful method of rewarding courtiers if used sparingly, but which in 'the late grasping days' had become a public scandal, with agents, promoters and informers taking their cut. In the last Parliament in 1597 the Queen had promised speedy redress by having existing patents scrutinized by the law officers and by undertaking to issue no more, but she had not kept her word. In preparation for the great debate there were placards and broadsheets in circulation, such as the following, of which Elizabeth was not ignorant:

The courtiers craved all
The Queen granted all
The Parliament passed all
The Keeper sealed all
The ladies ruled all
Monsieur Buyroome* spoiled all
The crafty intelligencer heard all
The bishops smoothed all
He that was, opposed himself against all
The judges pardoned all
Therefore unless your Majesty speedily amend all
Without the great Mercy of God the evil will have all.[22]

In the House Lawrence Hyde began a vigorous attack on the entire system of monopolies and Sir Robert Wroth read out the lengthy list of commodities involved, rapidly leading to the 'beggary and bondage of the subject' – from aniseed to vinegar. 'Is not bread there?' asked lawyer Hakewell. 'Bread?' asked others in amazement. 'No,' said Hakewell, 'If order be not taken for these, bread will be there before the next parliament.' Francis Bacon defended the issue of monopolies with a legalistic argument as being an essential part of the Queen's prerogative, 'the head pearl in her crown and diadem', and Cecil, who had excused ministers from earlier groping with the problem on the grounds that they had been too preoccupied with Essex's revolt, now in hectoring tone reproved Mr Speaker for receiving a bill on such a topic and the House for behaving more like 'a grammar school than a court of Parliament'. The House was in an uproar with leaders quite incapable of making progress with government business; and then, by sheer instinct, Elizabeth intervened, sending for the Speaker to convey a message to her faithful Commons. First she thanked them very fulsomely for their zealous loyalty in making 'so hasty and free a subsidy', though in fact the House had

* A euphemism for 'Mounseer Drybone', the nickname for syphilis.

deferred reading the subsidy bill! Then she triumphantly cut short
all the wrangling about monopolies by undertaking herself to reform affairs, repealing some of the patents, suspending others and
'none put in execution but such as should first have a trial according to the law for the good of the people.' In earnest of this she
promised a proclamation to this effect and it was in print by the
end of the week. Her timing was superb, she had taken the wind
out of the agitation and the House was overjoyed – like a pack of
grammar school boys let off their daily stint of construing – overjoyed not at its own victory, but at their Queen's magnanimity.
They wanted to send a deputation to thank her and she readily
agreed to give an audience to a hundred of their number; then the
House decided that their thankfulness was so great and unprecedented that they *all* wanted to be present, so the Queen said all
could come, though in fact no more than 150 actually attended on
her in the Council Chamber at Whitehall in the afternoon of 20
November, where the Speaker assured her 'the last drop of blood
in our hearts and the last spirit of breath in our nostrils' would be
for her safety.

She accepted their grateful thanks with as much joy as they had
in making it and went on to make what posterity has considered
her most remarkable parliamentary speech:

I do assure you there is no prince that loveth his subjects better, or
whose love can countervail our love. There is no jewel, be it of never
so rich a price, which I set before this jewel: I mean your love. For I do
esteem of it [more] than any treasure or riches; for *that* we know how to
prize, but *Love* and *Thanks* I count unvaluable. And, though God hath
raised me high, yet this I count the glory of my crown – that I have
reigned with your loves. This makes me that I do not so much rejoice,
that God hath made me to be a Queen, as to be a Queen over so thankful a people.

Therefore, I have cause to wish nothing more than to content the
subjects, and that is a duty which I owe. Neither do I desire to live
longer days than that I may see your prosperity, and that is my only
desire. And as I am that person that still, yet under God, hath delivered
you, so I trust by the Almighty power of God, that I still shall be his
instrument to preserve you from envy, peril, dishonour, shame,
tyranny and oppression; partly by means of your intended helps [the

subsidy] which we take very acceptably, because it manifests the largeness of your loves and loyalty to your sovereign.

Of myself I must say this, I was never any greedy, scraping grasper, nor a straight, fast-holding prince, nor yet a waster. My heart was never set on worldly goods, but only for my subjects' good. What you do bestow on me I will not hoard it up, but receive it to bestow on you again. Yea, my own properties I count yours, and to be expended for your good; and your eyes shall see the bestowing of all for your good. Therefore, render unto them from me, I beseech you, Mr Speaker, such thanks as you imagine my heart yieldeth, but my tongue cannot express.

Then she bade them all rise from their knees and spoke about monopolies, which she had only granted to some of her oldest servants who had deserved well of her, but now she fully understood that these had developed into a real and oppressive grievance, and 'our kingly dignity shall not suffer it.' Once she had heard the facts she could not hope for rest until she had reformed the scandals:

I have ever used to set the last Judgement-Day before my eyes, and so to rule as I shall be judged to answer before a higher judge, to whose judgement-seat I do appeal, that never thought was cherished in my heart that tended not to my people's good. . . . I know the title of a King is a glorious title. But assure yourself, that the shining glory of princely authority hath not so dazzled the eyes of our understanding, but that we well know and remember that we also are to yield an account of our actions before the Great Judge. To be a King and wear a Crown is a thing more glorious to them that see it than pleasing to them that bear it. For myself, I was never so much enticed with the glorious name of a King, or royal authority of a Queen, as delighted that God hath made me his instrument to maintain his truth and glory and to defend this Kingdom, as I said, from peril, dishonour, tyranny and oppression. There will never Queen sit in my seat with more zeal to my country, care for my subjects and that sooner with willingness will venture her life for your good and safety, than myself. For it is not my desire to live nor reign longer than my life and reign shall be for your good. And though you have had, and may have, many princes more mighty and wise, sitting in this state, yet you never had, or shall have, any that will be more careful and loving.

Shall I ascribe anything to myself, and my sexly weakness? I were not worthy to live then; and of all, most unworthy of the great mercies I have had from God, who hath ever yet given me a heart, which never yet feared foreign or home enemy. I speak it to give God the praise, as a testimony before you, and not to attribute anything to myself. For I, O Lord, What am I, whom practices and perils past should not fear? Or what can I do? That I should speak for any glory, God forbid.

Such was her message for Mr Speaker to convey to the whole House, but she asked the privy councillors to bring all those who had come to hear her to kiss her hand before the sessions ended.[23]

At the age of sixty-eight her touch was as sure as ever. Before Christmas her words to the deputation in the Council Chamber were in print and later generations were to call it her 'golden speech', for she had here put into words, without attempting a definition, the essence of that remarkable relationship between sovereign and people in the golden age of monarchy that passed with her death. It was not her last public speech,[24] for three weeks later she went in person to the Lords for the dissolution. In the interval the Commons had loyally responded with voting four subsidies and eight fifteenths and tenths, and the Puritan pressure group, a shadow of its former self, had attempted to bring in bills for Sabbath observance and for abolishing pluralities, which were killed, probably on the Queen's instructions. And now, before they dispersed to their homes for Christmas, she gave members 'notes for their observation' on domestic and foreign affairs, the main points of which she hoped they would pass on to their neighbours in shire and borough. This was much more than a wartime Christmas message; it was rather, a masterly survey of policy during her forty-four years as Queen, a statesman's swan-song, for with taxation voted for the next four years she knew, surely, she would be unlikely to survive to address another Parliament. Because England was still at war, she devoted most space to foreign affairs, but began by assuring them all – did they dare doubt it? – that her first cause had always been to rule uprightly to conserve her people's affection. She referred to the series of attempts to assassinate her and to that watershed of English politics, the rebellion in the north; yet characteristically she made no actual mention of religion, for church affairs were, as she might have put it, fundamental but not important. She dwelt on affairs in the Netherlands from the days of Alva, denying that she had made a practice of fishing in those troubled waters for political ends, and looked back with pride to the hectic days in the summer of 1588 when the overconfident Philip thought nothing could stop him crushing England. The fight, alas, continued under his son, but it was a just war, involving now the pacification of Ireland. She was ever thankful for their subsidies in this costly campaigning, for 'I have diminished my own revenue that I might add to your security and been content to be a taper of virgin wax to waste myself and spend my life that I might give light and comfort to those that live under me.' Such happily chosen words were better than bothering them with figures, though her hearers would have been amazed to know that since 1585 her aid to the Dutch had totalled £1,420,000, her assistance to Henry IV was £300.000, and the costs of dealing with Tyrone's rebellion were to reach nearly £2 million. Elizabeth would neither continue the war, nor make peace, unless it were for the good of the whole realm. 'This testimony I would have you carry hence for the world to know that your sovereign is more careful of you ... than of herself, and will daily crave of God that they wish you best may never wish in vain.' This was an anti-climax for those who had listened to the 'golden speech', and remarkable to us, if not to the men of 1601, in that Elizabeth breathed not a word on the question that had remained of key importance all her reign, the problem of the succession. Long ago she had forbidden Parliament to meddle with the succession, and yet with the passing of each month the topic became more and more topical.[25]

The weeks went quietly enough, if not quickly. Elizabeth told the French ambassador in June 1602 that she chose 'to sit in the dark and sometimes with shedding tears to bewail Essex', but next month the Scottish ambassador eavesdropped on her dancing alone in her room in front of a mirror. That summer in which she paid her visit to the Lord Keeper's at Harefield, welcomed by 'Time' and 'Place', she finished her translation of Horace's *Art of Poetry*; she was too old now to make her version of Ovid's *Art of Love*.

In October she was suffering from pains in her face, but the trouble was not serious. 'Her Majesty, thanks be to God, hath passed 17 November [her accession day] with as great an applause of multitudes as if they had never seen her before', wrote Cecil as she entered on the forty-fifth year of her reign. She passed Christmas comfortably enough at Whitehall, at the last moment cancelling her removal to Richmond, and enjoyed watching the round of plays and the dancing in the privy chamber. But close observers, such as Sir John Harington, were struck by her frailty and increasing melancholy. 'My royal godmother, and this state's natural mother, doth now bear show of human infirmity too fast for that evil which we shall get by her death, and too slow for that good which we shall get by her releasement from her pains and misery. I was bidden to her presence; I blessed that happy moment, and found her in a most pitiable state', he told his wife. The Queen asked about his writing and he read her some verses, yet only once did she smile and at the end admonished him; 'when thou dost feel creeping Time at thy gate, these fooleries will please thee less. I am past my relish for such matters. Thou seest my bodily meat doth not suit me well. I have eaten but one ill-tasted cake since yesternight' – and that was the third day of Christmas. In mid-January she was heavy with a cold, but when better insisted on setting out for Richmond, that 'warm winter-box to shelter her old age', as she described it; was it Dr Dee's uncanny hint that she must 'beware of Whitehall', or sheer determination to visit again the home of her grandfather, the first of the Tudors, with his enviable control of the nation's economy?[26]

She appeared in the best of form when Scaramelli, the Venetian ambassador, was given an audience on the first Sunday in February. He was a little awed when he came into the presence chamber, the musicians playing for dancing though it was Sunday, and saw the figure, in silver and white taffeta, trimmed with gold, blazing with jewels on her head, neck, wrists, and robes – 'great pearls like pears . . . vast quantity of gems' – who rose as he was announced. Why, she began in his own tongue, had the Venetian Republic waited until the forty-fifth year of her reign to honour her with a diplomatic representative – 'never has it given a sign of holding me or my kingdom in that esteem which other princes and other potentates have not refused. Nor am I aware that my sex has brought me this demerit, for my sex cannot diminish my prestige . . .' Then she smiled, spoke more graciously and said she would appoint commissioners to consult with him on commercial affairs, adding as a final tweak, 'I do not know if I have spoken Italian well, still I think so, for I learnt it when a child and believe I have not forgotten it.' Scaramelli agreed with her 'fame of past, though never quite lost, beauty.'[27]

On the last day of February, as the first signs of spring were showing in the park, she was taken ill and her ladies knew that, though she might pull through, the effort of doing so would so seriously weaken her heart that she would never be the same. The sudden death of Lady Nottingham, the admiral's wife, and one of her most devoted ladies of the privy chamber, moved her very deeply. 'I never beheld other show of sickness in the Queen than such as is proper to age', wrote Cecil, daily feeling the pulse of the palace, and confident that his own plans for King James's succession were too well-laid to founder. He denied she was in extreme peril, 'but because all flesh is subject to mortality, I must confess to you that she hath been so ill-disposed as I am fearful lest the continuance of such accident should bring Her Majesty to future weakness.' Her appetite returned in some sort, she had neither cough nor fever and had even taken walks in the gardens, but she was troubled by 'a heat in her breasts and dryness in her mouth and tongue, which kept her from sleep frequently, to her disgust.' Soon her bad nights were a byword among courtiers and she snatched at sleep in the day when she could, from chair, stool or cushions on the floor, and refused to go to bed, fearing wakefulness in the long, silent watches. Was the wretchedness of her mother Anne, of her cousin of Norfolk, of Mary of Scotland, of Essex, or of all those others down the years in the Tower for treason akin to hers now, as they in turn had awaited a royal warrant to hasten the sounding of the last trumpet? Hunsdon's son, Robert Carey, tried his best to cheer her. 'No, Robin. I *am not well*', she answered him, explaining her heaviness of heart in melancholy sentences punctuated by sighs. Another day she told

Howard, the Lord Admiral, 'My Lord I am tied with a chain of iron about my neck.' Howard reminded her how courageous she had always been, but she shook her head: 'I am tied, I am tied, and the case is altered with me.' Her thoughts surely darted back to an earlier admiral, and to another Howard; to her father in his last days with his sore leg, and Anjou who had dared to say, all of thirty years ago, that *she* was an old woman with a sore leg; to little Simier and Alençon with his pock marks, to her own attack of smallpox and how she had wanted to make Dudley Protector of the realm. She spared herself the effort of rereading his last letter in the little casket, for she knew it by heart. What a rich canvas of memory there was to dwell upon in those days of sleeplessness.[28]

Legend, naturally enough, surrounds the Queen's last days, with the inventions of Lady Southwell and others adding to the apocrypha. It is most unlikely, as Carey narrates in his memoirs and as Cecil maintained in the earliest days of the new reign, that she did in fact indicate James of Scotland as her successor, while the councillors stood round her great bed on 23 March; she certainly could not have *named* him, for she had lost her powers of speech. Journeying from Whitehall to Richmond ten weeks before she was reputed to have said to Howard 'I told you my seat has been the seat of kings and I will have no rascal to succeed me; and who should succeed me but a king?' It has an authentic ring, yet it is impossible that she went on, as the narratives maintain, with the further question 'Who but our cousin of Scotland?' For forty-four years she had stubbornly refused to name her successor, and she was too strong a character, even while life was ebbing so certainly, to go back on her word. What was the point of giving way now? What happened tomorrow was their affair and she would have no part in it. She was too shrewd to be unaware that the careful Cecil had long been making plans, even though she knew not the details; not long ago she had told the antiquary Lambarde, 'now the wit of the fox is everywhere on foot, so as hardly one faithful or virtuous man may be found.' By the beginning of that week 'every man's mouth' was full of the dangers to her life, and Arabella Stuart, closely watched at Hardwick Hall, was receiving daily reports about the condition of the sovereign at Richmond. To prevent panic, the Privy Council forbade news about the Queen's health to be circulated, for such could only be prejudicial to public order. There had been 'few dry eyes' at morning service in the chapel, where the bishops earnestly prayed for her recovery.[29] Throughout the day Archbishop Whitgift – 'her little black husband' whom she had especially favoured for his celibacy, the good house he maintained and the company of tall, young men about him – waited for a final summons. Elizabeth, realizing her hours were numbered, sent for him at 6 o'clock and by signs answered his catechism about her belief. He continued long in prayer, holding her hand: 'O most heavenly Father and God of all mercy, we most humbly beseech Thee to behold Thy servant our Queen with the eyes of pity and compassion. Give unto her the comfort of Thy Holy Spirit ... O Lord punish her not for her offences, neither punish us in her ...' She would not let him cease his intercession until, late in the evening, she fell asleep, at last at peace with the world. She died in her sleep about 3 o'clock in the morning of 24 March.

The eve of Lady Day, when the new year of grace then began, was a good day to die. As the clerk of the wardrobe who engrossed the account of her obsequies for passing to the Exchequer put it, 'Our late Sovereign Lady of Blessed memory, Queen Elizabeth, departed from this mortal life the 24 day of March, being the last day of the year of Our Lord after the computation of the Church of England 1602'* and his words would have pleased her – much more than the costs of her state funeral. Her body was brought by water from Richmond to Whitehall and each night until the funeral, five weeks later, was watched over by some of her ladies. All the trappings of royal mourning were prepared for her last progress to Westminster Abbey, not least the effigy, the head painted by Maximilian Colte, which was set on top of the coffin, fully robed, with crown, orb and sceptre and was so lifelike that it caused 'a general sighing, groaning and weeping' among the throngs of Londoners who could remember no ruler except

* That is, of course, 24th March 1603 under our system of chronology in which the year 1603 would begin on 1 January.

Elizabeth. History furnished no precedent for this universal grief, noted the chronicler Stow, for 'any people, time or state to make like lamentations for the death of their sovereign.' Elizabeth had reigned forty-four years and 127 days, longer by far than any monarch since Edward III and with her passing an epoch ended; she was the first English sovereign to give a name to an age and to her contemporaries 'represented England [in Bishop Creighton's words] as no other ruler ever did' – and this in spite of being a woman; such was the real measure of her achievement. The jingles of the ballad-mongers lamenting her death made the point:

> She rul'd this Nation by her self
> And was beholden to no man,
> O she bore the sway and of all affairs
> And yet she was but a woman.

The very use of the word 'nation' in such a verse speaks volumes for the remarkable growth of national consciousness during her reign, and another lament for the dead Queen, by Thomas Dekker, describes her as 'having brought up (even under her wing) a nation that was almost begotten and born under her.' She who had taken such pride in her 'mere Englishry' would have thought that the best of all epitaphs.[30]

NOTES

NOTES

(for list of abbreviations see p. 370)

CHAPTER I MERE ENGLISH

1 Chapuys to Granvelle, 23 February 1533, in Vienna State Archives (P.C. 228, ii, fo. 43). I am grateful to the Director for sending me a photo-copy of this dispatch, which is partially quoted by Paul Friedman in *Anne Boleyn* (1884), I, 190. Though often alluded to, it has never been printed in full.

2 This secret wedding is generally assigned to 25 January 1533 (as in Stow's *Chronicle*, 562). Holinshed, however, places the marriage on 14 November 1532, following Henry's and Anne's return from France (*Chronicle*, III, 777) and later editions of Hall also favour the earlier date. It is just possible that Elizabeth brought pressure to bear on Holinshed and the continuator of Hall to show that she was conceived in wedlock.

3 *A Chronicle of Henry VIII*, 12–13.

4 That same day Anne wrote to two friends, telling them of Elizabeth's birth (*L. and P. Henry VIII*, vi, no. 1089).

5 ibid., no. 1112.

6 Trinity XIII (*Galatians*, iii).

7 *L. and P.* vi, no. 111 (extract from Hall's *Chronicle*).

8 ibid., no. 1125.

9 ibid., x, nos. 1044, 1107.

10 ibid., vii, no. 939.

11 ibid., vi, no. 1486.

12 ibid., viii, nos. 440, 653.

13 ibid., vi, no. 1392.

14 ibid., no. 1558.

15 ibid., vii, nos. 38, 171, 373.

16 Madden, *Privy Purse Expenses of the Princess Mary* (1831), p. cxxxviii.

17 *L. and P.*, xi, no. 132.

18 ibid., ix, no. 913.

19 ibid., vii, no. 509; ix, no. 568.

20 ibid., x, no. 141.

21 S.P. 70/7, fo. 5.

22 Strype, *Ecclesiastical Memorials* (1822), I, iii, 255–8; B.M. Cotton MSS, Otho C.X. fo. 230.

23 *L. and P.*, xi, no. 312.

24 Strype, op. cit., II, i, 4–8.

25 *Remains of Edward VI*, Preface, cclxiii.

26 *L. and P.*, xi, i, nos. 815–16.

27 Madden, *Privy Purse Expenses*, 24, 88, 96, 178.

28 T. Hearne, *Syllogue Epistolarum* (1716), 149–51.

29 B.M. Cotton MSS, Otho C.X. fo. 231, printed in Hearne, op. cit., 164–5.

30 op. cit., 161–3.

31 B.M. Royal MSS, 7 D.X.

32 S.P. 12/289.

33 Plate 1. See Roy Strong, *The Portraits of Queen Elizabeth* (1963), 3, 53.

34 *The Legend of Sir Nicholas Throckmorton* (ed. Nicholls), 17.

35 The letter of 27 February 1547 in which Elizabeth declines Seymour's proposal (printed in Wood, *Letters of Illustrious Ladies*, III, 181–2), is undoubtedly a forgery of Leti's.

36 S.P. 46/1, fo. 14.

37 Ellis, *Original Letters*, 1st series, II, 150.

38 *Literary Remains of Edward VI*, 205.

39 Haynes, *Burghley State Papers*, 61.

40 Katherine Ashley's confession in S.P. 10/6, fo. 55 is more detailed on this incident than that given in Haynes, op. cit., 99–100.

41 Haynes, op. cit., 99–100.

42 ibid., 96.

43 S.P. 10/2, no. 25.

44 Lawrence V. Ryan, *Roger Ascham* (1963), 102–118; *Cal. S.P. Ven. 1554*, 539.

45 J. A. Giles, *Ascham's Works* (1865), I, lxiv.

46 ibid., lxii, lxiii; Ryan, op. cit., 107, 113; Strype, *Life of Aylmer* (1821), 196.

47 B.M. Royal MSS, 12A, xxv.

48 Haynes, op. cit., 62.

49 ibid., 102–3.

50 S.P. 10/6, fo. 57d.

51 Haynes, op. cit., 100.

52 ibid., 96.

53 S.P. 10/6, fo. 24; see S.P. 46/162, fo. 13.

54 Haynes, op. cit., 70–1.

55 ibid., 88–90.

56 ibid., 94–5; S.P. 10/6, fos. 55–8d.

57 Haynes, op. cit., 103, 108; Ellis; *Original Letters*, 1st series, II, 153–158.

58 B.M. Royal MSS, 16, E.1.

59 *Acts of Privy Council, 1547–50*, 251–2; Wood, *Letters*, III, 218.

60 *Cal. Patent Rolls, 1549–51*, pp. 238–42, 415.

61 Conyers Read, *Cecil*, 64.

62 *H.M.C. Cecil*, I, 114–15.

63 S.P. 10/8, fo. 117.

64 S.P. 10/10, fo. 73.

65 *Cal. S.P. Spain*, XI, 38; Baker's *Chronicle*, 84.

66 E. 179/69/69 lists Elizabeth's household in 1552–3.

67 *A.P.C. 1550–2*, 376; B.M., Cotton MSS, Vesp. F. iii, fo. 20. Ellis, *Original Letters*, 1st series, II, 147–8, 160–1.

68 R. Vertot, *Ambassades de M. de Noailles*, II.

CHAPTER 2 MUCH SUSPECTED

1 *Cal. S.P. Ven. 1554*, 539, 532.

2 *Cal. S.P. Spain, 1553*, 115, 151; Madden, *Privy Purse Expenses*, 194; S.P. 46/8, fo. 5; *H.M.C. Cecil*, I, 131. For a reminiscence of the Prince of Orange about Elizabeth carrying her sister's train see C. Read, *Lord Burghley and Queen Elizabeth*, 560, n. 16.

3 P.R.O. 31/3/20, Noailles to Henry II, 9 August 1553; *Cal. S.P. Spain, 1553*, 188.

4 ibid., 217, 220–1; P.R.O. 31/3/20, letters of 7 and 24 September 1553.

5 *Cal. S.P. Spain, 1553*, 393–4, 440; H.F.M. Prescott, *Spanish Tudor* (1940), 254.

6 *Cal. S.P. Ven. 1534–54,* 539.

7 *Cal. S.P. Spain, 1554,* 50; Hearne, *Syllogue,* 154–5; D.M.Loades, *Two Tudor Conspiracies* (1965), 93–4; H.F.M.Prescott, *Spanish Tudor* (1940), 324. For a discussion of the problem of the copy of Elizabeth's letter in the postbag see Appendix 1 of E.Harris Harbison, *Rival Ambassadors at the Court of Queen Mary* (1940).

8 P.R.Tytler, *England Under Edward VI and Mary* (1856), 426–7.

9 ibid., 306–12; *Machyn's Diary,* 57.

10 Loades, *Two Tudor Conspiracies,* 91–2; *Cal. S.P. Spain, 1554,* 151, 162. Persistent search has failed to produce the 'signed statement' of Wyatt's.

11 S.P. 11/4, fos. 3, 3d. Various slips appear in the version given in Ellis, *Original Letters,* 2nd series, II, 255. See plate 9.

Elizabeth did not date the letter, which was assigned to 16 March in *Cal. S.P. Dom. 1547–1580,* 62 and that date has generally been followed (though not by Froude). 16 March was in fact a Friday and it is abundantly clear from Renard (in *Cal. S.P. Spain, 1554,* 166–7), and Holinshed that the letter was written on the morning of the Saturday before Palm Sunday.

12 *Chronicle of Queen Jane and Queen Mary* (Camden Soc., Orig. series, vol. 48), 70–1; *Cal. S.P. Spain, 1554,* 166–7.

13 Loades, *Two Tudor Conspiracies,* 93–4; A.Strickland, *Queens of England,* III, 65.

14 *Cal. S.P. Spain, 1554,* 312, 319, 312; Foxe, *Church Historians,* VIII, ii, 614.

15 C.R.Manning, 'Papers relating to the captivity of the Princess Elizabeth at Woodstock' in *Norfolk Archaeology,* IV (1855), 149–54.

16 The story recounted by Lucy Aitkin, *The Court of Queen Elizabeth* (1819), I, 187–8, that Elizabeth was at Hampton Court for Christmas 1554 is not borne out by the evidence.

17 *Norfolk Archaeology,* IV, 192, 203–205, 208; Holinshed, *Chronicles of England,* IV, 133.

18 *Norfolk Archaeology,* IV, 223–4.

19 S.P. 46/124, fo. 222; *E.H.R.,* VII, 271–2.

20 *Cal. S.P. Spain, 1554–8,* 145; *Norfolk Archaeology,* IV, 214.

21 Foxe, *Church Historians,* VI, ii, 554; Holinshed, *Chronicles,* IV, 133.

22 *Cal. S.P. Venice, 1555–6,* 61; J.A. Froude, *History,* VI, 356–60.

23 ibid., 363; Foxe, op. cit., VIII, 621; *Cal. S.P. Spain, 1554–8,* 145; *Machyn's Diary,* 94.

24 *Cal. S.P. Venice, 1555–6,* 174.

25 Loades, op. cit., 177, 238–40; Harbison, *Rival Ambassadors,* 312–313; S.P. 11/8, fos. 108, 87d.

26 Loades, op. cit., 246; Harbison, op. cit., 290–1.

27 S.P. 11/8, fos. 91–2; *Cal. S.P. Venice, 1555–6,* 504–5, 510, 514; Nicholls, *Progresses of Queen Elizabeth,* I, 16.

28 A.Strickland, *Queens,* III, 89–90, quoting B.M. Lansdowne MSS, 1236, no. 37.

29 *Cal. S.P. Venice, 1557–8,* XXXV, 423, 1015, 1080; Harbison, *Rival Ambassadors,* 328; Prescott, *Spanish Tudor,* 492, 495.

30 Nicholls, *Progresses*, I, 16, 18; E. Jenkins, *Elizabeth the Great*, 59; N. Williams, *The Royal Residences* (1960), 163.

31 Prescott, op. cit., 480; S.P. 46/8, fos. 182–4.

32 J. E. Neale, 'Sir Nicholas Throckmorton's advice to Queen Elizabeth' in *E.H.R.*, 65 (1950), 91–8. Dr A. L. Rowse demonstrates that this memorandum was written earlier in the year than Mary's death (*Raleigh and the Throckmortons*, 25–6).

33 J. E. Neale, 'The Accession of Queen Elizabeth' in *Essays in Elizabethan History* (1958), 48–52; *H.M.C. Cecil*, IV, 189.

34 *Cal. S.P. Spain, 1558–67*, 2, 7; K. de Lettenhove, *Relations*, 280.

CHAPTER 3   GOD'S CREATURE

1 *Egerton Papers* (Camden Soc. Original Series, XII), 28; *Machyn's Diary* (ibid., XLII), 178; *Cal. S.P. For., 1559–60*, Introduction, ix.

2 Robert Naunton, *Fragmenta Regalia*; Strickland, *Queens*, III, 103; S.P. 12/1, fos. 13, 13d.

3 Read, *Cecil*.

4 *Machyn's Diary*; *Cal. S.P. Spain, 1558–67*, 5, 18.

5 *Acts of Privy Council, 1558–70*, 10.

6 E. 351/3032; A.O. 1/2339/1, 3.

7 The following paragraphs are based on my 'Coronation of Queen Elizabeth' in *Quarterly Review*, no. 597 (1953), 397–411. See also A. L. Rowse in *History Today*, III (1953), 301–10.

8 *Cal. S.P. Venice, 1558–80*, 16–17.

9 There are two main accounts of the service in the Abbey, but they contradict each other on points of detail. One was written by an Englishman who must himself have witnessed all that he chronicled; the other was a report made by a foreign resident in London. In 1907 a scholar scrutinized these two very different versions of the service (G. C. Bayne in *E.H.R.*, vol. 22) and compared their contents with the order of service in the '*Liber Regalis*', the service-book used at all coronations between 1307 and 1661 (indeed the volume has marginal notes in William Cecil's hand). He concluded that despite occasional slips which a layman might make when describing a long and very complicated service, the English account is by far the more reliable of the two, and it is this which is followed here.

CHAPTER 4   WINDOWS IN MEN'S SOULS

1 *De Maisse's Journal*, 59.

2 S.P. 12/1, fo. 150d.; Strype, *Annals*, I, i, 154; *The Wonders of England*, quoted in John C. Booty, *John Jewel as Apologist for the Church of England* (1963), 2.

3 Camden, *Historie*, 16.

4 *Zurich Letters*, I, 9, 10.

5 S.P. 12/28/6.

6 Strype, *Annals*, I, i, 56; *Cal. S.P. Spain, 1558–67*, 37; J. E. Neale in *E.H.R.*, vol. 65 (1950), 304–32.

7 *Zurich Letters*, I, 17, 18; *Cal. S.P. Spain, 1558–67*, 61–2.

8　*H.M.C. Cecil*, II, 121.

9　Booty, *John Jewel, passim*; Camden, *Historie*, I, 30.

10　S.P. 70/26, fo. 44; C. 66/1215, m. 28.

11　Strype, *Parker*, II, 121.

12　*Cal. Pat. Rolls, 1558–60*, 449; Claude Jenkins in *Journal of Theological Studies*, vol. 24 (1922), 1–32; V.J.K. Brook, *Matthew Parker*, 85–6; *History Today*, vol. 6, 686–692.

13　S.P. 12/16, fo. 10; Neale, *Elizabeth I and Her Parliaments, 1559–1581*, 116–21; *Parker's Correspondence*, 173–5.

14　S.P. 12/28/30.

15　Strype, *Parker*, 212–14; F.O. White, *Lives of the Elizabethan Bishops* (1898), 10, 44; Harington, *Briefe View of the State of the Church*, II, 16.

16　S.P. 12/36/7; White, *op. cit.*, 71–72, 405, 331, 337.

17　Christopher Hill, *Society and Puritanism*, 47; Gee and Hardy, *Documents of Church History*, lxxxi.

18　L. Tyerman, *Life and Times of John Wesley* (1886), III, 32.

19　S.P. 46/13, fo. 316d. This version considerably antedates the examples given by Sir John Neale in *Essays in Elizabethan History*, 102–103.

20　*Meditationes Variae et Preces piae.*

21　*Times Literary Supplement*, 12 October 1933, pp. 691–2.

22　*Zurich Letters*, I, 23–4; White, *Elizabethan Bishops*, 84; *Parker's Correspondence*, 97, 379.

23　*Cal. Pat. Rolls, 1560–3*, 279–80.

24　*Zurich Letters*, I, 175, 201; *Letters of Queen Elizabeth to King James VI of Scotland* (Camden Soc. Orig. Series, vol. 46, 1849), 63.

25　*Cal. S.P. Spain, 1558–67*, 17; *Cal. S.P. For., 1566–8*, 8.

26　White, *op. cit.*, 75–7; *Cal. S.P. Dom., 1581–90*, 108.

27　Holinshed, *Chronicles*, IV, 326–8; Stow, *Chronicle*, 680; C. 66/1127, m. 30.

28　S.P. 12/118/46–7; C. 66/1186, mm. 2, 3; C. 66/1283, m. 12.

29　Camden, *Historie*, 31.

30　The most fulsome account of her strained finances is in her instructions to John Mann, 20 February 1566, in S.P. 70/82, fos. 95–7.

31　I Eliz. cap. 19; Strype, *Annals*, I, 142–3; Christopher Hill, *Economic Problems of the Church* (1956), 15–20.

32　S.P. 12/259/47; S.P. 12/263/40; Hill, *op. cit.*, 24, 316; White, *Elizabethan Bishops*, 90–4, 310, 313, 361.

33　S.P. 12/76, fos. 1–20d.

34　*Hutton's Correspondence* (ed. Raine, Surtees Soc., 1834), 93–4.

CHAPTER 5　ANSWERS ANSWERLESS

1　Bodleian Library, Ashmole MSS, 858, 54; *Cal. S.P. For., 1558–9*, nos. 845, 868, 902. A coloured drawing of the arms sent from France is in B.M., Cotton MSS, Caligula, B X, 17.

2　*Cal. S.P. For., 1558–9*, p. 443; ibid., *1559–61*, 2, 3; *Hardwicke State Papers* (1778), I, 177; S.P. 46/10.

3　S.P. 12/29/63.

4　Wright, *Queen Elizabeth*, I, 207;

S.P. 12/37, fos. 25–7; S.P. 12/41/47.

5 S.P. 12/43, fos. 99–100; S.P. 12/69/17; *D.N.B.* s.v. Keys, Mary.

6 *Cal. S.P. Venice, 1556–8,* 1077; ibid., *1558–80,* 614; S.P. 12/44/50; S.P. 12/66, fo. 109.

7 B.M., Harleian MSS, 4774I.

8 The account in *Cal. S.P. Venice, 1592–1603,* 541, is far from trustworthy.

9 *Sadler Papers,* I, 10; *Cal. S.P. Spain, 1558–67,* 5, 6, 67.

10 ibid, 3, 5, 7, 10, 26–8, 37, 48.

11 J. E. Neale, *Elizabeth I and Her Parliaments, 1559–81* (1953), 47–50.

12 *D.N.B.* s.v. Pickering, W.; *Cal. S.P. Spain, 1558–67,* 67, 73, 79; *Cal. S.P. For., 1558–9,* no. 729.

13 *Cal. S.P. Spain, 1558–67,* 73, 96, 109; *Cal. S.P. For., 1559–60,* 2.

14 ibid., 60–1, 510; *Cal. S.P. Spain, 1558–67,* 19, 108, 155.

15 ibid., 93, 102, 108–9; *Cal. S.P. For., 1558–9,* 239, 372; ibid., *1560–1,* 211, 221, 230; *Zurich Letters,* I.

16 *Cal. S.P. For., 1560–1,* 193, 434–435, 437.

17 *Cal. S.P. Spain, 1558–67,* 63, 70, 72, 74–5; *Cal. S.P. For., 1558–9,* 298–300.

18 W. Camden, *Historie of Elizabeth* (1630), I, 44; *Harleian Miscellany,* IV, 474.

19 *Cal. S.P. Spain,* 1558–67, 57–8.

20 Haynes, *Burghley Papers,* 212

21 Camden, op. cit., 44.

22 *Cal. S.P. Spain, 1558–67,* 107, 113–14, 117; see my *Thomas Howard* (1964), 60.

23 S.P. 12/13, fos. 55–8; *Norfolk Archaeology,* 32 (1961), 80; *Acts of Privy Council, 1578–80,* 455.

24 *Cal. S.P. Spain,* 1558–67, 175.

25 Haynes, *Burghley Papers,* 361–2; Ian Aird in *E.H.R.,* 71 (1956), 69–79.

26 *Cal. S.P. For., 1560–1,* 348; S.P. 63/2, fos. 82, 82d.; *Cal. S.P. Spain, 1558–67,* 177.

27 *Hardwicke State Papers,* I, 121–3, 163–5, 167; *Cal. S.P. For., 1560–1,* 439, 523.

28 ibid., 462, 478; *Hardwicke State Papers,* I, 168.

29 *Cal. S.P. Spain, 1558–67,* 178, 181, 263.

30 ibid., 178, 181. Anent the Duchess of Suffolk's marriage, contracted in 1557, Elizabeth said, 'Has the woman so far forgotten herself as to marry a common groom?' (*Complete Peerage,* s.v. Dorset, 421n.)

31 *Cal. S.P. Spain, 1558–67,* 178, 208, 225, 245, 248, 531.

32 *History Today,* vol. 5, 543; S.P. 12/159/1.

33 N. Williams, *Thomas Howard,* 84–85. The sole source for the crisis among the councillors is De Quadra's correspondence in *Cal. S.P. Spain, 1558–67,* 261–3. The pages of the Privy Council Register between September 1562 and January 1563 are missing from the volume.

34 J. E. Neale, *Elizabeth I and Her Parliaments, 1559–81,* 107–10, 126–127.

35 C. Read, *Cecil,* 303–4.

36 *Cal. S.P. Scotland, 1563–9,* 19–20, 58.

CHAPTER 6

AS GOOD A COURAGE AS EVER MY FATHER HAD

1   S.P. 12/29/61.

2   S.P. 12/33/53.

3   *Melville's Memoirs* (Abbey classics edition), 51–3; S.P. 12/34, fos. 178d–9; *Cal. S.P. For., 1564–5,* no. 691.

4   *Melville's Memoirs,* 54–6; *Cal. S.P. For., 1564–5,* no. 723.

5   ibid., nos. 714, 757, 772, 961; S.P. 52/9/385; Read, *Cecil,* 310–14.

6   Wright, *Queen Elizabeth and Her Times,* I, 181; *Cal. S.P. Spain, 1558–67,* 233, 424.

7   *Cal. S.P. For., 1564–5,* nos. 1047, 1129; Read, *Cecil,* 315–16.

8   *Queen Elizabeth and Some Foreigners* (ed. V. Von Klarwill, 1928), 202–3, 206, 209, 211; *Cal. S.P. Spain, 1558–67,* 436–7.

9   *Queen Elizabeth and Some Foreigners,* 217, 231.

10   Read, *Cecil,* 328–9; *Queen Elizabeth and Some Foreigners,* 233. F. von Raumer, *Queen Elizabeth and Mary Queen of Scots* (1836), 35–7.

11   Murdin, *Burghley State Papers,* 760; R. Naunton, *Fragmenta Regalia.*

12   Haynes, *Cecil State Papers,* 444.

13   S.P. 52/10, fo. 68; Camden, *Historie,* I, 79; Wright, *Queen Elizabeth,* I, 209.

14   Von Raumer, op. cit., 37–9; S.P. 12/44/42; *Cal. S.P. For., 1564–5,* nos. 1657 (3), 1658; *Cal. S.P. Spain, 1558–67,* 504, 518.

15   *Cal. S.P. Spain, 1558–67,* 511, 518–19, 524, 544, 549, 571; Wright, op. cit., I, 225.

16   *Cal. S.P. For., 1566–8,* nos. 99, 111.

17   J.E. Neale, *Essays in Elizabethan History,* 95; *Cal. S.P. Spain, 1558–67,* 562–3; von Raumer, op. cit., 40; Camden, *Historie,* 83.

18   S.P. 70/82, fos. 195–7, Elizabeth's instructions to Dr John Man in Madrid, 20 February 1566.

19   Murdin, *Burghley State Papers,* 762; Neale, *Elizabeth I and Her Parliaments, 1559–81,* 136, quoting La Forêt's despatch.

20   *Cal. S.P. Spain, 1558–67,* 591–2.

21   J.E. Neale in *E.H.R.,* vol. 36, 514–17.

22   Neale, *Elizabeth I and Her Parliaments, 1559–81,* 163–4, 174–6.

23   *Queen Elizabeth and Some Foreigners,* 211, 240, 258, 265.

24   ibid., 267, 279; *Cal. S.P. For., 1566–8,* nos. 1296, 1327.

25   Camden, *Historie,* 101–2; *D.N.B.,* s.v. North, Roger; S.P. 12/44/42, 46; *H.M.C. Bath,* II, 17–18.

26   *Queen Elizabeth and Some Foreigners,* 299; *Cal. S.P. For., 1566–8,* nos. 1857–8, 1947; Haynes, *Burghley State Papers,* 464; N. Williams, *Thomas Howard, 4th Duke of Norfolk,* 129–32.

27   S.P. 52/13, fo. 30, original in French (*Cal. S.P. Scot., 1563–9,* 316).

28   Read, *Cecil,* 377–8; Robert Keith, *The History of the Affairs of Church and State in Scotland* (ed. 1844), II, 667; *Cal. S.P. Scot., 1563–9,* 361, 375.

29 *Cal. S.P. For.*, *1566–8*, 458; *Cal. S.P. Spain*, *1568–79*, 36; S.P. 12/2; *Cal. S.P. Scot.*, *1563–9*, 701–4; Labanoff, *Lettres de Marie Stuart*, II, 73–7; Von Raumer, op. cit., 138–9.

30 Froude, *History*, IX (1866), 247–8; *Cal. S.P. Scot.*, *1563–9*, 426.

31 *Cal. S.P. Spain*, *1568–79*, 50.

32 Anderson, *Collections Relating to Mary Queen of Scotland* (1728), IV, i, 3–32; Melville, *Memoirs*, 104–6; *Cal. S.P. Scot.*, *1563–9*, 530–5; *Dépêches de Fénélon* (ed. C.P. Cooper, 1838), I, 17–18; Strickland, *Queens*, III, 207.

33 The text of the casket letters will be found in the Appendix to *Cal. S.P. Scot.*, *1563–9*.

CHAPTER 7 MANIFEST DANGER

1 F. Peck, *Desiderata Curiosa* (1732), I, 15–16.

2 *Cal. S.P. Spain*, *1568–79*, 111.

3 Read, *Cecil*, 442, quoting the French ambassador's report.

4 Haynes, *Cecil State Papers*, 541–3.

5 I have discussed these overlapping conspiracies in my *Thomas Howard, Fourth Duke of Norfolk*, 149–52.

6 S.P. 12/51, fos. 9–13; Fénélon, *Dépêches*, II, 127–8.

7 *Cal. S.P. Scotland*, *1569–71*, 674.

8 H.M.C. Cecil, I, 414; *State Trials*, I, 997; Froude, *History*, IV, 470; Williams, *Howard*, 164–5.

9 *Cal. S.P. Dom. Addenda*, *1566–71*, 362; Cuthbert Sharp, *Memorials of the Rebellion of 1569* (1840), 13, 156; S.P. 15/14, nos. 94, 99, 100, 104; ibid., vol. 15, nos. 3, 12, 14, 54.

10 Sharp, *Memorials*, 199; *Cal. S.P. Dom. Addenda*, *1566–71*, 108–9; R.R. Reid in *Trans. Royal Hist. Soc.*, new ser., vol. 20 (1906).

11 Williams, *Howard*, 173–5; S.P. 12/66, fos. 147–52d.

12 E. 164/37 & 38; E. 137/133/1; Strickland, *Queens*, III, 218; Sharp, *Memorials*, 219, 230–40, 330–3.

13 Read, *Walsingham*, I, 68–74.

14 Haynes, *Cecil State Papers*, 572; S.P. 12/67, fos. 7–12; S.P. 15/19/1.

15 Williams, *Howard*, 195–205.

16 ibid., 205–25; Froude, *History*, X, 279; Murdin, *Burghley State Papers*, 18–61.

17 Williams, *Howard*, 232–7, 247–51.

18 *Cal. S.P. Scotland*, *1569–71*, 40; Neale, *Parliaments*, 269.

CHAPTER 8 'LA PLUS FINE FEMME DU MONDE'

1 *Dépêches de Fénélon*, IV, 411–12; Lettenhove, VI, 350; Camden, *Historie*, 52 says, wrongly, her illness was smallpox.

2 *Cal. S.P. For.*, *1569–71*, no. 1253; Fénélon, op. cit., III, 424–5.

3 ibid., III, 418–19; Camden, *Historie*, II, 21.

4   Fénélon, III, 438–9.

5   ibid., III, 462–7. During the absence of a Spanish ambassador Fénélon's despatches are of key importance for diplomatic history, especially for negotiations for the French match.

6   Digges, *Compleat Ambassador*, (1658), 47, 63; Read, *Burghley*, 32–3.

7   ibid., 64; Camden, *Historie*, II, 23.

8   Murdin, *Burghley State Papers*, 204.

9   S.P. 12/91/45 and 52.

10   E. St John Brooks, *Sir Christopher Hatton* (1946), 83–4.

11   S.P. 12/92/16; Brooks, op. cit., 99.

12   loc. cit.

13   Camden, *Historie*, II, 46; R.B. Wernham, *Before the Armada*, 316–17; Read, *Walsingham*, I, 195.

14   ibid., I, 256.

15   *Cal. S.P. Spain, 1568–79*, 403–10; Read, *Burghley*, 87–9.

16   Wernham, op. cit., 324–7.

17   Camden, *Histoire*, II, 57–8; Fénélon, op. cit., VI, 318.

18   *Cal. S.P. For., 1575–7*, nos. 617, 829, 1072; Read, *Walsingham*, I, 285.

19   *Cal. S.P. For., 1575–7*, nos. 315, 738; Read, *Burghley*, 169, 145.

20   Wernham, op. cit., 247–51

21   *Cal. S.P. For., 1575–7*, no. 1478.

22   *H.M.C. Rutland*, I, 107; Harington, *Nugae Antiquae*, I, 359–60; Neale, *Parliaments*, 366, prints a better version of the speech than that in Harington, op. cit., sent by the Queen 'to boy Jack'.

23   Camden, *Histoire*, II, 90, 95; *Cal. S.P. For., 1578–9*, 506.

24   Strickland, *Queens of England*, III, 320.

25   S.P. 12/131/50; C. 66/1188, m. 4.

26   C. 66/1214, m. 40.

27   *Cal. S.P. Spain, 1568–79*, 692; Strickland, op. cit., 321.

28   Camden, *Historie*, III, 10 (placed wrongly under 1581).

29   Read, *Burghley*, 210–11.

30   See Martin Hume, *Courtship of Queen Elizabeth*, 360–7. Fénélon in 1569 thought Elizabeth could not bear children because of an accident to her legs (II, 122), but he changed his mind later. The story of Ben Jonson in *Conversations with Drummond*, 484–5, is worthless.

31   The evidence mustered by A.F. Pollard, *Political History of England, 1558–1603*, 181, is of little weight.

32   *Cal. S.P. Spain, 1568–79*, 702.

33   Read, *Burghley*, 220–1; *Cal. S.P. Spain, 1568–79*, 704–5.

34   ibid., *1580–6*, 14, 31.

35   Read, *Burghley*, 275.

36   *Cal. S.P. Spain, 1580–6*, 95, 101.

37   Holinshed, *Chronicle*, III, 1315.

38   Nichols, *Progresses*, II, 310.

39   Camden, *Historie*, III, 7–8; *Cal. S.P. Spain, 1580–6, Egerton Papers* (Camden Soc. O.S. vol. 12), 78 seq.

40   ibid., 226–7, 229; Camden, *Histoire*, III, 8.

41   *Cal. S.P. Spain, 1580–6*, 244, 281.

42   ibid., 243, 281; Nichols, *Progresses*, II, 346.

43   'A.H.' in Introduction to Digges' *Compleat Ambassador* (1658).

44   *Cal. S.P. For., 1583–4*, 533.

CHAPTER 9   THE SPLENDIFEROUS PLANET

1 S.P. 46/13/71; Brooks, *Hatton*, 17.

2 Neale, *Elizabeth*, 73.

3 Muriel St Clare Byrne, *Elizabethan Life in Town and Country*, 3–4.

4 Quoted in Neale, *Essays*, 73.

5 A.O. 1/380/2, 3.

6 See my *Royal Residences of Great Britain* (1960), 1–7, 20, 102.

7 E. 101/429/2.

8 A.O. 1/380/1, 2.

9 Allegra Woodworth, 'Purveyance for the Royal Household in the Reign of Queen Elizabeth' in *Trans. American Philosophical Society* (Philadelphia, 1945), N.S., vol. 35, pt. 1, 11–12, 17.

10 ibid., 16–17, 38.

11 ibid., 62–6.

12 de Maisse, *Journal*, 14; Nichols, *Progresses*, II, 78, 271, 498–500; ibid., III, 49.

13 C. 115/L.2/6697, 19; E. 407/4/1, 4. Van Hesse also bought from the Queen a gold anchor. One wonders whether this was the same ornament which was given to her again two years later by Egerton (see above, p. 244).

14 C. 115/L.2/6697.

15 de Maisse, *Journal*, 36–7, 25.

16 ibid., 35–6; Paul Hentzner's description in 1598, see my *Royal Residences*, 94–5; Wright, *Queen Elizabeth and Her Times*, II, 174.

17 A.O. 1/380/3; Lambarde, *Perambulation of Kent* (1573).

18 R. Crawford, *The King's Evil*, 64.

19 Birch, *Memoirs of Queen Elizabeth*, I, 154–5.

20 Allegra Woodworth, op. cit., 13; S.P. 12/148/34.

21 See my articles on 'Sessions of the Clerk of the Market of the Household' in *Trans. of the London and Middlesex Arch. Soc.*, vol. 19 (1957), 1–14, and on 'The Master of the Royal Tents and his Records' in *Journal of the Society of Archivists*, 2 (1960).

22 *Cal. S.P. Spain, 1568–79*, 50–1; Puttenham, II, 22; Nichols, *Progresses*, III, 121.

23 Lodge, *Illustrations*, II, 75; Nichols, op. cit., I, 601.

24 F. Peck, *Desiderata Curiosa*, 25; *Egerton Papers*, 340–56; Lodge, *Illustrations*, III, 132; E. K. Chambers, *Elizabethan Stage*, 113, 117.

25 Nichols, *Progresses*, 101–21; de Maisse, *Journal*, 14; *Chamberlain's Letters*, 161.

26 *H.M.C. Hatfield*, IV, 136, 504.

27 *H.M.C. Pepys*, 178–9; Nichols, op. cit., I, 500–5.

28 Chambers, *Elizabethan Stage*, I, 127–8; Williams, *Thomas Howard*, 88–9.

29 Chambers, loc. cit.; C. 115/L.2/6697, 23.

30 Nichols, *Progresses*, III, 168–9; *Complete Peerage*; sv. Norreys.

31 *Sydney Papers*, II, 210; *Chamberlain's Letters*, 166, 169.

32 Harington, op. cit., I, 314.

33 *Chamberlain's Letters*, I, 160; Nichols, *Progresses*, III, 486–95; Chambers, op. cit., IV, 67–8.

34 *Chamberlain's Letters*, I, 160; S.P. 12/284/97.

35 Cooper, *Athene Cantabrigienses*, I, 311; A.O. 1/380/3.

36 C. 66/1209, mm. 2–3; C. 66/1225, mm. 16–18; C. 66/1231,

m. 22; J. S. Bumpus, *English Cathedral Music*, I, 43, 63.

37 *Melville's Memoirs*, 55–6; de Maisse, *Journal*, 55, 95; John Hawkins, *History of Music* (1853), 452.

38 Nichols, op. cit., II, 577; C. 66/1113, m. 29.

39 Chambers, *Elizabethan Stage*, I, 159, 243; II, 34, 44.

40 S.P. 12/215, fo. 218.

41 Birch, I, 146; A. L. Rowse, *William Shakespeare*, 125, 205.

42 'Journey Through England and Scotland made by Lupold von Wedel in 1584 and '85', in *Trans. R. H. Soc.*, 2 ser., IX (1895), 236, 258–9.

43 Chambers, op. cit., IV, 112.

CHAPTER 10   THE DAUGHTER OF DEBATE

1 S.P. 12/155/42; S.P. 12/173, fo. 187; Digges quoted in Neale, *Parliaments, 1584–1601*, 44; C. C. Jones, *Court Fragments* (1828), II, 43; Castelnau, *Mémoires* (1731), I, 539; *Cal. S.P. Spain, 1580–6*, 588.

2 Read, *Burghley*, 245–50.

3 ibid., 247; Neale, *Parliaments, 1559–81*, 388–90; Hugh Bowler, *Recusant Roll No. 2* (Catholic Record Soc., 1965), xii–xx.

4 *Cal. S.P. Scot., 1581–3*, 56; ibid., *1585–6*, 68; von Raumer, *Queen Elizabeth and Mary Queen of Scots*, 230–1.

5 *Cal. S.P. Scot., 1581–3*, 397–8, 630–1; ibid., *1584–5*, 314–17, 479.

6 Fuller, *Worthies of England*, 133; William M. Wallace, *Sir Walter Raleigh* (1959), 20–42.

7 The poems are discussed by Walter Oakeshott, *The Queen and the Poet*, by A. L. Rowse, *Raleigh and the Throgmortons*, pp. 150–60; by Wallace, op. cit., 68 seq.

8 Meyer, *England and the Catholic Church under Queen Elizabeth*, 271; K.B. 8/45; *D.N.B.*, s.v. Somerville, J.; *Cal. S.P. Dom., 1581–90*, 206.

9 Conyers Read, *Mr. Secretary Walsingham and The Policy of Queen Elizabeth*, II, chapter xi; Camden, *Historie*, III, 20–1; Naunton, *Fragmenta Regalia*, 36; *Cal. S.P. For., 1583–4*, Intro. vi.

10 Read, *Walsingham*, II, 376–81; *Cal. S.P. Spain, 1580–6*, 351; Camden, op. cit., II, 34.

11 Rowse, *Raleigh and the Throgmortons*, 101–2; S.P. 12/163/65.

12 *Cal. S.P. Spain, 1580–6*, xliii, 336, 397.

13 *Cal. S.P. For., 1583–4*, 599, 606–607; ibid., *1584–5*, 525; *Cal. S.P. Dom., 1581–90*, 210.

14 S.P. 12/174 passim. The stages of drafting the Bond are described by Neale in *Parliaments, 1584–1601*, 16–18.

15 ibid., 34–7; Read, *Burghley*, 299.

16 ibid., 299–302; Neale, op. cit., 39–41.

17 K.B. 8/46; S.P. 12/176/47; *Cal. S.P. For., 1583–4*, 638; Brooks, *Hatton*, chapter 22.

18 ibid., 242; *Cal. S.P. For., 1584–5*, 386–7; *Cal. S.P. Dom., 1581–90*, 248.

19 Statutes of the Realm, IV, i, 704–705; S.P. 12/176/68; Neale, *Parliaments*, 51–2.

20 ibid., 98–100.

21 *Cal. S.P. Scot., 1584–5,* 550; *Cal. S.P. For., 1585–6,* 374.

22 An enormous literature has grown up around the Babington plot. The fullest modern accounts are in Read, *Walsingham,* II; and in Brooks, *Hatton,* 260–97. The most authoritative study by a Roman Catholic historian is the Jesuit J. H. Pollen's *Mary Queen of Scots and the Babington Plot* (Scottish Hist. Soc., 1922). Read's edition of *The Bardon Papers* (Royal Hist. Soc., 1909) is important.

23 *Cal. S.P. For., 1585–6,* 475; Read, *Burghley,* 394.

24 *Cal. S.P. Scot., 1584–5,* 597.

25 S.P. 12/194, fo. 69.

26 Von Raumer, *Queen Elizabeth and Mary Queen of Scots,* 340–1; *Cal. S.P. For., 1568–8,* 120, 137.

27 Neale, *Parliaments, 1584–1601,* 126–31; *Holinshed Chronicle,* IV, 938–40.

28 *Cal. S.P. Scot., 1586–9,* 394; Nicholas, *Life of William Davison* (1823), 79.

29 ibid., 236–7.

30 ibid., 86–7.

31 ibid., 104, 267, 276–8; *Acts of Privy Council, 1586–7,* 317.

32 Read, *Burghley,* 368–70; C. 66/1103, m. 11.

33 Camden Soc., vol. 46, 42–3. The appointment of the three commissioners to act for the Queen at the opening of the Parliament of 1586–7 is duly enrolled on the Patent Rolls, but not the later commissioners to act for her at the closing sessions, when Burghley, in disgrace, was left off. Similarly there is no official record of the commissioners to try Davison. Much mystery still surrounds the official documentation of the whole affair (see *E.H.R.,* vol. 35, p. 103 seq.).

CHAPTER II   IN THE MIDST AND HEAT OF THE BATTLE

1 *Cal. S.P. For., 1584–5,* 514–15 (cp. 337–8).

2 Read, *Burghley,* 323.

3 Read, *Walsingham,* II, 172.

4 *Cal. S.P. For., 1584–5,* 671, 691; Camden, *Historie,* III, 59; C.R. Markham, *The Fighting Veres,* 69.

5 S.P. 12/182, fo. 41; ibid., no. 32; *Cal. S.P. For., 1585–6,* 193, 197; Bruce, *Leycester Correspondence,* 110.

6 C. 66/1302, m. 30.

7 C. 66/1301, m. 38; G. B. Harrison, *Essex,* 30–1; *Cal. S.P. Spain, 1587–1603,* 127.

8 C. G. Cruickshank, *Elizabeth's Army,* chapter 1; *Cal. S.P. For., 1583 and Addenda,* no. 471.

9 F. C. Dietz, *The Exchequer in Elizabeth's Reign* (Smith College Studies, vol. 8, 2), 86, 98–100.

10 J. A. Williamson, *The Age of Drake,* esp. chapter 14.

11 G. Mattingly, *The Defeat of the Armada,* 83.

12 See Burghley's Memorandum in *Cal. S.P. For., 1569–71,* 513.

13 *Acts of Privy Council, 1587–8,* 175, 193, 252; J. K. Laughton, *The Defeat of the Spanish Armada* (Navy Record Soc., 1894), I, lvii, lxvii.

14   Mattingly, *Armada*, chapter 15.

15   *Cal. S.P. Spain, 1587–1603*, 451.

16   S.P. 46/35, fo. 29; Wernham, *Foreign Policy*, 404–5; Read, *Burghley*, 424–5.

17   Camden, *Historie*, III, 133–6; Laughton, op. cit., I, 219; Mattingly, *Armada*, 292.

18   Laughton, op. cit., 217, 220, 225; Camden, op. cit., III, 141.

19   ibid., 140; Nichols, *Progresses*, II, 536; S.P. 46/125, fo. 175.

20   Nichols, loc. cit.; *Acts of Privy Council*, 1588, 241; *Cal. S.P. Spain, 1587–1603*, 431; S.P. 12/215, no. 65.

21   S.P. 46/18, fo. 113; C.H. Firth, *Tudor Tracts*; Firth in *Trans. Royal Hist. Soc.* (3rd ser., 1909); III, 102; Camden, op. cit., III, 144.

22   The 1588 has on the reverse: 'Tranquilla per Undas' (Tranquil amidst violent waters). The 1589 medal has on the obverse 'Ditior in Toto Non Alter Circulus Orbe' (No other circle more rich in the whole world), and on the reverse 'Non Pericula Tangent' (Not even dangers affect it).

23   Goodman, *Court of King James I*, I, 163.

24   Harrison, *Essex*, 32–3; Birch, *Queen Elizabeth and Her Times*, I, 56.

25   R.B. Wernham, 'The Portugal Expedition' in *E.H.R.*, vol. 66 (1951), 1–26, 194–218.

26   Wernham, loc. cit.; S.P. 12/225/15; W.B. Devereux, *Lives and Letters of the Devereux Earls of Essex*, I, 204; A.L. Rowse, *The Expansion of Elizabethan England*, 286.

27   Harrison, *Essex*, 47; Carey, *Memoirs*, 17; Devereux, op. cit., I, 244.

28   Brooks, *Hatton*, 353; Camden, *Historie*, IV, 34.

29   G.C. Williamson, *George, 3rd Earl of Cumberland*, 78–9; Rowse, *Expansion*, 293–4.

30   Wallace, *Raleigh*, 92–6.

31   Harrison, *Essex*, 95–101.

32   ibid., 105–33; Rowse, *Expansion*, 305–13.

33   Read, *Burghley*, 522; H.M.C. *Cecil*, VII, 41.

34   Harington, *Nugae Antiquae*, II, 216.

35   The audience which some historians have placed in 1596 was on 25 July 1597. Cecil's report to Essex, then on the Islands Voyage, is printed in von Raumer, *Queen Elizabeth*, 436–7. The Latin text of the Queen's spontaneous speech was later set down and a copy is in S.P. 88/2, fo. 15, of which Cecil's version is a fair translation.

36   Neale, *Parliaments, 1583–1601*, 322.

CHAPTER 12   THE GREAT LIONESS

1   Strickland, *Queens of England*, III, 499; *Cal. S.P. Dom.*, 1597–8, 487; H.M.C. *Cecil*, VIII, 385; ibid., X, 288.

2   Strype, *Life of Aylmer*, 192–3.

3   *Cal. S.P. Venice, 1592–1603*, 532. See my *Powder and Paint*, 26–8; E. 190/3/2, fo. 11, for imported rose water.

4   S.P. 12/268/82–3; K.B. 8/55;

Camden, *Historie*, IV, 132; *D.N.B.*, s.v. Squier, E.

5   Spedding, *Life of Bacon*, II, 40.

6   G. B. Harrison, *Essex*, 161–2; *H.M.C. Cecil*, VII, 306.

7   Neale, *Essays in Elizabethan History*, 82; S.P. 46/125, fo. 251; S.P. 12/265/10.

8   L. Stone, *Crisis of the Aristocracy*, 100–1; Read, *Burghley*, 437; *H.M.C. De Lisle and Dudley*, II, 317; *Sydney Papers*, II, 75, 77.

9   Camden, op. cit., IV, 126.

10 *H.M.C. Cecil*, XIII, 21–2; *Cal. Carew Papers, 1575–88*, xv.

11 Camden, op. cit., IV, 127; Devereux, *Lives of the Devereux Earls of Essex*, I, 493.

12 *H.M.C. Cecil*, VIII, 355.

13 Wallace, *Raleigh*, 160–1; *D.N.B.*, s.v. Hayward, J.

14 *Cal. S.P. Ireland*, IV, 150; Harrison, *Essex*, 227–50.

15 ibid., 160–1.

16 ibid., 270–5.

17 ibid., 281–322.

18 C. H. Firth in *T.R.H.S.*, 3rd ser., III, 116–17; S.P. 46/23, fo. 130.

19 P. M. Handover, *The Second Cecil*, 234–5; D. H. Willson, *James VI and I*, 152–3; *H.M.C. Cecil*, X, 288; *Correspondence of Elizabeth and James VI* (Camden Soc. Orig. Ser., 46), 125, 135–6.

20 *Sydney Papers*, II, 122; *D.N.B.*, s.v. Fitton, M.; *Cal. S.P. Dom., 1601–3*, 19; *Cal. Carew Papers,*

1601–3, 20; *H.M.C. Cecil*, XI, 201–2.

21 S.P. 91/1, fos. 170, 179; *H.M.C. Cecil*, XI, 388.

22 S.P. 46/26, fo. 148.

23 S.P. 12/282/65–7; H. Townshend, *Historical Collections* (1680), 262–6; cp. Neale, *Parliaments, 1584–1601*, 388–92.

24 As in Black, *The Reign of Elizabeth*, 194.

25 Neale, *Parliaments*, 428–31; *H.M.C. Cecil*, XIII, 21–2.

26 E. P. Cheyney, *History of England from the Defeat of the Armada to the Death of Elizabeth*, II, 566; *H.M.C. Cecil*, XII, 439, 495, 610; Harington, *Nugae Antiquae*, I, 320.

27 *Cal. S.P. Venice, 1592–1603*, 531–533, 565.

28 *H.M.C. 7th Report*, 528; *H.M.C. Cecil*, XII, 667.

29 Nichols, *Bibliotheca Topographica*, I, 525–6; *H.M.C. Cecil*, XII, 693; Cheyney, op. cit., II, 573; Neale, *Essays in Elizabethan History*, 106–112.

30 S.P. 12/185/79; P. M. Dawley, *Whitgift*, 225–6; *Cal. S.P. Venice, 1592–1603*, 566; L.C. 2/4/4 (The funeral cost £11,305 1s. 0d.); Stow, *Chronicle of London* (ed. Howes, 1631), p. 815; Ashmole MS, 36, fo. 296 quoted in M. St Clare Byrne, *Elizabethan Life in Town and Country*, 19; Dekker, *Wonderfull Year* (1603).

ABBREVIATIONS USED IN THE NOTES

B.M.	British Museum.
Cal. S.P. Dom.	*Calendar of State Papers, Domestic Series.*
Cal. S.P. For.	*Calendar of State Papers, Foreign Series.*
Cal. S.P. Scot.	*Calendar of State Papers, Scotland.*
Cal. S.P. Spain	*Calendar of State Papers, Spanish.*
Cal. S.P. Ven.	*Calendar of State Papers, Venetian.*
D.N.B.	*Dictionary of National Biography.*
E.H.R.	*English Historical Review.*
H.M.C.	*Historical Manuscripts Commission Reports.*
L. and P.	*Letters and Papers, Foreign and Domestic, Henry VIII.*
MSS	Manuscripts.
N.S.	New Series.
O.S.	Original Series.
Ser.	Series.
Soc.	Society publications.
Trans.	*Transactions.*
T.R.H.S.	*Transactions of the Royal Historical Society.*

KEY TO PUBLIC RECORD OFFICE REFERENCES

A.O. 1	Audit Office, Declared Accounts.
C. 66	Chancery, Patent Rolls.
C. 115	Chancery, Master's Exhibits, Scudamore (or Duchess of Norfolk) Deeds.
E. 101	Exchequer, King's Remembrancer, Accounts Various.
E. 351	Exchequer, Pipe Office, Declared Accounts.
E. 407	Exchequer of Receipt, Miscellanea.
K.B. 8	King's Bench, Baga de Secretis.
P.R.O. 31	Public Record Office, Transcripts from Foreign Archives.
S.P. 10	State Papers Domestic, Edward VI.
S.P. 11	State Papers Domestic, Mary.
S.P. 12	State Papers Domestic, Elizabeth I.
S.P. 15	State Papers Domestic, Addenda, Edward VI to Elizabeth I.
S.P. 46	State Papers Supplementary.
S.P. 70	State Papers Foreign, General Series, Elizabeth I.
S.P. 78	State Papers Foreign, France.
S.P. 91	State Papers Foreign, Russia.

A HUNDRED BOOKS
on the Reign of Queen Elizabeth I

The following list of a hundred important, readable books on the Queen and her reign has been selected from the very extensive literature on Elizabethan England. Source material has been included somewhat sparingly, but those wishing to read even further should consult Conyers Read's *Bibliography of British History, Tudor Period, 1485–1603*, which classifies 6,543 books and articles in periodicals, some 4,000 of them relating to the period 1558–1603.

ALLEN, J.W., *A History of Political Thought in the Sixteenth Century* (1928).

AUERBACH, ERNA, *Tudor Artists* (1954).

BIRCH, T., *Memoirs of the Reign of Queen Elizabeth* (covering the years from 1581; 2 vols., 1764).

BLACK, J.B., *The Reign of Elizabeth, 1558–1603* (Oxford History of England, 1936; 2nd edition, revised 1959).

BOOTY, JOHN E., *John Jewel as Apologist for the Church of England* (1963).

BOURNE, H.R. FOX, *Sir Philip Sidney* (1891).

BRAUDEL, F., *La Méditérranée et la monde méditérranéen à l'époque de Philippe II* (1949).

BROOK, V.J.K., *Life of Archbishop Parker* (1962).

BURGON, J.W., *The Life and Times of Sir Thomas Gresham* (2 vols., 1839).

BYRNE, MURIEL ST CLAIRE, *Elizabethan Life in Town and Country* (1925; revised edition 1961; also issued as a paperback).

CAMDEN, WILLIAM, *The Historie of the Life and Reigne of the Most Revered and Victorious Princess Elizabeth, late Queene of England* (trans. Benjamin Fisher, 1630).

CARAMAN, PHILIP, *John Gerrard; Autobiography of an Elizabethan* (1951).

CECIL, ALGERNON, *A Life of Robert Cecil, First Earl of Salisbury* (1915).

CHAMBERS, E.K. *The Elizabethan Stage* (4 vols., 1923).

CHAMBERS, E.K., *William Shakespeare* (1930).

CHEYNEY, E.P., *A History of England from the Defeat of the Armada to the Death of Elizabeth* (2 vols., 1914, 1918).

CLAPHAM, JOHN, *Elizabeth of England; Certain Observations Concerning the Life and Reign of Queen Elizabeth* (ed. E.P.Read and Conyers Read, 1951).

CORBETT, JULIAN S., *Drake and The Tudor Navy* (2 vols., 1898–9).

CREIGHTON, MANDELL, *Queen Elizabeth* (1896; also a paperback edition with an introduction by G. R. Elton, 1966).

CRUIKSHANK, C.G., *Elizabeth's Army* (1946).

DEVEREUX, W.B., *Lives and Letters of the Devereux, Earls of Essex* (2 vols., 1853).

DEWAR, MARY, *Sir Thomas Smith* (1964).

Elizabethan Government and Society; Essays Presented to Sir John Neale (ed. S.T.Bindoff, J.Hurstfield and C.H.Williams, 1961).

ELTON, G.R., *England Under the Tudors* (1956).

EMMISON, F.G., *Tudor Secretary* (a life of Sir William Petre, 1961).

FELLOWES, E.H., *The English Madrigal Composers* (1921).

FROUDE, J.A., *History of England from the Fall of Wolsey to the Defeat of the Spanish Armada* (1856–70, vols. vii–xii; also available in Everyman's Library).

HAKLUYT, RICHARD, *Principal Navigations etc.* (ed. W.Raleigh, 12 vols., 1903–5; also available in Everyman's Library).

HANDOVER, P.M., *The Second Cecil, 1563–1604* (1959).

HARINGTON, JOHN, *Nugae Antiquae* (ed. T.Peck, 2 vols., 1769).

HARRISON, G.B. (ed.), *The Letters of Queen Elizabeth* (a useful collection but by no means exhaustive; 1935).

HARRISON, G.B., *The Life and Death of Robert Devereux, Earl of Essex* (1937).

HARRISON, WILLIAM, *An Historicall Description of the Iland of Britaine* (1577, reprinted 1908).

HENDERSON, T.F., *Mary Queen of Scots* (2 vols., 1905).

HILL, CHRISTOPHER, *Economic Problems of the Church* (1956).

HILL, CHRISTOPHER, *Society and Puritanism* (1964).

HOOKER, RICHARD, *On the Lawes of Ecclesiasticall Politie* (ed. J.Keble revised by W.Church and F.Paget, 1888; also available in Everyman's Library).

HURSTFIELD, JOEL, *Elizabeth I and the Unity of England* (1960).

HURSTFIELD, JOEL, *The Queen's Wards* (1958).

JUDGES, A.V., *The Elizabethan Underworld* (reprints of tracts and ballads; 1930).

KLARWILL, V. VON, *Queen Elizabeth and Some Foreigners* (trans. T.N. Nash, 1928).

KNAPPEN, M.M., *Tudor Puritanism* (1939).

MAISSE, ANDRÉ HURAULT, SIEUR DE, *Journal, 1597* (trans. G. B. Harrison and R. A. Jones, 1931).

MARKHAM, CLEMENTS R., *The Fighting Veres* (1888).

MATTINGLY, GARRETT, *The Defeat of the Spanish Armada* (1959).

MEYER, A.O., *England and the Catholic Church under Queen Elizabeth* (trans. McKee, 1916).

MILLER, AMOS C., *Sir Henry Killigrew* (1963).

NAUNTON, ROBERT, *Fragmenta Regalia* (ed. E. Arber, 1895).

NEALE, J.E., *Elizabeth I and Her Parliaments, 1559-81* (1953; also a paperback edition).

NEALE, J.E., *Elizabeth I and Her Parliaments, 1584-1601* (1957; also a paperback edition).

NEALE, J. E., *Essays in Elizabethan History* (1958).

NEALE, J. E., *Queen Elizabeth* (1934; also a paperback edition).

NEALE, J. E., *The Elizabethan House of Commons* (1949).

NICHOLAS, HARRIS, *The Memoirs of the Life and Times of Sir Christopher Hatton* (1847).

NICHOLS, JOHN, *The Progresses and Public Processions of Queen Elizabeth* (3 vols., 1823).

PEARSON, A.F.SCOTT, *Thomas Cartwright and Elizabethan Puritanism* (1925).

POLLARD, A.F., *Political History of England, 1547-1603* (1910).

POLLEN, J.H., *The English Catholics in the Reign of Queen Elizabeth* (1920).

PRESCOTT, H.F.M., *Spanish Tudor; the Life of Bloody Mary* (1940).

RAMSAY, G.D., *English Overseas Trade during the Centuries of Emergence* (1957).

READ, CONYERS, *Lord Burghley and Queen Elizabeth* (1960; also a paperback edition).

READ, CONYERS, *Mr. Secretary Cecil and Queen Elizabeth* (1955; also a paperback edition).

READ, CONYERS, *Mr. Secretary Walsingham and the Policy of Queen Elizabeth* (3 vols., 1925).

REID, R.R., *The King's Council in the North* (1921).

ROWSE, A.L., *Raleigh and the Throckmortons* (1962).

ROWSE, A.L., *Sir Richard Grenville of 'The Revenge'* (1937).

ROWSE, A.L., *The England of Elizabeth* (1950).

ROWSE, A.L., *The Expansion of Elizabethan England* (1953).

ROWSE, A.L., *Tudor Cornwall* (1941).

ROWSE, A.L., *William Shakespeare* (1963).

RYAN, LAWRENCE V., *Roger Ascham* (1963).

SITWELL, EDITH, *The Queen and the Hive* (1962; also a paperback edition).

SMITH, LACEY BALDWIN, *The Elizabethan Epic* (1966).

STONE, LAWRENCE, *An Elizabethan; Sir Horatio Palavicino* (1956).

STONE, LAWRENCE, *The Crisis of the Aristocracy* (1965).

STOPES, C.C., *The Life of Henry, 3rd Earl of Southampton, Shakespeare's Patron* (1922).

STRACHEY, LYTTON, *Elizabeth and Essex* (1928).

STRICKLAND, AGNES, *The Queens of England*, vol. 3 (1866).

STRONG, ROY, *The Portraits of Queen Elizabeth I* (1963).

STUBBES, PHILIP, *Anatomy of Abuses* (ed. F.J.Furnivall, New Shakespere Society, 1877).

TAWNEY, R.H., *Religion and the Rise of Capitalism* (1926; also a paperback edition).

TAWNEY, R.H., *The Agrarian Problem in the Sixteenth Century* (1912).

TAYLOR, E.G.R., *Late Tudor and Early Stuart Geography* (1934).

TAYLOR, H.O., *Thought and Expression in the Sixteenth Century* (1920).

THOMSON, GLADYS SCOTT, *Lords Lieutenant in the Sixteenth Century* (1923).

TILLYARD, E.M.W., *The Elizabethan World Picture* (1943).

TRIMBLE, W.R., *The Catholic Laity in Elizabethan England* (1964).

UNWIN, GEORGE, *Studies in Economic History* (ed. R.H.Tawney, 1927).

WALLACE, WILLARD M., *Sir Walter Raleigh* (1959).

WARD, B.M., *The Seventeenth Earl of Oxford* (1928).

WERNHAM, R.B., *Before the Armada; the Growth of English Foreign Policy, 1485-1588* (1966).

WHITE, F.O., *Lives of the Elizabethan Bishops* (1898).

WILLIAMSON, G.C., *George, 3rd Earl of Cumberland* (1920).

WILLIAMSON, J.A., *Sir John Hawkins* (1927, revised edition 1949).

WILLSON, D.H., *King James VI and I* (1956).

WILSON, F.P., *The Plague in Shakespeare's London* (1927).

WILSON, THOMAS, *A Discourse upon Usury* (ed. R.H.Tawney, 1926).

WILSON, THOMAS, *The State of England A.D. 1600* (ed. F.J.Fisher, Camden Society, *Miscellany*, xv, 1936).

WRIGHT, T., *Queen Elizabeth and Her Times* (2 vols., 1838).

Zurich Letters (ed. Hastings Robinson, Parker Society; vol. 1, 1558–79; vol. 2, 2nd series, 1558–1602, published 1842–5).

INDEX